ROUTLEDGE · E[...]
GENERAL EDITOR

SPENSER

Selected Writings

ROUTLEDGE · ENGLISH · TEXTS
GENERAL EDITOR · JOHN DRAKAKIS

WILLIAM BLAKE: *Selected Poetry and Prose* ed. David Punter
EMILY BRONTË: *Wuthering Heights* ed. Heather Glen
ROBERT BROWNING: *Selected Poetry* ed. Aidan Day
GEOFFREY CHAUCER: *The Tales of the Clerk and the Wife of Bath* ed. Marion Wynne-Davies
JOHN CLARE: *Selected Poetry and Prose* ed. Merryn and Raymond Williams
JOSEPH CONRAD: *Selected Literary Criticism and The Shadow-Line* ed. Allan Ingram
CHARLES DICKENS: *Hard Times* ed. Terry Eagleton
JOHN DONNE: *Selected Poetry and Prose* ed. T. W. and R. J. Craik
GEORGE ELIOT: *The Mill on the Floss* ed. Sally Shuttleworth
HENRY FIELDING: *Joseph Andrews* ed. Stephen Copley
BEN JONSON: *The Alchemist* ed. Peter Bement
D. H. LAWRENCE: *Selected Poetry and Non-fictional Prose* ed. John Lucas
ANDREW MARVELL: *Selected Poetry and Prose* ed. Robert Wilcher
JOHN MILTON: *Selected Poetry and Prose* ed. Tony Davies
WILFRED OWEN: *Selected Poetry and Prose* ed. Jennifer Breen
ALEXANDER POPE: *Selected Poetry and Prose* ed. Robin Sowerby
PERCY BYSSHE SHELLEY: *Selected Poetry and Prose* ed. Alasdair D. F. Macrae
OSCAR WILDE: *The Importance of Being Earnest and Related Writings* ed. Joseph Bristow
WILLIAM WORDSWORTH: *Selected Poetry* ed. Philip Hobsbaum

SPENSER
Selected Writings

Edited by Elizabeth Porges Watson

LONDON AND NEW YORK

*First published 1992
by Routledge
11 New Fetter Lane,
London EC4P 4EE*

*Simultaneously published in the USA
and Canada
by Routledge, a division of
Routledge, Chapman and Hall, Inc.
29 West 35th Street, New York, NY 10001*

*Introduction, critical commentary and
notes © 1992 Elizabeth Porges Watson*

*Printed and bound in Great Britain by
Cox & Wyman Ltd., Reading, Berkshire*

*All rights reserved. No part of this book
may be reprinted or reproduced or utilized
in any form or by any electronic,
mechanical, or other means, now known or
hereafter invented, including photocopying
and recording, or in any information storage
or retrieval system, without permission in
writing from the publishers.*

British Library Cataloguing in
Publication Data
Spenser, Edmund, 1552?-1599
   Selected writings.
   I. Title II. Watson, Elizabeth Porges
   821.3

Library of Congress Cataloging in
Publication Data
Spenser, Edmund, 1552?-1599.
   [Selections. 1992]
   Spenser, selected writings/
   edited by Elizabeth Porges Watson.
   p. cm. – *(Routledge English texts)*
   Includes bibliographical references and
   index.
   I. Watson, Elizabeth Porges.
   II. Title. III. Series.
   PR2352.W38 1992
   821'.3–dc20   91-28662

ISBN 0 415 01636 3

For Stephen Windos,
whose mirror Spenser made, but not his Book

Contents

A note on the text — ix
Abbreviations used — xi
Introduction — 1

SPENSER: SELECTED WRITINGS

The Shepheardes Calender

June — 33
October — 42

The Faerie Queene: Book I — 54

Canto i — 57
Canto ii — 77
Canto iii — 93
Canto iv — 108
Canto v — 126
Canto vi — 145
Canto vii — 162
Canto viii — 180
Canto ix — 197
Canto x — 217
Canto xi — 241
Canto xii — 260

The Faerie Queene: Dedicatory Sonnets

To Lord Grey 277
To Sir Walter Raleigh 278
To the Countesse of Penbroke 279

The Faerie Queene: A Letter of the Authors to Sir Walter Raleigh
280

Complaints

Muiopotmos, or the Fate of the Butterflie 285
Visions of the Worlds Vanitie 302

Colin Clouts Come Home Againe
310

Epithalamion
342

Prothalamion
357

Two Cantos of Mutabilitie

Canto vi 365
Canto vii 386
Canto viii 'unperfite' 408

Notes 409
Critical commentary 453
Select bibliography 496

A note on the text

Almost all Spenser's work was printed during his lifetime, the exceptions being the *Two Cantos of Mutabilitie*, included with the first folio of *The Faerie Queene* published by Mathew Lownes in 1609, and the *Veue of the Present State of Ireland*, which was first printed by Sir James Ware in Dublin, 1633. Spenser himself saw much of his work through the press. As a proof-reader he was no perfectionist, leaving a number of obvious errors still standing, but in the absence of any manuscript authority later editors have in the main worked from these early editions.

The importance of archaisms, colloquialisms and even of coinages in Spenser's writing makes any modernization of the text impossible. Spenser's original spelling has therefore been kept to throughout, except for the sixteenth-century convention of printing i for j and u for v, and vice versa which has been changed in accordance with modern English usage. I have supplied, page by page, a gloss of words unfamiliar in themselves or likely to appear so by reason of their spelling. I have also included brief identifications of mythological and historical references, where these are made allusively: both ranges of material receive fuller treatment in the Critical Commentary and Notes.

Representative examples and illustrations given in the Notes and in each section of the Critical Commentary are taken as far as possible from the texts selected for this book; other references to Spenser's work are cited where appropriate by way of comparison or explication.

The present text is heavily indebted to both the *Variorum* edition of Spenser's *Works*, 1932-57, and the edition of the *Poetical Works* by Smith and de Selincourt, Oxford, 1912: see below.

ix

Further reading under each heading of the Critical Commentary is suggested in the appropriate section of the Bibliography.

Important editions of Spenser's work are:

The Faerie Queene: Disposed into twelve books ... (Books I–III), London, 1590.
The Faerie Queene ... with *The Second Part of the Faerie Queene* ... (Books I–VI), 2 vols, London, 1596.
The Faerie Queene, disposed into XII bookes fashioning 12 Moral Virtues (Books I–VI). First folio: first appearance of *Mutabilitie*, London, 1609.
The Faerie Queene: The Shepheardes Calender: Together with the other Works of Englands Arch-Poet, Edm. Spenser, London, 1611. First appearance of the *Shepheardes Calender* under Spenser's own name.
Spenser, *Works*, ed. John Hughes, 6 vols, London, 1715.
The Faerie Queene: A New Edition with a Glossary, and Notes explanatory and critical, ed. John Upton, 2 vols, London, 1758.
Spenser, *Works with the Principal Illustrations of Various Commentators*, ed. H.J. Todd, 8 vols, London, 1805. The first Variorum edition.
Minor Poems, ed. Ernest de Selincourt, Oxford, 1909.
The Faerie Queene, ed. J.C. Smith, 2 vols, Oxford, 1909.
Spenser: *Works ... A Variorum Edition*, ed. Edwin Greenlaw, C.G. Osgood and F.M. Padelford, Baltimore, 1932–57.
Poetical Works, ed. J.C. Smith and Ernest de Selincourt, Oxford, 1912.
The Faerie Queene, ed. Thomas P. Roche, Jr, Penguin Books, 1978.

Abbreviations used

The following standard abbreviations are used in references to Spenser's works throughout:

CCCHA	*Colin Clouts Come Home Againe*
Epith.	*Epithalamion*
FQ	*The Faerie Queene*
HB	*Hymne in Honoure of Beauty*
HHB	*Hymne of Heavenly Beautie*
HHL	*Hymne of Heavenly Love*
HL	*Hymne in Honour of Love*
Letter	*A Letter of the Authors . . . to Sir Walter Raleigh*
MHT	*Mother Hubberds Tale*
Muio.	*Muiopotmos, or the Fate of the Butterflie*
Mutabilitie	*Two Cantos of Mutabilitie*
Proth.	*Prothalamion*
SC	*The Shepheardes Calender*
TM	*Teares of the Muses*
Veue	*Veue of the Present State of Ireland*
VG	*Virgils Gnat*
VWV	*Visions of the Worlds Vanitie*

Other abbreviations used:

Fr.	French
Ital.	Italian

Lat.	Latin
ME	Middle English
Nativity	*On the Morning of Christ's Nativity*
OE	Old English
OED	*Oxford English Dictionary*
PL	*Paradise Lost*
Variorum	*Spenser: Works ... A Variorum Edition*, ed. Edwin Greenlaw, C.G. Osgood and F.M. Padelford, Baltimore, 1932–57.
Works	*Spenser: Poetical Works*, ed. J.C. Smith and Ernest de Selincourt, Oxford, 1912.

Introduction

(i) SPENSER'S LIFE AND TIMES

Spenser's life has so far attracted no full-scale biography, though one is now proposed by a consortium of American scholars. His work, however, has stimulated a good deal of biographical speculation. Helena Shires has put the situation very clearly:

> Our information is such that over his life-time an important fact may be known — his passing from the service of the Earl of Leicester to take up an appointment in Ireland — but we cannot interpret it. We cannot tell for certain why this came about, either for what reasons or for what end; nor can we ascertain whether the choice was his, or what disappointment, acquiescence, gratitude, anxiety or satisfaction it aroused in the young poet. Yet the event rightly understood may be the key to his life story.[1]

She has chosen a crucial instance; one where some internal evidence does appear to exist, legitimately inviting attempts to interpret it. Of this and other known facts of Spenser's life, however, it remains true that any such exercise must be ultimately confined to the careful assessment of probabilities.

Spenser was almost certainly born in 1552, the year before the death of Edward VI and the accession of Mary. He was one of three children, having a brother and a sister. His father, John Spenser, had come to London from Lancashire, and was a free journeyman of the

Merchant Taylors' Company. In *Proth.*, 1596, Spenser says that he was born in London:

> mery London, my most kyndly Nurse,
> That to me gave this Lifes first native sourse.

A very little is known of his background. In the same passage he adds:

> Though from another place I take my name,
> An house of aunceint fame.

This was the family of the Spencers of Althorp, Northampton, Spenser had claimed kinship with them before, notably in *CCCHA* 536–71, and also in his dedications of *Muio.*, *MHT* and *TM* to the 'sisters three', daughters of Sir John Spencer, there celebrated as '*Phillis, Charillis* and sweet *Amarylis*'. A distant relationship is not impossible, and certainly the dedications and compliment were accepted. By the time they were offered the assumed connection might well have appeared mutually gratifying. Spenser's immediate family, however, seem to have been of quite humble station, and by no means affluent. Edmund, like his brother John, was a scholarship boy in his schooldays and later at Cambridge,[2] and certainly in matters of property, finance and advancement he seems to have kept all his life the sensibility as well as the practical anxieties natural to a self-made man.

In 1561 Spenser went to the newly founded Merchant Taylors' School, where he may well have been among its first intake of pupils. He and his fellow pupils were fortunate in the school's first headmaster. Richard Mulcaster was at this time about thirty years old, a fine humanist scholar, with a fresh and energetic feel for education, its problems and ideals. Some twenty years later he drew on his experience for two books: *The Positions*, 1581, and *The Elementarie*, 1582. When Spenser was his pupil he must still have been experimenting with methods and ideas, but his central belief, that education is a privilege carrying with it social and public responsibility, certainly comes to be reflected in Spenser's deeply purposive view of his own poetic vocation.

Mulcaster's pupils were well grounded in the classical languages and literatures and even in Hebrew, but English, not Latin, was the teaching language. The respect for the vernacular encouraged by

Mulcaster may be one reason why Spenser, unlike Milton in the century following, never seems even briefly to have considered the possibility of writing his major work in Latin. There is little evidence that Spenser continued to read widely in Greek in later life: much Greek literature was in any case available in Latin translation. His proficiency, however, remained such as to be remarked by Lodovick Bryskett, with whom he was working in Ireland in the 1580s, who praises him as being 'perfect in the Greek tongue'.[3] The school curriculum included mathematics, and Spenser's continuing and evident interest in the natural sciences may first have been stimulated at this time. Mulcaster was also convinced of the importance in education of the performing arts. Acting, in his opinion, developed self-confidence and deportment as well as elocution and fluency in spoken Latin, which was still the language of diplomacy as well as of learning. The school presented a play each year before the Court: it is likely that Spenser first saw Queen Elizabeth face to face on such an occasion. Music was taught also, vocal and instrumental, as well as the theory, taken as a branch of mathematics. At this time anyone with pretensions to education was expected to have some skill in performance, extending at least to the sight-reading of a new madrigal. Spenser's own knowledge of music was, technically at least, considerable, as his wide and exact use of musical reference and terminology indicates. For some reason this is an aspect of his writing that has received little critical attention.

When Spenser first went to school Elizabeth had been on the throne for three years. His own memories of her sister Mary's reign — the desperate attempts to return England to Catholicism, the accompanying persecutions, the feverish uncertainty, both religious and political — must have been sketchy, but neither the fears nor the reminiscence of his parents' generation were nullified simply by Mary's death. During his childhood and schooldays Spenser must have heard and read a great deal of what had happened in England so recently; of what might still recur and of what was actually happening elsewhere. There was at this time a steady output of pamphlets and ephemera on religious issues. More substantially, in 1561 Calvin's *Institutio* was translated into English, and John Knox, returned from exile in Geneva six years before, had overseen the drawing up of the Confessions of the Faith of the Church of Scotland. John Foxe's

Commentarii, 10 appeared in English in 1563, as *Actes and Monuments of these latter perilous times touching matters of the Church*. This was the influential, emotive and partisan *Book of Martyrs*, recalling the miseries of Mary's reign with emphasis heightened by contemporary awareness. On the Continent, confrontation between Catholic and Protestant and between different Protestant factions was brutally uncompromising. Political and nationalist feeling of a kind with which our own century is bitterly familiar was still secondary to the overriding impetus of religious conviction. Each side believed, with terrifying sincerity, that its opponents were damned or damnable, to be saved or purged by a foretaste of eternal agony. That in England the tensions of controversy never collapsed into the bloodthirsty outrage evinced in the French Wars of Religion or the persecutions conducted in the Netherlands by the Spanish Inquisition was due in large measure to Elizabeth's conscious policy of moderation. To a number of her loyal subjects this seemed dangerous; a lull inviting the storm. Such unease was not only felt within the growing Puritan faction; it also affected a number of convinced Anglicans, laymen and divines. Among them were Archbishop Grindal, Leicester, his nephew Sidney and, in due course, Spenser.

From 1559 on through his schooldays and indeed his life Spenser would have worshipped according to Cranmer's Book of Common Prayer as revised under Elizabeth. His daily familiarity with the Psalms in particular, and with the Bible generally, is evident in his writing and typical of his period. Of his family's precise religious position within the Church of England we know nothing. The year 1569, however, in which he left school and proceeded to Cambridge, saw Spenser's first printed work: an undertaking clearly indicative of his own sympathies at this time, and very probably contributing to his maturer opinions. This was the translation of part of Jan Baptista van der Noodt's *A Theatre for Worldlings*.

Van der Noodt himself was a Protestant refugee from Spanish persecution in the Netherlands, with some reputation as a poet and scholar. His *Theatre* had first appeared in 1558, in Flemish and then in French. In the following year he arranged for and perhaps commissioned an English translation. The work consists of twenty-two poems, each accompanied by a woodcut, followed by a prose commentary developed as a savage indictment of the Roman Church.

The prose was translated apparently by a Theodore Roest, whose name suggests that he may have been a fellow countryman. The poems were translated by Spenser. How he received the commission, whether through family contact or even on Mulcaster's recommendation, is not known, but that he did so was to prove important in a number of ways. The poems themselves comprise one of Petrarch's *Canzoni* (1-6);[4] the *Songe* of Joachim du Bellay (7-17, omitting 6,8,13,14 of the original);[5] and four sonnets by van der Noodt himself on passages from the Apocalypse.[6] Petrarch's work originally lamented the death of his beloved Laura, and is here slanted by inference to highlight the vulnerability of beauty and goodness in this world. The sonnets of du Bellay's *Songe* present a series of 'visions' encapsulating the decay of ancient Roman glory into the corruption of the Roman Church. The Apocalyptic poems rely on the common Protestant exegesis of this time, by which the Whore of Babylon typifies the Catholic Church of Rome as the New Jerusalem does the reformed churches: 'There growes lifes fruit unto the Churches good.'[7]

Each poem, together with its woodcut, makes up an 'emblem', a picture 'interpreted' by an accompanying verse, which was a popular form for the didactic epigram at this time and later.

Spenser rendered the Petrarchan section into sonnets of the 'Shakespearian' form, and the du Bellay sonnets and those of van der Noodt himself into blank verse. Very probably he consulted the original Italian and French of Petrarch and du Bellay. The result is rather better than good prentice work, but its interest goes beyond this. Van der Noodt's Apocalyptic visions recur, richly expanded, in Book I of *FQ*, most vividly in Canto viii. Possibly during his time at Cambridge but certainly before 1591 Spenser revised his versions of the poems of Petrarch and du Bellay, in the latter case using the sonnet form and adding the poems omitted by van der Noodt. These appeared in his volume of *Complaints*, 1591, as *The Visions of Bellay* and *The Visions of Petrarch, formerly translated*. The latter may in fact be the *Dreames*, one of the 'lost' works.[8] *The Ruines of Rome*, a rather freer version of du Bellay's *Antiquitez de Rome*, to which the *Songe* is in the original an appendix, also appeared in *Complaints*, as did *The Ruines of Time* and also *Visions of the Worlds Vanitie*. Both these latter works derive recognizably from the translated *Visions*. *The Ruines of Rome* transfers the theme of transcience from Rome itself to the Roman city

5

of Verulam, St Albans, of which it presents a tragic historical retrospect culminating in specific laments for the deaths of Robert Dudley, Earl of Leicester (d.1588) and his nephew Sir Philip Sidney (d.1586), 'Immortal spirit of *Philisides*', using the name Sidney had taken for himself in his *Arcadia*. This melancholy and strongly orchestrated poem may again be one of the 'lost' works, or a version of it, under another name: the *Stemma Dudleiana*. The *Visions of the Worlds Vanitie* are, like those of Petrarch, eclectic: they are Spenser's own exercise in the genre, his own choice of examples to illustrate the world's despight, owing a great deal to the emblem tradition with which he had first worked in the *Theatre*. His earliest work had long-lasting and exciting repercussions, perhaps paradoxically the stronger for the flat kind of concentration needed for the apparently straightforward task he was given in hand.

On 20 May 1569 Spenser matriculated at Pembroke Hall, Cambridge, as a sizar; that is, a student receiving his upkeep in return for performing certain domestic duties in the college. Pembroke Hall was at this time a small college, with about one hundred residents including the senior members and domestic staff. Students attended lectures in other colleges besides their own, as indeed they still do.

For the first three years the university curriculum followed by Spenser came under three interrelated headings. Rhetoric dealt with the use of language; the technical skills of speech and literature. The precepts of Quintilian and Cicero in Latin and of Aristotle in Greek were fundamental reading. Literature, classical and also modern, supplied material for exemplary analysis and highly informed appreciation. Logic was taught using humanist techniques of dialectic ultimately derived from Plato's *Dialogues*.[9] In Cambridge these had come largely to displace the older Aristotelean scholasticism. Philosophy included practical exercises in disputation and speech-making as well as study of the works of Plato and Aristotle in particular. Spenser took his BA in 1573, and in 1574 left Cambridge for a time during an outbreak of plague. He returned to work for his MA, which he took in 1576, for which the curriculum extended his previous philosophical studies, especially through the Italian Neoplatonists of the previous generation and earlier. Scientific theory, or 'natural philosophy', including astronomy, was given complementary weight.

During his time at Cambridge Spenser seems to have suffered from recurrent ill-health,[10] though this cannot greatly have affected his studies. The delighted breadth of his reading, his intricate fascination with the nuances of thought, image and expression, are evident in all his writing. Certain of his specific areas of interest and his approaches to them are considered in the Critical Commentary. His greatest debt to Cambridge, however, is inclusive and curiously simple, owing as much to the form of study as to its content: an intelligent awareness of the Creation as meaningfully coherent at every level of actuality, perception, thought. Without it the revelatory structures of *SC* and later of *FQ* could not have been conceived, much less maintained.

Academic discipline has never been the exclusive focus of university life. The Cambridge of Spenser's time was a centre for political and religious controversy as well as learning, with current opinion running strongly towards Puritanism. Spenser was probably in sympathy with the principles underlying such a position; less so with some of its manifestations. He may well have been a witness of the riots in Cambridge that followed on the news of the Massacre of Saint Bartholomew in 1572, when Mass books and church ornaments were burnt in the streets. Certainly in *FQ* VI.xii.25 he assigns such destructive activity to the Blatant Beast, one of his most loathsome creations:

> From thence into the sacred Church he broke,
> And robd the Chancell, and the deskes downe threw,
> And Altars fouled, and blasphemy spoke,
> And th' Images for all their goodly hew,
> Did cast to ground ...

Spenser here presents iconoclasm as a hideous side-effect of reform, dangerous as well as demeaning.

Spenser must have had friends and acquaintances among his contemporaries but only one can be named, and that tentatively. 'E.K.', who supplied the introductory Epistle and Argument to *SC* as well as the *Glosse*, has often been identified as being a fellow student, Edward Kirke, though Helena Shires for one has pointed out that the initials may well stand for *Edmundus Kalendarius*: Edmund the Calendar-maker; that is, for Spenser himself. Kirke, like Spenser, was certainly taught by Gabriel Hervey, who was elected Fellow of Pembroke in 1570, and whose friendship with the poet was important and long-lasting. Hervey was a sound if opinionated scholar, strongly Puritan in his views and of irascible temperament. He had a facility for making enemies, and is perhaps best known for his public quarrel with one of them; his exchange of pamphlets with Thomas Nashe took place in the 1590s, when Hervey proved no match for Nashe's professional vituperation. His reputation has suffered unfairly in consequence. His company can never have been less than stimulating, and what we know of his continued friendship with Spenser shows that he was capable of intellectual generosity as well as affection.

Spenser left Cambridge after taking his MA, and in 1577 may briefly have visited Northern Ireland. He also travelled for a time in Northamptonshire and Lancashire, where he very possibly made contact with various family connections. In the following year he took up the post of secretary to John Young, who had been Master of Pembroke since 1567 and who was consecrated Bishop of Rochester on 1 April 1578. How well Spenser might have come to know Young during his time at Cambridge is doubtful; Young was in London a great deal, and seems to have conducted the affairs of the college largely *in absentia*. However, he had been of assistance to Hervey in settling some troublesome disputes with his colleagues, for which Hervey had professed gratitude,[11] and in *SC* the *Glosse* to 'June' 18 indicates that Spenser took the post on Hervey's advice: 'the Poete ... removing out of the Northparts came in to the South, as Hobbinoll indeede advised him privately'. Young's principal residence was at Bromley, in Kent. Hobbinoll is Spenser's name for Hervey in *SC*.

SC is Spenser's first published work, if we except his translations for the *Theatre for Worldlings*. It is an extraordinary achievement, brilliantly experimental and delicately orchestrated, its twelve eclogues with their various emphases interrelated with extreme subtlety. We cannot know just how long it took in the writing, though the text gives some indication of structural revision.[12] It appeared in 1579, and a number of specific references indicate that it was brought into its final form during Spenser's time as Young's secretary.[13] More generally, Spenser's daily contact with church affairs and theological issues very probably served to bring this range of his material into a heightened focus.

By the time *SC* was published Spenser had left Rochester and was in service with Leicester, as appears from his correspondence with Hervey.[14] Possibly he had considered and abandoned a career in the church, but nothing of the circumstances is known. At the this time he made the acquaintance of Leicester's nephew, Sir Philip Sidney, and of at least one other of the poets prominent at Court, Sir Edward Dyer.[15] Again, the extent of their intimacy is uncertain. Spenser's admiration for both poets, their common interest in English letters and in particular the techniques of English versification, probably did not amount to close friendship. Certainly Sidney did not receive the dedication to him of *SC* with any kind of enthusiasm:[16] its authorship was clearly known to him as to other of Spenser's immediate acquaintance, although to its general readership this remained for some considerable time mysterious.[17] At this time he was also working on *FQ*. Sidney and other of Spenser's friends may well have seen parts of the work in progress: certainly Hervey did, and perhaps not surprisingly found its avoidance of a purely classical idiom, and the derivation of much of its material from popular romance, distasteful in the first instance:

> If so be the *Faerye Queene* be fairer in your eie than the *Nine Muses*, and *Hobgoblin* runne away with the Garland from *Apollo*: Marke what I saye, and yet I will not say that I thought, but there an end for this once, and fare you well, till God or some good Aungell putte you in a better mind.[18]

This is the reaction of shock rather than an expression of settled prejudice: Spenser's epic writing was revolutionary in style, structure and content. Hervey later changed his opinion, and contributed one of the most delightful of the Commendatory Verses appended to Books I–III on their publication in 1590, signing it *Hobynoll*. On 17 October 1579 Spenser married a lady named Machabyas Childe at St Margaret's, Westminster.[19] He may well have hoped that through Leicester he would receive advancement and an assured career in England. The reasons why he in fact left Leicester's service in 1580 to take up the post of private secretary to Lord Grey, the newly appointed Lord Deputy in Ireland, remain obscure. There are strong indications that he did, or more probably wrote, something which unintentionally caused Leicester grave offence. Several passages in his works as we have them have been interpreted as being the occasion for this, as indeed one or more of them may be.[20] It is possible, however, that it actually occurred in one of the 'lost' works: either truly lost or so reworked as to excise the offending content. Certainly Spenser never refers to Leicester directly or indirectly without admiration and gratitude. Whatever kind of misunderstanding may have occurred, that it was the direct occasion of Spenser's taking up the Irish post, one by no means disgraceful in itself, remains no more than a fairly likely hypothesis. That he did so, however, was in more than one way decisive. His future career lay in Ireland; there he made his home, and there the greater part of his work was written or prepared for the press.

Arthur, Lord Grey of Wilton, took up his post in August 1580, and Spenser sailed with him. So did his wife, or she may have joined him later: his children, Sylvanus and Katherine, were both born in Ireland in or around 1582 and 1584: Machabyas seems to have died shortly after the birth of their daughter.

Spenser's position placed him at the tragic crux of the Irish problem at a time when it was heightened by international pressure. Catholic Ireland was violently disaffected; torn by internal feud, the clans united only in rebellion under Desmond in the south: a potential gateway for Spain. Shortly after Grey's arrival an attempt was made to force it: 600 Spanish and papal troops landed in Kerry, assured of Desmond's support against the English rule, and fortified a base in Smerwick. Grey's conviction that the only way with the Irish was the decisive use of military force was brutally confirmed by this very real threat. Spenser accompanied him on the campaigns that directly resulted: the first countermarch towards Wicklow, frustrated by an ambush in the mountains, and the siege of Smerwick itself. Here Grey was successful. The Spanish garrison surrendered, and the common soldiers were massacred. While it is certainly true that to convey so many prisoners through hostile country would have been strategically near impossible Grey's savagery here was horrifyingly in keeping with his policy as a whole: to overcome immediate resistance by the sword, backed by a scorched-earth policy by which crops were burned and cattle slaughtered, reducing the rebel population to starvation, even in some dreadfully recorded instances to cannibalism.[21]

Spenser admired Grey. His *Veue*, written some years later, expresses the deepest horror at scenes of which he must have been an eye-witness, but he thought he saw beyond this terrible necessity to an eventually peaceful Ireland, rebuilt and in his own terms civilized.

Underlying all political and religious exacerbations of the English feeling for Ireland at this time was an essential clash of cultures. The clan system, its real nature, strengths and weaknesses, was literally incomprehensible to Spenser among many others as a system, however they might make themselves familiar with its workings, as Spenser for one certainly did; his analysis of Irish customs in the *Veue* is both careful and observant. What they saw was a fair and potentially fruitful land given over to nomadic barbarism. The Irish, their traditions, dress and manners, were a standard of comparison for any newly encountered primitive or ill-conditioned peoples: the Russians, or certain tribes of America.[22] Such assumptions were clearly well established by 1560, when Archbishop Parker urged the proliferation of clerical appointments in the north of Ireland, lest the English settlers should be 'too much Irish and savage', and the 'wild Irish' were proverbial at least until the time of Milton.[23]

Civilization meant in practice Anglicization: the establishment through settlement, colonization in fact, of stable land tenure, primogeniture, humanist education and the ascendancy of English as the language of government. Spenser himself admired certain of the characteristics and customs of the Irish people as he saw them, though he interpreted what he saw as the corrupt relics of a nobler and more ancient state.[24] He drew on Irish tradition and folklore in his writing.[25] Such positives he believed would find their true place and fulfilment in the future. But the only way to that future as he saw it was through such a policy as Grey's: the uncompromising extirpation of all contraries. He was not alone in this belief, in his own time or later. Sir John Davies, drawing on his own experience in Ireland at the beginning of James I's reign, provides both confirmation and retrospect:

> The *Defects* which hindered the *Perfection* of the Conquest of *Ireland*, were of two kinds, and consisted; first, *in the faint prosecution of the warre*, and next, *in the loosenesse of the civill Government*. For, the Husbandman must first break the Land, before it be made capable of good seede: and when it is thoroughly broken and manured, if he do not forthwith cast good seed into it, it will grow wilde againe, and beare nothing but Weeds. So a barbarous country must first be broken by a warre, before it will be capable of good Government; and when it is fully subdued and conquered, if it bee not well planted and governed after the Conquest, it will eft-soones return to the former Barbarisme.[26]

Wars of whatever kind are expensive. Elizabeth was not prepared to finance Grey's policy, and whatever her feelings may have been on the outcome of Smerwick in particular, where a foreign invasion was in question, it is probable that she was genuinely shocked by reports she received of his brutality elsewhere. Grey was recalled in 1582.

Spenser remained in Ireland, whether out of a sense of commitment, or because he saw small chance of advancement in England as a member of Grey's discredited administration we cannot be certain. It was not in him to conceal or deny his own opinions. He saw Grey's actions as right and necessary in their time and place, and admired him also as a man whom he knew well. In the *Veue* he offers a strongly reasoned defence of both. His political arguments may well have gained edge and definition from his disgusted experience of Grey's successors, but his sympathy for him as a man is personal as well as perceptive and still worth consideration; Spenser not only addressed to him one of the Dedicatory Sonnets to *FQ* but took him in due course as his co-relative in contemporary history for Artegall, knight and patron of justice in Book V of that work. His comments on Grey in the *Veue* show that his doing so went beyond mere partisanship: he saw Grey's character and situation as aptly mirroring the hard condition of the one virtue that is operative only in a fallen world:

> In the meane tyme all that was formerlye done with longe laboure and toile was ... in a moment undone, and that good Lorde blotted with the name of a bloddye man, whom whoe that well knewe, knewe to be moste gentle, affable and temperate. But that the necessitye of present state of things forced him to that violence and allmoste Changed his verye natural disposicion, But otherwise he was so farr from delightinge in blodd that oftentimes he suffered not just vengeance to fall wheare it was deserved and even some of those which weare afterweardes his accusers had tasted so much of his mercye, and weare from the gallowes broughte to be his accusers.[27]

From the time of Grey's recall Spenser's loyalty to the man as to his policies was unwavering.

Later in 1582 he obtained a twenty-one year lease of New Abbey, a forfeited rebel property; some indication that he was thinking of his stay in Ireland as being permanent, or at any rate long term. Over the next few years he held a number of minor civil service posts as well as carrying out his obligation as a landholder to act as a commissioner of musters in the County of Kildare. In 1589 he succeeded Lodovick Bryskett as clerk of the Council of Munster, the function of which was to divide the confiscated Desmond lands into estates. These were then granted to English beneficiaries as a mark of royal favour, or sold to English settlers, in the hope that by this means the countryside might be subdued and brought to civilized prosperity. Sir Walter Raleigh, who had served under Grey in the action at Smerwick, had received one of the largest of these grants, amounting in all to about 40,000 acres. Spenser himself had received the manor and castle of Kilcolman in Cork; 3,028 acres, with six English settlers under him. It was not a rich estate, being neglected and beset by law-suits. From about 1587 this was his home and perhaps the first he had thought of as being such. He built a new house there, which might have been a matter merely of convenience. More tellingly, he also made its setting that of some of his greatest poetry, where the natural splendour of its forests, streams and mountains is lovingly enriched by local legend and the reciprocal play of his own humanist imagination.

Spenser's situation was far from being unusual in the Ireland of this time. A number of men, intelligent, even learned, were in positions similar to his own, and we have one clear picture of at least one kind of the social intercourse that resulted. It occurs in Lodovick Bryskett's *A Discourse of Civil Life* which, although it was not published until 1606, must by internal reference have been written before 1589. It is dedicated to Lord Grey, of whom Bryskett took a view similar to that of Spenser. The occasion of his writing the *Discourse* was, he says, 'The visitation of certain gentlemen to my little cottage which I had built near to Dublin' at a time when he was in poor health. Among the company, which also included Doctor Long, the Primate of Armagh, and 'M. Dormer, the Queen's Solicitor', as well as a number of officers, captains in the standing army, was 'M. Edmond Spenser late your lordship's secretary'. It was Spenser whom Bryskett singled out for his learning, asking him 'to spend this time which we have now destined to familiar discourse and conversation, in declaring to us the great benefits which men obtained by the knowledge of Morall Philosophie'; a proposal which no matter how it was put originally strikingly suggests the oasis of refreshment and relief from day-to-day tension and responsibility expected by such a gathering from purely intellectual exercise. Spenser's excuse as recorded by Bryskett should be seen in the light of this: 'it is not unknowne unto you, that I have already undertaken a work tending to the same effect, which is in *heroical verse* under the title of a *Faerie Queene*'. His creative and imaginative energies may well have been concentrated by having little in the way of any casual outlet.

Spenser evidently continued his practice of circulating parts of his work in progress among his friends: Bryskett adds that 'some parcels had been by some of them seene', before reverting to the discussion of his own work. Spenser, or one of his acquaintance, must also have sent parts of *FQ* to England, to Hervey or others, since the first lines of the work to appear in print occur in *The Arcadian Rhetoric* of Abraham Fraunce, 1588: *FQ* II.iv.35.

By some time in 1589 Spenser had Books I–III of his great poem completed and ready for publication. In the autumn of that year Sir Walter Raleigh, who had earlier incurred the queen's disfavour[28] and had removed himself to Ireland for a time accordingly, visited Spenser at Kilcolman. Their acquaintance, which may have begun as early as 1580 when both were in Leicester's service, and which must have continued at least intermittently during Grey's campaigns, now developed into firm friendship. They had many political opinions and national ambitions in common, especially with regard to the New World, where Raleigh had himself founded Virginia, naming it in honour of the queen. More immediately, both were poets, and each was deeply impressed by the other's work. Spenser wrote his Introductory Epistle to *FQ* he says, at Raleigh's instigation, and was easily persuaded to accompany him to England. Their journey and its outcome are the subject of Spenser's poem *CCCHA*, written, or at least completed, on his return to Ireland, in which he pays Raleigh the graceful compliment of borrowing the name he gives to the queen in his own writing: Cynthia. Raleigh presented Spenser to Elizabeth. He was graciously received, and on 1 December the first three Books of his poem were entered at the Stationers' Hall, with the formal dedication to the queen, as well as the *Letter* and seventeen Dedicatory Sonnets, including that to Lord Grey. It appeared early in 1590, and Spenser remained in England for the greater part of that year. In the first instance he was anxious to see his work through the press, indeed *FQ* is the first major work in English whose author gave it that care; that he did so marks Spenser as a new kind of poet, a professional. The circulation and casual copying of manuscripts was a commonplace, and Spenser took part in this, as we have seen. To oversee the actual business of printing was another matter, and dispensed with any convention of graceful and dismissive modesty. It is an important indication of Spenser's attitude to his work and to its importance; one for which all his editors subsequently have been grateful.

He took the opportunity while in England of renewing acquaintance at Court and elsewhere, as a number of the dedications to poems published around this time indicate, and of enjoying his success and new reputation. He also prepared for publication his volume of *Complaints*, combining some earlier work now revised with newer pieces.[29] *Daphnaida*, an elegy on the death of Sir Arthur Gorges's young wife who had died in the summer of 1590, was also printed in 1591.[30] If he had hoped for preferment in England, however, he was disappointed; at a time when almost any position carried political weight his unflinching loyalty to friends and opinions out of favour, or at least discordant with prevailing policies, was a sufficient bar to anything of the kind. To overcome it he would have had to temporize, as he saw others do and despised them for doing. There may even have been a certain relief in the final dashing of hopes for him so ambiguous.[31] In the following year he did receive recognition: whether or not Elizabeth recognized in his work the greatest compliment ever paid to any living sovereign, she rewarded him not ungenerously with an annual pension of £50 a year. It is difficult to transpose this sum into modern figures, but had Spenser had no other income at all it would at that time have been enough to live on decently.[32]

Once back in Ireland Spenser again took up the clerkship of the Council of Munster and the management of his estate, where there was some backlog of litigation. His work on *FQ* continued, and Book VI appears to have been near completion in 1594.

Spenser had by this time been a widower for some years. It is not known just when or in what circumstances he first met Elizabeth Boyle, whose home was at Kilcolran, no very great distance from Kilcolman: *Amoretti*, the sonnet sequence in which he traces the progress of his courtship, does so in terms of the convention employed.[33] Temporal reference is, however, central to its structure, and the passage of time indicated is something over a year. They were married on 11 June 1594, and his gift to the bride,

> made in lieu of many ornaments,
> With which my love should duly have bene dect,

was his marvellous celebration of their wedding day, *Epithalamion*.

During the year following he completed work on Books IV–VI of *FQ* and made some minor revisions to the earlier Books, as well as writing, or at least completing, the *Fowre Hymnes*. He made another visit to London in the winter of 1595 and remained there until 1597. During this time he saw his new work through the press, and also wrote *Prothalamion* in celebration of the forthcoming double marriage of the two daughters of the Earl of Worcester. His main energies at this time were probably taken up in giving final shape to the mass of material he had been collecting over the years since Grey's recall for his tract *A Veue of the Present State of Ireland*. It takes the form of a dialogue between Eudoxus 'Knowledgeable' and Irenius 'Peaceable', and its scope is historical and economic as well as immediately political. The arguments are brilliantly and forcefully concentrated on a defence of Grey's policy as typifying the only hope of attaining lasting peace and prosperity in Ireland, whose ills are 'some of them ... of verye great antiquitye and long Continuance, Others more late and of lesse endurance; Others dailie growinge and increasinge Continuallye as the evill occacions are everye daie offered.'[34] The correlative to Spenser's endorsement of a discredited administration is his undisguised contempt for Grey's successors in office. The *Veue* was finally entered at the Stationers' Register in 1598, when it was not surprisingly rejected for publication. It was not printed until 1633, when it appeared in Dublin.

On his return to Ireland Spenser was for a time without office, having resigned his clerkship to his wife's kinsman, Sir Richard Boyle, later first Earl of Cork. In 1598 the queen recommended him to be sheriff of Cork, a post carrying military as well as administrative responsibility. His deep feeling for the idyllic beauty of Kilcolman is evident in *Mutabilitie*, of which it is the setting; so is the underlying tension and unease which he expressed very differently in the *Veue*. For Spenser, living there with a wife and four children, two of whom were very young, this anxiety must have been inescapable. *Mutabilitie* was probably his last work, complete in itself, whether or not it was intended as part of a later Book of *FQ*. In October 1598 the Tyrone rebellion spread to Munster and flared into general insurrection. Kilcolman was burned, and Spenser and his family fled to Cork, probably losing almost all of their possessions. It has been conjectured that later Books of *FQ* were destroyed in the fire. However, *Mutabilitie* survived, and anything completed by 1595-7 would have been printed or at least taken to England on Spenser's second visit there; on returning to Ireland in 1597 he had little time left for substantial work. The disaster in Munster was not unheralded: there had been news of Tyrone's defeat of the English in Armagh in August; it must have been clear that rebellion would spread, and though the rising in Munster itself was sudden it was the fulfilment of long-felt dread.

Shortly after his escape to Cork, Spenser was sent to England with dispatches, among which was included his own report, *A briefe discourse of*

Ireland, addressed to the queen. It is in effect a précis of the arguments put forward in the *Veue* to which events had given an edge of painful desperation most apparent in the conclusion:

> But if your highnesse will dispose your selfe to be inclined to any such milder dealing with them or to temporize any longer with pardons and proteccions as hath bene done by your governours here then we humbly beseeche your Majestie to call us your poore subjectes alltogether away from hence that at least we may die in our Countrie and not see the horrable calamities which will thereby come upon all this land.[35]

This last wish at least was to be granted, and not by the queen. Spenser had little opportunity to put his plea in person. He arrived in London at Christmas and was taken ill a few days later; he was weakened by shock, exhaustion and hard travel. He died on 16 January 1599 and was buried in Westminster Abbey, not far from Chaucer. He had apparently come to England very poorly provided; presumably whatever had been salvaged from Kilcolman had been left in Cork for the support of his family. His funeral expenses were paid by the Earl of Essex.

(ii) LANGUAGE AND STYLE

Spenser's language attracted immediate attention.[36] After about 1650 this became focused almost entirely and for the most part unsympathetically on his use of archaisms. Only comparatively recently has this attention become at all precise. It remains the most immediately apparent aspect of Spenser's handling of language: deceptively so, in that for a modern reader any sixteenth-century text, unmodernized, will appear 'archaic', and the distinctions Spenser himself recognized be blurred with their effects. Sidney's objection to the linguistic experiments of *SC*, and Ben Jonson's comment in *Timber*, printed in 1640, that '*Spencer* in affecting the Ancients, writ no Language', which may also have had that work principally in mind, arise from specific examples rather than from Spenser's general usage. There are comparatively few words in Spenser's work that are not used more or less commonly by his contemporaries. The exceptions fall into four main categories to be considered presently, of which the first two in some degree overlap: genuine archaisms, that is ME words or forms that had passed out of current usage; dialect terms; adoptions from languages other than English; coinages verbal and semantic. It is, however, true that where two forms of a word are available to him Spenser tends to use the older with rather more consistency than do most of his contemporaries. Examples occurring in *FQ* I include: *bewray* 'betray, disclose', iv.39; *charret* 'chariot', v.38; *libbard* 'leopard', vi.3; *mo* 'more', ix.44; *nouriture* 'nurture, upbringing', ix.5; *nosethrill* 'nostril', xi.22; *scape* 'to escape', iv.3; *swounde* 'swoon', i.41; *whyleare* 'erewhile, formerly', iv.28; all of which recur in Spenser's work and would have been familiar to his readers. Similarly the *y*- prefix, as in *ymounted* 'mounted', ii.29; *yplast* 'placed', iv.28, and the *-en* ending, as in *woxen* past participle 'become', iv.34; *eyen* plural 'eyes', ii.27 were in common use. These usages, together with the availability of such alternative forms as *embay/baye[s]* 'bathe', x.27, vii.30; *emperst/perst* 'pierced' xi.53, iii.1, contribute to metrical fluidity as well as to verbal texture, an important factor in any consideration of Spenser's handling of language. He uses the same freedom as his contemporaries in deploying such elements as *em-* (*im-*, *in-*) and also *a-*, *adowne* 'down', vii.24, *dis-*, *dispiteous* 'unpitying', ii.15, *-head*, *hardyhed* 'audacity', iv.38, *-ment*, *rablement* 'rabble', vi.8, but their contribution to the dynamics of his versification, especially in *FQ*, draws the reader's attention to them as characteristic of his style.

Ben Jonson, who was generally dubious about 'Words borrowe'd of Antiquity', extending his disapproval to Lucretius as being 'scabrous and rough in these' as opposed to Virgil's moderation, evidently had in mind the first of the four categories mentioned, 'Chaucerismes' as he terms them, whether or not he took these as being inclusive of the second: dialect terms. Sidney's complaint is certainly directed at the latter, since he says that Virgil, for one, made no such use of 'olde rusticke language' as Spenser does in *SC*. Virgil does on occasion use old forms to be found in earlier writers such as Ennius. The distinction here seems to be one partly at least of literary currency.

E.K. has in some ways over-anticipated such a response as that of Sidney. In 'June' for example he very fairly glosses not only '*Syte* "situation and place"', which *OED* gives as the first recorded instance of what is later a common meaning, and the rare use of '*Spring* "not of water, but of young trees springing"', for which *OED* gives only three earlier and two later examples besides noting its nineteenth-century appearance in Suffolk and Northamptonshire glossaries. However, he also glosses '*To make* "to versifie"', a usage established from the fourteenth to the mid seventeenth centuries, and '*wite* "blame"', which *OED* shows to have been established from OE, the first citation given being from King Alfred. More interesting is the careful gloss of '*underfonge* "undermine and deceive by false suggestion"'. *OED* has this as the first of only three examples having this meaning, one of which occurs in *FQ* V.ii.7, and the other in an eclogue by John Davies of Hereford, 1614, which may well show Spenser's influence. As such it has moved effectively into the fourth category of coinages. Spenser's only other use of the word occurs in 'November', where it has the more usual meaning of 'undertake', for which there are no later instances given in *OED*. It is used in this sense by both Chaucer and Lydgate, both of whom are cited elsewhere by E.K. as good precedent. The most famous example occurs in 'Maye': '*Chevisaunce* "sometime of Chaucer used for gaine: sometime of other for spoyle, or bootie, or enterprise, and sometime for chiefdome."' In 'Maye' *chevisaunce* signifies 'bargain'; a primary meaning in ME. It has no connection with chiefdom except by false etymology which may be E.K.'s own. Spenser uses it on three other occasions, all in *FQ*: II.ix.8; III.vii.45; III.xi.24, in every one of which it has an entirely new meaning: 'chivalric enterprise'. The parallel example of *underfong* suggests that Spenser felt in no way bound by earlier usage. He understood and used the original meanings of both words, but felt free to redeploy them.

Both these examples might be expected to recall older literature and to provide specifically archaic effect accordingly. A good many other words were probably intended similarly to be reminiscent of earlier writing, and of Chaucer in particular, so implying a living continuity of English literary tradition. Many of the words used in *FQ* to denote weaponry and parts of armour are 'out of date', and so constitute effective archaisms. Some of these were certainly derived from romance sources and were probably intended to carry 'antique' chivalric associations. It was an effect Spenser used sparingly, however. A surprisingly slight proportion of Spenser's vocabulary is deliberately archaic in any of these senses, even including some of the dialect terms.

Like his predecessor John Skelton (?1460–1529) Spenser is credited by *OED* with the 'first appearance' of a surprisingly large number of words and, as in Skelton's case a high proportion of these are dialect or colloquial. *OED* is a rough guide at best, but both poets seem to have drawn deliberately on vocabulary which was non-literary, and that Spenser took his poetic pseudonym in *SC*, Colin Cloute, from Skelton suggests that he identified his own names with what he took to be those of the earlier poet, at least in part. E.K., in 'Januarie', glosses Colin Cloute as: 'a name not greatly used, and yet have I sene a Poesie of M. Skeltons under that title'.

Skelton was a priest and scholar writing before the Reformation in England, but in his satires he inveighs bitterly against ecclesiastical abuse at every level, concentrating his attacks above all on Cardinal Wolsey. The utterance of the titular persona of his poem *Colin Cloute* is larded with the 'Satyrical bitternesse' which E.K., in his General Argument finds in the eclogues he calls moral, in vitriolic concentration. Skelton's poetry was not held in critical favour by Spenser's generation, but Spenser may well have read him as a precursor of Protestant dialectic, in much the same way as many Elizabethan writers, for example the author of the non-Shakespearian *Troublesome Raigne*, saw King John's defiance of papal authority as heralding that of Henry VIII.

Skelton's Colin is representative of the common people. His use of colloquial diction is therefore appropriate in itself, and may have suggested wider possibilities to Spenser, who does not confine his experiments in this kind to the satiric eclogues. In the Epistle E.K.'s defence of the language of *SC* tacitly assumes that his poet is using two distinct categories of 'good and naturall English words, as have ben long time out of use and almost cleane disherited': those with a literary pedigree, 'used of most excellent Authors and most famous Poetes', and those without, 'because such olde and obsolete wordes are most used of country folke'. For the former case he can argue from authority, since Cicero himself, in *De Oratore*, 'sayth that oft-times an auncient worde maketh the style seeme grave, and as it were reverend'. For the latter he has two defensive positions and one attacking: from decorum, such language being 'fittest for such rusticall rudenesse of shepheards'; by artistic and musical analogy, for just as 'in most exquisite pictures' the very contrast between 'the daintie lineaments of beautye' and a setting of 'rude thickets and craggy clifts' is delightful. 'Even so doe those rough and harsh termes enlumine and make more clearly to appeare the brightnesse of brave and glorious words. So oftentimes a dischorde in Musick maketh a comely concordaunce.' Finally national pride allows a pre-emptive sally:

Other some not so wel seene in the English tonge as perhaps in other

> languages, if they happen to here an olde worde albeit very natural and significant, crye out streight way, that we speak no English ... Whose first shame is, that they are not ashamed, in their own mother tongue straungers to be counted and alienes.

E.K.'s rather finicky care with the *Glosse* is the counterpart to this tripartite defence, though neither prevented the disparagement both he and Spenser clearly anticipated.

Spenser seems generally to have confined his use of words he himself regarded as dialect or colloquial to *SC*: when they do recur it is often with a different meaning or in a different form. In 'June' E.K. glosses: '*Nis* "is not"'; which appears also in 'Maye' and 'November', but not elsewhere, and the phrase: *Poynte of worthy wight* 'the pricke of deserved blame', the separate elements of which recur in the later poems, though *wight* elsewhere appears as *wite*, which is E.K.'s spelling of it in his gloss. Spenser may later have dropped the spelling *wight* in order to avoid confusion with its distinct meaning, 'person'. In 'October' *dapper* 'pretye', is a nonce usage. So is *pend*, though in the form used by E.K., *pent* 'shut up in slouth as in a coupe or cage', it recurs, *FQ*. V.ix.10, with the meaning 'sunken': 'hollow eyes deepe pent'. *Ligge* and *layd*, *Ligge so layde* 'lye so faynt and unlustye', both recur in *SC* only; *ligge* in 'Maye' and 'September', *layd* in its literal sense of 'reduced' again in 'October': 'And when my Gates shall han their bellies layd', where *gate* for 'goat', used also in 'Maye', may also be a dialect form.

In his 'Januarie' gloss E.K. suggests an additional derivation for Spenser's pseudonym: 'But indeed the word Colin is Frenche, and used of the French Poete Marot ... in a certein Æglogue.' Clement Marot, 1496-1544, had introduced the eclogue with other forms into French, and had strong Protestant sympathies besides. Spenser may well have seen many of their aims as parallel. 'November' is based on Marot's elegy on the death of Queen Loys of Savoy, and E.K. may here be calling attention to this interplay with recent European writing. In the later poetry this extends to language, but not in *SC*. The emphasis placed by E.K. in the Epistle on the native qualities of Spenser's diction in *SC* is borne out by the fact that under a dozen words in the poem can be traced as having direct foreign origin, and of these one is *Elysian*, in 'November', and another *Melampode*, in 'Julye' (Lat. *melampodium* 'black hellebore'). Another occurs in 'June', *Tamburin*, glossed by E.K. as: '*Tamburines* "an olde kind of instrument, which of some is supposed to be the Clarion"'. *OED* finds its derivation and therefore Spenser's exact meaning uncertain, but takes it to be a percussion instrument perhaps similar to the modern tambourine: 'The earlier names for this or a similar instrument mentioned in the Bible were *timbre* or *timbrel*', to be found in biblical translation from the time of Coverdale. Spenser uses *timbrel* elsewhere, as in *Epith.* 143. Ben Jonson uses *Timburine* in *The Sad Shepherd*, 1637. Both poets may have chosen the form as avoiding biblical overtones irrelevant to a given pastoral context.

In *SC* Spenser in fact tends to minimize his use even of commonly established words obviously of foreign origin. 'June' exemplifies the norm in this respect: words such as *pleasaunt, christall, discurtesee* occur sparingly, and have for Spenser's generation older English rather than foreign connotations. The vocabulary of 'October' ranges rather more widely: the theme, poetry and poetic aspiration, demands virtuoso expression both satiric and exemplary. In the Epistle E.K.'s attack on 'the rakehellye route of our ragged rymers (for so themselves use to hunt the letter)', may have been inspired by Spenser's own wicked parody of contemporary taste in poetry:

Or it mens follies must be forst to fayne,
And rolle with rest in rymes of rybaudrye.

The second of these lines recurs in Thalia's diatribe in *TM* against the 'scoffing Scurrilitie' by which Comedy is being degraded: in both passages complaint is directed equally against content and style. *Rybaudrye* 'obscenity' occurs only in these passages. In 'October' Piers and Cuddie set the current state of poetry in England, here unkindly illustrated, against both its classical past and its immediate potential. The Rome of Virgil is evoked by direct and indirect reference. Virgil himself is 'the Romish *Tityrus*', to distinguish him from Chaucer to whom Spenser gives this name elsewhere in *SC*. Virgil is the supreme type of pastoral and epic poet, as Maecenas and Augustus, neither of whom are mentioned elsewhere in *SC*, are of private and royal patronage respectively. The readiness as well as the present frustration of the English genius is conveyed by argument and more subtly by verbal and mythological inference: Piers's reference to Orpheus' rescue of Eurydice 'From *Plutoes* balefull bowre' recalls particularly Virgil's fourth *Georgic*, exemplifying the highest range of pastoral. Mars, as the god of war, is cited in the context of possible contemporary epic themes, making a direct connection with classical epic presently to be mentioned. Bacchus is invoked as inspiring the ecstasy of tragedy and Bellona, goddess of war, as representative of its matter:

> How I could reare the Muse on stately stage,
> And teache her tread aloft in bus-kin fine,
> With queint Bellona in her equipage.

None of these mythological figures appears elsewhere in *SC*. This passage is cited by *OED* as giving the first examples of *bus-kin*, in the sense of 'tragic style' and of *equipage* with the meaning 'retinue'. E.K.'s gloss expresses its intention and effect:

> He seemeth here to be ravished with a Poetical furie. For (if one rightly mark) the numbers rise so ful, and the verse groweth so big, that it seemeth he hath forgot the meanenesse of shepheards state and stile.

In the later poems Spenser draws more freely on both ancient and modern languages, though still moderately by comparison with some of his contemporaries. Among the words for which Spenser provides the earliest citation in *OED* and which also occur in the present selection the following may give some indication of his methods and purpose: *aemule* 'to emulate', *CCCHA* 72,73, and *horrid* 'bristling, rough', *FQ* I.vii.31, come both from classical Lat., *aemulare, horridus*. Spenser drops their verbal and inflexional endings and uses their primary senses. *Trinal* 'threefold', *FQ* I.xii.39, is taken from late Lat. *trinalis*. The elegantly varied phrase 'trinall triplicities' for the ninefold Angelic Hierarchies, is repeated in *HHL*. *Canto*, Ital., is used by Dante, Ariosto and Tasso to denote a subdivision of a long poem: Spenser uses it in the same sense, as formally indicating his Italian sources and as being appropriate to the structure of *FQ*. *Counterfeisance* 'deceit', *FQ* I.viii.49, is Fr. *contrefaisance*, Anglicized only in the second element; *enfouldred* 'thundery' reinforces Fr. *fouldre (foudre)* with the *en-* prefix; *paravant* 'first of all', *CCCHA* 941, is the Fr. word unchanged. Adoptions of this kind were intended to be recognized, and their aptness to context, clarity of meaning, mode of Anglicization, formal analogues already established all taken into account. The critical temper of the time was as sensitive to innovation as to archaism. Roger Ascham, writing on Sallust in *The Scholemaster*, 1570, quotes the great humanist scholar Sir John Cheke as attributing '*Sallustes* roughnesse and darknesse' to 'new wordes' even more than to 'those smellyng of an older store' as well as to his affectation of Greek syntax, 'as a man would say, English talk, placed and framed outlandish like'. Spenser's foreign derivations received no criticism of this kind in his own time when they were still clearly recognizable as being the very opposite of archaic. The paradox by which later readers have largely taken them as such is itself indicative: Spenser's diction is a compound, not a mixture. Its elements are interactive with varying emphasis and effect, never merely curious or decorative, E.K.'s complaint that some writers 'have made our English tongue, a gallimaufray or hodgepodge of al other speches' could be applied no more to *FQ* than to *SC*.

Spenser's coinages are the final contributory element to be considered: words where form and or meaning have been so far modified as to have radically new connotations. Two examples by which this process can be measured have been already considered: *underfong*, and *chevisaunce*, the first extending its primary meaning to a new, figurative conclusion; the second shifting ground entirely by semantic association, here with 'chivalry' and its cognates. *Chevisaunce* in its new meaning retained a limited currency through to the Romantic period, when its attractively archaic form proved useful to writers of historical fiction, then virtually a new genre. Only one other of Spenser's coinages has had a comparable career as notorious: in 'October' E.K. glosses '*In derring doe* "In manhoode and chevalrie"'. *OED* gives the full history of this term, from the misprinting of Lydgate's use of *dorryng do* 'daring to do' as *derryng do* in the editions of 1513 and 1555 to Spenser's understanding of it in that form as a substantive phrase, as glossed by E.K.: 'Modern romantic writers, led by Sir W[alter] Scott, have taken it from Spenser, printed it *derring-do* and accentuated the erroneous use.' It is still used, now generally for humorous effect. Spenser uses it once again in *SC*: in 'December', where its meaning of 'energetic enterprise' carries no chivalric overtones. It occurs twice in *FQ* II.iv.42, where it means 'audacity', with no added sense of 'praiseworthy'; and VI.v.37, where there is such a sense. In the form *derring doers* it is used once, *FQ* IV.ii.38, of a gathering of noble knights, rivals in love: *der-doing* is used adjectively, *FQ* II.vii.10, qualifying *armes* 'knightly weapons'.

These two examples are famous by reason of their very oddity. For most readers today Spenser's coinages fall into two categories: those hardly recognized as such, for example *trophy* 'token of victory', *Mutabilitie* vii.56, *spangles* 'of frost', *FQ* I.x.48, and those which, like *underfong*, having never gained such currency, are now actually what they seem to be: archaisms.

Spenser was surprisingly successful in his aim of doubly enriching the language: by rehabilitating old words, often extending their meanings, and by introducing new words and forms. Some credit for the fact that many of both kinds remain in familiar use must go to Milton, whose debt to Spenser's vocabulary, pastoral and epic, merits detailed attention. Latinisms such as *horrid*, a word he uses frequently, or *transfix* (*FQ* I.v.50; *PL* I.328), Milton might certainly have derived for himself, though he would have known Spenser's earlier use of them. Among the minor poems *Lycidas* in particular draws on the vocabulary of *SC* extensively and probably for deliberate effect. *Oaten* (in 'Januarie', 'June'), *daffadillies* ('Januarie', 'Aprill', and also in *FQ*) are instances of words still familiar where *OED* also gives Spenser as the earliest example. *Equipage* (*PL* VII.204), *trinal* (*Nativity* II) and *arboret* ('little tree', *FQ* II.vi.12; *PL* IX.436) exemplify Milton's use of Spenserian words derived from foreign sources other than classical Latin. Writing when he did Milton's use of these and many other of Spenser's words went far towards establishing them, often not only in poetic usage. Even without his assistance such introductions as *blandishment* (*FQ* I.ix.14); *duress* ('constraint', *FQ* IV.viii.19): *lambkin* ('December'); *unsound* (of reasoning; *Epith.*), remain in common use, with no hint of sheepfold or inkhorn about them.

Spenser's 'choyse of old and unwonted words' both literary and colloquial is not confined to *SC* and is motivated beyond linguistic experiment or expansion considered simply as such. E.K. indicates as much by the wording of his reference to Cicero: old words give a peculiar quality to style, making it, 'as it were it were reverend: no otherwise then we honour and reverence gray heares for a certein religious regard, which we have of old age'. Some words or forms might certainly be expected to recall a specific author, such as Chaucer, or genre, such as chivalric romance, but by no means all. Such language very often carries a different and essentially anonymous kind of authority: the proverbial. The prevalence and importance of proverbial reference and diction in Spenser's work is considerably greater than is general in the writing of this period, when proverbs, aphorisms and *sententiae* made an important contribution to the school curriculum, as appears from the text-book collections in existence from at least as early as 1540. Erasmus' name, and those of the classical authors on whom he drew, had given more specific authority to the Latin *sententiae* used in schools and in anthologies of proverbs generally, much as the name of Aesop had long graced the genre of beast fable, but the vernacular tradition carried its own credence, 'reverend' in the sense of meriting respect. Interwoven with all innovation and 'strangenesse' of vocabulary, form, structure there runs throughout Spenser's work the firm thread of 'morall wisenesse', in E.K.'s phrase: the pithy, the familiar, the controvertible utterance. Three rather different examples, all of which occur in this selection, may give some indication of range and function. The first is a commonplace traceable to Sallust and Seneca:

> Yet never day so long, but late would pass.
>
> (*Epith.* 273)

Here it qualifies a state of mind proverbial in itself: the bridegroom's impatient longing for nightfall.

> All ends that was begonne
>
> (*FQ* I.ix.42)

applies or rather misapplies the same concept to a very different end: the very fact of mortality is here taken by Despaire as proving the pointlessness of existence.

The second example occurs four times in Spenser's writing, always with the meaning of smooth hypocrisy:

> And well could file his tongue
>
> (*FQ* I.i.35)

is said of Archimago. Spenser took the phrase probably from Chaucer, who uses it more than once: it occurs also in Gower and Skelton among others. The wording here is as important as the meaning; recognition confers authority.

The last example has Erasmus as an immediate source, though it is much older:

> Untroubled night, they say, gives counsell best,
>
> (*FQ* I.i.33)

where the speaker, Archimago again, colours his feigned hospitality with proverbial consensus. 'They say' aligns him with accepted truth: an effective contribution to his disguise.

The wording, variation and application of such *sententiae* would be at once recognized and appreciated by Spenser's contemporaries. It is also

possible that the natural syntax of many of the La[tin texts known to]
Spenser may account in part for the inversions t[hat are so]
characteristic of his English style and of which the [example]
given above may serve as an example. Phrasing of thi[s kind is]
an associative device, calling rhetorical attention [to some]
element in his work, and to its importance. Certainly Spenser's writing becomes itself a mine for proverbs and *sententiae* from as early as 1602: some indication of the contribution they were recognized as making to its tough underlying structure. At once subtle and uncompromising, it evoked constant and familiar awareness of the primary moral intention against which linguistic play and enrichment of every other kind was to be appreciated and its purpose understood.

NOTES

1. Helena Shires, *A Preface to Spenser*, London, 1978.
2. Edmund and his brother John both received financial help from the Nowell family of Lancashire while at school and university. See A.B. Grosart, *The Complete Works ... of Edmund Spenser*, London, 1883–4, vol. I, pp. xxvi–xxvii, xxxiii, xxxv, xli; 13–14, 28–9.
3. Lodovick Bryskett, *A Discourse of Civil Life*, London, 1606, p. 25.
4. Petrarch, 'Standomi un giorno solo alla fenestra'. Van der Noodt used the French translation by Clement Marot: *Des Visions de Petrarque*, which had first appeared in his *La Suite de l'Adolescence Clementine*, 1533. Spenser seems to have used this as well as the original. See *Variorum*, 'Minor Poems', vol. 2, pp. 273–7.
5. Joachim du Bellay, *Premier livre des Antiquitez de Rome ... Plus un Songe ou Vision sur le mesme subject*, 1558.
6. Revelations 13:1–15; 17:3–6 to 18:1–2; 19:11–20; 21:1–22 to 22:1–2.
7. Spencer, *A Theatre for Worldlings*, 1569, Sonnet XV.
8. There are a number of references in Spenser's writing and elsewhere to works by him that have not survived, or not under the titles given them. For a complete list of these, and a range of critical opinion concerning possible revisions and assimilations of certain of them into *FQ* in particular, see *Variorum*, 'Minor Poems', vol. 2, pp. 270, 510–20.
9. These techniques had been synthesized by the French scholar Petrus Ramus (Pierre de la Ramee) in his *Dialectica*, 1543, enlarged 1544, and recently introduced into England. They were taken up in Cambridge with rapid enthusiasm; Oxford was more conservative.

Spenser's name occurs five times in the Pembroke records as being a recipient of financial allowances made because of illness between 1571 and 1574.

11 *Letter-Book of Gabriel Hervey, 1573-80*, ed. Edward J.L. Scott, Camden Society Publications, 1884 (NS 33), pp. 2-34.

12 For example the reference in 'November' to the sun being 'in *Fishes haske*' suggests that this eclogue was originally intended for February, under the sign of Pisces.

13 Young himself, *Episcopus Roffensis*, appears in 'September' as 'Roffyn', and there are besides a number of clear references to contemporary church issues. See p. 000.

14 *Works*, pp. 612, 623, 636, 638: the passages referring in most detail to his activities and new acquaintance.

15 Sir Edward Dyer, ?1540-?1607, was a close friend of Sidney who in his will divided his books between him and Fulke Greville. His poetry is finely lyric, and deserves to be better known.

16 'The *Sheapheards Kalender* hath much Poetrie in his Eglogues: indeede worth the reading, if I be not deceived. That same framing of his stile to an old rustick language I dare not alowe, sith neither *Theocritus* in Greeke, *Virgill* in Latine, nor *Sanazar* in Italian did affect it.' From Sidney's *The Apology for Poetrie*, c.1583 (printed 1585). However they may have agreed on poetic theory, the originality of Spenser's practice seemed to Sidney merely misguided.

17 William Webbe, in *A Discourse of English Poetrie*, 1586, comes close, identifying 'the rightest English Poet that ever I read, that is, the Author of the Sheepeheardes Kalender ... whether it was Master *Sp.* or what rare Scholler in Pembroke Hall soever, because himself and his freendes, for what respect I knowe not, would not reveale it, I force not greatly to sette downe'. George Puttenham, in *The Arte of English Poesie*, 1589, Chapter xxxi, praises as writers of pastoral Sidney, Sir Thomas Chaloner and 'that other Gentleman who wrote the late shepheardes Callender'.

18 *Works*, p. 628.

19 See Shires, *Preface to Spenser*, p. 17.

20 De Selincourt suggests that Leicester found Spenser's attack on Burghley in *MHT* a political embarrassment; see *Works*, pp. xxii-xxiii. Shires, *Preface to Spenser*, pp. 45-6, finds in 'March' a reference to the death of Leicester's first wife so tactless as to be incredible if it were so intended. The wording of the dedication of *VG* 'Long since ... to ... the Earle of Leicester, late deceased' makes it clear that some good intention of the poet's was wrongly taken: 'Wrong'd, yet not daring to expresse my paine'.

21 Spenser himself says: 'That did eat the dead Carrions, happie wheare they

Coulde finde them, Yea and one another sone after, in so muche as the verye carkasses they spare not to scrape out of theire graves', *Veue* 3248-70. Other instances are cited; see *Variorum*, 'Prose Works', p. 382.

22   See David Beers Quinn, *The Elizabethans and the Irish*, New York, 1966, pp. 22ff.

23   See Charles G. Smith, *Spenser's Proverb Lore*, Cambridge, Mass., 1970, p. 157.

24   Spenser (as Irenius) takes the Irish to be descended from the Scythians; see *Veue*, 1145ff. Eudoxus comments on his arguments: 'Neither have youe sure anie more dishonoured the Irishe for you have broughte them from verye greate and anciente nacions as anie weare in the worlde', *Veue* 1380-3. Spenser evidently planned a work specifically on 'the Antiquities of Ireland' (*Veue* 5513); his present handling of such material is dictated by his immediate purpose: 'Heare onelye it shall suffice to tuche suche Customes of the Irishe as seme offensive and repugnant to the good government of that realme', *Veue* 1139-41.

25   In particular Spenser has drawn on Irish topographical tradition for the river-myths in *CCCHA* and *Mutabilitie*. See pp. 310-16 and 379-86.

26   Sir John Davies, *A Discovery of the true causes why Ireland was never entirely subdued ... until the beginning of his Majesties happy reign*, 1612, paragraph iv.

27   *Veue* 3324-34.

28   The causes of Raleigh's temporary eclipse at this time are not known. Far more serious was the disgrace into which he fell in 1592, which may have been connected with the circumstances of his marriage in that year to Elizabeth Throckmorton, one of the queen's maids of honour. See *The Poems of Sir Walter Raleigh*, ed. Agnes M.C. Latham, London, 1951, pp. xvi-xvii. Spenser gives a delicate extrapolation of this episode in the relationship of Timias and Belphoebe; see *FQ* III.v; IV.vii-viii.

29   *Muio.* may well have been written during Spenser's time in England, and it is likely that *MHT* in particular was so radically revised as to be a new work. See n. 20.

30   Gorges later paid Spenser the posthumous compliment of interweaving ll. 215-492 of *Daphnaida* with ll. 1060-88 of his own elegy written on the death of Prince Henry, *The Olympian Catastrophe*, 1612.

31   See in particular *CCCHA* 648-75. A more general and conventional expression of the same feeling is uttered by Meliboe in *FQ* VI.ix.24-5.

32   The rent of New Abbey, Kildare, was £3 for example. The prices of goods generally rose during Elizabeth's reign, partly owing to the influx into Europe of precious metals from the New World, but in the 1590s a pair of Spanish leather pumps cost 1s 2d, a simple shirt 1s; starch was 3d per 1b and tobacco from 12s to 64s per lb, according to quality; 420 oranges cost 2s 4d. There was considerable fluctuation in the price of other basic commodities

especially in the 1590s; but all prices in Ireland would vary from those in England to some extent, luxury goods tending to be dearer and much farm produce cheaper. See M. St Clare Byrne, *Elizabethan Life in Town and Country*, London, 1925, revised edn 1950, appendix III, and, for more detailed exploration of the economic situation as a whole, Sir William Beveridge, *Prices and Wages in England from the Twelfth to the Nineteenth Century*, vol. I, London, 1939.

33 It has been suggested on stylistic and other grounds that some of the sonnets in *Amoretti* were in fact written considerably earlier; see for example *Variorum*, 'Minor Poems', vol. 2, pp. 637–8, and J.W. Lever's chapter on *Amoretti* in *The Elizabethan Love Sonnet*, London, 1956. The sequence as it stands is, however, coherent in itself, the conventions it exploits being deployed with originality as well as elegance.

34 *Veue* 48–51.

35 *A briefe discourse of Ireland* 270–6.

36 A great deal of work has been done on all aspects of Spenser's use of language. Full and detailed lists of books and articles are to be found in any of the comprehensive bibliographies of Spenser listed at the head of the Select Bibliography, in addition to the works there cited in the appropriate section.

SPENSER
Selected Writings

The Shepheardes Calender

JUNE

Ægloga sexta

Argument

This Æglogue is wholly vowed to the complayning of Colins ill successe in his love. For being (as is aforesaid) enamoured of a Country lasse

Rosalind, and having (as seemeth) founde place in her heart, he lamenteth to his deare frend Hobbinoll, that he is nowe forsaken unfaithfully, and in his steede Menalcas, another shepheard received disloyally. And this is the whole Argument of this Æglogue.

HOBBINOL   COLIN CLOUTE

Lo *Colin*, here the place, whose pleasaunt syte
From other shades hath weand my wandring mynde.
Tell me, what wants me here, to work delyte?
The simple ayre, the gentle warbling wynde,
So calme, so coole, as no where else I fynde:
The grassye ground with daintye Daysies dight,
The Bramble bush, where Byrds of every kynde
To the waters fall their tunes attemper right.

COLLIN

O happy *Hobbinoll*, I blesse thy state,
That Paradise has found, whych *Adam* lost.   10
Here wander may thy flock early or late,
Withouten dreade of Wolves to bene ytost:
Thy lovely layes here mayst thou freely boste.
But I unhappy man, whom cruell fate,
And angry Gods pursue from coste to coste,
Can nowhere fynd, to shroude my lucklesse pate.

---

1 *syte* see Glosse
2 *weand* drawn
3 *what wants me* what do I lack
4 *simple* pure
6 *dight* decked
8 *attemper* harmonize
12 *ytost* harried
13 *boste* utter
16 *shroude ... pate* to shelter my luckless head

*Numbers in square brackets refer to pages on which notes may be found.

HOBBINOLL

Then if by me thou list advised be,
Forsake the soyle, that so doth thee bewitch:
Leave me those hilles, where harbrough nis to see,
Nor holybush, nor brere, nor winding witche: 20
And to the dales resort, where shepheards ritch,
And fruictfull flocks bene every where to see.
Here no night Ravens lodge more black than pitche,
Nor elvish ghosts, nor gastly owles doe flee.

But frendly Faeries, met with many Graces,
And lightfote Nymphes can chace the lingering night,
With Heydeguyes, and trimly trodden traces,
Whilst systers nyne, which dwell on *Parnasse* hight,
Doe make them musick, for their more delight:
And *Pan* himselfe to kisse their christall faces, 30
Will pype and daunce, when *Phœbe* shineth bright:
Such pierlesse pleasures have we in these places.

COLLIN

And I, whylst youth, and course of carelesse yeeres
Did let me walke withouten lincks of love,
In such delights did joy amongst my peeres:

18 *soyle* place; see *Glosse*
19 *where harbrough nis to see* where no refuge is to be found
20 *brere* briar rose; *witche* witch-elm
23 *night Ravens* see *Glosse*
24 *gastly* of ill omen; *flee* fly
27 *Heydeguyes* see *Glosse*; *traces* paths
28 *systers nyne* the Muses; *Parnasse hight* Mount Parnassus
30 *Pan* the god of the pastoral world
31 *Phoebe* the moon
32 *pierlesse* unequalled
33 *carelesse* carefree
35 *peeres* see *Glosse*

But ryper age such pleasures doth reprove,
My fancye eke from former follies move
To stayed steps: for time in passing weares
(As garments doen, which wexen old above)
And draweth newe delightes with hoary heares. 40

Tho couth I sing of love, and tune my pype
Unto my plaintive pleas in verses made:
Tho would I seeke for Queene apples unrype,
To give my *Rosalind*, and in Sommer shade
Dight gaudy Girlonds, was my comen trade,
To crowne her golden locks, but yeeres more rype,
And losse of her, whose love as lyfe I wayd,
Those weary wanton toyes away dyd wype.

HOBBINOLL

Colin, to heare thy rymes and roundelayes,
Which thou were wont on wastfull hylls to singe, 50
I more delight, then larke in Sommer dayes:
Whose Echo made the neyghbour groves to ring,
And taught the byrds, which in the lower spring
Did shroude in shady leaves from sonny rayes,
Frame to thy songe their chereful cheriping,
Or hold theyr peace, for shame of thy swete layes.

---

36 *reprove* disdain
37 *eke* also
38 *stayed* sober
41 *Tho* then; *couth* could
43 *Queene apples* quinces
45 *gaudy* bright; *comen trade* usual occupation
48 *weary* tedious; *wanton* foolish
49 *roundelayes* short songs, with refrains
50 *wastfull* desolate
52 *neyghbour groves* nearby woodland; see *Glosse*
53 *spring* see *Glosse*

I sawe *Calliope* wyth Muses moe,
Soone as thy oaten pype began to sound,
Theyr yvory Luyts and Tamburins forgoe:
And from the fountaine, where they sat around,   60
Renne after hastely thy silver sound.
But when they came, where thou thy skill didst showe,
They drewe abacke, as halfe with shame confound,
Shepheard to see, them in theyr art outgoe.

COLLIN

Of Muses *Hobbinol*, I conne no skill:
For they bene daughters of the hyghest *Jove*,
And holden scorne of homely shepheards quill.
For sith I heard, that *Pan* with *Phœbus* strove,
Which him to much rebuke and Daunger drove:
I never lyst presume to *Parnasse* hyll,   70
But pyping lowe in shade of lowly grove,
I play to please my selfe, all be it ill.

Nought weigh I, who my song doth prayse or blame,
Ne strive to winne renowne, or passe the rest:
With shepheard sittes not, followe flying fame:
But feede his flocke in fields, where falls hem best.
I wrote my rymes bene rough, and rudely drest:
The fytter they, my carefull case to frame:

57 *Calliope* muse of epic poetry
59 *Tamburins* tabors
60 *the fountaine* Hippocrene, on Mount Helicon
61 *Renne after hastely* run quickly after
63 *confound* confounded
65 *conne* know
66 *Jove* Jupiter
71 *lowe* modestly
73 *Nought weigh I* I care not
75 *sittes not* does not suit
76 *where falls hem best* where is best for them
77 *rough, and rudely drest* rustic and unpolished
78 *carefull* sorrowful

Enough is me to paint out my unrest,
And poore my piteous plaints out in the same. 80

The God of Shepheards *Tityrus* is dead,
Who taught me homely, as I can, to make.
He, whilst he lived, was the soueraigne head
Of shepheards all, that bene with love ytake:
Well couth he wayle hys Woes, and lightly slake
The flames, which love within his heart had bredd,
And tell us mery tales, to keepe us wake,
The while our sheepe about us safely fedde.

Nowe dead he is, and lyeth wrapt in lead,
(O why should death on hym such outrage showe?) 90
And all hys passing skil with him is fledde,
The fame whereof doth dayly greater growe.
But if on me some little drops would flowe,
Of that the spring was in his learned hedde,
I soone would learne these woods, to wayle my woe,
And teache the trees, their trickling teares to shedde.

Then should my plaints, causd of discurtesee,
As messengers of all my painfull plight,
Flye to my love, where ever that she bee,
And pierce her heart with poynt of worthy wight: 100
As shee deserves, that wrought so deadly spight.
And thou *Menalcas*, that by trecheree
Didst underfong my lasse, to wexe so light,
Shouldest well be knowne for such they villanee.

But since I am not, as I wish I were,
Ye gentle shepheards, which your flocks do feede,

80 *poore* pour
82 *to make* see *Glosse*
84 *ytake* overcome
95 *learne* teach
100 *poynt of worthy wight* see *Glosse*
103 *underfong* see *Glosse*; *wexe so light* become so false

Whether on hylls, or dales, or other where,
Beare witnesse all of thys so wicked deede:
And tell the lasse, whose flowre is woxe a weede,
And faultlesse fayth, is turned to faithlesse fere, 110
That she the truest shepheards hart made bleede,
That lyves on earth, and loved her most dere.

HOBBINOL

O carefull *Colin*, I lament thy case,
Thy teares would make the heardest flint to flowe.
Ah faithlesse Rosalind, and voide of grace,
That art the roote of all this ruthfull woe.
But now is time, I gesse, homeward to goe:
Then ryse ye blessed flocks, and home apace,
Least night with stealing steppes doe you forsloe,
And wett your tender Lambes, that by you trace. 120

Colins Embleme
Gia speme spenta

Glosse

1 Syte) situation and place.
10 Paradise) A Paradise in Greeke signifieth a Garden of pleasure, or place of delights. So he compareth the soile, wherein Hobbinoll made his abode, to that earthly Paradise, in scripture called Eden; wherein Adam in his first creation was placed. Which of the most learned is thought to be in Mesopotamia, the most fertile and pleasaunte country in the world (as may appeare by Diodorus Syculus description of it, in 130 the hystorie of Alexanders conquest thereof) lying betweene the two famous Ryvers (which are sayd in scripture to flowe out of Paradise) Tygris and Euphrates, whereof it is so denominate.
18 Forsake the the soyle) This is no poetical fiction, but unfeynedly

110 *fere* companion
115 *voide* lacking
116 *ruthfull* pitiable
119 *forsloe* hinder
120 *wett* refresh
133 *denominate* named

spoken of the Poete selfe, who for speciall occasion of private affayres (as I have bene partly of himselfe informed) and for his more preferment removing out of the Northparts came into the South, as Hobbinoll indeede advised him privately.

19 Those hylles) that is the North countrye, where he dwelt.
N'is) is not.

21 The Dales) The Southpartes, where he nowe abydeth, which thoughe they be full of hylles and woodes (for Kent is very hyllye and woodye; and therefore so called: for Kantsh in the Saxons tongue signifieth woodie) yet in respecte of the Northpartes they be called dales. For indede the North is counted the higher countrye.

23 Night Ravens &c.) by such hatefull byrdes, hee meaneth all misfortunes (Whereof they be tokens) flying every where.

25 Frendly faeries) the opinion of Faeries and elfes is very old, and yet sticketh very religiously in the myndes of some. But to roote that rancke opinion of Elfes oute of mens hearts, the truth is, that there be no such thinges, nor yet the shadowes of the things, but onely by a sort of bald Friers and knavish shavelings so feigned; which as in all other things, so in that, soughte to nousell the comen people in ignorounce, least being once acquainted with the truth of things, they woulde in tyme smell out the untruth of theyr packed pelfe and Massepenie religion. But the sooth is, that when all Italy was distraicte into the Factions of the Guelfes and the Gibelins, being two famous houses in Florence, the name began through their great mischiefes and many outrages, to be so odious or rather dreadfull in the peoples eares, that if theyr children at any time were frowarde and wanton, they would say to them that the Guelfe or the Gibeline came. Which words nowe from them (as many thinge els) be come into our usage, and for Guelfes and Gibelines, we say Elfes and Goblins. No otherwise then the Frenchmen used to say of that valiaunt captain, the very scourge of Fraunce, the Lord Thalbot, afterward Erle of Shrewsbury; whose noblesse bred such a terrour in the hearts of the French, that oft times even great armies were defaicted and put to flyght at the onely hearing

149 *religiously* inextricably; *to roote that rancke opinion* to extirpate that pernicious belief
151 *sort* crowd
152 *knavish shavelings* dishonest (tonsured) monks; *feigned* invented
153 *nousell* foster
155 *packed pelfe* horded wealth; *Massepenie* a gift of money made at Mass: here 'hired'
160 *frowarde* disobedient
167 *defaicted* defeated; *at the onely hearing* only by hearing

of hys name. In somuch that the French wemen, to affray theyr chyldren, would tell them that the Talbot commeth.

25 Many Graces) though there be indeede but three Graces or Charites (as afore is sayd) or at the utmost but foure, yet in respect of many gyftes of bounty, there may be sayde more. And so Musæus sayth, that in Heroes eyther eye there satte a hundred graces. And by that authoritye, thys same Poete in his Pageaunts sayth.

An hundred Graces on her eyeledde satte. &c.

27 Haydeguies) A country daunce or rownd. The conceipt is, that the Graces and Nymphes doe daunce unto the Muses, and Pan his musicke all night by Moonelight. To signifie the pleasauntnesse of the soyle.
35 Peeres) Equalles and felow shepheards.
43 Queneapples unripe) imitating Virgils verse.

Ipse ego cana legam tenera lanugine mala.

52 Neighbour groves) a straunge phrase in English, but word for word expressing the Latine *vicina nemora*.
53 Spring) not of water, but of young trees springing.
57 Calliope) afforesayde. Thys staffe is full of verie poetical invention.
59 Tamburines) an olde kind of instrument, which of some is supposed to be the Clarion.
68 Pan with Phæbus) the tale is well knowne, howe that Pan and Apollo striving for excellencye in musicke, chose Midas for their judge. Who being corrupted wyth partiall affection, gave the victorye to Pan undeserved: for which Phœbus sette a payre of Asses eares upon hys head &c.
81 Tityrus) That by Tityrus is meant Chaucer, hath bene already sufficiently sayde, and by thys more playne appeareth, that he sayth, he tolde merye tales. Such as be hys Canterburie tales. Whom he called the God of Poetes for hys excellencie, so as Tullie calleth Lentulus, Deum vitæ suæ .s. the God of hys lyfe.
82 To make) to versifie.
90 O why) A pretye Epanorthosis or correction.
97 Discurtesie) he meaneth the falsenesse of his lover Rosalinde, who forsaking hym, hadde chosen another.
100 Poynte of worthy wite) the pricke of deserved blame.
102 Menalcas) the name of a shephearde in Virgile; but here is meant a

---

185 *staffe* verse
199 *Epanorthosis* rhetorical term: 'amendment'

person unkowne and secrete, agaynst whome he often bitterly invayeth.
103 underfonge) undermine and deceive by false suggestion.

Embleme

You remember, that in the fyrst Æglogue, Colins Poesie was Anchora speme: for that as then there was hope of favour to be found in tyme. But nowe being cleane forlorne and rejected of her, as whose hope, that was, is cleane extinguished and turned into despeyre, he renounceth all comfort and hope of goodnesse to come. Which is all the meaning of thys Embleme.

OCTOBER

Ægloga decima

Argument

In Cuddie is set out the prefecte paterne of a Poete, whiche finding no maintenaunce of his state and studies, complayneth of the contempte of Poetrie, and the causes thereof: Specially having bene in all ages, and even

205 *invayeth* complains

amongst the most barbarous alwayes of singular accounpt and honor, and being indede so worthy and commendable an arte: or rather no arte, but a divine gift and heavenly instinct not to bee gotten by laboure and learning, but adorned with both: and poured into the witte by a certaine ἐνθουσιασμὸς. and celestiall inspiration, as the Author hereof els where at large discourseth, in his booke called the English Poete, which booke being lately come to my hands, I mynde also by Gods grace upon further advisement to publish.

PIERCE   CUDDIE

Cuddie, for shame hold up thy heavye head,
And let us cast with what delight to chace,
And weary thys long lingring *Phœbus* race.
Whilome thou wont the shepheards laddes to leade,
In rymes, in ridles, and in bydding base:
Now they in thee, and thou in sleepe art deade.

CUDDYE

Piers, I have pyped erst so long with payne,
That all mine Oten reedes bene rent and wore:
And my poore Muse hath spent her spared store,
Yet little good hath got, and much lesse gayne.   10
Such pleasaunce makes the Grashopper so poore,
And ligge so layd, when Winter doth her straine:

The dapper ditties, that I wont devise,
To feede youthes fancie, and the flocking fry,

Argument *accounpt* esteem; ἐνθουσιασμὸς inspiration; *advisement* consideration
  2 *cast* plan
  3 *Phœbus race* time of daylight
  4 *whilome* formerly
  7 *erst* lately
  9 *spared* hoarded
 12 *ligge so layd* see *Glosse; straine* oppress
 13 *dapper* see *Glosse*
 14 *fry* young people, and see *Glosse*

Delighten much: what I the bett for thy?
They han the pleasure, I a sclender prise.
I beate the bush, the byrds to them doe flye:
What good thereof to Cuddie can arise?

PIRES

Cuddie, the prayse is better, then the price,
The glory eke much greater then the gayne: 20
O what an honor is it, to restraine
The lust of lawlesse youth with good advice:
Or pricke them forth with pleasaunce of thy vaine,
Whereto thou list their trayned willes entice.

Soone as thou gynst to sette thy notes in frame,
O how the rurall routes to thee doe cleave:
Seemeth thou dost their soule of sence bereave,
All as the shepheard, that did fetch his dame
From *Plutoes* balefull bowre withouten leave:
His musicks might the hellish hound did tame. 30

CUDDIE

So praysen babes the Peacoks spotted traine,
And wondren at bright *Argus* blazing eye:
But who rewards him ere the more for thy?
Or feedes him once the fuller by a graine?
Sike prayse is smoke, that sheddeth in the skye,
Sike words bene wynd, and wasten soone in vayne.

15 *what I the bett for thy?* how am I the better for that?
23 *pricke them forth* enliven them
24 *trayned* fascinated
25 *gynst* begin
26 *routes* crowds
33 *ere* ever
35 *Sike* such; *sheddeth* disperses
36 *wasten* dissipate

PIERS

Abandon then the base and viler clowne,
Lyft up thy selfe out of the lowly dust:
And sing of bloody Mars, of wars, of giusts,
Turne thee to those, that weld the awful crowne. 40
To doubted Knights, whose woundlesse armour rusts,
And helmes unbruzed wexen dayly browne.

There may thy Muse display her fluttryng wing,
And stretch her selfe at large from East to West:
Wither thou list in fayre *Elisa* rest,
Or if thee please in bigger notes to sing,
Advaunce the worthy whome shee loveth best,
That first the white beare to the stake did bring.

And when the stubborne stroke of stronger stounds,
Has somewhat slackt the tenor of thy string: 50
Of love and lustihead tho mayst thou sing,
And carrol lowde, and leade the Myllers rownde,
All were *Elisa* one of thilke same ring.
So mought our *Cuddies* name to Heaven sownde.

CUDDYE

Indeede the Romish *Tityrus*, I heare,
Through his *Mecœnas* left his Oaten reede,

---

37 *the base and viler clowne* the modest vocation of a pastoral poet
39 *giusts* jousts
40 *weld* wear; *awful* awe-inspiring
41 *doubted* famous; *woundlesse* pristine, and see *Glosse*
46 *bigger* grander
49 *stounds* conflicts
50 *slackt* see *Glosse*
51 *lustihead* pleasure
52 *Myllers rownde* see *Glosse*
53 *All were Elisa* even if Elisa were; *thilke* that
54 *mought* might

Whereon he earst had taught his flocks to feede,
And laboured lands to yield the timely eare,
And eft did sing of warres and deadly drede,
So as the Heavens did quake his verse to here.   60

But ah *Mecœnas* is yclad in claye,
And great *Augustus* long ygoe is dead:
And all the worthies liggen wrapt in leade,
That matter made for Poets on to play:
For ever, who in derring doe were dreade,
The loftie verse of hem was loved aye.

But after vertue gan for age to stoupe,
And mighty manhode brought a bedde of ease:
The vaunting Poets found nought worth a pease,
To put in preace emong the learned troupe.   70
The gan the streames of flowing wittes to cease,
And sonnebright honour pend in shamefull coupe.

And if that any buddes of Poesie,
Yet of the old stocke gan to shoote agayne:
Or it mens follies mote by forst to fayne,
And rolle with rest in rymes of rybaudrye:
Or as it sprong, it wither must agayne:
Tom Piper makes us better melodie.

61 *yclad* wrapped
63 *liggen* lie
65 *ever* always; *derring doe* see *Glosse*
66 *hem* them
67 *after* later
68 *a bedde* to a bed
69 *vaunting* aspiring; *pease* pease-straw: of no value
70 *put in preace* to test their art
75 *mote* must
76 *rybaudrye* obscenity

46

PIERS

O pierlesse Poesye, where is then thy place?
If nor in Princes pallace thou doe sitt: 80
(And yet is Princes pallace the most fitt)
Ne brest of baser birth doth thee embrace.
Then make thee winges of thine aspyring wit,
And, whence thou camst, flye backe to heaven apace.

CUDDIE

Ah *Percy* it is all to weake and wanne,
So high to sore, and make so large a flight:
Her peeced pyneons bene not so in plight,
For *Colin* fittes such famous flight to scanne:
He, were he not with love so ill bedight,
Would mount as high, and sing as soote as Swanne.   90

PIERS

Ah fon, for love does teach him climbe so hie,
And lyftes him up out of the loathsome myre:
Such immortall mirrhor, as he doth admire,
Would rayse ones mynd above the starry skie.
And cause a caytive corage to aspire,
For lofty love doth loath a lowly eye.

---

85 *wanne* faint
87 *peeced pyneons* tattered flight-feathers
88 *scanne* attempt
89 *bedight* afflicted
90 *soote* sweet
91 *fon* fool
95 *caytive* base

CUDDIE

All otherwise the state of Poet stands,
For lordly love is such a Tyranne fell:
That where he rules, all power he doth expell.
The vaunted verse a vacant head demaundes, 100
Ne wont with crabbed care the Muses dwell.
Unwisely weaves, that takes two webbes in hand.

Who ever casts to compasse weightye prise,
And thinks to throwe out thondring words of threate:
Let powre in lavish cups and thriftie bitts of meate,
For *Bacchus* fruite is frend to *Phœbus* wise.
And when with Wine the braine begins to sweate,
The nombers flowe as fast as spring doth ryse.

Thou kenst not *Percie* howe the ryme should rage.
O if my temples were distaind with wine, 110
And girt in girlonds of wild Yvie twine,
How I could reare the Muse on stately stage,
And teache her tread aloft in bus-kin fine,
With queint *Bellona* in her equipage.

But ah my corage cooles ere it be warme,
For thy, content us in thys humble shade:
Where no such troublous tydes han us assayde,
Here we our slender pipes may safely charme.

98 *Tyranne fell* fearful tyrant
100 *vacant* untroubled
103 *Who...prise* whoever tries to achieve great things
104 *threate* denunciation
106 *Bacchus* god of wine
112 *reare* raise up
113 *bus-kin* see *Glosse*
114 *queint Bellona* strange Bellona, and see *Glosse*
118 *charme* tune

PIRES

And when my Gates shall han their bellies layd:
Cuddie shall have a Kidde to store his farme.   120

> Cuddies Embleme
> *Agitante calescimus illo &c.*

Glosse

This Æglogue is made in imitation of Theocritus his xvi. Idilion, wherein hee reproved the Tyranne Hiero of Syracuse for his nigardise towarde Poetes, in whome is the power to make men immortal for theyr good dedes, or shameful for their naughty lyfe. And the lyke also is in Mantuane, The style hereof as also that in Theocritus, is more loftye then the rest, and applyed to the heighte of Poeticall witte.

Cuddie) I doubte whether by Cuddie be specified the authour selfe, or   130
some other. For in the eyght Æglogue the same person was brought in, singing a Cantion of Colins making, as he sayth. So that some doubt, that the persons be different.

4 Whilome) sometime.   8 Oaten reedes) Avena.

12 Ligge so layde) lye so faynt and unlustye.   13 Dapper) pretye.

14 Frye) is a bold Metaphore, forced from the spawning fishes. For the multitude of young fish to be called the frye.

21 To restraine.) This place seemeth to conspyre with Plato, who in his first booke de Legibus sayth, that the first invention of Poetry was of very vertuous intent. For at what time an infinite number of youth usually   140
came to theyr great solemne feastes called Panegyrica, which they used every five yeere to hold, some learned man being more hable than the rest, for speciall gyftes of wytte and Musicke, would take upon him to sing fine verses to the people, in prayse eyther of vertue or of victory or of immortality or such like. At whose wonderful gyft al men being astonied and as it were ravished, with delight, thinking (as it was indeed) that he was inspired from above, called him vatem: which kinde of men afterwarde framing their verses to lighter musick (as of musick be many kinds, some sadder, some lighter, some martiall, some

119 *Gates* goats; *layd* unburdened
132 *Cantion* song
139 *de Legibus* The Laws
147 *vatem* Lat. *vates*, prophet

[411-13]

heroical: and so diversely eke affect the mynds of men) found out lighter matter of Poesie also, some playing wyth love, some scorning at mens fashions, some powred out in pleasures, and so were called Poetes or makers.

27 Sence bereave) what the secrete working of Musick is in the myndes of men, aswell appeareth, hereby, that some of the aunciente Philosophers, and those the moste wise, as Plato and Pythagoras held for opinion, that the mynd was made of a certaine harmonie and musicall nombers, for the great compassion and likenes of affection in thone and in the other as also by that memorable history of Alexander: to whom when as Timotheus the great Musitian playd the Phrygian melodie, it is said, that he was distraught with such unwonted fury, that streight way rysing from the table in great rage, he caused himselfe to be armed, as ready to goe to warre (for that musick is very war like:) And immediately whenas the Musitian chaunged his stroke into the Lydian and Ionique harmony, he was so furr from warring, that he sat as styl, as if he had bene in matters of counsell. Such might is in musick. Wherefore Plato and Aristotle forbid the Arabian Melodie from children and youth. For that being altogither on the fyft and vii, tone, it is of great force to molifie and quench the kindly courage, which useth to burne in yong brests. So that it is not incredible which the Poete here sayth, that Musick can bereave the soule of sence.

28 The shepheard that) Orpheus: of whom is sayd, that by his excellent skil in Musick and Poetry, he recovered his wife Eurydice from hell.

32 Argus eyes) of Argus is before said, that Iuno to him committed hir husband Jupiter his Paragon Iô, bicause he had an hundred eyes: but afterwarde Mercury wyth hys Musick lulling Argus aslepe, slew him and brought Iô away, whose eyes it is sayd that Juno for his eternall memory placed in her byrd the Peacocks tayle. For those coloured spots indeede resemble eyes.

41 Woundlesse armour) unwounded in warre, doe rust through long peace.

43 Display) A poeticall metaphore: whereof the meaning is, that if the Poet list showe his skill in matter of more dignitie, then is the homely Æglogue, good occasion is him offered of higher veyne and more Heroical argument, in the person of our most gratious soveraign, whom (as before) he calleth Elisa. Or if matter of knighthoode and chevalrie please him better, that there be many Noble and valiaunt men, that are both worthy of his payne in theyr deserved prayses, and also favourers of hys skil and faculty.

169 *kindly* natural

47 The worthy) he meaneth (as I guesse) the most honorable and renowmed the Erle of Leycester, whom by his cognisance (although the same be also proper to other) rather than by his name he bewrayeth, being not likely, that the names of noble princes be known to country clowne.

50 Slack) that is when thou chaungest thy verse from stately discourse, to matter of more pleasaunce and delight.

52 The Millers) a kind of daunce.   53 Ring) company of dauncers.

55 The Romish Tityrus) wel knowen to be Virgile, who by Mecænas means was brought into the favour of the Emperor Augustus, and by him moved to write in loftier kinde, then he erst had doen.

57 Whereon) in these three verses are the three severall workes of Virgile intended. For in teaching his flocks to feede, is meant his Æglogues. In labouring of lands, is hys Georgiques. In singing of wars and deadly dreade, is his divine Æneis figured.

65 In derring doe) In manhoode and chevalrie.   For ever) He sheweth the cause, why Poetes were wont be had in such honor of noble men; that is, that by them their worthines and valor shold through theyr famous Posies be commended to al posterities. Wherfore it is sayd, that Achilles had never bene so famous, as he is, but for Homeres immortal verses. Which is the only advantage, which he had of Hector. And also that Alexander the great comming to his tombe in Sigeus, with naturall teares blessed him, that ever was his hap to be honoured with so excellent a Poets work: as so renowmed and ennobled onely by hys meanes. Which being declared in a most eloquent Oration of Tullies, is of Petrarch no lesse wortheley sette forth in a sonet

> Giunto Alexandro a la famosa tomba
> Del fero Achille sospirando disse
> O fortunato che si chiara tromba.   Trouasti &c.

And that such account hath bene always made of Poetes, as well sheweth this that the worthy Scipio in all his warres against Carthage and Numantia had evermore in his company, and that in a most familiar sort the good olde Poet Ennius: as also that Alexander destroying Thebes, when he was enformed that the famous Lyrick Poet Pindarus was borne in that citie, not onely commaunded streightly, that no man should upon payne of death do any violence to that house by fire or otherwise: but also specially spared most, and some highly rewarded, that were of hys kinne. So favoured he the only name of a

208 *Posies* poems

Poete. Whych prayse otherwise was in the same man no lesse famous, that when he came to ransacking of king Darius coffers, whom he lately had overthrowen, he founde in a little coffer of silver the two bookes of Homers works, as layd up there for speciall jewells and richesse, which he taking thence, put one of them dayly in his bosome, and thother every night layde under his pillowe. Such honor have Poetes alwayes found in the sight of princes and noble men. Which this author here very well sheweth, as els where more notably.

67 But after) he sheweth the cause of contempt of Poetry to be idlenesse and basenesse of mynd.

72 Pent) shut up in slouth, as in a coope or cage.

78 Tom Piper) An Ironicall Sarcasmus, spoken in derision of these rude wits, whych make more account of a ryming rybaud, then of skill grounded upon learning and judgment.

82 Ne brest) the meaner sort of men.

87 Her peeced pineons) unperfect skil.
Spoken wyth humble modestie.

90 As soote as Swanne) The comparison seemeth to be strange: for the swanne hath ever wonne small commendation for her swete singing: but it is sayd of the learned that the swan a little before hir death, singeth most pleasantly, as prophecying by a secrete instinct her neere destinie As wel sayth the Poete elswhere in one of his sonetts.

> The silver swanne doth sing before her dying day
> As shee that feeles the deepe delight that is in death &c.

93 Immortall myrrhour) Beauty, which is an excellent object of Poeticall spirites, as appareth by the worthy Petrachs saying.

> Fiorir faceva il mio debile ingegno
> A la sua ombra, et crescer ne gli affanni.

95 A caytive corage) a base and abject minde.

96 For lofty love) I think this playing with the letter to be rather a fault then a figure, aswel in our English tongue, as it hath bene alwayes in the Latine, called Cacozelon.

100 A vacant) imitateth Mantuanes saying. vacuum curis divina cerebrum Poscit.

105 Lavish cups) Resembleth that comen verse Fæcundi calices quem non fecere disertum.

110 O if my) He seemeth here to be ravished with a Poetical furie. For (if

240 *Sarcasmus* gibe

one rightly mark) the numbers rise so ful, and the verse groweth so big, that it seemeth he hath forgot the meanenesse of shepheards state and stile.

111 Wild yvie) for it is dedicated to Bacchus and therefore it is sayd that the Mænades (that is Bacchus franticke priestes) used in theyr sacrifice to carry Thyrsos, which were pointed staves of Javelins, wrapped about with yvie.

113 In buskin) it was the manner of Poetes and plaiers in tragedies to were buskins, as also in Comedies to use stockes and light shoes. So that the buskin in Poetry is used for tragical matter, as is said in Virgile. Sola sophocleo tua carmina digna cothurno. And the like in Horace, Magnum loqui, nitique cothurno.

114 Queint) strange Bellona; the goddesse of battaile, that is Pallas, which may therefore wel be called queint for that (as Lucian saith) when Jupiter hir father was in traveile of her, he caused his sonne Vulcane with his axe to hew his head. Out of which leaped forth lustely a valient damsell armed at all poyntes, whom seeing Vulcane so faire and comely, lightly leaping to her, proferred her some cortesie, which the Lady disdeigning, shaked her speare at him, and threatned his saucinesse. Therefore such straungeness is well applyed to her.

Æquipage.) order.

117 Tydes) seasons.

118 Charme) temper and order. For Charmes were wont to be made by verses as Ovid sayth. Aut si carminibus.

Embleme

Hereby is meant, as also in the whole course of this Æogue, that Poetry is a divine instinct and unnatural rage passing the reache of comen reason. Whom Piers answereth Epiphonematicos as admiring the excellencye of the skyll whereof in Cuddie hee hadde alreadye hadde a taste.

---

291 *Unnatural rage* supernatural energy

TO
THE MOST HIGH,
MIGHTIE
And
MAGNIFICENT
EMPRESSE RENOW-
MED FOR PIETIE, VER-
TUE, AND ALL GRATIOUS
GOVERNMENT ELIZABETH BY
THE GRACE OF GOD QUEENE
OF ENGLAND FRANCE AND
IRELAND AND OF VIRGI-
NIA, DEFENDOUR OF THE
FAITH, &c. HER MOST
HUMBLE SERVAUNT
EDMUND SPENSER
DOTH IN ALL HU-
MILITIE DEDI-
CATE, PRE-
SENT
AND CONSECRATE THESE
HIS LABOURS TO LIVE
WITH THE ETERNI-
TIE OF HER
FAME.

renowmed renowned
government behaviour

The First
Booke of The
Faerie Queene

Contayning
**The Legende of the
Knight of the Red Crosse,**
or
of Holinesse

1

Lo I the man, whose Muse whilome did maske,
   As time her taught, in lowly Shepheards weeds,
   Am now enforst a far unfitter taske,
   For trumpets sterne to chaunge mine Oaten reeds,
   And sing of Knights and Ladies gentle deeds;
   Whose prayses having slept in silence long,
   Me, all too meane, the sacred Muse areeds
   To blazon broad emongst her learned throng:
Fierce warres and faithfull loves shall moralize my song.

2

Helpe then, O holy Virgin chiefe of nine,
   Thy weaker Novice to performe they will,
   Lay forth out of thine everlasting scryne
   The antique rolles, which there lye hidden still,
   Of Faerie knights and fairest *Tanaquill*,
   Whom that most noble Briton Prince so long

---

1 *whilome* formerly; *did maske* disguised herself
2 *As time her taught* as fitted the occasion
3 *Am now enforst* have now forced upon me; *unfitter* less suited to my skill
10 *holy Virgin chiefe of nine* Clio, muse of history
12 *scryne* book-chest

Sought through the world, and suffered so much ill,
   That I must rue his undeserved wrong:
O helpe thou my weake wit, and sharpen my dull tong.

3

And thou most dreaded impe of highest *Jove*,
   Faire *Venus* sonne, that with thy cruell dart
   At that good knight so cunningly didst rove,
   That glorious fire it kindled in his hart,
   Lay now thy deadly Heben bow apart,
   And with they mother milde come to mine ayde:
   Come both, and with you bring triumphant *Mart*,
   In loves and gentle jollities arrayd,
After his murdrous spoiles and bloudy rage allayd.

4

And with them eke, O Goddesse heavenly bright,
   Mirrour of grace and Majestie divine,
   Great Lady of the greatest Isle, whose light
   Like *Phœbus* lampe throughout the world doth shine,
   Shed thy faire beames into my feeble eyne,
   And raise my thoughts too humble and too vile,
   To thinke of that true glorious type of thine,
   The argument of mine afflicted stile:
The which to heare, vouchsafe, O dearest dred a-while.

19 *impe* offspring
20 *Faire Venus sonne* Cupid
23 *Heben* ebony
25 *Mart* Mars
30 *Great Lady* Queen Elizabeth I
31 *Phœbus* Apollo: the sun
35 *afflicted* humble

CANTO i

The Patron of true Holinesse,
Foule Errour doth defeate:
Hypocrisie him to entrapp;
Doth to his home entreate.

1

A Gentle Knight was pricking on the plaine,
　Y cladd in mightie armes and silver shielde,
　Wherein old dints of deepe wounds did remaine,
　The cruell markes of many' a bloudy fielde;
　Yet armes till that time did he never wield:
　His angry steede did chide his foming bitt,
　As much disdayning to the curbe to yield:
　Full jolly knight he seemd, and faire did sitt,
As one for knightly giusts and fierce encounters fitt.

2

But on his brest a bloudie Crosse he bore,   10
　The deare remembrance of his dying Lord,
　For whose sweete sake that glorious badge he wore,
　And dead as living ever him ador'd:
　Upon his shield the like was also scor'd,
　For soveraine hope, which in his helpe he had:
　Right faithful true he was in deede and word,
　But of his cheere did seeme too solemne sad;
Yet nothing did he dread, but ever was ydrad.

　1　*Gentle* noble; *pricking* riding fast
　8　*jolly* gallant
　9　*giusts* jousts
14　*scor'd* engraved
18　*ydrad* feared

3

Upon a great adventure he was bond,
   That greatest *Gloriana* to him gave,
   The greatest Glorious Queene of *Faerie* lond,
   To winne him worship, and her grace to have,
   Which of all earthly things he most did crave;
   And ever as he rode, his hart did earne
   To prove his puissance in battell brave
   Upon his foe, and his new force to learne;
Upon his foe, a Dragon horrible and stearne.

4

A lovely Ladie rode him faire beside,
   Upon a lowly Asse more white then snow,
   Yet she much whiter, but the same did hide
   Under a vele, that wimpled was full low,
   And over all a blacke stole she did throw,
   As one that inly mournd: so was she sad,
   And heavie sat upon her palfrey slow:
   Seemed in heart some hidden care she had,
And by her in a line a milke white lambe she lad.

5

So pure an innocent, as that same lambe,
   She was in life and every vertuous lore,
   And by descent from Royall lynage came
   Of ancient Kings and Queenes, that had of yore
   Their scepters stretcht from East to Westerne shore,
   And all the world in their subjection held;
   Till that infernall feend with foule uprore

19 *bond* bound
25 *puissance* might
34 *palfrey* mount (usually a horse) suitable for a lady
38 *lore* doctrine

[413–14]

Forwasted all their land, and them expeld:
Whom to avenge, she had this Knight from far compeld.

6

Behind her farre away a Dwarfe did lag,
   That lasie seemd in being ever last,
   Or wearied with bearing of her bag
   Of needments at his backe. Thus as they past,
   The day with cloudes was suddeine overcast,   50
   And angry *Jove* an hideous storme of raine
   Did poure into his Lemans lap so fast,
   That every wight to shroud it did constrain,
And this faire couple eke to shroud themselves were fain.

7

Enforst to seeke some covert nigh at hand,
   A shadie grove not far away they spide,
   That promist ayde the tempest to withstand:
   Whose loftie trees yclad with sommers pride,
   Did spred so broad, that heavens light did hide,
   Not perceable with power of any starre: 60
   And all within were pathes and alleies wide,
   With footing worne, and leading inward farre:
Faire harbour that them seemes; so in they entred arre.

8

And foorth they passe, with pleasure forward led,
   Joying to heare the birdes sweete harmony,
   Which therein shrouded from the tempest dred,

45 *compeld* brought
51 *Jove* Jupiter: the sky
52 *his Lemans* his lover's: the earth
53 *to shroud* to shroud themselves
60 *perceable* able to be pierced

    Seemd in their song to scorne the cruell sky.
    Much can they prayse the trees so straight and hy,
        The sayling Pine, the Cedar proud and tall,
        The vine-prop Elme, the Poplar never dry,   70
        The builder Oake, sole king of forrests all,
The Aspine good for staves, the Cypresse funerall.

9

The Laurell, meed of mightie Conquerours
    And Poets sage, the Firre that weepeth still,
    The Willow worne of forlorne Paramours,
    The Eugh obedient to the benders will,
    The Birch for shaftes, the Sallow for the mill,
    The Mirrhe sweete bleeding in the bitter wound,
    The warlike Beech, the Ash for nothing ill,
    The fruitfull Olive, and the Platane round,   80
The carver Holme, the Maple seeldom inward sound.

10

Led with delight, they thus beguile the way,
    Untill the blustring storme is overblowne;
    When weening to returne, whence they did stray,
    They cannot finde that path, which first was showne,
    But wander too and fro in wayes unknowne,
    Furthest from end then, when they neerest weene,
    That makes them doubt, their wits be not their owne:
    So many pathes, so many turnings seene,
That which of them to take, in diverse doubt they been.   90

11

At last resolving forward still to fare,
    Till that some end they finde or in or out,

76 *Eugh* yew
77 *Sallow* pussy willow
80 *Platane* Oriental plane tree

That path they take, that beaten seemd most bare,
And like to lead the labyrinth about;
Which when by tract they hunted had throughout,
At length it brought them to a hollow cave,
Amid the thickest woods. The Champion stout
Eftsoones dismounted from his courser brave,
And to the Dwarfe a while his needlesse spere he gave.

12

Be well aware, quoth then that Ladie milde, 100
   Least suddaine mischiefe ye too rash provoke:
   The danger hid, the place unknowne and wilde,
   Breedes dreadfull doubts: Oft fire is without smoke,
   And perill without show: therefore your stroke
   Sir knight with-hold, till further triall made.
   Ah Ladie (said he) shame were to revoke
   The forward footing for an hidden shade:
Vertue gives her selfe light, through darkenesse for to wade.

13

Yea but (quoth she) the perill of this place
   I better wot then you, though now too late 110
   To wish you backe returne with foule disgrace,
   Yet wisedome warnes, whilest foot is in the gate,
   To stay the steppe, ere forced to retrate.
   This is the wandring wood, this *Errours den*,
   A monster vile, whom God and man does hate:
   Therefore I read beware. Fly fly (quoth then
The fearefull Dwarfe:) this is no place for living men.

---

97 *stout* brave
99 *needlesse spere* his lance, useless to him when on foot
106 *revoke* withdraw
116 *read* advise

14

But full of fire and greedy hardiment,
    The youthfull knight could not for ought be staide,
    But forth unto the darksome hole he went,
    And looked in: his glistring armor made
    A litle glooming light, much like a shade,
    By which he saw the ugly monster plaine,
    Halfe like a serpent horribly displaide,
    But th'other halfe did womans shape retaine,
Most lothsom, filthie, foule, and full of vile disdaine.

15

And as she lay upon the durtie ground,
    Her huge long taile her den all overspred,
    Yet was in knots and many boughtes upwound,
    Pointed with mortall sting. Of her there bred
    A thousand yong ones, which she dayly fed,
    Sucking upon her poisonous dugs, eachone
    Of sundry shapes, yet all ill favored:
    Soone as that uncouth light upon them shone,
Into her mouth they crept, and suddain all were gone.

16

Their dam upstart, out of her den effraide,
    And rushed forth, hurling her hideous taile
    About her cursed head, whose folds displaid
    Were stretcht now forth at length without entraile.
    She lookt about, and seeing one in mayle
    Armed to point, sought backe to turne againe;

---

118 *greedy hardiment* eager courage
124 *displaide* stretched out
129 *boughtes* coils
136 *effraide* startled
139 *without entraile* straight

For light she hated as the deadly bale,
    Ay wont in desert darknesse to remaine,
Where plaine none might her see, nor she see any plaine.

17

Which when the valiant Elfe perceiv'd, he lept
    As Lyon fierce upon the flying pray,
    And with his trenchand blade her boldly kept
    From turning backe, and forced her to stay:
    Therewith enrag'd she loudly gan to bray,
    And turning fierce, her speckled taile advaunst,   150
    Threatning her angry sting, him to dismay:
    Who nought aghast, his mightie hand enhaunst:
The stroke down from her head unto her shoulder glaunst.

18

Much daunted with that dint, her sence was dazd,
    Yet kindling rage, her selfe she gathered round,
    And all attonce her beastly body raizd
    With doubled forces high above the ground:
    Tho wrapping up her wrethed sterne arownd,
    Lept fierce upon his shield, and her huge traine
    All suddenly about his body wound,   160
    That hand or foot to stirre he strove in vaine:
God helpe the man so wrapt in *Errours* endlesse traine.

19

His Lady sad to see his sore constraint,
    Cride out, Now now Sir knight, shew what ye bee,
    Add faith unto your force, and be not faint:
    Strangle her, else she sure will strangle thee.
    That when he heard, in great perplexitie,
    His gall did grate for griefe and high disdaine,

---

147 *trenchand* sharp
168 *gall* bile: angry resentment

    And knitting all his force got one hand free,
        Wherewith he grypt her gorge with so great paine,   170
That soone to loose her wicked bands did her constraine.

20

Therewith she spewd out of her filthy maw
    A floud of poyson horrible and blacke,
    Full of great lumpes of flesh and gobbets raw,
    Which stunck so vildly, that it forst him slacke
    His grasping hold, and from her turne him backe:
    Her vomit full of bookes and papers was,
    With loathly frogs and toades, which eyes did lacke,
    And creeping sought way in the weedy gras:
Her filthy parbreake all the place defiled has.   180

21

As when old father *Nilus* gins to swell
    With timely pride above the *Aegyptian* vale,
    His fattie waves do fertile slime outwell,
    And overflow each plaine and lowly dale:
    But when his later spring gins to avale,
    Huge heapes of mudd he leaves, wherein there breed
    Ten thousand kindes of creatures, partly male
    And partly female of his fruitfull seed;
Such ugly monstrous shapes elsewhere may no man reed.

22

The same so sore annoyed has the knight,   190
    That welnigh choked with the deadly stinke,
    His forces faile, ne can no longer fight.

---

180 *parbreake* vomit
185 *avale* sink
189 *reed* perceive
190 *annoyed* distressed

Whose corage when the feend perceiv'd to shrinke,
   She poured forth out of her hellish sinke
   Her fruitfull cursed spawne of serpents small,
   Deformed monsters, fowle, and blacke as inke,
   Which swarming all about his legs did crall,
And him encombred sore, but could not hurt at all.

23

As gentle Shepheard in sweete even-tide,
   When ruddy *Phœbus* gins to welke in west,   200
   High on an hill, his flocke to vewen wide,
   Markes which do byte their hasty supper best;
   A cloud of combrous gnattes do him molest,
   All striving to infixe their feeble stings,
   That from their noyance he no where can rest,
   But with his clownish hands their tender wings
He brusheth oft, and oft doth mar their murmurings.

24

Thus ill bestedd, and fearefull more of shame,
   Then of the certaine perill he stood in,
   Halfe furious unto his foe he came,   210
   Resolv'd in minde all suddenly to win,
   Or soone to lose, before he once would lin;
   And strooke at her with more then manly force,
   That from her body full of filthie sin
   He raft her hatefull head without remorse;
A streame of cole black bloud forth gushed from her corse.

---

200 *welke* dim
203 *combrous* harassing
208 *ill bestedd* hard-pressed
212 *lin* cease
215 *raft* cut off

25

Her scattred brood, soone as their Parent deare
    They saw so rudely falling to the ground,
    Groning full deadly, all with troublous feare,
    Gathred themselves about her body round,
    Weening their wonted entrance to have found
    At her wide mouth: but being there withstood
    They flocked all about her bleeding wound,
    And sucked up their dying mothers blood,
Making her death their life, and eke her hurt their good.

26

That detestable sight him much amazde,
    To see th'unkindly Impes of heaven accurst,
    Devoure their dam; on whom while so he gazd,
    Having all satisfide their bloudy thurst,
    Their bellies swolne he saw with fulnesse burst,
    And bowels gushing forth: well worthy end
    Of such as drunke her life, the which them nurst;
    Now needeth him no lenger labour spend,
His foes have slaine themselves, with whom he should contend.

27

His Ladie seeing all, that chaunst, from farre
    Approcht in hast to greet his victorie,
    And said, Faire knight, borne under happy starre,
    Who see your vanquisht foes before you lye:
    Well worthy be you of that Armorie,
    Wherein ye have great glory wonne this day,
    And proov'd your strength on a strong enimie,
    Your first adventure: many such I pray,
And henceforth ever wish, that like succeed it may.

---

227 *Impes* offspring

28

Then mounted he upon his Steede againe,
   And with the Lady backward sought to wend;
   That path he kept, which beaten was most plaine,
   Ne ever would to any by-way bend,
   But still did follow one unto the end,
   The which at last out of the wood them brought.
   So forward on his way (with God to frend)   250
   He passed forth, and new adventure sought;
Long way he travelled, before he heard of ought.

29

At length they chaunst to meet upon the way
   An aged Sire, in long blacke weedes yclad,
   His feete all bare, his beard all hoarie gray,
   And by his belt his booke he hanging had;
   Sober he seemde, and very sagely sad,
   And to the ground his eyes were lowly bent,
   Simple in shew, and voyde of malice bad,
   And all the way he prayed, as he went,   260
And often knockt his brest, as one that did repent.

30

He faire the knight saluted, louting low,
   Who faire him quited, as that courteous was:
   And after asked him, if he did know
   Of straunge adventures, which abroad did pas.
   Ah my deare Sonne (quoth he) how should, alas,
   Silly old man, that lives in hidden cell,
   Bidding his beades all day for his trespas,

257 *sad* solemn
262 *faire* graciously; *louting* bowing
263 *him quited* replied to him in kind
267 *Silly* simple
268 *Bidding* telling

         Tydings of warre and worldly trouble tell?
With holy father sits not with such things to mell.   270

31

But if of daunger which hereby doth dwell,
    And homebred evill ye desire to heare,
    Of a straunge man I can you tidings tell,
    That wasteth all this countrey farre and neare.
    Of such (said he) I chiefly do inquere,
    And shall you well reward to shew the place,
    In which that wicked wight his dayes doth weare:
    For to all knighthood it is foule disgrace,
That such a cursed creature lives so long a space.

32

Far hence (quoth he) in wastfull wildernesse   280
    His dwelling is, by which no living wight
    May ever passe, but thorough great distresse.
    Now (sayd the Lady) draweth toward night,
    And well I wote, that of your later fight
    Ye all forwearied be: for what so strong,
    But wanting rest will also want of might?
    The Sunne that measures heaven all day long,
At night doth baite his steedes the *Ocean* waves emong.

33

Then with the Sunne take Sir, your timely rest,
    And with new day new worke at once begin: 290
    Untroubled night they say gives counsell best.
    Right well Sir knight ye have advised bin,
    (Quoth then that aged man;) the way to win

270 *mell* meddle
273 *straunge* foreign
288 *baite* feed

Is wisely to advise: now day is spent;
  Therefore with me ye may take up your In
  For this same night. The knight was well content:
So with that godly father to his home they went.

34

A little lowly Hermitage it was,
  Downe in a dale, hard by a forests side,
  Far from resort of people, that did pas   300
  In travell to and froe: a little wyde
  There was an holy Chappell edifyde,
  Wherein the Hermite dewly wont to say
  His holy things each morne and eventyde:
  Thereby a Christall streame did gently play,
Which from a sacred fountaine welled forth alway.

35

Arrived there, the little house they fill,
  Ne looke for entertainement, where none was:
  Rest is their feast, and all things at their will;
  The noblest mind the best contentment has,   310
  With faire discourse the evening so they pas:
  For that old man of pleasing wordes had store,
  And well could file his tongue as smooth as glas;
  He told of Saintes and Popes, and evermore
He strowd an *Ave-Mary* after and before.

36

The drouping Night thus creepeth on them fast,
  And the sad humour loading their eye liddes,

301 *wyde* distance away
302 *edifyde* built
313 *file* polish
315 *an Ave-Mary* a Hail Mary
317 *humour* moisture

[413-14]

    As messenger of *Morpheus* on them cast
    Sweet slombring deaw, the which to sleepe them biddes.
    Unto their lodgings then his guestes he riddes: 320
    Where when all drownd in deadly sleepe he findes,
    He to his study goes, and there amiddes
    His Magick bookes and artes of sundry kindes,
He seekes out mighty charmes, to trouble sleepy mindes.

37

Then choosing out few wordes most horrible,
    (Let none them read) thereof did verses frame,
    With which and other spelles like terrible,
    He bad awake blacke *Plutoes* griesly Dame,
    And cursed heaven, and spake reprochfull shame
    Of highest God, the Lord of life and light;   330
    A bold bad man, that dar'd to call by name
    Great *Gorgon*, Prince of darknesse and dead night,
At which *Cocytus* quakes, and *Styx* is put to flight.

38

And forth he cald out of deepe darknesse dred
    Legions of Sprights, the which like little flyes
    Fluttring about his ever damned hed,
    A-waite whereto their service he applyes,
    To aide his friends, or fray his enimies:
    Of those he chose out two, the falsest twoo,
    And fittest for to forge true-seeming lyes;   340
    The one of them he gave a message too,
The other by him selfe staide other worke to doo.

---

318 *Morpheus* god of sleep
320 *riddes* ushers
328 *blacke Plutoes griesly Dame* Pluto is god of the underworld. His wife is Proserpina
332 *Gorgon* a deity of the underworld
333 *Cocytus...Styx* rivers of Hades
338 *fray* affright

39

He making speedy way through spersed ayre,
   And through the world of waters wide and deepe,
   To *Morpheus* house doth hastily repaire.
   Amid the bowels of the earth full steepe,
   And low, where dawning day doth never peepe,
   His dwelling is; there *Tethys* his wet bed
   Doth ever wash, and *Cynthia* still doth steepe
   In silver deaw his ever-drouping hed,   350
Whiles sad Night over him her mantle black doth spred.

40

Whose double gates he findeth locked fast,
   The one faire fram'd of burnisht Yvory,
   The other all with silver overcast;
   And wakefull dogges before them farre to lye,
   Watching to banish Care their enimy,
   Who oft is wont to trouble gentle Sleepe.
   By them the Sprite doth passe in quietly,
   And unto *Morpheus* comes, whom drowned deepe
In drowsie fit he findes: of nothing he takes keepe.   360

41

And more, to lulle him in his slumber soft,
   A trickling streame from high rocke tumbling downe
   And ever-drizling raine upon the loft,
   Mixt with a murmuring winde, much like the sowne
   Of swarming Bees, did cast him in a swowne:
   No other noyse, nor peoples troublous cryes,
   As still are wont t'annoy the walled towne,

---

343 *spersed* scattered
348 *Tethys* a sea goddess: the sea
349 *Cynthia* 'goddess of the waves': the moon
364 *sowne* sound

    Might there be heard: but carelesse Quiet lyes,
Wrapt in eternall silence farre from enemyes.

42

The messenger approching to him spake,   370
    But his wast wordes returned to him in vaine:
    So sound he slept, that nought mought him awake.
    Then rudely he him thrust, and pusht with paine,
    Whereat he gan to stretch: but he againe
    Shooke him so hard, that forced him to speake.
    As one then in a dreame, whose dryer braine
    Is tost with troubled sights and fancies weake,
He mumbled soft, but would not all his silence breake.

43

The Sprite then gan more boldly him to wake,
    And threatned unto him the dreaded name   380
    Of *Hecate*: whereat he gan to quake,
    And lifting up his lumpish head, with blame
    Halfe angry asked him, for what he came.
    Hither (quoth he) me *Archimago* sent,
    He that the stubborne Sprites can wisely tame,
    He bids thee to him send for his intent
A fit false dreame, that can delude the sleepers sent.

44

The God obayde, and calling forth straight way
    A diverse dreame out of his prison darke,
    Delivered it to him, and downe did lay   390
    His heavie head, devoide of carefull carke,

---

371 *wast* wasted
381 *Hecate* goddess of witchcraft
382 *lumpish* heavy
391 *carke* sorrow

Whose sences all were straight benumbd and starke.
He backe returning by the Yvorie dore,
Remounted up as light as chearefull Larke,
And on his litle winges the dreame he bore
In hast unto his Lord, where he him left afore.

45

Who all this while with charmes and hidden artes,
  Had made a Lady of that other Spright,
  And fram'd of liquid ayre her tender partes
  So lively, and so like in all mens sight, 400
  That weaker sence it could have ravisht quight:
  The maker selfe for all his wondrous witt,
  Was nigh beguiled with so goodly sight:
  Her all in white he clad, and over it
Cast a blacke stole, most like to seeme for *Una* fit.

46

Now when that ydle dreame was to him brought,
  Unto that Elfin knight he bad him fly,
  Where he slept soundly void of evill thought,
  And with false shewes abuse his fantasy,
  In sort as he him schooled privily: 410
  And that new creature borne without her dew,
  Full of the makers guile, with usage sly
  He taught to imitate that Lady trew,
Whose semblance she did carrie under feigned hew.

47

Thus well instructed, to their worke they hast,
  And comming where the knight in slomber lay,

406 *ydle* empty
409 *fantasy* imagination
412 *usage* behaviour

[413–14]

The one upon his hardy head him plast,
And made him dreame of loves and lustfull play,
That nigh his manly hart did melt away,
Bathed in wanton blis and wicked joy: 420
Then seemed him his Lady by him lay,
And to him playnd, how that false winged boy
Her chast hart had subdewd, to learne Dame Pleasures toy.

48

And she her selfe of beautie soveraigne Queene,
  Faire *Venus* seemde unto his bed to bring
Her, whom he waking evermore did weene
To be the chastest flowre, that ay did spring
On earthly braunch, the daughter of a king,
Now a loose Leman to vile service bound:
And eke the *Graces* seemed all to sing, 430
  Hymen iō Hymen, dauncing all around,
Whilst freshest *Flora* her with Yvie girlond crownd.

49

In this great passion of unwonted lust,
  Or wonted feare of doing ought amis,
He started up, as seeming to mistrust
Some secret ill, or hidden foe of his:
Lo there before his face his Lady is
Under blake stole hyding her bayted hooke,
And as halfe blushing offred him to kis,
  With gentle blandishment and lovely looke, 440
Most like that virgin true, which for her knight him took.

---

423 *toy* game
425 *Venus* goddess of love and beauty
429 *loose Leman* promiscuous woman
430 *the Graces* attendants on Venus
431 *Hymen* ... invocation to Hymen, god of marriage
432 *Flora* goddess of flowers and fertility

50

All cleane dismayd to see so uncouth sight,
   And halfe enraged at her shamelesse guise,
   He thought have slaine her in his fierce despight:
   But hasty heat tempring with sufferance wise,
   He stayde his hand, and gan himselfe advise
   To prove his sense, and tempt her faigned truth.
   Wringing her hands in wemens pitteous wise,
   Tho can she weepe, to stirre up gentle ruth,
Both for her noble bloud, and for her tender youth.   450

51

And said, Ah Sir, my liege Lord and my love,
   Shall I accuse the hidden cruell fate,
   And mightie causes wrought in heaven above,
   Or the blind God, that doth me thus amate,
   For hoped love to winne me certaine hate?
   Yet thus perforce he bids me do, or die.
   Die is my dew: yet rew my wretched state
   You, whom my hard avenging destinie
Hath made judge of my life or death indifferently.

52

Your owne deare sake forst me at first to leave   460
   My Fathers kingdome, There she stopt with teares;
   Her swollen hart her speach seemd to bereave,
   And then againe begun, My weaker yeares
   Capiv'd to fortune and frayle worldly feares,
   Fly to your faith for succour and sure ayde:
   Let me not dye in languor and long teares.

---

442 *Uncouth* unprecedented
454 *the blind God* Cupid; *amate* overwhelm
466 *languor* sorrow

    Why Dame (quoth he) what hath ye thus dismayd?
What frayes ye, that were wont to comfort me affrayd?

53

Love of your selfe, she said, and deare constraint
    Lets me not sleepe, but wast the wearie night
    In secret anguish and unpittied plaint,
    Whiles you in carelesse sleepe are drowned quight.
    Her doubtfull words made that redoubted knight
    Suspect her truth: yet since no'untruth he knew,
    Her fawning love with foule disdainefull spight
    He would not shend, but said, Deare dame I rew,
That for my sake unknowne such griefe unto you grew.

54

Assure your selfe, it fell not all to ground;
    For all so deare as life is to my hart,
    I deeme your love, and hold me to you bound;
    Ne let vaine feares procure your needlesse smart,
    Where cause is none, but to your rest depart.
    Not all content, yet seemd she to appease
    Her mournefull plaintes, beguiled of her art,
    And fed with words, that could not chuse but please,
So slyding softly forth, she turned as to her ease.

55

Long after lay he musing at her mood,
    Much griev'd to thinke that gentle Dame so light,
    For whose defence he was to shed his blood.
    At last dull wearinesse of former fight

---

468 *frayes* dismays
476 *shend* humiliate
488 *light* shameless

[414–15]

Having yrockt a sleepe his irkesome spright,
That troublous dreame gan freshly tosse his braine,
With bowres, and beds, and Ladies deare delight:
But when he saw his labour all was vaine,
With that misformed spright he backe returnd againe.

CANTO ii

The guilefull great Enchaunter parts
 The Redcrosse Knight from Truth:
 Into whose stead faire falshood steps,
 And workes him wofull ruth.

1

By this the Northerne wagoner had set
 His sevenfold teme behind the stedfast starre,
That was in Ocean waves yet never wet,
But firme is fixt, and sendeth light from farre
To all, that in the wide deepe wandring arre:
And chearefull Chaunticlere with his note shrill
Had warned once, that *Phœbus* fiery carre
In hast was climbing up the Easterne hill,
Full envious that night so long his roome did fill.

2

When those accursed messengers of hell,   10
 That feigning dreame, and that faire-forged Spright
 Came to their wicked maister, and gan tell

---

491 *his irkesome spright* his weary mind
495 *misformed spright* the false Una
  1 *the Notherne wagoner* the constellation Bootes
  2 *sevenfold teme* the stars of the constellation of the Plough; *the stedfast starre* the pole star
  6 *Chaunticlere* the cock

Their bootelesse paines, and ill succeeding night:
   Who all in rage to see his skilfull might
   Deluded so, gan threaten hellish paine
   And sad *Proserpines* wrath, them to affright.
   But when he saw his threatning was but vaine,
He cast about, and searcht his balefull bookes againe.

3

Eftsoones he tooke that miscreated faire,
   And that false other Spright, on whom he spred
   A seeming body of the subtile aire,
   Like a young Squire, in loves and lusty-hed
   His wanton dayes that ever loosely led,
   Without regard of armes and dreaded fight:
   Those two he tooke, and in a secret bed,
   Covered with darknesse and misdeeming night,
Them both together laid, to joy in vaine delight.

4

Forthwith he runnes with feigned faithfull hast
   Unto his guest, who after troublous sights
   And dreames, gan now to take more sound repast,
   Whom suddenly he wakes with fearefull frights,
   As one aghast with feends or damned sprights,
   And to him cals, Rise rise unhappy Swaine,
   That here wex old in sleepe, whiles wicked wights
   Have knit themselves in *Venus* shamefull chaine;
Come see, where your false Lady doth her honour staine.

---

13 *bootlesse paines* useless efforts
16 *sad* gloomy
18 *balefull* deadly
19 *that miscreated faire* the spright given Una's shape
21 *subtile* delicate
26 *misdeeming* ill-judging

5

All in amaze he suddenly up start
   With sword in hand, and with the old man went;
   Who soone him brought into a secret part,
   Where that false couple were full closely ment   40
   In wanton lust and lewd embracement:
   Which when he saw, he burnt with gealous fire,
   The eye of reason was with rage yblent,
   And would have slaine them in his furious ire,
But hardly was restreined of that aged sire.

6

Returning to his bed in torment great,
   And bitter anguish of his guiltie sight,
   He could not rest, but did his stout heart eat,
   And wast his inward gall with deepe despight,
   Yrkesome of life, and too long lingring night.   50
   At last faire *Hesperus* in highest skie
   Had spent his lampe, and brought forth dawning light,
   Then up he rose, and clad him hastily;
The Dwarfe him brought his steed: so both away do fly.

7

Now when the rosy-fingred Morning faire,
   Weary of aged *Tithones* saffron bed,
   Had spred her purple robe through deawy aire,
   And the high hils *Titan* discovered,
   The royall virgin shooke off drowsy-hed,
   And rising forth out of her baser bowre,   60
   Lookt for her knight, who far away was fled,

   40 *ment* mingled
   43 *yblent* blinded
   51 *Hesperus* the morning (sometimes the evening) star
   58 *Titan* Apollo: the sun

And for her Dwarfe, that wont to wait each houre;
Then gan she waile and weepe, to see that woefull stowre.

8

And after him she rode with so much speede
   As her slow beast could make; but all in vaine:
   For him so far had borne his light-foot steede,
   Pricked with wrath and fiery fierce disdaine,
   That him to follow was but fruitlesse paine;
   Yet she her weary limbes would never rest,
   But every hill and dale, each wood and plaine   70
   Did search, sore grieved in her gentle brest,
He so ungently left her, whom she loved best.

9

But subtill *Archimago*, when his guests
   He saw divided into double parts,
   And *Una* wandring in woods and forrests,
   Th'end of his drift, he praisd his divelish arts,
   That had such might over true meaning harts;
   Yet rests not so, but other meanes doth make,
   How he may worke unto her further smarts:
   For her he hated as the hissing snake,   80
And in her many troubles did most pleasure take.

10

He then devisde himselfe how to disguise;
   For by his mightie science he could take
   As many formes and shapes in seeming wise,
   As ever *Proteus* to himselfe could make:
   Sometime a fowle, sometime a fish in lake,
   Now like a foxe, now like a dragon fell,

---

63 *woefull stowre* occasion of distress

[414–15]

That of himselfe he oft for feare would quake,
And oft would flie away. O who can tell
The hidden power of herbes, and might of Magicke spell? 90

11

But now seemde best, the person to put on
    Of that good knight, his late beguiled guest:
    In mighty armes he was yclad anon,
    And silver shield: upon his coward brest
    A bloudy crosse, and on his craven crest
    A bounch of haires discoloured diversly:
    Full jolly knight he seemde, and well addrest,
    And when he sate upon his courser free,
Saint George himself ye would have deemed him to be.

12

But he the knight, whose semblaunt he did beare, 100
    The true *Saint George* was wandred far away,
    Still flying from his thoughts and gealous feare;
    Will was his guide, and griefe led him astray.
    At last him chaunst to meete upon the way
    A faithlesse Sarazin all arm'd to point,
    In whose great shield was writ with letters gay
    Sans foy: full large of limbe and every joint
He was, and cared not for God or man a point.

13

He had a faire companion of his way,
    A goodly Lady clad in scarlot red, 110
    Purfled with gold and pearle of rich assay,
    And like a *Persian* mitre on her hed

105 *Sarazin* saracen
107 *Sans foy* Without faith
111 *Purfled* bordered

> She wore, with crownes and owches garnished,
> The which her lavish lovers to her gave;
> Her wanton palfrey all was overspred
> With tinsell trappings, woven like a wave,
> Whose bridle rung with golden bels and bosses brave.

14

> With faire disport and courting dalliaunce
> She intertainde her lover all the way:
> But when she saw the knight his speare advaunce,
> She soone left off her mirth and wanton play,
> And bad her knight addresse him to the fray:
> His foe was nigh at hand. He prickt with pride
> And hope to winne his Ladies heart that day,
> Forth spurred fast: adowne his coursers side
> The red bloud trickling staind the way, as he did ride.

15

> The knight of the *Redcrosse* when him he spide,
> Spurring so hote with rage dispiteous,
> Gan fairely couch his speare, and towards ride:
> Soone meete they both, both fell and furious,
> That daunted with their forces hideous,
> Their steeds do stagger, and amazed stand,
> And eke themselves too rudely rigorous,
> Astonied with the stroke of their owne hand,
> Do backe rebut, and each to other yeeldeth land.

16

> As when two rams stird with ambitious pride,
> Fight for the rule of the rich fleeced flocke,
> Their horned fronts so fierce on either side

113 *owches* clasps
135 *rebut* recoil

>   Do meete, that with the terrour of the shocke
>   Astonied both, stand sencelesse as a blocke, 140
>   Forgetfull of the hanging victory:
>   So stood these twaine, unmoved as a rocke,
>   Both staring fierce, and holding idely
> The broken reliques of their former cruelty.

17

> The *Sarazin* sore daunted with the buffe
>   Snatcheth his sword, and fiercely to him flies;
>   Who well it wards, and quyteth cuff with cuff:
>   Each others equall puissaunce envies,
>   And through their iron sides with cruell spies
>   Does seeke to perce: repining courage yields 150
>   No foote to foe. The flashing fier flies
>   As from a forge out of their burning shields,
> And streames of purple bloud new dies the verdant fields.

18

> Curse on that Crosse (quoth then the *Sarazin*)
>   That keepes thy body from the bitter fit;
>   Dead long ygoe I wote thou haddest bin,
>   Had not that charme from thee forwarned it:
>   But yet I warne thee now assured sitt,
>   And hide thy head. Therewith upon his crest
>   With rigour so outrageous he smitt, 160
>   That a large share it hewd out of the rest,
> And glauncing downe his shield, from blame him fairely blest.

19

> Who thereat wondrous wroth, the sleeping spark
>   Of native vertue gan eftsoones revive,

141 *hanging* undecided
162 *blame* hurt

    And at his haughtie helmet making mark,
      So hugely stroke, that it the steele did rive,
      And cleft his head. He tumbling downe alive,
      With bloudy mouth his mother earth did kis,
      Greeting his grave: his grudging ghost did strive
      With the fraile flesh; at last it flitted is,   170
Whither the soules do fly of men, that live amis.

20

The Lady when she saw her champion fall,
    Like the old ruines of a broken towre,
    Staid not to waile his woefull funerall,
    But from him fled away with all her powre;
    Who after her as hastily gan scowre,
    Bidding the Dwarfe with him to bring away
    The *Sarazins* shield, signe of the conqueroure.
    Her soone he overtooke, and bad to stay,
For present cause was none of dread her to dismay.   180

21

She turning backe with ruefull countenaunce,
    Cride, Mercy mercy Sir vouchsafe to show
    On silly Dame, subject to hard mischaunce,
    And to your mighty will. Her humblesse low
    In so ritch weedes and seeming glorious show,
    Did much emmove his stout heroïcke heart,
    And said, Deare dame, your suddein overthrow
    Much rueth me; but now put feare apart,
And tell, both who ye be, and who that tooke your part.

22

Melting in teares, then gan she thus lament;   190
    The wretched woman, whom unhappy howre

---

176 *scowre* pursue

Hath now made thrall to your commandement,
Before that angry heavens list to lowre,
And fortune false betraide me to your powre,
Was, (O what now availeth that I was!)
Borne the sole daughter of an Emperour,
He that the wide West under his rule has
And high hath set his throne, where *Tiberis* doth pas.

23

He in the first flowre of my freshest age,
   Betrothed me unto the onely haire
   Of a most mighty king, most rich and sage;
   Was never Prince so faithfull and so faire,
   Was never Prince so meeke and debonaire;
   But ere my hoped day of spousall shone,
   My dearest Lord fell from high honours staire,
   Into the hands of his accursed fone,
And cruelly was slaine, that shall I ever mone.

24

His blessed body spoild of lively breath,
   Was afterward, I know not how, convaid
   And fro me hid: of whose most innocent death
   When tidings came to me unhappy maid,
   O how great sorrow my sad soule assaid.
   Then forth I went his woefull corse to find,
   And many yeares throughout the world I straid,
   A virgin widow, whose deepe wounded mind
With love, long time did languish as the striken hind.

---

193 *lowre* frown
206 *fone* foe

25

At last it chaunced this proud *Sarazin*
    To meete me wandring, who perforce me led
    With him away, but yet could never win
    The Fort, that Ladies hold in soveraigne dread.   220
    There lies he now with foule dishonour dead,
    Who whiles he liv'de, was called proud *Sans foy*,
    The eldest of three brethren, all three bred
    Of one bad sire, whose youngest is *Sans joy*,
And twixt them both was borne the bloudy bold *Sans loy*.

26

In this sad plight, friendlesse, unfortunate,
    Now miserable I *Fidessa* dwell,
    Craving of you in pitty of my state,
    To do none ill, if please ye not do well.
    He in great passion all this while did dwell,   230
    More busying his quicke eyes, her face to view,
    Then his dull eares, to heare what she did tell;
    And said, Faire Lady hart of flint would rew
The undeserved woes and sorrowes, which ye shew.

27

Henceforth in safe assurance may ye rest,
    Having both found a new friend you to aid,
    And lost an old foe, that did you molest:
    Better new friend then an old foe is said.
    With chaunge of cheare the seeming simple maid
    Let fall her eyen, as shamefast to the earth,   240
    And yeelding soft, in that she nought gain-said,
    So forth they rode, he feining seemely merth,
And she coy lookes: so dainty they say maketh derth.

224 *Sans joy* Without joy
225 *Sans loy* Without law
239 *seeming* apparently

28

Long time they thus together traveiled,
    Till weary of their way, they came at last,
    Where grew two goodly trees, that faire did spred
    Their armes abroad, with gray mosse overcast,
    And their greene leaves trembling with every blast,
    Made a calme shadow far in compasse round:
    The fearefull Shepheard often there aghast
    Under them never sat, ne wont there sound
His mery oaten pipe, but shund th'unlucky ground.

29

But this good knight soone as he them can spie,
    For the coole shade him thither hastly got:
    For golden *Phœbus* now ymounted hie,
    From fiery wheeles of his faire chariot
    Hurled his beame so scorching cruell hot,
    That living creature mote it not abide;
    And his new Lady it endured not.
    There they alight, in hope themselves to hide
From the fierce heat, and rest their weary limbs a tide.

30

Faire seemely pleasaunce each to other makes,
    With goodly purposes there as they sit:
    And in his falsed fancy he her takes
    To be the fairest wight, that lived yit;
    Which to expresse, he bends his gentle wit,
    And thinking of those braunches greene to frame
    A girlond for her dainty forehead fit,
    He pluckt a bough; out of whose rift there came
Small drops of gory bloud, that trickled downe the same.

261 *a tide* a while

31

Therewith a piteous yelling voyce was heard,
    Crying, O spare with guilty hands to teare
    My tender sides in this rough rynd embard,
    But fly, ah fly far hence away, for feare
    Least to you hap, that happened to me heare,
    And to this wretched Lady, my deare love,
    O too deare love, love bought with death too deare.
    Astond he stood, and up his haire did hove,
And with that suddein horror could no member move.

32

At last whenas the dreadfull passion
    Was overpast, and manhood well awake,
    Yet musing at the straunge occasion,
    And doubting much his sence, he thus bespake;
    What voyce of damned Ghost from *Limbo* lake,
    Or guilefull spright wandring in empty aire,
    Both which fraile men do oftentimes mistake,
    Sends to my doubtfull eares these speaches rare,
And ruefull plaints, me bidding guiltlesse bloud to spare?

33

Then groning deepe, Nor damned Ghost, (quoth he,)
    Nor guilefull sprite to thee these wordes doth speake,
    But once a man *Fradubio*, now a tree,
    Wretched man, wretched tree; whose nature weake,
    A cruell witch her cursed will to wreake,
    Hath thus transformd, and plast in open plaines,
    Where *Boreas* doth blow full bitter bleake,
    And scorching Sunne does dry my secret vaines:
For though a tree I seeme, yet cold and heat me paines.

273 *embard* confined
284 *Limbo lake* depths of hell
295 *Boreas* the north wind

34

Say on *Fradubio* then, or man, or tree,
    Quoth then the knight, by whose mischievous arts
    Art though misshaped thus, as now I see?
    He oft finds med'cine, who his griefe imparts;
    But double griefs afflict concealing harts,
    As raging flames who striveth to suppresse.
    The author then (said he) of all my smarts,
    Is one *Duessa* a false sorceresse,
That many errant knights hath brought to wretchednesse.

35

In prime of youthly yeares, when corage hot
    The fire of love and joy of chevalree
    First kindled in my brest, it was my lot
    To love this gentle Lady, whom ye see,
    Now not a Lady, but a seeming tree;
    With whom as once I rode accompanyde,
    Me chaunced of a knight encountred bee,
    That had a like faire Lady by his syde,
Like a faire Lady, but did fowle *Duessa* hyde.

36

Whose forged beauty he did take in hand,
    All other Dames to have exceeded farre;
    I in defence of mine did likewise stand,
    Mine, that did then shine as the Morning starre:
    So both to battell fierce arraunged arre,
    In which his harder fortune was to fall
    Under my speare: such is the dye of warre:
    His Lady left as a prise martiall,
Did yield her comely person, to be at my call.

37

So doubly lov'd of Ladies unlike faire,
    Th'one seeming such, the other such indeede,
    One day in doubt I cast for to compare,
    Whether in beauties glorie did exceede;
    A Rosy girlond was the victors meede:
    Both seemde to win, and both seemde won to bee,   330
    So hard the discord was to be agreede.
    Frælissa was as faire, as faire mote bee,
And ever false *Duessa* seemde as faire as shee.

38

The wicked witch now seeing all this while
    The doubtfull ballaunce equally to sway,
    What not by right, she cast to win by guile,
    And by her hellish science raisd streight way
    A foggy mist, that overcast the day,
    And a dull blast, that breathing on her face,
    Dimmed her former beauties shining ray,   340
    And with foule ugly forme did her disgrace:
Then was she faire alone, when none was faire in place.

39

Then cride she out, Fye, fye, deformed wight,
    Whose borrowed beautie now appeareth plaine
    To have before bewitched all mens sight;
    O leave her soone, or let her soone be slaine.
    Her loathly visage viewing with disdaine,
    Eftsoones I thought her such, as she me told,
    And would have kild her; but with faigned paine,
    The false witch did my wrathfull hand with-hold;   350
So left her, where she now is turned to treen mould.

---

351 *treen mould* wooden shape

40

Thens forth I tooke *Duessa* for my Dame,
    And in the witch unweeting joyd long time,
    Ne ever wist, but that she was the same,
    Till on a day (that day is every Prime,
    When Witches wont do penance for their crime)
    I chaunst to see her in her proper hew,
    Bathing her selfe in origane and thyme:
    A filthy foule old woman I did vew,
That ever to have toucht her, I did deadly rew.   360

41

Her neather partes misshapen, monstruous,
    Were hidd in water, that I could not see,
    But they did seeme more foule and hideous,
    Then womans shape man would beleeve to bee.
    Thens forth from her most beastly companie
    I gan refraine, in minde to slip away,
    Soone as appeard safe opportunitie:
    For danger great, if not assur'd decay
I saw before mine eyes, if I were knowne to stray.

42

The divelish hag by chaunges of my cheare   370
    Perceiv'd my thought, and drownd in sleepie night,
    With wicked herbes and ointments did besmeare
    My bodie all, through charmes and magicke might,
    That all my senses were bereaved quight:
    Then brought she me into this desert waste,
    And by my wretched lovers side me pight,
    Where now enclosd in wooden wals full faste,
Banisht from living wights, our wearie dayes we waste.

355 *Prime* spring: the first day of the new moon
358 *origane* oregano
376 *pight* placed

43

But how long time, said then the Elfin knight,
   Are you in this misformed house to dwell?
   We may not chaunge (quoth he) this evil plight,
   Till we be bathed in a living well;
   That is the terme prescribed by the spell.
   O how, said he, mote I that well out find,
   That may restore you to your wonted well?
   Time and suffised fates to former kynd
Shall us restore, none else from hence may us unbynd.

44

The false *Duessa*, now *Fidessa* hight,
   Heard how in vaine *Fradubio* did lament,
   And knew well all was true. But the good knight
   Full of sad feare and ghastly dreriment,
   When all this speech the living tree had spent,
   The bleeding bough did thrust into the ground,
   That from the bloud he might be innocent,
   And with fresh clay did close the wooden wound:
Then turning to his Lady, dead with feare her found.

45

Her seeming dead he found with feigned feare,
   As all unweeting of that well she knew,
   And paynd himselfe with busie care to reare
   Her out of carelesse swowne. Her eylids blew
   And dimmed sight with pale and deadly hew
   At last she up gan lift: with trembling cheare
   Her up he tooke, too simple and too trew,
   And oft her kist. At length all passed feare,
He set her on her steede, and forward forth did beare.

391 *dreriment* grief
400 *carelesse* untroubled

[415]

CANTO iii

Forsaken Truth long seekes her love,
And makes the Lyon mylde,
Marres blind Devotions mart, and fals
In hand of leachour vylde.

1

Nought is there under heav'ns wide hollownesse,
    That moves more deare compassion of mind,
    Then beautie brought t'unworthy wretchednesse
    Through envies snares or fortunes freakes unkind:
    I, whether lately through her brightnesse blind,
    Or through alleageance and fast fealtie,
    Which I do owe unto all woman kind,
    Feele my heart perst with so great agonie,
When such I see, that all for pittie I could die.

2

And now it is empassioned so deepe,   10
    For fairest *Unaes* sake, of whom I sing,
    That my fraile eyes these lines with teares do steepe,
    To thinke how she through guileful handeling,
    Though true as touch, though daughter of a king,
    Though faire as ever living wight was faire,
    Though nor in word nor deede ill meriting,
    Is from her knight divorced in despaire
And her due loves deriv'd to that vile witches share.

---

  4 *freakes* caprice
 13 *handeling* plotting
 14 *touch* touchstone
 18 *And her due loves...share* and the love due to her transferred to Duessa

3

Yet she most faithfull Ladie all this while
   Forsaken, wofull, solitaire mayd
   Farre from all peoples prease, as in exile,
   In wildernesse and wastfull deserts strayed,
   To seeke her knight; who subtilly betrayd
   Through that late vision, which th'Enchaunter wrought,
   Had her abandond. She of nought affrayd,
   Through woods and wastnesse wide him daily sought;
Yet wished tydings none of him unto her brought.

4

One day nigh wearie of the yrkesome way,
   From her unhastie beast she did alight,
   And on the grasse her daintie limbes did lay
   In secret shadow, farre from all mens sight:
   From her faire head her fillet she undight,
   And laid her stole aside. Her angels face
   As the great eye of heaven shyned bright,
   And made a sunshine in the shadie place;
Did never mortall eye behold such heavenly grace.

5

It fortuned out of the thickest wood
   A ramping Lyon rushed suddainly,
   Hunting full greedie after salvage blood;
   Soone as the royall virgin he did spy,
   With gaping mouth at her ran greedily,
   To have attonce devour'd her tender corse:
   But to the pray when as he drew more ny,

---

21 *prease* company
32 *fillet...undight* unbound her veil
34 *eye of heaven* the sun
39 *salvage blood* the blood of wild beasts

His bloudie rage asswaged with remorse,
And with the sight amazd, forgat his furious forse.

6

In stead thereof he kist her wearie feet,
 And lickt her lilly hands with fawning tong,
 As he her wronged innocence did weet.
 O how can beautie maister the most strong,
 And simple truth subdue avenging wrong?   50
 Whose yeelded pride and proud submission,
 Still dreading death, when she had marked long,
 Her hart gan melt in great compassion,
And drizling teares did shed for pure affection.

7

The Lyon Lord of everie beast in field,
 Quoth she, his princely puissance doth abate,
 And mightie proud to humble weake does yield,
 Forgetfull of the hungry rage, which late
 Him prickt, in pittie of my sad estate:
 But he my Lyon, and my noble Lord,   60
 How does he find in cruell hart to hate
 Her that him lov'd, and ever most adord,
As the God of my life? why hath he me abhord?

8

Redounding teares did choke th'end of her plaint,
 Which softly ecchoed from the neighbour wood;
 And sad to see her sorrowfull constraint
 The kingly beast upon her gazing stood;
 With pittie calmd, downe fell his angry mood.
 At last in close hart shutting up her paine,

48 *weet* understand
59 *prickt* urged

    Arose the virgin borne of heavenly brood,   70
    And to her snowy Palfrey got againe,
To seeke her strayed Champion, if she might attaine.

9

The Lyon would not leave her desolate,
    But with her went along, as a strong gard
    Of her chast person, and a faithfull mate
    Of her sad troubles and misfortunes hard:
    Still when she slept, he kept both watch and ward,
    And when she wakt, he waited diligent,
    With humble service to her will prepard:
    From her faire eyes he tooke commaundement,   80
And ever by her lookes conceived her intent.

10

Long she thus traveiled through deserts wyde,
    By which she thought her wandring knight shold pas,
    Yet never shew of living wight espyde;
    Till that at length she found the troden gras,
    In which the tract of peoples footing was,
    Under the steepe foot of a mountaine hore;
    The same she followes, till at last she has
    A damzell spyde slow footing her before,
That on her shoulders sad a pot of water bore.   90

11

To whom approching she to her gan call,
    To weet, if dwelling place were nigh at hand;
    But the rude wench her answer'd nought at all,
    She could not heare, nor speake, nor understand;
    Till seeing by her side the Lyon stand,
    With suddaine feare her pitcher downe she threw,

  90 *sad* drooping

[415]

And fled away: for never in that land
  Face of faire Ladie she before did vew,
And that dread Lyons looke her cast in deadly hew.

12

Full fast she fled, ne ever lookt behynd,   100
  As if her life upon the wager lay,
  And home she came, whereas her mother blynd
  Sate in eternall night: nought could she say,
  But suddaine catching hold, did her dismay
  With quaking hands, and other signes of feare:
  Who full of ghastly fright and cold affray,
  Gan shut the dore. By this arrived there
Dame *Una*, wearie Dame, and entrance did requere.

13

Which when none yeelded, her unruly Page
  With his rude clawes and wicket open rent,   110
  And let her in; where of his cruell rage
  Nigh dead with feare, and faint astonishment,
  She found them both in darkesome corner pent;
  Where that old woman day and night did pray
  Upon her beades devoutly penitent;
  Nine hundred *Pater nosters* every day,
And thrise nine hundred *Aves* she was wont to say.

14

And to augment her painefull pennance more,
  Thrise every weeke in ashes she did sit,
  And next her wrinkled skin rough sackcloth wore,   120
  And thrise three times did fast from any bit:
  But now for feare her beads she did forget.

115 *beades* rosary
116 *Pater nosters* Our Fathers: the Lord's Prayer

Whose needlesse dread for to remove away,
Faire *Una* framed words and count'nance fit:
Which hardly doen, at length she gan them pray,
That in their cotage small, that night she rest her may.

15

The day is spent, and commeth drowsie night,
When every creature shrowded is in sleepe;
Sad *Una* downe her laies in wearie plight,
And at her feet the Lyon watch doth keepe:
In stead of rest, she does lament, and weepe
For the late losse of her deare loved knight,
And sighes, and grones, and evermore does steepe
Her tender brest in bitter teares all night,
All night she thinks too long, and often lookes for light.

16

Now when *Aldeboran* was mounted hie
Above the shynie *Cassiopeias* chaire,
And all in deadly sleepe did drowned lie,
One knocked at the dore, and in would fare;
He knocked fast, and often curst, and sware,
That readie entrance was not at his call:
For on his backe a heavy load he bare
Of nightly stelths and pillage severall,
Which he had got abroad by purchase criminall.

17

He was to weete a stout and sturdie thiefe,
Wont to robbe Churches of their ornaments,
And poore mens boxes of their due reliefe,
Which given was to them for good intents;

---

143 *pillage severall* different thefts

>   The holy saints of their rich vestiments
>   He did disrobe, when all men carelesse slept,
>   And spoild the Priests of their habiliments,
>   Whiles none the holy things in safety kept;
> Then he by cunning sleights in at the window crept.

150

18

> And all that he by right or wrong could find,
>   Unto this house he brought, and did bestow
>   Upon the daughter of this woman blind,
>   *Abessa* daughter of *Corceca* slow,
>   With whom he whoredome usd, that few did know,
>   And fed her fat with feast of offerings,
>   And plentie, which in all the land did grow;
>   Ne spared he to give her gold and rings:
> And now he to her brought part of his stolen things.

160

19

> Thus long the dore with rage and threats he bet,
>   Yet of those fearefull women none durst rize,
>   The Lyon frayed them, him in to let:
>   He would no longer stay him to advize,
>   But open breakes the dore in furious wize,
>   And entring is; when that disdainful beast
>   Encountring fierce, him suddaine doth surprize,
>   And seizing cruell clawes on trembling brest,
> Under his Lordly foot him proudly hath supprest.

170

20

> Him booteth not resist, nor succour call,
>   His bleeding hart is in the vengers hand,
>   Who streight him rent in thousand peeces small,

172 *Him booteth not* it is useless for him

    And quite dismembered hath: the thirstie land
    Drunke up his life; his corse left on the strand.
    His fearefull friends weare out the wofull night,
    Ne dare to weepe, nor seeme to understand
    The heavie hap, which on them is alight,
Affraid, least to themselves the like mishappen might.   180

21

Now when broad day the world discovered has,
    Up *Una* rose, up rose the Lyon eke,
    And on their former journey forward pas,
    In wayes unknowne, her wandring knight to seeke,
    With paines farre passing that long wandring *Greeke*,
    That for his love refused deitie;
    Such were the labours of this Lady meeke,
    Still seeking him, that from her still did flie,
Then furthest from her hope, when most she weened nie.

22

Soone as she parted thence, the fearefull twaine,   190
    That blind old woman and her daughter deare
    Came forth, and finding *Kirkrapine* there slaine,
    For anguish great they gan to rend their heare,
    And beat their brests, and naked flesh to teare.
    And when they both had wept and wayld their fill,
    Then forth they ranne like two amazed deare,
    Halfe mad through malice, and revenging will,
To follow her, that was the causer of their ill.

23

Whom overtaking, they gan loudly bray,
    With hollow howling, and lamenting cry,   200
    Shamefully at her rayling all the way,

---

185 *that long wandring Greeke* Ulysses; see Notes

And her accusing of dishonesty,
    That was the flowre of faith and chastity;
    And still amidst her rayling, she did pray,
    That plagues, and mischiefs, and long misery
    Might fall on her, and follow all the way,
And that in endlesse error she might ever stray.

24

But when she saw her prayers nought prevaile,
    She backe returned with some labour lost;
    And in the way as she did weepe and waile,
    A knight her met in mighty armes embost,
    Yet knight was not for all his bragging bost,
    But subtill *Archimag*, that *Una* sought
    By traynes into new troubles to have tost:
    Of that old woman tydings he besought,
If that of such a Ladie she could tellen ought.

25

Therewith she gan her passion to renew,
    And cry, and cure, and raile, and rend her heare,
    Saying, that harlot she too lately knew,
    That causd her shed so many a bitter teare,
    And so forth told the story of her feare:
    Much seemed he to mone her haplesse chaunce,
    And after for that Ladie did inquere;
    Which being taught, he forward gan advaunce
His fair enchaunted steed, and eke his charmed launce.

26

Ere long he came, where *Una* traveild slow,
    And that wilde Champion wayting her besyde:

---

207 *in endlesse error ... stray* might wander without ever finding her way
214 *traynes* plots

Whom seeing such, for dread he durst not show
   Himselfe too nigh at hand, but turned wyde
   Unto an hill; from whence when she him spyde, 230
   By his like seeming shield, her knight by name
   She weend it was, and towards him gan ryde:
   Approching nigh, she wist it was the same,
And with faire fearefull humblesse towards him shee came.

27

And weeping said, Ah my long lacked Lord,
   Where have ye bene thus long out of my sight?
   Much feared I to have bene quite abhord,
   Or ought have done, that ye displeasen might,
   That should as death unto my deare hart light:
   For since mine eye your joyous sight did mis, 240
   My chearefull day is turnd to chearelesse night,
   And eke my night of death the shadow is;
But welcome now my light, and shining lampe of blis.

28

He thereto meeting said, My dearest Dame,
   Farre be it from your thought, and fro my will,
   To thinke that knighthood I so much should shame,
   As you to leave, that have me loved still,
   And chose in Faery court of meere goodwill,
   Where noblest knights were to be found on earth:
   The earth shall sooner leave her kindly skill 250
   To bring forth fruit, and make eternall derth,
Then I leave you, my liefe, yborne of heavenly berth.

29

And sooth to say, why I left you so long,
   Was for to seeke adventure in strange place,
   Where *Archimago* said a felon strong
   To many knights did daily worke disgrace;

But knight he now shall never more deface:
   Good cause of mine excuse; that mote ye please
   Well to accept, and evermore embrace
   My faithfull service, that by land and seas 260
Have vowd you to defend, now then your plaint appease.

30

His lovely words her seemd due recompence
   Of all her passed paines: one loving howre
   For many yeares of sorrow can dispence:
   A dram of sweet is worth a pound of sowre:
   She has forgot, how many a wofull stowre
   For him she late endur'd; she speakes no more
   Of past: true is, that true love hath no powre
   To looken backe; his eyes be fixt before.
Before her stands her knight, for whom she toyld so sore. 270

31

Much like, as when the beaten marinere,
   That long hath wandered in the *Ocean* wide,
   Oft soust in swelling *Tethys* saltish teare,
   And long time having tand his tawney hide
   With blustring breath of heaven, that none can bide,
   And scorching flames of fierce *Orions* hound,
   Soone as the port from farre he has espide,
   His chearefull whistle merrily doth sound,
And *Nereus* crownes with cups; his mates him pledg around.

32

Such joy made *Una*, when her knight she found; 280
   And eke th'enchaunter joyous seemd no lesse,

273 *Tethys* a sea goddess
276 *fierce Orions hound* Sirius, the dog star
279 *Nereus* a sea god

Then the glad marchant, that does vew from ground
His ship farre come from watrie wildernesse,
He hurles out vowes, and *Neptune* oft doth blesse:
So forth they past, and all the way they spent
Discoursing of her dreadfull late distresse,
In which he ask her, what the Lyon ment:
Who told her all that fell in journey as she went.

33

They had not ridden farre, when they might see
    One pricking towards them with hastie heat,   290
    Full strongly armd, and on a courser free,
    That through his fiercenesse fomed all with sweat,
    And the sharpe yron did for anger eat,
When his hot ryder spurd his chauffed side;
    His looke was sterne, and seemed still to threat
    Cruell revenge, which he in hart did hyde,
And on his shield *Sans loy* in bloudie lines was dyde.

34

When nigh he drew unto this gentle payre
    And saw the Red-crosse, which the knight did beare,
    He burnt in fire, and gan eftsoones prepare   300
    Himselfe to battell with his couched speare.
Loth was that other, and did faint through feare,
    To taste th'untryed dint of deadly steele;
    But yet his Lady did so well him cheare,
    That hope of new good hap he gan to feele;
So bent his speare, and spurnd his horse with yron heele.

---

284 *Neptune* ruling god of the sea
293 *the sharpe yron* his bit
294 *chauffed* heated
300 *eftsoones* at once

35

But that proud Paynim forward came so fierce,
   And full of wrath, that with his sharp-head speare
   Through vainely crossed shield he quite did pierce,
   And had his staggering steede not shrunke for feare,
   Through shield and bodie eke he should him beare:
   Yet so great was the puissance of his push,
   That from his saddle quite he did him beare:
   He tombling rudely downe to ground did rush,
And from his gored wound a well of bloud did gush.

36

Dismounting lightly from his loftie steed,
   He to him lept, in mind to reave his life,
   And proudly said, Lo there the worthie meed
   Of him, that slew *Sansfoy* with bloudie knife;
   Henceforth his ghost freed from ripining strife,
   In peace may passen over *Lethe* lake,
   When morning altars purgd with enemies life,
   The blacke infernall *Furies* doen aslake:
Life from *Sansfoy* thou tookst, *Sansloy* shall from thee take.

37

Therewith in haste his helmet gan unlace,
   Till *Una* cride, O hold that heavie hand,
   Deare Sir, what ever that thou be in place:
   Enough is, that thy foe doth vanquisht stand
   Now at thy mercy: Mercie not withstand:
   For he is one the truest knight alive,

---

307 *Paynim* heathen
309 *vainely crossed shield* marked with the cross falsely, as a disguise
321 *Lethe lake* river Lethe, in Hades. Its waters gave forgetfulness
323 *Furies* infernal ministers of vengeance

Though conquered now he lie on lowly land,
And whilest him fortune favour, faire did thrive
In bloudie field: therefore of life him not deprive.

38

Her piteous words might not abate his rage,
   But rudely rending up his helmet, would
   Have slaine him straight: but when he sees his age,
   And hoarie head of *Archimago* old,
   His hastie hand he doth amazed hold,
   And halfe ashamed, wondred at the sight:
   For the old man well knew he, though untold,   340
   In charmes and magicke to have wondrous might,
Ne ever wont in field, ne in round lists to fight.

39

And said, Why *Archimago*, lucklesse syre,
   What doe I see? what hard mishap is this,
   That hath thee hither brought to taste mine yre?
   Or thine the fault, or mine the error is,
   In stead of foe to wound my friend amis?
   He answered nought, but in a traunce still lay,
   And on those guilefull dazed eyes of his
   The cloud of death did sit. Which doen away,   350
He left him lying so, ne would no lenger stay.

40

But to the virgin comes, who all this while
   Amased stands, her selfe so mockt to see
   By him, who has the guerdon of his guile,
   For so misfeigning her true knight to bee:
   Yet is she now in more perplexitie,
   Left in the hand of that same Paynim bold,

---

354 *guerdon* reward

From whom her booteth not at all to flie;
   Who by her cleanly garment catching hold,
Her from her Palfrey pluckt, her visage to behold.   360

41

But her fierce servant full of kingly awe
   And high disdaine, whenas his soveraine Dame
   So rudely handled by her foe he sawe,
   With gaping jawes full greedy at him came,
   And ramping on his shield, did weene the same
   Have reft away with his sharpe rending clawes:
   But he was stout, and lust did now inflame
   His corage more, than from his griping pawes
He hath his shield redeem'd, and foorth his swerd he drawes.

42

O then too weake and feeble was the forse   370
   Of salvage beast, his puissance to withstand:
   For he was strong, and of so mightie corse,
   As ever wielded speare in warlike hand,
   And feates of armes did wisely understand.
   Eftsoones he perced through his chaufed chest
   With thrilling point of deadly yron brand,
   And launcht his Lordly hart: with death opprest
He roar'd aloud, whiles life forsooke his stubborne brest.

43

Who now is left to keepe the forlorne maid
   From raging spoile of lawlesse victors will?   380
   Her faithfull gard remov'd, her hope dismaid,
   Her selfe a yeelded pray to save or spill.

---

365 *ramping on* rearing up against
375 *chaufed* heated, enraged
377 *launcht* pierced

He now Lord of the field, his pride to fill,
   With foule reproches, and disdainfull spight
   Her vildly entertaines, and will or nill,
   Beares her away upon his courser light:
Her prayers nought prevaile, his rage is more of might.

44

And all the way, with great lamenting paine,
   And piteous plaints she filleth his dull eares,
   That stony hart could riven have in twaine, 390
   And all the way she wets with flowing teares:
   But he enrag'd with rancor, nothing heares.
   Her servile beast yet would not leave her so,
   But followes her farre off, ne ought he feares
   To be partaker of her wandring woe,
More mild in beastly kind, then that her beastly foe.

CANTO iv

To sinfull house of Pride, Duessa
   guides the faithfull knight,
Where brothers death to wreak Sansjoy
   doth chalenge him to fight.

1

Young knight, what ever that dost armes professe,
   And through long labours huntest after fame,
   Beware of fraud, beware of ficklenesse,
   In choice, and change of thy deare loved Dame,
   Least thou of her beleeve too lightly blame,
   And rash misweening doe thy hart remove:
   For unto knight there is no greater shame,

392 *rancor* bitterness
396 *More mild ... foe* more merciful by his animal nature than her depraved enemy
 1 *Young knight* a prospective reader

Then lightnesse and inconstancie in love;
That doth this *Redcrosse* knights ensample plainly prove.

2

Who after that he had faire *Una* lorne,
   Through light misdeeming of her loialtie,
   And false *Duessa* in her sted had borne,
   Called *Fidess'*, and so supposd to bee;
   Long with her traveild, till at last they see
   A goodly building, bravely garnished,
   The house of mightie Prince it seemd to bee:
   And towards it a broad high way that led,
All bare through peoples feet, which thither traveiled.

3

Great troupes of people traveild thitherward
   Both day and night, of each degree and place,
   But few returned, having scaped hard,
   With balefull beggerie, or foule disgrace,
   Which ever after in most wretched case,
   Like loathsome lazars, by the hedges lay.
   Thither *Duessa* bad him bend his pace:
   For she is wearie of the toilesome way,
And also nigh consumed is the lingring day.

4

A stately Pallace built of squared bricke,
   Which cunningly was without morter laid,
   Whose wals were high, but nothing strong, nor thick,
   And golden foile all over them displaid,

9 *ensample* example
10 *lorne* deserted
11 *light* too easy
24 *lazars* lepers

That purest skye with brightnesse they dismaid:
High lifted up were many loftie towres,
And goodly galleries farre over laid,
   Full of faire windowes, and delightfull bowres;
And on the top a Diall told the timely howres.

5

It was a goodly heape for to behould,
   And spake the praises of the workmans wit;
   But full great pittie, that so faire a mould
   Did on so weake foundation ever sit: 40
   For on a sandie hill, that still did flit,
   And fall away, it mounted was full hie,
   That every breath of heaven shaked it:
   And all the hinder parts, that few could spie,
Were ruinous and old, but painted cunningly.

6

Arrived there they passed in forth right;
   For still to all the gates stood open wide,
   Yet charge of them was to a Porter hight
   Cald *Malvenù*, who entrance none denide:
   Thence to the hall, which was on every side 50
   With rich array and costly arras dight:
   Infinite sorts of people did abide
   There waiting long, to win the wished sight
Of her, that was the Lady of that Pallace bright.

7

By them they passe, all gazing on them round,
   And to the Presence mount; whose glorious vew
   Their frayle amazed senses did confound:

41 *flit* shift; see Notes
49 *Malvenù* ill-come

    In living Princes court none ever knew
    Such endlesse richesse, and so sumptuous shew;
    Ne *Persia* selfe, the nourse of pompous pride
    Like ever saw. And there a noble crew
    Of Lordes and Ladies stood on every side,
Which with their presence faire, the place much beautifide.

8

High above all a cloth of State was spred,
    And a rich throne, as bright as sunny day,
    On which there sate most brave embellished
    With royall robes and gorgeous array,
    A mayden Queene, that shone as *Titans* ray,
    In glistring gold, and peerelesse pretious stone:
    Yet her bright blazing beautie did assay
    To dim the brightnesse of her glorious throne,
As envying her selfe, that too exceeding shone.

9

Exceeding shone, like *Phœbus* fairest childe,
    That did presume his fathers firie wayne,
    And flaming mouthes of steedes unwonted wilde
    Through highest heaven with weaker hand to rayne;
    Proud of such glory and advancement vaine,
    While flashing beames do daze his feeble eyen,
    He leaves the welkin way most beaten plaine,
    And rapt with whirling wheeles, inflames the skyen,
With fire not made to burne, but fairely for to shyne.

10

So proud she shyned in her Princely state,
    Looking to heaven; for earth she did disdayne,
    And sitting high; for lowly she did hate:

79 *welkin* sky

    Lo underneath her scornefull feete, was layne
    A dreadfull Dragon with an hideous trayne,
    And in her hand she held a mirrhour bright,
    Wherein her face she often vewed fayne,
    And in her selfe-lov'd semblance tooke delight;
For she was wondrous faire, as any living wight.   90

11

Of griesly *Pluto* she the daughter was,
    And sad *Proserpina* the Queene of hell;
    Yet did she thinke her pearelesse worth to pas
    That parentage, with pride so did she swell,
    And thundring *Jove*, that high in heaven doth dwell,
    And wield the world, she claymed for her syre,
    Or if that any else did *Jove* excell:
    For to the highest she did still aspyre,
Or if ought higher were then that, did it desyre.

12

And proud *Lucifera* men did her call,   100
    That made her selfe a Queene, and crownd to be,
    Yet rightfull kingdome she had none at all,
    Ne heritage of native soveraintie,
    But did usurpe with wrong and tyrannie
    Upon the scepter, which she now did hold:
    Ne ruld her Realmes with lawes, but pollicie,
    And strong advizement of six wisards old,
That with their counsels bad her kingdome did uphold.

13

Soone as the Elfin knight in presence came,
    And false *Duessa* seeming Lady faire,   110

---

95 *Jove* Jupiter, king of the gods
106 *pollicie* intrigue

A gentle Husher, *Vanitie* by name
   Made rowme, and passage for them did prepaire:
   So goodly brought them to the lowest staire
   Of her high throne, where they on humble knee
   Making obeyssance, did the cause declare,
   Why they were come, her royall state to see,
To prove the wide report of her great Majestee.

14

With loftie eyes, halfe loth to looke so low,
   She thanked them in her disdainefull wise,
   Ne other grace vouchsafed them to show   120
   Of Princesse worthy, scarse them bad arise.
   Her Lordes and Ladies all this while devise
   Themselves to setten forth to straungers sight:
   Some frounce their curled haire in courtly guise,
   Some prancke their ruffes, and others trimly dight
Their gay attire: each others greater pride does spight.

15

Goodly they all that knight do entertaine,
   Right glad with him to have increast their crew:
   But to *Duess'* each one himselfe did paine
   All kindnesse and faire courtesie to shew;   130
   For in that court whylome her well they knew:
   Yet the stout Faerie mongst the middest crowd
   Thought all their glorie vaine in knightly vew,
   And that great Princesse too exceeding prowd,
That to strange knight no better countenance allowd.

---

124 *frounce...guise* dress elaborately, as fashionable at Court
125 *prancke* pleat intricately
135 *countenance* acknowledgement

16

Suddein upriseth from her stately place
    The royall Dame, and for her coche doth call:
    All hurtlen forth, and she with Princely pace,
    As faire *Aurora* in her purple pall,
    Out of the East the dawning day doth call: 140
    So forth she comes: her brightnesse brode doth blaze;
    The heapes of people thronging in the hall,
    Do ride each other, upon her to gaze:
Her glorious glitterand light doth all mens eyes amaze.

17

So forth she comes, and to her coche does clyme,
    Adorned all with gold, and girlonds gay,
    That seemd as fresh as *Flora* in her prime,
    And strove to match, in royall rich array,
    Great *Junoes* golden chaire, the which they say
    The Gods stand gazing on, when she does ride   150
    To *Joves* high house through heavens bras-paved way
    Drawne of faire Pecocks, that excell in pride,
And full of *Argus* eyes their tailes dispredden wide.

18

But this was drawne of six unequall beasts,
    On which her six sage Counsellours did ryde,
    Taught to obay their bestiall beheasts,
    With like conditions to their kinds applyde:
    Of which the first, that all the rest did guyde,
    Was sluggish *Idlenesse* the nourse of sin;
    Upon a slouthfull Asse he chose to ryde,   160

---

138 *hurtlen* rush
139 *Aurora* goddess of the dawn
143 *ride* climb over
149 *Junoes* Juno was queen of the gods

Arayd in habit blacke, and amis thin,
Like to an holy Monck, the service to begin.

19

And in his hand his Portesse still he bare,
   That much was worne, but therein little red,
   For of devotion he had little care,
   Still drownd in sleepe, and most of his dayes ded;
   Scarse could he once uphold his heavie hed,
   To looken, whether it were night or day:
   May seeme the wayne was very evill led,
   When such an one had guiding of the way,   170
That knew not, whether right he went, or else astray.

20

From worldly cares himselfe he did esloyne,
   And greatly shunned manly exercise,
   From every worke he chalenged essoyne,
   For contemplation sake: yet otherwise,
   His life he led in lawlesse riotise;
   By which he grew to grievous malady;
   For in his lustlesse limbs through evill guise
   A shaking fever raignd continually:
Such one was *Idlenesse*, first of this company.   180

21

And by his side rode loathsome *Gluttony*,
   Deformed creature, on a filthie swyne,
   His belly was up-blowne with luxury,

---

161 *amis* cape
163 *Portesse* breviary
172 *esloyne* withdraw
174 *essoyne* exemption
178 *lustlesse* lethargic

[415-16]

And eke with fatnesse swollen were his eyne,
And like a Crane his necke was long and fyne,
With which he swallowed up excessive feast,
For want whereof poore people oft did pyne;
And all the way, most like a brutish beast,
He spued up his gorge, that all did him deteast.

22

In greene vine leaves he was right fitly clad; 190
For other clothes he could not weare for heat,
And on his head an yvie girland had,
From under which fast trickled downe the sweat:
Still as he rode, he somewhat still did eat,
And in his hand did beare a bouzing can,
Of which he supt so oft, that on his seat
His dronken corse he scarse upholden can,
In shape and life more like a monster, then a man.

23

Unfit he was for any worldly thing,
And eke unhable once to stirre or go, 200
Not meet to be of counsell to a king,
Whose mind in meat and drinke was drowned so,
That from his friend he seldome knew his fo:
Full of diseases was his carcas blew,
And a dry dropsie through his flesh did flow:
Which by misdiet daily greater grew:
Such one was *Gluttony*, the second of that crew.

24

And next to him rode lustfull *Lechery*,
Upon a bearded Goat, whose rugged haire,
And whally eyes (the signe of gelosy,) 210

195 *bouzing can* tankard
210 *whally* with a greenish tinge

Was like the person selfe, whom he did beare:
Who rough, and blacke, and filthy did appeare,
Unseemely man to please faire Ladies eye;
Yet he of Ladies oft was loved deare,
When fairer faces were bid standen by:
O who does know the bent of womens fantasy?

25

In a greene gowne he clothed was full faire,
   Which underneath did hide his filthinesse,
   And in his hand a burning hart he bare,
   Full of vaine follies, and new fanglenesse: 220
For he was false, and fraught with ficklenesse,
   And learned had to love with secret lookes,
   And well could daunce, and sing with ruefulnesse,
   And fortunes tell, and read in loving bookes,
And thousand other wayes, to bait his fleshly hookes.

26

Inconstant man, that loved all he saw,
   And lusted after all, that he did love,
   Ne would his looser life be tide to law,
   But joyd weake wemens hearts to tempt and prove
If from their loyal loves he might then move; 230
   Which lewdnesse fild him with reprochfull paine
   Of that fowle evill, which all men reprove,
   That rots the marrow, and consumes the braine:
Such one was *Lecherie*, the third of all this traine.

27

And greedy *Avarice* by him did ride,
   Upon a Camell loaden all with gold;
   Two iron coffers hong on either side,
   With precious mettall full, as they might hold,
And in his lap an heape of coine he told;

[415-16]

> For of his wicked pelfe his God he made, 240
> And unto hell him selfe for money sold;
> Accursed usurie was all his trade,
> And right and wrong ylike in equall ballaunce waide.

28

> His life was nigh unto deaths doore yplast,
> And thred-bare cote, and cobled shoes he ware,
> Ne scarse good morsell all his life did tast,
> But both from backe and belly still did spare,
> To fill his bags, and richesse to compare;
> Yet chylde ne kinsman living had he none
> To leave them to; but thorough daily care 250
> To get, and nightly feare to lose his owne,
> He led a wretched life unto him selfe unknowne.

29

> Most wretched wight, whom nothing might suffise,
> Whose greedy lust did lacke in greatest store,
> Whose need had end, but no end covetise,
> Whose wealth was want, whose plenty made him pore,
> Who had enough, yet wished ever more;
> A vile disease, and eke in foote and hand
> A grievous gout tormented him full sore,
> That well he could not touch, nor go, nor stand: 260
> Such one was *Avarice*, the fourth of this faire band.

30

> And next to him malicious *Envie* rode,
> Upon a ravenous wolfe, and still did chaw
> Betweene his cankred teeth a venemous tode,

240 *pelfe* money
245 *cobled* mended
252 *unto him selfe unknowne* unaware of it
264 *cankred* poisonous

That all the poison ran about his chaw;
But inwardly he chawed his owne maw
At neighbours wealth, that made him ever sad;
For death it was, when any good he saw,
And wept, that cause of weeping none he had,
But when he heard of harme, he wexed wondrous glad. 270

31

All in a kirtle of discolourd say
    He clothed was, ypainted full of eyes;
    And in his bosome secretly there lay
    An hatefull Snake, the which his taile uptyes
    In many folds, and mortall sting implyes.
    Still as he rode, he gnasht his teeth, to see
    Those heapes of gold with griple Covetyse,
    And grudged at the great felicitie
Of proud *Lucifera*, and his owne companie.

32

He hated all good workes and vertuous deeds, 280
    And him no lesse, that any like did use,
    And who with gracious bread the hungry feeds,
    His almes for want of faith he doth accuse;
    So every good to bad he doth abuse:
    And eke the verse of famous Poets witt
    He does backebite, and spightfull poison spues
    From leprous mouth on all, that ever writt:
Such one vile *Envie* was, that fifte in row did sitt.

33

And him beside rides fierce revenging *Wrath*,
    Upon a Lion, loth for to be led; 290

---

271 *discolourd say* silky cloth of mixed colours

[415–16]

And in his hand a burning brond he hath,
The which he brandisheth about his hed;
His eyes did hurle forth sparkles fiery red,
And stared sterne on all, that him beheld,
As ashes pale of hew and seeming ded;
And on his dagger still his hand he held,
Trembling through hasty rage, when choler in him sweld.

34

His ruffin raiment all was staind with blood,
   Which he had spilt, and all to rags yrent,
   Through unadvized rashnesse woxen wood;   300
   For of his hands he had no governement,
   Ne car'd for bloud in his avengement:
   But when the furious fit was overpast,
   His cruell facts he often would repent;
   Yet wilfull man he never would forecast,
How many mischieves should ensue his heedlesse hast.

35

Full many mischiefes follow cruell *Wrath*;
   Abhorred bloudshed, and tumultuous strife,
   Unmanly murder, and unthrifty scath,
   Bitter despight, with rancours rusty knife,   310
   And fretting griefe the enemy of life;
   All these, and many evils moe haunt ire,
   The swelling Splene, and Frenzy raging rife,
   The shaking Palsey, and Saint *Fraunces* fire:
Such one was *Wrath*, the last of this ungodly tire.

---

298 *ruffin* disordered
300 *woxen wood* become mad
301 *governement* control
304 *facts* deeds

36

And after all, upon the wagon beame
    Rode *Sathan*, with a smarting whip in hand,
    With which he forward lasht the laesie teme,
    So oft as *Slowth* still in the mire did stand.
    Huge routs of people did about them band, 320
    Showting for joy, and still before their way
    A foggy mist had covered all the land;
    And underneath their feet, all scattered lay
Dead sculs and bones of men, whose life had gone astray.

37

So forth they marchen in this goodly sort,
    To take the solace of the open aire,
    And in fresh flowring fields themselves to sport;
    Emongst the rest rode that false Lady faire,
    The fowle *Duessa*, next unto the chaire
    Of proud *Lucifera*, as one of the traine: 330
    But that good knight would not so nigh repaire,
    Him selfe estraunging from their joyaunce vaine,
Whose fellowship seemd far unfit for warlike swaine.

38

So having solaced themselves a space
    With pleasaunce of the breathing fields yfed,
    They backe returned to the Princely Place;
    Whereas an errant knight in armes ycled,
    And heathnish shield, wherein with letters red
    Was writ *Sans joy*, they new arrived find:
    Enflam'd with fury and fiers hardy-hed, 340
    He seemd in hart to harbour thoughts unkind,
And nourish bloudy vengeaunce in his bitter mind.

332 *estraunging* keeping away

39

Who when the shamed shield of slaine *Sans foy*
    He spide with that same Faery champions page,
    Bewraying him, that did of late destroy
    His eldest brother, burning all with rage
    He to him lept, and that same envious gage
    Of victors glory from him snatcht away:
    But th'Elfin knight, which ought that warlike wage,
    Disdaind to loose the meed he wonne in fray,   350
And him rencountring fierce, reskewd the noble pray.

40

Therewith they gan to hurtlen greedily,
    Redoubted battaile ready to darrayne,
    And clash their shields, and shake their swords on hy,
    That with their sturre they troubled all the traine;
    Till that great Queene upon eternall paine
    Of high displeasure, that ensewen might,
    Commaunded them their fury to refraine,
    And if that either to that shield had right,
In equall lists they should the morrow next it fight.   360

41

Ah dearest Dame, (quoth then the Paynim bold,)
    Pardon the errour of enraged wight,
    Whom great griefe made forget the raines to hold
    Of reasons rule, to see this recreant knight,
    No knight, but treachour full of false despight

349 *which ought* to whom was due
350 *meed* reward
351 *rencountring* encountering
353 *darrayne* prepare for battle
355 *sturre* tumult
364 *recreant* backsliding
365 *treachour* traitor

And shamefull treason, who through guile hath slayn
   The prowest knight, that ever field did fight,
   Even stout *Sans foy* (O who can then refrayn?)
Whose shield he bares renverst, the more to heape disdayn.

42

And to augment the glorie of his guile, 370
   His dearest love the faire *Fidessa* loe
   Is there possessed of the traytour vile,
   Who reapes the harvest sowen by his foe,
   Sowen in bloudy field, and bought with woe:
   That brothers hand shall dearely well requight
   So be, O Queene, you equall favour showe.
   Him litle answerd th'angry Elfin knight;
He never meant with words, but swords to plead his right.

43

But threw his gauntlet as a sacred pledge,
   His cause in combat the next day to try: 380
   So been they parted both, with harts on edge,
   To be aveng'd each on his enimy.
   That night they pas in joy and jollity,
   Feasting and courting both in bowre and hall;
   For Steward was excessive *Gluttonie*,
   That of his plenty poured forth to all;
Which doen, the Chamberlain *Slowth* did to rest them call.

44

Now whenas darkesome night had all displayd
   Her coleblacke curtein over brightest skye,
   The warlike youths on dayntie couches layd, 390
   Did chace away sweet sleepe from sluggish eye,
   To muse on meanes of hoped victory.

369 *renverst* reversed; see Notes

But whenas *Morpheus* had with leaden mace
Arrested all that courtly company,
Up-rose *Duessa* from her resting place,
And to the Paynims lodging comes with silent pace.

45

Whom broad awake she finds, in troublous fit,
   Forecasting, how his foe he might annoy,
   And him amoves with speaches seeming fit:
   Ah deare *Sans joy*, next dearest to *Sans foy*,   400
   Cause of my new griefe, cause of my new joy,
   Joyous, to see his ymage in mine eye,
   And greev'd, to thinke how foe did him destroy,
   That was the flowre of grace and chevalrye;
Lo his *Fidessa* to thy secret faith I flye.

46

With gentle wordes he can her fairely greet,
   And bad say on the secret of her hart.
   Then sighing soft, I learne that litle sweet
   Oft tempred is (quoth she) with muchell smart:
   For since my brest was launcht with lovely dart   410
   Of deare *Sansfoy*, I never joyed howre,
   But in eternall woes my weaker hart
   Have wasted, loving him with all my powre,
And for his sake have felt full many an heavie stowre.

47

At last when perils all I weened past,
   And hop'd to reape the crop of all my care,
   Into new woes unweeting I was cast,

---

398 *annoy* trouble
409 *muchell* great
414 *stowre* strife

    By this false faytor, who unworthy ware
    His worthy shield, whom he with guilefull snare
    Entrapped slew, and brought to shamefull grave.   420
    Me silly maid away with him he bare,
    And ever since hath kept in darksome cave,
For that I would not yeeld, that to *Sans-foy* I gave.

48

But since faire Sunne hath sperst that lowring clowd,
    And to my loathed life now shewes some light,
    Under your beames I will me safely shrowd,
    From dreaded storme of his disdainfull spight:
    To you th'inheritance belongs by right
    Of brothers prayse, to you eke longs his love.
    Let not his love, let not his restlesse spright   430
    Be unreveng'd, that calles to you above
From wandring *Stygian* shores, where it doth endlesse move.

49

Thereto said he, Faire Dame be nought dismaid
    For sorrowes past; their griefe is with them gone:
    Ne yet of present perill be affraid;
    For needlesse feare did never vantage none,
    And helplesse hap it booteth not to mone.
    Dead is *Sans-foy*, his vitall paines are past,
    Though greeved ghost for vengeance deepe do grone:
    He lives, that shall him pay his dewties last,   440
And guiltie Elfin bloud shall sacrifice in hast.

---

418 *faytor* impostor; *ware* wears
421 *silly* simple
424 *sperst* dispersed
432 *Stygian shores* shores of the River Styx
438 *vitall* living

50

O but I feare the fickle freakes (quoth shee)
  Of fortune false, and oddes of armes in field.
  Why dame (quoth he) what oddes can ever bee,
  Where both do fight alike, to win or yield?
  Yea but (quoth she) he beares a charmed shield,
  And eke enchaunted armes, that none can perce,
  Ne none can wound the man, that does them wield.
  Charmd or enchaunted (answerd he then ferce)
I no whit reck, ne you the like need to reherce. 450

51

But faire *Fidessa*, sithens fortunes guile,
  Or enimies powre hath now captived you,
  Returne from whence ye came, and rest a while
  Till morrow next, that I the Elfe subdew,
  And with *Sans-foyes* dead dowry you endew.
  Ay me, that is a double death (she said)
  With proud foes sight my sorrow to renew:
  Where ever yet I be, my secrete aid
Shall follow you. So passing forth she him obaid.

CANTO v

*The faithfull knight in equall field
subdewes his faithlesse foe,
Whom false Duessa saves, and for
his cure to hell does goe.*

1

The noble hart, that harbours vertuous thought,
  And is with child of glorious great intent,

---

455 *And with ... you endew* and give you what Sans foy would have had, had he lived

Can never rest, until it forth have brought
Th'eternal brood of glorie excellent:
Such restlesse passion did all night torment
The flaming corage of that Faery knight,
Devizing, how that doughtie turnament
With greatest honour he atchieven might;
Still did he wake, and still did watch for dawning light.

2

At last the golden Orientall gate
    Of greatest heaven gan to open faire,
    And *Phœbus* fresh, as bridegrome to his mate,
    Came dauncing forth, shaking his deawie haire:
    And hurld his glistring beames through gloomy aire.
    Which when the wakeful Elfe perceiv'd, streight way
    He started up, and did him selfe prepare,
    In sun-bright armes, and battailous array:
For with that Pagan proud he combat will that day.

3

And forth he comes into the commune hall,
    Where earely waite him many a gazing eye,
    To weet what end to straunger knights may fall.
    There many Minstrales maken melody,
    To drive away the dull melancholy,
    And many Bardes, that to the trembling chord
    Can tune their timely voices cunningly,
    And many Chroniclers, that can record
Old loves, and warres for Ladies doen by many a Lord.

---

8 *atchieven* win
21 *straunger* from elsewhere
25 *timely* keeping time; *cunningly* knowledgeably

4

Soone after comes the cruell Sarazin,
   In woven maile all armed warily,
   And sternly lookes at him, who not a pin
   Does care for looke of living creatures eye.
   They bring them wines of *Greece* and *Araby*,
   And daintie spices fetcht from furthest *Ynd*,
   To kindle heat of corage privily:
   And in the wine a solemne oth they bynd
T'observe the sacred lawes of armes, that are assynd.

5

At last forth comes that far renowmed Queene,
   With royall pomp and Princely majestie;
   She is ybrought unto a paled greene,
   And placed under stately canapee,
   The warlike feates of both those knights to see.
   On th'other side in all mens open vew
   Duessa placed is, and on a tree
   Sans-foy his shield is hangd with bloudy hew:
Both those the lawrell girlonds to the victor dew.

6

A shrilling trompet sownded from on hye,
   And unto battaill bad them selves addresse:
   Their shining shieldes about their wrestes they tye,
   And burning blades about their heads do blesse,
   The instruments of wrath and heavinesse:
   With greedy force each other doth assayle,
   And strike so fiercely, that they do impresse

---

33 *Ynd* India
36 *assynd* laid down
39 *paled* fenced in
49 *blesse* brandish

Deepe dinted furrowes in the battred mayle;
The yron walles to ward their blowes are weake and fraile.

7

The Sarazin was stout, and wondrous strong,
   And heaped blowes like yron hammers great:
   For after bloud and vengeance he did long.
   The knight was fiers, and full of youthly heat:
   And doubled strokes, like dreaded thunders threat:
   For all for prayse and honour he did fight. 60
   Both stricken strike, and beaten both do beat,
   That from their shields forth flyeth firie light,
And helmets hewen deepe, shew marks of eithers might.

8

So th'one for wrong, the other strives for right:
   As when a Gryfon seized of his pray,
   A Dragon fiers encountreth in his flight,
   Through widest ayre making his ydle way,
   That would his rightfull ravine rend away:
   With hideous horrour both together smight,
   And souce so sore, that they the heavens affray: 70
   The wise Southsayer seeing so sad sight,
Th'amazed vulgar tels of warres and mortall fight.

9

So th'one for wrong, the other strives for right,
   And each to deadly shame would drive his foe:
   The cruell steele so greedily doth bight
   In tender flesh, that streames of bloud down flow,
   With which the armes, that earst so bright did show,
   Into a pure vermillion now are dyde:

70 *souce* strike
72 *Th'amazed vulgar* the terrified populace

>   Great ruth in all the gazers harts did grow,
>   Seeing the gored woundes to gape so wyde,   80
> That victory they dare not wish to either side.
>
>
> 10
>
> At last the Paynim chaunst to cast his eye,
>   His suddein eye, flaming with wrathfull fyre,
>   Upon his brothers shield, which hong thereby:
>   Therewith redoubled was his raging yre,
>   And said, Ah wretched sonne of wofull syre,
>   Doest thou sit wayling by black *Stygian* lake,
>   Whilest here thy shield is hangd for victors hyre,
>   And sluggish german doest thy forces slake,
> To after-send his foe, that him may overtake?   90
>
>
> 11
>
> Goe caytive Elfe, him quickly overtake,
>   And soone redeeme from his long wandring woe;
>   Goe guiltie ghost, to him my message make,
>   That I his shield have quit from dying foe.
>   Therewith upon his crest he stroke him so,
>   That twise he reeled, readie twise to fall;
>   End of the doubtfull battell deemed tho
>   The lookers on, and lowd to him gan call
> The false *Duessa*, Thine the shield, and I, and all.
>
>
> 12
>
> Soone as the Faerie heard his Ladie speake,   100
>   Out of his swowning dreame he gan awake,
>   And quickning faith, that earst was woxen weake,
>   The creeping deadly cold away did shake:

89 *german* kinsman
91 *caytive* villainous
102 *earst* before; *woxen* become

Tho mov'd with wrath, and shame, and Ladies sake,
   Of all attonce he cast avengd to bee,
   And with so'exceeding furie at him strake,
   That forced him to stoupe upon his knee;
Had he not stouped so, he should have cloven bee.

13

And to him said, Goe now proud Miscreant,
   Thy selfe thy message doe to german deare,   110
   Alone he wandring thee too long doth want:
   Goe say, his foe thy shield with his doth beare.
   Therewith his heavie hand he high gan reare
   Him to have slaine; when loe a darkesome clowd
   Upon him fell: he no where doth appeare,
   But vanisht is. The Elfe him cals alowd,
But answer none receives: the darknes him does shrowd.

14

In haste *Duessa* from her place arose,
   And to him running said, O prowest knight,
   That ever Ladie to her love did chose,   120
   Let now abate the terror of your might,
   And quench the flame of furious despight,
   And bloudie vengeance; lo th'infernall powres
   Covering your foe with cloud of deadly night,
   Have borne him hence to *Plutoes* balefull bowres.
The conquest yours, I yours, the shield, and glory yours.

15

Not all so satisfide, with greedie eye
   He sought all round about, his thirstie blade
   To bath in bloud of faithlesse enemy;
   Who all that while lay hid in secret shade: 130

---

110 *doe* bear

He standes amazed, how he thence should fade.
At last the trumpets Triumph sound on hie,
And running Heralds humble homage made,
Greeting him goodly with new victorie,
And to him brought the shield, the cause of enmitie.

16

Wherewith he goeth to that soveraine Queene,
  And falling her before on lowly knee,
  To her makes present of his service seene:
  Which she accepts, with thankes, and goodly gree,
  Greatly advauncing his gay chevalree.   140
  So marcheth home, and by her takes the knight,
  Whom all the people follow with great glee,
  Shouting, and clapping all their hands on hight,
That all the aire it fils, and flyes to heaven bright.

17

Home is he brought, and laid in sumptuous bed:
  Where many skilfull leaches him abide,
  To salve his hurts, that yet still freshly bled.
  In wine and oyle they wash his woundes wide,
  And softly can embalme on every side.
  And all the while, most heavenly melody   150
  About the bed sweet musicke did divide,
  Him to beguile of griefe and agony:
And all the while *Duessa* wept full bitterly.

18

As when a wearie traveller that strayes
  By muddy shore of broad seven-mouthed *Nile*,

139 *gree* favour
146 *leaches* doctors
151 *did divide* sang in descant

[416–17]

    Unweeting of the perillous wandring wayes,
    Doth meet a cruell craftie Crocodile,
    Which in false griefe hyding his harmefull guile,
    Doth weepe full sore, and sheddeth tender teares:
    The foolish man, that pitties all this while   160
    His mournefull plight, is swallowed up unwares,
Forgetfull of his owne, that mindes anothers cares.

19

So wept *Duessa* untill eventide,
    That shyning lampes in *Joves* high house were light:
    Then forth she rose, ne lenger would abide,
    But comes unto the place, where th'Hethen knight
    In slombring swownd nigh voyd of vitall spright,
    Lay cover'd with inchaunted cloud all day:
    Whom when she found, as she him left in plight,
    To wayle his woefull case she would not stay,   170
But to the easterne coast of heaven makes speedy way.

20

Where griesly *Night*, with visage deadly sad,
    That *Phœbus* chearefull face durst never vew,
    And in a foule blacke pitchie mantle clad,
    She findes forth comming from her darkesome mew,
    Where she all day did hide her hated hew.
    Before the dore her yron charet stood,
    Alreadie harnessed for journey new;
    And coleblacke steedes yborne of hellish brood,
That on their rustie bits did champ, as they were wood.   180

---

175 *mew* den
177 *charet* chariot
180 *wood* mad

21

Who when she saw *Duessa* sunny bright,
    Adornd with gold and jewels shining cleare,
    She greatly grew amazed at the sight,
    And th'unacquainted light began to feare:
    For never did such brightnesse there appeare,
    And would have backe retyred to her cave,
    Untill the witches speech she gan to heare,
    Saying, Yet O thou dreaded Dame, I crave
Abide, till I have told the message, which I have.

22

She stayd, and foorth *Duessa* gan proceede,   190
    O thou most aunciert Grandmother of all,
    More old then *Jove*, whom thou at first didst breede,
    Or that great house of Gods cælestiall,
    Which wast begot in *Dæmogorgons* hall,
    And sawst the secrets of the world unmade,
    Why suffredst thou thy Nephewes deare to fall
    With Elfin sword, most shamefully betrade?
Lo where the stout *Sansjoy* doth sleepe in deadly shade.

23

And him before, I saw with bitter eyes
    The bold *Sansfoy* shrinke underneath his speare;   200
    And now the pray of fowles in field he lyes,
    Nor wayld of friends, nor laid on groning beare,
    That whylome was to me too dearely deare.
    O what of Gods then boots it to be borne,
    If old *Aveugles* sonnes so evill heare?
    Or who shall not great *Nightes* children scorne,
When two of three her Nephews are so fowle forlorne.

194 *Dæmogorgons* see I.i.37n.
205 *Aveugles* Blind: darkness

24

Up then, up dreary Dame, of darknesse Queene,
  Go gather up the reliques of thy race,
  Or else goe them avenge, and let be seene,   210
  That dreaded *Night* in brightest day hath place,
  And can the children of faire light deface.
  Her feeling speeches some compassion moved
  In hart, and chaunge in that great mothers face:
  Yet pittie in her hart was never proved
Till then: for evermore she hated, never loved.

25

And said, Deare daughter rightly may I rew
  The fall of famous children borne of mee,
  And good successes, which their foes ensew:
  But who can turne the streame of destinee,   220
  Or breake the chayne of strong necessitee,
  Which fast is tyde to *Joves* eternall seat?
  The sonnes of Day he favoureth, I see,
  And by my ruines thinkes to make them great:
To make one great by others losse, is bad excheat.

26

Yet shall they not escape so freely all;
  For some shall pay the price of others guilt:
  And he the man that made *Sansfoy* to fall,
  Shall with his owne bloud price that he hath spilt.
  But what art thou, that telst of Nephews kilt?   230
  I that do seeme not I, *Duessa* am,
  (Quoth she) how ever now in garments gilt,
  And gorgeous gold arayd I to thee came;
Duessa I, the daughter of Deceipt and Shame.

225 *excheat* exchange
229 *price* pay for

27

Then bowing downe her aged backe, she kist
    The wicked witch, saying; In that faire face
    The false resemblance of Deceipt, I wist
    Did closely lurke; yet so true-seeming grace
    It carried, that I scarse in darkesome place
    Could it discerne, though I the mother bee   240
    Of falshood, and root of *Duessaes* race.
    O welcome child, whom I have longd to see,
And now have seene unwares. Lo now I go with thee.

28

Then to her yron wagon she betakes,
    And with her beares the fowle welfavourd witch:
    Through mirkesome aire her readie way she makes.
    Her twyfold Teme, of which two blacke as pitch,
    And two were browne, yet each to each unlich,
    Did softly swim away, ne ever stampe,
    Unlesse she chaunst their stubborne mouths to twitch;   250
    Then foming tarre, their bridles they would champe,
And trampling the fine element, would fiercely rampe.

29

So well they sped, that they be come at length
    Unto the place, whereas the Paynim lay,
    Devoid of outward sense, and native strength,
    Coverd with charmed cloud from vew of day,
    And sight of men, since his late luckelesse fray.
    His cruell wounds with cruddy bloud congealed,
    They binden up so wisely, as they may,
    And handle softly, till they can be healed: 260
So lay him in her charet, close in night concealed.

---

252 *rampe* rear
258 *cruddy* clotted

30

And all the while she stood upon the ground,
    The wakefull dogs did never cease to bay,
    As giving warning of th'unwonted sound,
    With which her yron wheeles did them affray,
    And her darke griesly looke them much dismay;
    The messenger of death, the ghastly Owle
    With drearie shriekes did also her bewray;
    And hungry Wolves continually did howle,
At her abhorred face, so filthy and so fowle.   270

31

Thence turning backe in silence soft they stole,
    And brought the heavie corse with easie pace
    To yawning gulfe of deepe *Avernus* hole.
    By that same hole an entrance darke and bace
    With smoake and sulphure hiding all the place,
    Descends to hell: there creature never past,
    That backe returned without heavenly grace;
    But dreadfull *Furies*, which their chaines have brast,
And damned sprights sent forth to make ill men aghast.

32

By that same way the direfull dames doe drive   280
    Their mournefull charet, fild with rusty blood,
    And downe to *Plutoes* house are come bilive:
    Which passing through, on every side them stood
    The trembling ghosts with sad amazed mood,
    Chattring their yron teeth, and staring wide
    With stonie eyes; and all the hellish brood
    Of feends infernall flockt on every side,
To gaze on earthly wight, that with the Night durst ride.

282 *bilive* quickly

33

They pas the bitter waves of *Acheron*,
   Where many soules sit wailing woefully,   290
   And come to fiery flood of *Phlegeton*,
   Whereas the damned ghosts in torments fry,
   And with sharpe shrilling shriekes doe bootlesse cry,
   Cursing high *Jove*, the which them thither sent.
   The house of endlesse paine is built thereby,
   In which ten thousand sorts of punishment
The cursed creatures doe eternally torment.

34

Before the threshold dreadfull *Cerberus*
   His three deformed heads did lay along,
   Curled with thousand adders venemous,   300
   And lilled forth his bloudie flaming tong:
   At them he gan to reare his bristles strong,
   And felly gnarre, untill dayes enemy
   Did him appease; then downe his taile he hong
   And suffered them to passen quietly:
For she in hell and heaven had power equally.

35

There was *Ixion* turned on a wheele,
   For daring tempt the Queene of heaven to sin;
   And *Sisyphus* an huge round stone did reele
   Against an hill, ne might from labour lin;   310
   There thirstie *Tantalus* hong by the chin;
   And *Tityus* fed a vulture on his maw;
   Typhœus joynts were stretched on a gin,

---

293 *bootlesse* uselessly
303 *felly gnarre* snarl threateningly
310 *lin* rest
313 *gin* rack

[416-17]

Theseus condemned to endlesse slouth by law,
And fifty sisters water in leake vessels draw.

36

They all beholding worldly wights in place,
    Leave off their worke, unmindfull of their smart,
    To gaze on them; who forth by them doe pace,
    Till they be come unto the furthest part:
    Where was a Cave ywrought by wondrous art,   320
    Deepe, darke, uneasie, dolefull, comfortlesse,
    In which sad *Æsculapius* farre a part
    Emprisond was in chaines remedilesse,
For that *Hippolytus* rent corse he did redresse.

37

Hippolytus a jolly huntsman was,
    That wont in charet chace the foming Bore;
    He all his Peeres in beautie did surpas,
    But Ladies love as losse of time forbore:
    His wanton stepdame loved him the more,
    But when she saw her offred sweets refused   330
    Her love she turnd to hate, and him before
    His father fierce of treason false accused,
And with her gealous termes his open eares abused.

38

Who all in rage his Sea-god syre besought,
    Some cursed vengeance on his sonne to cast:
    From surging gulf two monsters straight were brought,
    With dread whereof his chasing steedes aghast,
    Both charet swift and huntsman overcast.
    His goodly corps on ragged cliffs yrent,

315 *leake* leaky
324 *redresse* cure

    Was quite dismembred, and his members chast   340
      Scattered on every mountaine, as he went,
That of *Hippolytus* was left no moniment.

39

His cruell stepdame seeing what was donne,
    Her wicked dayes with wretched knife did end,
    In death avowing th'innocence of her sonne.
    Which hearing his rash Syre, began to rend
    His haire, and hastie tongue, that did offend:
    Tho gathering up the relicks of his smart
    By *Dianes* meanes, who was *Hippolyts* frend,
    Them brought to *Æsculape*, that by his art   350
Did heale them all againe, and joyned every part.

40

Such wondrous science in mans wit to raine
    When *Jove* avizd, that could the dead revive,
    And fates expired could renew againe,
    Of endlesse life he might him not deprive,
    But unto hell did thrust him downe alive,
    With flashing thunderbolt ywounded sore:
    Where long remaining, he did alwaies strive
    Himselfe with salves to health for to restore,
And slake the heavenly fire, that raged evermore.   360

41

There aunciant Night arriving, did alight
    From her nigh wearie waine, and in her armes
    To *Æsculapius* brought the wounded knight:
    Whom having softly disarayd of armes,

---

340 *chast* chaste
353 *avizd* perceived
362 *waine* carriage

Tho gan to him discover all his harmes,
Beseeching him with prayer, and with praise,
If either salves, or oyles, or herbes, or charmes
A fordonne wight from dore of death mote raise,
He would at her request prolong her nephews daies.

42

Ah Dame (quoth he) thou temptest me in vaine, 370
    To dare the thing, which daily yet I rew,
    And the old cause of my continued paine
    With like attempt to like end to renew.
    Is not enough, that thrust from heaven dew
    Here endlesse penance for one fault I pay,
    But that redoubled crime with vengeance new
    Thou biddest me to eeke? Can Night defray
The wrath of thundring *Jove*, that rules both night and day?

43

Not so (quoth she) but sith that heavens king
    From hope of heaven hath thee excluded quight, 380
    Why fearest thou, that canst not hope for thing,
    And fearest not, that more thee hurten might,
    Now in the powre of everlasting Night?
    Goe to then, O thou farre renowmed sonne
    Of great *Apollo*, shew they famous might
    In medicine, that else hath to thee wonne
Great paines, and greater praise, both never to be donne.

368 *fordonne* mortally wounded
377 *eeke* augment
379 *sith* since
384 *Goe to* proceed

44

Her words prevaild: And then the learned leach
   His cunning hand gan to his wounds to lay,
   And all things else, the which his art did teach:
   Which having seene, from thence arose away
   The mother of dread darknesse, and let stay
   Aveugles sonne there in the leaches cure,
   And backe returning tooke her wonted way,
   To runne her timely race, whilst *Phœbus* pure
In westerne waves his wearie wagon did recure.

45

The false *Duessa* leaving noyous Night,
   Returnd to stately pallace of dame Pride;
   Where when she came, she found the Faery knight
   Departed thence, albe his woundes wide
   Not throughly heald, unreadie were to ride.
   Good cause he had to hasten thence away;
   For on a day his wary Dwarfe had spide,
   Where in a dongeon deepe huge numbers lay
Of caytive wretched thrals, that wayled night and day.

46

A ruefull sight, as could be seene with eie;
   Of whom he learned had in secret wise
   The hidden cause of their captivitie,
   How mortgaging their lives to *Covetise*,
   Through wastefull Pride, and wanton Riotise,
   They were by law of that proud Tyrannesse
   Provokt with *Wrath*, and *Envies* false surmise,

---

396 *recure* refresh
397 *noyous* noxious
400 *albe* although
405 *thrals* prisoners

    Condemned to that Dongeon mercilesse,
Where they should live in woe, and die in wretchednesse.

47

There was that great proud king of *Babylon*,
    That would compell all nations to adore,
    And him as onely God to call upon,
    Till through celestiall doome throwne out of dore,
    Into an Oxe he was transform'd of yore:
    There also was king *Crœsus*, that enhaunst   420
    His heart too high through his great riches store;
    And proud *Antiochus*, the which advaunst
His cursed hand gainst God, and on his altars daunst.

48

And them long time before, great *Nimrod* was,
    That first the world with sword and fire warrayd;
    And after him old *Ninus* farre did pas
    In princely pompe, of all the world obayd;
    There also was that mightie Monarch layd
    Low under all, yet above all in pride,
    That name of native syre did fowle upbrayd,   430
    And would as *Ammons* sonne be magnifide,
Till scornd of God and man a shamefull death he dide.

49

All these together in one heape were throwne,
    Like carkases of beasts in butchers stall.
    And in another corner wide were strowne
    The antique ruines of the *Romaines* fall:
    Great *Romulus* the Grandsyre of them all,
    Proud *Tarquin*, and too lordly *Lentulus*,
    Stout *Scipio*, and stubborne *Hanniball*,
    Ambitious *Sylla*, and sterne *Marius*,   440
High *Cæsar*, great *Pompey*, and fierce *Antonius*.

50

Amongst these mighty men were wemen mixt,
    Proud wemen, vaine, forgetfull of their yoke:
    The bold *Semiramis*, whose sides transfixt
    With sonnes owne blade, her fowle reproches spoke;
    Faire *Sthenobœa*, that her selfe did choke
    With wilfull cord, for wanting of her will;
    High minded *Cleopatra*, that with stroke
    Of Aspes sting her selfe did stoutly kill:
And thousands moe the like, that did that dongeon fill.   450

51

Besides the endlesse routs of wretched thralles,
    Which thither were assembled day by day,
    From all the world after their wofull falles,
    Through wicked pride, and wasted wealthes decay.
    But most of all, which in that Dongeon lay
    Fell from high Princes courts, or Ladies bowres,
    Where they in idle pompe, or wanton play,
    Consumed had their goods, and thriftlesse howres,
And lastly throwne themselves into these heavy stowres.

52

Whose case when as the carefull Dwarfe had tould,   460
    And made ensample of their mournefull sight
    Unto his maister, he no lenger would
    There dwell in perill of like painefull plight,
    But early rose, and ere that dawning light
    Discovered had the world to heaven wyde,
    He by a privie Posterne tooke his flight,

---

443 *their yoke* their subordinate status
459 *stowres* miseries
466 *Posterne* back-door

That of no envious eyes he mote be spyde:
For doubtlesse death ensewd, if any him descryde.

53

Scarse could he footing find in that fowle way,
   For many corses, like a great Lay-stall 470
   Of murdred men which therein strowed lay,
   Without remorse, or decent funerall:
   Which all through that great Princesse pride did fall
   And came to shamefull end. And them beside
   Forth ryding underneath the castell wall,
   A donghill of dead carkases he spide,
The dreadfull spectacle of that sad house of *Pride*.

CANTO vi

From lawlesse lust by wondrous grace
* fayre Una is releast:*
Whom salvage nation does adore,
* and learnes her wise beheast.*

1

As when a ship, that flyes faire under saile,
   An hidden rocke escaped hath unwares,
   That lay in waite her wrack for to bewaile,
   The Marriner yet halfe amazed stares
   At perill past, and yet in doubt ne dares
   To joy at his foole-happie oversight:
   So doubly is distrest twixt joy and cares
   The dreadlesse courage of this Elfin knight,
Having escapt so sad ensamples in his sight.

468 *ensewd* would follow
470 *Lay-stall* refuse-heap
  3 *wrack* wreck
  8 *dreadlesse* fearless

[418]

2

Yet sad he was that his too hastie speed
    The faire *Duess'* had forst him leave behind;
    And yet more sad, that *Una* his deare dreed
    Her truth had staind with treason so unkind;
    Yet crime in her could never creature find,
    But for his love, and for her owne selfe sake,
    She wandred had from one to other *Ynd*,
    Him for to seeke, ne ever would forsake,
Till her unwares the fierce *Sansloy* did overtake.

3

Who after *Archimagoes* fowle defeat,
    Led her away into a forrest wilde,
    And turning wrathfull fire to lustfull heat,
    With beastly sin thought her to have defilde,
    And made the vassall of his pleasures vilde.
    Yet first he cast by treatie, and by traynes,
    Her to perswade, that stubborne fort to yilde:
    For greater conquest of hard love he gaynes,
That workes it to his will, then he that it constraines.

4

With fawning wordes he courted her a while,
    And looking lovely, and oft sighing sore,
    Her constant hart did tempt with diverse guile:
    But wordes, and lookes, and sighes she did abhore,
    As rocke of Diamond stedfast evermore.
    Yet for to feed his fyrie lustfull eye,
    He snatcht the vele, that hong her face before;

---

12 *deare dreed* honoured dear one
16 *from one to other Ynd* From India to the Indies
24 *treatie* entreaty; *traynes* cunning
25 *that stubborne fort* her virginity

Then gan her beautie shine, as brightest skye,
And burnt his beastly hart t'efforce her chastitye.

5

So when he saw his flatt'ring arts to fayle,
    And subtile engines bet from batteree,
    With greedy force he gan the fort assayle,
    Whereof he weend possessed soone to bee,   40
    And win rich spoile of ransackt chastetee.
    Ah heavens, that do this hideous act behold,
    And heavenly virgin thus outraged see,
    How can ye vengeance just so long withhold,
And hurle not flashing flames upon that Paynim bold?

6

The pitteous maiden carefull comfortlesse,
    Does throw out thrilling shriekes, and shrieking cryes,
    The last vaine helpe of womens great distresse,
    And with loud plaints importuneth the skyes,
    That molten starres do drop like weeping eyes;   50
    And *Phœbus* flying so most shamefull sight,
    His blushing face in foggy cloud implyes,
    And hides for shame. What wit of mortall wight
Can now devise to quit a thrall from such a plight?

7

Eternall providence exceeding thought,
    Where none appeares can make her selfe a way:
    A wondrous way it for this Lady wrought,
    From Lyons clawes to pluck the griped pray.
    Her shrill outcryes and shriekes so loud did bray,
    That all the woodes and forestes did resownd;   60

---

38 *engines bet from batteree* siege engines beaten back from their bombardment
52 *implyes* wraps

A troupe of *Faunes* and *Satyres* far away
   Within the wood were dauncing in a rownd,
Whiles old *Sylvanus* slept in shady arber sownd.

8

Who when they heard that pitteous strained voice,
   In hast forsooke their rurall meriment,
   And ran towards the far rebownded noyce,
   To weet, what wight so loudly did lament.
   Unto the place they come incontinent:
   Whom when the raging Sarazin espide,
   A rude, misshapen, monstrous rablement,   70
   Whose like he never saw, he durst not bide,
But got his ready steed, and fast away gan ride.

9

The wyld woodgods arrived in the place,
   There find the virgin dolefull desolate,
   With ruffled rayments, and faire blubbred face,
   As her outrageous foe had left her late,
   And trembling yet through feare of former hate;
   All stand amazed at so uncouth sight,
   And gin to pittie her unhappie state,
   All stand astonied at her beautie bright,   80
In their rude eyes unworthie of so wofull plight.

10

She more amaz'd in double dread doth dwell;
   And every tender part for feare does shake:
   As when a greedie Wolfe through hunger fell

66 *rebownded* echoing
68 *incontinent* in haste
81 *rude* rustic

A seely Lambe farre from the flocke does take,
Of whom he meanes his bloudie feast to make,
A Lyon spyes fast running towards him,
The innocent pray in hast he does forsake,
Which quit from death yet quakes in every lim
With chaunge of feare, to see the Lyon looke so grim.   90

11

Such fearefull fit assaid her trembling hart,
Ne word to speake, ne joynt to move she had:
The salvage nation feele her secret smart,
And read her sorrow in her count'nance sad;
Their frowning forheads with rough hornes yclad,
And rusticke horror all a side doe lay,
And gently grenning, shew a semblance glad
To comfort her, and feare to put away,
Their backward bent knees teach her humbly to obey.

12

The doubtfull Damzell dare not yet commit   100
Her single person to their barbarous truth,
But still twixt feare and hope amazd does sit,
Late learnd what harme to hastie trust ensu'th
They in compassion of her tender youth,
And wonder of her beautie soveraine,
Are wonne with pitty and unwonted ruth,
And all prostrate upon the lowly plaine,
Do kisse her feete, and fawne on her with count'nance faine.

---

85 *seely* innocent
96 *horror* roughness
97 *grenning* grinning
99 *backward bent knees* Fauns and satyrs have goats' legs
108 *faine* loving

13

Their harts she ghesseth by their humble guise,
    And yields her to extremitie of time;   110
    So from the ground she fearelesse doth arise,
    And walketh forth without suspect of crime:
    They all as glad, as birdes of joyous Prime,
    Thence lead her forth, about her dauncing round,
    Shouting, and singing all a shepheards ryme,
    And with greene braunches strowing all the ground,
Do worship her, as Queene, with olive girlond cround.

14

And all the way their merry pipes they sound,
    That all the woods with doubled Eccho ring,
    And with their horned feet do weare the ground,   120
    Leaping like wanton kids in pleasant Spring.
    So towards old *Sylvanus* they her bring;
    Who with the noyse awaked, commeth out,
    To weet the cause, his weake steps governing,
    And aged limbs on Cypresse stadle stout,
And with an yvie twyne his wast is girt about.

15

Far off he wonders, what them makes so glad,
    Or *Bacchus* merry fruit they did invent,
    Or *Cybeles* franticke rites have made them mad;
    They drawing nigh, unto their God present   130
    That flowre of faith and beautie excellent.
    The God himselfe vewing that mirrhour rare,
    Stood long amazd, and burnt in his intent;

---

112 *crime* wrong
113 *Prime* spring
125 *stadle* staff
128 *Bacchus merry fruit* grapes; *invent* find

His owne faire *Dryope* now he thinkes not faire,
And *Pholoe* fowle, when her to this he doth compaire.

16

The woodborne people fall before her flat,
    And worship her as Goddesse of the wood;
    And old *Sylvanus* selfe bethinkes not, what
    To thinke of wight so faire, but gazing stood,
    In doubt to deeme her borne of earthly brood; 140
    Sometimes Dame *Venus* selfe he seemes to see,
    But *Venus* never had so sober mood;
    Sometimes *Diana* he her takes to bee,
But misseth bow, and shaftes, and buskins to her knee.

17

By vew of her he ginneth to revive
    His ancient love, and dearest *Cyparisse*,
    And calles to mind his pourtraiture alive,
    How faire he was, and yet not faire to this,
    And how he slew with glauncing dart amisse
    A gentle Hynd, the which the lovely boy 150
    Did love as life, above all wordly blisse;
    For griefe whereof the lad n'ould after joy,
But pynd away in anguish and selfe-wild annoy.

18

The wooddy Nymphes, faire *Hamadryades*
    Her to behold do thither runne apace,
    And all the troupe of light-foot *Naiades*,
    Flocke all about to see her lovely face:
    But when they vewed have her heavenly grace,

144 *buskins* high boots
149 *dart* arrow
153 *selfe-wild annoy* self-indulgent grief

They envie her in their malitious mind,
And fly away for feare of fowle disgrace: 160
But all the *Satyres* scorne their woody kind,
And henceforth nothing faire, but her on earth they find.

19

Glad of such lucke, the luckelesse lucky maid,
Did her content to please their feeble eyes,
And long time with that salvage people staid,
To gather breath in many miseries.
During which time her gentle wit she plyes,
To teach them truth, which worshipt her in vaine,
And made her th'Image of Idolatryes;
But when their bootlesse zeale she did restraine 170
From her own worship, they her Asse would worship fayn.

20

It fortuned a noble warlike knight
By just occasion to that forrest came,
To seeke his kindred, and the lignage right,
From whence he tooke his well deserved name:
He had in armes abroad wonne muchell fame,
And fild far landes with glorie of his might,
Plaine, faithfull, true, and enimy of shame,
And ever lov'd to fight for Ladies right,
But in vaine glorious frayes he litle did delight. 180

21

A Satyres sonne yborne in forrest wyld,
By straunge adventure as it did betyde,
And there begotten of a Lady myld,
Faire *Thyamis* the daughter of *Labryde*,

---

165 *salvage* wild

[418]

That was in sacred bands of wedlocke tyde
To *Therion*, a loose unruly swayne;
Who had more joy to raunge the forrest wyde,
And chase the salvage beast with busie payne,
Then serve his Ladies love, and wast in pleasure vayne.

22

The forlorne mayd did with loves longing burne, 190
    And could not lacke her lovers company,
    But to the wood she goes, to serve her turne,
    And seeke her spouse, that from her still does fly,
    And followes other game and venery:
    A Satyre chaunst her wandring for to find,
    And kindling coles of lust in brutish eye,
    The loyall links of wedlocke did unbind,
And made her person thrall unto his beastly kind.

23

So long in secret cabin there he held
    Her captive to his sensuall desire, 200
    Till that with timely fruit her belly sweld,
    And bore a boy unto that salvage sire:
    Then home he suffred her for to retire,
    For ransome leaving him the late borne childe;
    Whom till to ryper yeares he gan aspire,
    He noursled up in life and manners wilde,
Emongst wild beasts and woods, from lawes of men exilde.

24

For all he taught the tender ymp, was but
    To banish cowardize and bastard feare;

194 *venery* hunting
206 *noursled* nurtured
208 *ymp* child

153

His trembling hand he would him force to put 210
  Upon the Lyon and the rugged Beare,
  And from the she Beares teats her whelps to teare;
  And eke wyld roring Buls he would him make
  To tame, and ryde their backes not made to beare;
  And the Robuckes in flight to overtake,
That every beast for feare of him did fly and quake.

25

Thereby so fearelesse, and so fell he grew,
  That his owne sire and maister of his guise
  Did often tremble at his horrid vew,
  And oft for dread of hurt would him advise, 220
  The angry beasts not rashly to despise,
  Nor too much to provoke; for he would learne
  The Lyon stoup to him in lowly wise,
  (A lesson hard) and make the Libbard sterne
Leave roaring, when in rage he for revenge did earne.

26

And for to make his powre approved more,
  Wyld beasts in yron yokes he would compell;
  The spotted Panther, and the tusked Bore,
  The Pardale swift, and the Tigre cruell;
  The Antelope, and Wolfe both fierce and fell; 230
  And them constraine in equall teme to draw.
  Such joy he had, their stubborne harts to quell,
  And sturdie courage tame with dreadfull aw,
That his beheast they feared, as a tyrans law.

224 *Libbard* leopard
225 *earne* yearn
229 *Pardale* panther

27

His loving mother came upon a day
    Unto the woods, to see her little sonne;
And chaunst unwares to meet him in the way,
After his sportes, and cruell pastime donne,
When after him a Lyonesse did runne,
    That roaring all with rage, did lowd requere   240
    Her children deare, whom he away had wonne:
    The Lyons whelpes she saw how he did beare,
And lull in rugged armes, withouten childish feare.

28

The fearefull Dame all quaked at the sight,
    And turning backe, gan fast to fly away,
Untill with love revokt from vaine affright,
She hardly yet perswaded was to stay,
And then to him these womanish words gan say;
    Ah *Satyrane*, my dearling, and my joy,
    For love of me leave off this dreadfull play;   250
    To dally thus with death, is no fit toy,
Go find some other play-fellowes, mine own sweet boy.

29

In these and like delights of bloudy game
    He trayned was, till ryper yeares he raught,
And there abode, whilst any beast of name
Walkt in that forest, whom he had not taught
To feare his force: and then his courage haught
    Desird of forreine foemen to be knowne,
    And far abroad for straunge adventures sought:
    In which his might was never overthrowne,   260
But through all Faery lond his famous worth was blown.

30

Yet evermore it was his manner faire,
    After long labours and adventures spent,
    Unto those native woods for to repaire,
    To see his sire and ofspring aunctient.
    And now he thither came for like intent;
    Where he unwares the fairest *Una* found,
    Straunge Lady, in so straunge habiliment,
    Teaching the Satyres, which her sat around,
Trew Sacred lore, which from her sweet lips did redound.   270

31

He wondred at her wisedome heavenly rare,
    Whose like in womens wit he never knew;
    And when her curteous deeds he did compare,
    Gan her admire, and her sad sorrowes rew,
    Blaming of Fortune, which such troubles threw,
    And joyd to make proofe of her crueltie
    On gentle Dame, so hurtlesse, and so trew:
    Thenceforth he kept her goodly company,
And learnd her discipline of faith and veritie.

32

But she all vowd unto the *Redcrosse* knight,   280
    His wandring perill closely did lament,
    Ne in this new acquaintaunce could delight,
    But her deare heart with anguish did torment,
    And all her wit in secret counsels spent,
    How to escape. At last in privie wise
    To *Satyrane* she shewed her intent;
    Who glad to gain such favour, gan devise,
How with that pensive Maid he best might thence arise.

265 *ofspring* origin
277 *hurtlesse* harmless

33

So on a day when Satyres all were gone,
  To do their service to *Sylvanus* old,
The gentle virgin left behind alone
He led away with courage stout and bold.
Too late it was, to Satyres to be told,
Or ever hope recover her againe:
In vaine he seekes that having cannot hold.
  So fast he carried her with carefull paine,
That they the woods are past, and come now to the plaine.

34

The better part now of the lingring day,
  They traveild had, when as they farre espide
A wearie wight forwandring by the way,
And towards him they gan in hast to ride,
To weet of newes, that did abroad betide,
Or tydings of her knight of the *Redcrosse*.
But he them spying, gan to turne aside,
  For feare as seemd, or for some feigned losse;
More greedy they of newes, fast towards him do crosse.

35

A silly man, in simple weedes forworne,
  And soild with dust of the long dried way;
His sandales were with toilesome travell torne,
And face all tand with scorching sunny ray,
As he had traveild many a sommers day,
Through boyling sands of *Arabie* and *Ynde*;
And in his hand a *Jacobs* staffe, to stay
  His wearie limbes upon: and eke behind,
His scrip did hang, in which his needments he did bind.

---

313 *Jacobs staffe* pilgrim's staff
315 *scrip* bag; *needments* necessities

36

The knight approching nigh, of him inquerd
    Tydings of warre, and of adventures new;
    But warres, nor new adventures none he herd.
    Then *Una* gan to aske, if ought he knew,
    Or heard abroad of that her champion trew,   320
    That in his armour bare a croslet red.
    Aye me, Deare dame (quoth he) well may I rew
    To tell the sad sight, which mine eies have red:
These eyes did see that knight both living and eke ded.

37

That cruell word her tender hart so thrild,
    That suddein cold did runne through every vaine,
    And stony horrour all her sences fild
    With dying fit, that downe she fell for paine.
    The knight her lightly reared up againe,
    And comforted with curteous kind reliefe: 330
    Then wonne from death, she bad him tellen plaine
    The further processe of her hidden griefe;
The lesser pangs can beare, who hath endur'd the chiefe.

38

Then gan the Pilgrim thus, I chaunst this day,
    This fatall day, that shall I ever rew,
    To see two knights in travell on my way
    (A sory sight) arraung'd in battell new,
    Both breathing vengeaunce, both of wrathfull hew:
    My fearefull flesh did tremble at their strife,
    To see their blades so greedily imbrew,   340
    That drunke with bloud, yet thristed after life:
What more? the *Redcrosse* knight was slaine with Paynim knife.

325 *thrild* pierced
340 *imbrew* thrust
341 *thristed* thirsted

39

Ah dearest Lord (quoth she) how might that bee,
  And he the stoutest knight, that ever wonne?
  Ah dearest dame (quoth he) how might I see
  The thing, that might not be, and yet was donne?
  Where is (said *Satyrane*) that Paynims sonne,
  That him of life, and us of joy hath reft?
  Not far away (quoth he) he hence doth wonne
  Foreby a fountaine, where I late him left   350
Washing his bloudy wounds, that through the steele were cleft.

40

Therewith the knight thence marched forth in hast,
  Whiles *Una* with huge heavinesse opprest,
  Could not for sorrow follow him so fast;
  And soone he came, as he the place had ghest,
  Whereas that *Pagan* proud him selfe did rest,
  In secret shadow by a fountaine side:
  Even he it was, that earst would have supprest
  Faire *Una*: whom when *Satyrane* espide,
With fowle reprochfull words he boldly him defide.   360

41

And said, Arise thou cursed Miscreaunt,
  That hast with knightlesse guile and trecherous train
  Faire knighthood fowly shamed, and doest vaunt
  That good knight of the *Redcrosse* to have slain:
  Arise, and with like treason now maintain
  Thy guilty wrong, or else thee guilty yield.
  The Sarazin this hearing, rose amain,
  And catching up in hast his three square shield,
And shining helmet, soone him buckled to the field.

349 *wonne* stay
367 *amain* at once
368 *three square* three-cornered

42

And drawing nigh him said, Ah misborne Elfe, 370
  In evill houre thy foes thee hither sent,
  Anothers wrongs to wreake upon thy selfe:
  Yet ill thou blamest me, for having blent
  My name with guile and traiterous intent;
  That *Redcrosse* knight, perdie, I never slew,
  But had he beene, where earst his armes were lent,
  Th'enchaunter vaine his errour should not rew:
But thou his errour shalt, I hope now proven trew.

43

Therewith they gan, both furious and fell,
  To thunder blowes, and fiersly to assaile 380
  Each other bent his enimy to quell,
  That with their force they perst both plate and maile,
  And made wide furrowes in their fleshes fraile,
  That it would pitty any living eie.
  Large floods of bloud adowne their sides did raile;
  But floods of bloud could not them satisfie:
Both hungred after death: both chose to win, or die.

44

So long they fight, and fell revenge pursue,
  That fainting each, themselves to breathen let,
  And oft refreshed, battell oft renue: 390
  As when two Bores with rancling malice met,
  Their gory sides fresh bleeding fiercely fret,
  Til breathlesse both them selves aside retire,
  Where foming wrath, their cruell tuskes they whet,
  And trample th'earth, the whiles they may respire;
Then backe to fight againe, new breathed and entire.

373 *blent* stained
385 *raile* run
392 *fret* gore

45

So fiersly, when these knights had breathed once,
   They gan to fight returne, increasing more
   Their puissant force, and cruell rage attonce,
   With heaped strokes more hugely, then before,   400
   That with their drerie wounds and bloudy gore
   They both deformed, scarsely could be known.
   By this sad *Una* fraught with anguish sore,
   Led with their noise, which through the aire was thrown,
Arriv'd, where they in erth their fruitles bloud had sown.

46

Whom all so soone as that proud Sarazin
   Espide, he gan revive the memory
   Of his lewd lusts, and late attempted sin,
   And left the doubtfull battell hastily,
   To catch her, newly offred to his eie: 410
   But *Satyrane* with strokes him turning, staid,
   And sternely bad him other businesse plie,
   Then hunt the steps of pure unspotted Maid:
Wherewith he all enrag'd, these bitter speaches said.

47

O foolish faeries sonne, what furie mad
   Hath thee incenst, to hast thy dolefull fate?
   Were it not better, I that Lady had,
   Then that thou hadst repented it too late?
   Most sencelesse man he, that himselfe doth hate,
   To love another. Lo then for thine ayd   420
   Here take thy lovers token on they pate.
   So they to fight; the whiles the royall Mayd
Fled farre away, of that proud Paynim sore afrayd.

---

402 *deformed* were disfigured

48

But that false *Pilgrim*, which that leasing told,
  Being in deed old *Archimage*, did stay
  In secret shadow, all this to behold,
  And much rejoyced in their bloudy fray:
  But when he saw the Damsell passe away
  He left his stond, and her pursewd apace,
  In hope to bring her to her last decay. 430
  But for to tell her lamentable cace,
And eke this battels end, will need another place.

CANTO vii

*The Redcrosse knight is captive made
By Gyaunt proud opprest,
Prince Arthur meets with Una great-
ly with those newes distrest.*

1

What man so wise, what earthly wit so ware,
  As to descry the crafty cunning traine,
  By which deceipt doth maske in visour faire,
  And cast her colours dyed deepe in graine,
  To seeme like Truth, whose shape she well can faine,
  And fitting gestures to her purpose frame,
  The guiltlesse man with guile to entertaine?
  Great maistresse of her art was that false Dame,
The false *Duessa*, cloked with *Fidessaes* name.

2

Who when returning from the drery *Night*, 10
  She fownd not in that perilous house of *Pryde*,

424 *leasing* lie
 3 *visour* mask

Where she had left, the noble *Redcrosse* knight,
    Her hoped pray, she would no lenger bide,
    But forth she went, to seeke him far and wide.
    Ere long she fownd, whereas he wearie sate,
    To rest him selfe, foreby a fountaine side,
    Disarmed all of yron-coted Plate,
And by his side his steed the grassy forage ate.

3

He feedes upon the cooling shade, and bayes
    His sweatie forehead in the breathing wind,   20
    Which through the trembling leaves full gently playes
    Wherein the cherefull birds of sundry kind
    Do chaunt sweet musick, to delight his mind:
    The Witch approching gan him fairely greet,
    And with reproch of carelesnesse unkind
    Upbrayd, for leaving her in place unmeet,
With fowle words tempring faire, soure gall with hony sweet.

4

Unkindnesse past, they gan of solace treat,
    And bathe in pleasaunce of the joyous shade,
    Which shielded them against the boyling heat,   30
    And with greene boughes decking a gloomy glade,
    About the fountaine like a girlond made;
    Whose bubbling wave did ever freshly well,
    Ne ever would through fervent sommer fade:
    The sacred Nymph, which therein wont to dwell,
Was out of *Dianes* favour, as it then befell.

19 *bayes* bathes

5

The cause was this: one day when *Phœbe* fayre
    With all her band was following the chace,
    This Nymph, quite tyr'd with heat of scorching ayre
    Sat down to rest in middest of the race: 40
    The goddesse wroth gan fowly her disgrace,
    And bad the waters, which from her did flow,
    Be sure as she her selfe was then in place.
    Thenceforth her waters waxed dull and slow,
And all that drunke thereof, did faint and feeble grow.

6

Hereof this gentle knight unweeting was,
    And lying downe upon the sandie graile,
    Drunke of the streame, as cleare as cristall glas;
    Eftsoones his manly forces gan to faile,
    And mightie strong was turnd to feeble fraile. 50
    His chaunged powres at first them selves not felt,
    Till crudled cold his corage gan assaile,
    And chearefull bloud in faintnesse chill did melt,
Which like a fever fit through all his body swelt.

7

Yet goodly court he made still to his Dame,
    Pourd out in loosnesse on the grassy grownd,
    Both carelesse of his health, and of his fame:
    Till at the last he heard a dreadfull sownd,
    Which through the wood loud bellowing, did rebownd,
    That all the earth for terrour seemd to shake, 60
    And trees did tremble. Th'Elfe therewith astownd,

37 *Phœbe* Diana
47 *graile* gravel
52 *crudled* curdled
54 *swelt* raged

Upstarted lightly from his looser make,
And his unready weapons gan in hand to take.

8

But ere he could his armour on him dight,
    Or get his shield, his monstrous enimy
    With sturdie steps came stalking in his sight,
    An hideous Geant horrible and hye,
    That with his talnesse seemd to threat the skye,
    The ground eke groned under him for dreed;
    His living like saw never living eye,   70
    Ne durst behold: his stature did exceed
The hight of three the tallest sonnes of mortall seed.

9

The greatest Earth his uncouth mother was,
    And blustring *Æolus* his boasted sire,
    Who with his breath, which through the world doth pas,
    Her hollow womb did secretly inspire,
    And fild her hidden caves with stormie yre,
    That she conceiv'd; and trebling the dew time,
    In which the wombes of women do expire,
    Brought forth this monstrous masse of earthly slime,   80
Puft up with emptie wind, and fild with sinfull crime.

10

So growen great through arrogant delight
    Of th'high descent, whereof he was yborne,
    And through presumption of his matchlesse might,
    All other powres and knighthood he did scorne.
    Such now he marcheth to this man forlorne,

---

62 *make* companion
73 *uncouth* unknowing
74 *Aeolus* god of the winds

    And left to losse: his stalking steps are stayde
        Upon a snaggy Oke, which he had torne
        Out of his mothers bowelles, and it made
His mortall mace, wherewith his foemen he dismayde.   90

11

That when the knight he spide, he gan advance
        With huge force and insupportable mayne,
        And towardes him with dreadfull fury praunce;
        Who haplesse, and eke hopelesse, all in vaine
        Did to him pace, sad battaile to darrayne,
        Disarmd, disgrast, and inwardly dismayde,
        And eke so faint in every joynt and vaine,
        Through that fraile fountaine, which him feeble made,
That scarsely could he weeld his bootlesse single blade.

12

The Geaunt strooke so maynly mercilesse,   100
        That could have overthrowne a stony towre,
        And were not heavenly grace, that him did blesse,
        He had beene pouldred all, as thin as flowre:
        But he was wary of that deadly stowre,
        And lightly lept from underneath the blow:
        Yet so exceeding was the villeins powre,
        That with the wind it did him overthrow,
And all his sences stound, that still he lay full low.

13

As when that divelish yron Engin wrought
        In deepest Hell, and framd by *Furies* skill,   110

  92 *mayne* strength
  95 *darrayne* prepare
103 *pouldred* powdered
104 *stowre* danger
109 *divelish yron Engin* cannon

[418–19]

With windy Nitre and quick Sulphur fraught,
    And ramd with bullet round, ordaind to kill,
    Conceiveth fire, the heavens it doth fill
    With thundring noyse, and all the ayre doth choke,
    That none can breath, nor see, nor heare at will,
    Through smouldry cloud of duskish stincking smoke,
That th'onely breath him daunts, who hath escapt the stroke.

14

So daunted when the Geaunt saw the knight,
    His heavie hand he heaved up on hye,
    And him to dust thought to have battred quight, 120
    Until *Duessa* loud to him gan crye;
    O great *Orgoglio*, greatest under skye,
    O hold thy mortall hand for Ladies sake,
    Hold for my sake, and do him not to dye,
    But vanquisht thine eternal bondslave make,
And me thy worthy meed unto thy Leman take.

15

He hearkned, and did stay from further harmes,
    To gayne so goodly guerdon, as she spake:
    So willingly she came into his armes,
    Who her as willingly to grace did take, 130
    And was possessed of his new found make.
    Then up he tooke the slombred sencelesse corse,
    And ere he could out of his swowne awake,
    Him to his castle brought with hastie forse,
And in a Dongeon deepe him threw without remorse.

16

From that day forth *Duessa* was his deare,
    And highly honourd in his haughtie eye,

117 *th'onely breath* the breath alone
126 *Leman* lover

>He gave her gold and purple pall to weare,
>And triple crowne set on her head full hye,
>And her endowd with royall majestye: 140
>Then for to make her dreaded more of men,
>And peoples harts with awfull terrour tye,
>A monstrous beast ybred in filthy fen
>He chose, which he had kept long time in darksome den.

17

Such one it was, as that renowmed Snake
>Which great *Alcides* in *Stremona* slew,
>Long fostred in the filth of *Lerna* Lake,
>Whose many heads out budding ever new,
>Did breed him endlesse labour to subdew:
>But this same Monster much more ugly was; 150
>For seven great heads out of his body grew,
>An yron brest, and backe of scaly bras,
And all embrewd in bloud, his eyes did shine as glas.

18

His tayle was stretched out in wondrous length,
>That to the house of heavenly gods it raught,
>And with extorted powre, and borrow'd strength,
>The ever-burning lamps from thence it brought,
>And prowdly threw to ground, as things of nought;
>And underneath his filthy feet did tread
>The sacred things, and holy heasts foretaught. 160
>Upon this dreadfull Beast with sevenfold head
He set the false *Duessa*, for more aw and dread.

19

The wofull Dwarfe, which saw his maisters fall,
>Whiles he had keeping of his grasing steed,

160 *heasts* commandments

   And valiant knight became a caytive thrall,
     When all was past, tooke up his forlorne weed,
     His mightie armour, missing most at need;
     His silver shield, now idle maisterlesse;
     His poynant speare, that many made to bleed,
     The ruefull moniments of heavinesse,   170
And with them all departes, to tell his great distresse.

20

He had not travaild long, when on the way
     He wofull Ladie, wofull *Una* met,
     Fast flying from the Paynims greedy pray,
     Whilest *Satyrane* him from pursuit did let:
     Who when her eyes she on the Dwarfe had set,
     And saw the signes, that deadly tydings spake,
     She fell to ground for sorrowfull regret,
     And lively breath her sad brest did forsake,
Yet might her pitteous hart be seene to pant and quake.   180

21

The messenger of so unhappie newes
     Would faine have dyde: dead was his hart within,
     Yet outwardly some little comfort shewes:
     At last recovering hart, he does begin
     To rub her temples, and to chaufe her chin,
     And every tender part does tosse and turne:
     So hardly he the flitted life does win,
     Unto her native prison to retourne:
Then gins her grieved ghost thus to lament and mourne.

---

166 *his forlorne weed* his abandoned accoutrements
169 *poynant* sharp
170 *ruefull moniments of heavinesse* sad reminders of grief
185 *chaufe* rub
189 *ghost* spirit

22

Ye dreary instruments of dolefull sight, 190
   That doe this deadly spectacle behold,
   Why do ye lenger feed on loathed light,
   Or liking find to gaze on earthly mould,
   Sith cruell fates the carefull threeds unfould,
   The which my life and love together tyde?
   Now let the stony dart of senselesse cold
     Perce to my hart, and pas through every side,
And let eternall night so sad sight fro me hide.

23

O lightsome day, the lampe of highest *Jove*,
   First made by him, mens wandring wayes to guyde, 200
   When darknesse he in deepest dongeon drove,
   Henceforth thy hated face for ever hyde,
   And shut up heavens windowes shyning wyde:
   For earthly sight can nought but sorrow breed,
   And late repentance, which shall long abyde.
   Mine eyes no more on vanitie shall feed,
But seeled up with death, shall have their deadly meed.

24

Then downe againe she fell unto the ground;
   But he her quickly reared up againe:
   Thrise did she sinke adowne in deadly swownd, 210
   And thrise he her reviv'd with busie paine:
   At last when life recover'd had the raine,
   And over-wrestled his strong enemie,
   With foltring tong, and trembling every vaine,
   Tell on (quoth she) the wofull Tragedie,
The which these reliques sad present unto mine eie.

---

194 *the carefull threeds unfould* the sorrowful threads untwine
207 *seeled up* sewn up

25

Tempestuous fortune hath spent all her spight,
    And thrilling sorrow throwne his utmost dart;
    Thy sad tongue cannot tell more heavy plight,
    Then that I feele, and harbour in mine hart:
    Who hath endur'd the whole, can beare each part.
    If death it be, it is not the first wound,
    That launched hath my brest with bleeding smart.
    Begin, and end the bitter balefull stound;
If lesse, then that I feare, more favour I have found.

26

Then gan the Dwarfe the whole discourse declare,
    The subtill traines of *Archimago* old;
    The wanton loves of false *Fidessa* faire,
    Bought with the bloud of vanquisht Paynim bold:
    The wretched payre trasform'd to treen mould;
    The house of Pride, and perils round about;
    The combat, which he with *Sansjoy* did hould;
    The lucklesse conflict with the Gyant stout,
Wherein captiv'd, of life or death he stood in doubt.

27

She heard with patience all unto the end,
    And strove to maister sorrowfull assay,
    Which greater grew, the more she did contend,
    And almost rent her tender hart in tway;
    And love fresh coles unto her fire did lay:
    For greater love, the greater is the losse.
    Was never Ladie loved dearer day,
    Then she did love the knight of the *Redcrosse*;
For whose deare sake so many troubles her did tosse.

224 *stound* sorrow
230 *treen* trees

28

At last when fervent sorrow slaked was,
    She up arose, resolving him to find
    A live or dead: and forward forth doth pas,
    All as the Dwarfe the way to her assynd:
    And evermore in constant carefull mind
    She fed her wound with fresh renewed bale;
    Long tost with stormes, and bet with bitter wind,   250
    High over hils, and low adowne the dale,
She wandred many a wood, and measurd many a vale.

29

At last she chaunced by good hap to meet
    A goodly knight, faire marching by the way
    Together with his Squire, arayed meet:
    His glitterand armour shined farre away,
    Like glauncing light of *Phœbus* brightest ray;
    From top to toe no place appeared bare,
    That deadly dint of steele endanger may:
    Athwart his brest a bauldrick brave he ware,   260
That shynd, like twinkling stars, with stons most pretious rare.

30

And in the midst thereof one pretious stone
    Of wondrous worth, and eke of wondrous mights,
    Shapt like a Ladies head, exceeding shone,
    Like *Hesperus* emongst the lesser lights,
    And strove for to amaze the weaker sights;
    Thereby his mortall blade full comely hong
    In yvory sheath, ycarv'd with curious slights;

---

249 *bale* grief
260 *bauldrick* shoulder-belt
263 *mights* powers
268 *slights* designs

Whose hilts were burnished gold, and handle strong
Of mother pearle, and buckled with a golden tong.

31

His haughtie helmet, horrid all with gold,
  Both glorious brightnesse, and great terrour bred;
  For all the crest a Dragon did enfold
  With greedie pawes, and over all did spred
  His golden wings: his dreadfull hideous hed
  Close couched on the bever, seem'd to throw
  From flaming mouth bright sparkles fierie red,
  That suddeine horror to faint harts did show;
And scaly tayle was stretcht adowne his backe full low.

32

Upon the top of all his loftie crest,
  A bunch of haires discolourd diversly,
  With sprincled pearle, and gold full richly drest,
  Did shake, and seem'd to daunce for jollity,
  Like to an Almond tree ymounted hye
  On top of greene *Selinis* all alone,
  With blossomes brave bedecked daintily;
  Whose tender locks do tremble every one
At every little breath, that under heaven is blowne.

33

His warlike shield all closely cover'd was,
  Ne might of mortall eye be ever seene;
  Not made of steele, nor of enduring bras,
  Such earthly mettals soone consumed bene:
  But all of Diamond perfect pure and cleene
  It framed was, one massie entire mould,
  Hewen out of Adamant rocke with engines keene,

271 *haughtie* high; *horrid* embossed
295 *Adamant* diamond

That point of speare it never percen could,
Ne dint of direfull sword divide the substance would.

34

The same to wight he never wont disclose,
    But when as monsters huge he would dismay,
    Or daunt unequall armies of his foes,   300
    Or when the flying heavens he would affray;
    For so exceeding shone his glistring ray,
    That *Phœbus* golden face it did attaint,
    As when a cloud his beames doth over-lay;
    And silver *Cynthia* wexed pale and faint,
As when her face is staynd with magicke arts constraint.

35

No magicke arts hereof had any might,
    Nor bloudie wordes of bold Enchaunters call,
    But all that was not such, as seemd in sight,
    Before that shield did fade, and suddeine fall: 310
    And when him list the raskall routes appall,
    Men into stones therewith he could transmew,
    And stones to dust, and dust to nought at all;
    And when him list the prouder lookes subdew,
He would them gazing blind, or turne to other hew.

36

Ne let it seeme, that credence this exceedes,
    For he that made the same, was knowne right well
    To have done much more admirable deedes.
    It *Merlin* was, which whylome did excell
    All living wightes in might of magicke spell: 320

---

311 *raskall routes* barbarous hordes
312 *transmew* transform
316 *credence* belief

Both shield, and sword, and armour all he wrought
For this young Prince, when first to armes he fell;
But when he dyde, the Faerie Queene it brought
To Faerie lond, where yet it may be seene, if sought.

37

A gentle youth, his dearely loved Squire
　His speare of heben wood behind him bare,
　Whose harmefull head, thrice heated in the fire,
　Had riven many a brest with pikehead square;
　A goodly person, and could menage faire
　His stubborne steed with curbed canon bit,
　Who under him did trample as the aire,
　And chauft, that any on his backe should sit;
The yron rowels into frothy fome he bit.

38

When as this knight nigh to the Ladie drew,
　With lovely court he gan her entertaine;
　But when he heard her answers loth, he knew
　Some secret sorrow did her heart distraine:
　Which to allay, and calme her storming paine,
　Faire feeling words he wisely gan display,
　And for her humour fitting purpose faine,
　To tempt the cause it selfe for to bewray;
Wherewith emmov'd, these bleeding words she gan to say.

39

What worlds delight, or joy of living speach
　Can heart, so plung'd in sea of sorrowes deepe,

---

329 *menage* control
330 *curbed canon bit* smooth round bit with a curb
332 *chauft* chafed
333 *rowels* knobs on the bit

    And heaped with so huge misfortunes, reach?
        The carefull cold beginneth for to creepe,
        And in my heart his yron arrow steepe,
        Soone as I thinke upon my bitter bale:
        Such helplesse harmes yts better hidden keepe,
        Then rip up griefe, where it may not availe,   350
My last left comfort is, my woes to weepe and waile.

40

Ah Ladie deare, quoth then the gentle knight,
    Well may I weene, your griefe is wondrous great;
    For wondrous great griefe groneth in my spright,
    Whiles thus I heare you of your sorrowes treat.
    But wofull Ladie let me you intrete,
    For to unfold the anguish of your hart:
    Mishaps are maistred by advice discrete,
    And counsell mittigates the greatest smart;
Found never helpe, who never would his hurts impart.   360

41

O but (quoth she) great griefe will not be tould,
    And can more easily be thought, then said.
    Right so; (quoth he) but he, that never would,
    Could never: will to might gives greatest aid.
    But griefe (quoth she) does greater grow displaid,
    If then it find not helpe, and breedes despaire.
    Despaire breedes not (quoth he) where faith is staid.
    No faith so fast (quoth she) but flesh does paire.
Flesh may empaire (quoth he) but reason can repaire.

42

His goodly reason, and well guided speach   370
    So deepe did settle in her gratious thought,
    That her perswaded to disclose the breach,
    Which love and fortune in her heart had wrought,

[418-19]

And said; Faire Sir, I hope good hap hath brought
You to inquire the secrets of my griefe,
Or that your wisedome will direct my thought,
Or that your prowesse can me yield reliefe:
Then heare the storie sad, which I shall tell you briefe.

43

The forlorne Maiden, whom your eyes have seene
　The laughing stocke of fortunes mockeries, 380
　Am th'only daughter of a King and Queene,
　Whose parents deare, whiles equall destinies
　Did runne about, and their felicities
　The favourable heavens did not envy,
　Did spread their rule through all the territories,
　Which *Phison* and *Euphrates* floweth by,
And *Gehons* golden waves doe wash continually.

44

Till that their cruell cursed enemy,
　An huge great Dragon horrible in sight,
　Bred in the loathly lakes of *Tartary*, 390
　With murdrous ravine, and devouring might
　Their kingdome spoild, and countrey wasted quight:
　Themselves, for feare into his jawes to fall,
　He forst to castle strong to take their flight,
　Where fast embard in mightie brasen wall,
He has them now foure yeres besieged to make them thrall.

45

Full many knights adventurous and stout
　Have enterprizd that Monster to subdew;
　From every coast that heaven walks about,
　Have thither come the noble Martiall crew,
　That famous hard atchievements still pursew,
　Yet never any could that girlond win,

But all still shronke, and still he greater grew:
   All they for want of faith, or guilt of sin,
The pitteous pray of his fierce crueltie have bin.

46

At last yledd with farre reported praise,
   Which flying fame throughout the world had spred,
   Of doughtie knights, whom Faery land did raise,
   That noble order hight of Maidenhed,
   Forthwith to court of *Gloriane* I sped,
   Of *Gloriane* great Queene of glory bright,
   Whose kingdomes seat *Cleopolis* is red,
   There to obtaine some such redoubted knight,
That Parents deare from tyrants powre deliver might.

47

It was my chance (my chance was faire and good)
   There for to find a fresh unproved knight,
   Whose manly hands imbrew'd in guiltie blood
   Had never bene, ne ever by his might
   Had throwne to ground the unregarded right:
   Yet of his prowesse proofe he since hath made
   (I witnesse am) in many a cruell fight;
   The groning ghosts of many one dismaide
Have felt the bitter dint of his avenging blade.

48

And ye the forlorne reliques of his powre,
   His byting sword, and his devouring speare,
   Which have endured many a dreadfull stowre,
   Can speake his prowesse, that did earst you beare,
   And well could rule: now he hath left you heare,
   To be the record of his ruefull losse,

417 *imbrew'd* stained

And of my dolefull disaventurous deare: 430
   O heavie record of the good *Redcrosse*,
Where have you left your Lord, that could so well you tosse?

49

Well hoped I, and faire beginnings had,
   That he my captive langour should redeeme,
   Till all unweeting, an Enchaunter bad
   His sence abusd, and made him to misdeeme
   My loyalty, not such as it did seeme;
   That rather death desire, then such despight.
   Be judge ye heavens, that all things right esteeme,
   How I him lov'd, and love with all my might, 440
So thought I eke of him, and thinke I thought aright.

50

Thenceforth me desolate he quite forsooke,
   To wander, where wilde fortune would me lead,
   And other bywaies he himselfe betooke,
   Where never foot of living wight did tread,
   That brought not backe the balefull body dead;
   In which him chaunced false *Duessa* meete,
   Mine onely foe, mine onely deadly dread,
   Who with her witchcraft and misseeming sweete,
Inveigled him to follow her desires unmeete. 450

51

At last by subtill sleights she him betraid
   Unto his foe, a Gyant huge and tall,
   Who him disarmed, dissolute, dismaid,
   Unwares surprised, and with mightie mall

430 *my dolefull disaventurous deare* my unhappy and unfortunate beloved
434 *langour* sorrow
453 *dissolute* enfeebled
454 *mall* club

The monster mercilesse him made to fall,
    Whose fall did never foe before behold;
    And now in darkesome dungeon, wretched thrall,
    Remedilesse, for aie he doth him hold;
This is my cause of griefe, more great, then may be told.

52

Ere she had ended all, she gan to faint:
    But he her comforted and faire bespake,
    Certes, Madame, ye have great cause of plaint,
    That stoutest heart, I weene, could cause to quake.
    But be of cheare, and comfort to you take:
    For till I have acquit your captive knight,
    Assure your selfe, I will you not forsake.
    His chearefull words reviv'd her chearelesse spright,
So forth they went, the Dwarfe them guiding ever right.

CANTO viii

Faire virgin to redeeme her deare
    brings Arthur to the fight:
Who slayes the Gyant, wounds the beast,
    and strips Duessa quight.

1

Ay me, how many perils doe enfold
    The righteous man, to make him daily fall?
    Were not, that heavenly grace doth him uphold,
    And stedfast truth acquite him out of all.
    Her love is firme, her care continuall,
    So oft as he through his owne foolish pride,
    Or weaknesse is to sinfull bands made thrall:
    Else should this *Redcrosse* knight in bands have dyde,
For whose deliverance she this Prince doth thither guide.

465 *acquit* set free
  8 *bands* bonds

2

They sadly traveild thus, until they came
    Nigh to a castle builded strong and hie:
    Then cryde the Dwarfe, lo yonder is the same,
    In which my Lord my liege doth lucklesse lie,
    Thrall to that Gyants hatefull tyrannie:
    Therefore, deare Sir, your mightie powres assay.
    The noble knight alighted by and by
    From loftie steede, and bad the Ladie stay,
To see what end of fight should him befall that day.

3

So with the squire, th'admirer of his might,
    He marched forth towards that castle wall;
    Whose gates he found fast shut, ne living wight
    To ward the same, nor answere commers call.
    Then tooke that Squire an horne of bugle small,
    Which hong adowne his side in twisted gold,
    And tassels gay. Wyde wonders over all
    Of that same hornes great vertues weren told,
Which had approved bene in uses manifold.

4

Was never wight, that heard that shrilling sound,
    But trembling feare did feele in every vaine;
    Three miles it might be easie heard around,
    And Ecchoes three answerd it selfe againe:
    No false enchauntment, nor deceiptfull traine
    Might once abide the terror of that blast,
    But presently was voide and wholly vaine:
    No gate so strong, no locke so firme and fast,
But with that percing noise flew open quite, or brast.

26 *vertues* powers
34 *voide* useless
36 *brast* shattered

5

The same before the Geants gate he blew,
    That all the castle quaked from the ground,
    And every dore of freewill open flew.
    The Gyant selfe dismaied with that sownd,   40
    Where he with his *Duessa* dalliance fownd,
    In hast came rushing forth from inner bowre,
    With staring countenance sterne, as one astownd,
    And staggering steps, to weet, what suddein stowre
Had wrought that horror strange, and dar'd his dreaded powre.

6

And after him the proud *Duessa* came,
    High mounted on her manyheaded beast,
    And every head with fyrie tongue did flame,
    And every head was crowned on his creast,
    And bloudie mouthed with late cruell feast.   50
    That when the knight beheld, his mightie shild
    Upon his manly arme he soone addrest,
    And at him fiercely flew, with courage fild,
And eger greedinesse through every member thrild.

7

Therewith the Gyant buckled him to fight,
    Inflam'd with scornefull wrath and high disdaine,
    And lifting up his dreadfull club on hight,
    All arm'd with ragged snubbes and knottie graine,
    Him thought at first encounter to have slaine.
    But wise and warie was that noble Pere,   60
    And lightly leaping from so monstrous maine,
    Did faire avoide the violence him nere;
It booted nought, to thinke, such thunderbolts to beare.

---

39 *of freewill* by itself
54 *greedinesse* fierceness
58 *snubbes* snags

8

Ne shame he thought to shunne so hideous might:
    The idle stroke, enforcing furious way,
    Missing the marke of his misaymed sight
    Did fall to ground, and with his heavie sway
    So deepely dinted in the driven clay,
    That three yardes deepe a furrow up did throw:
    The sad earth wounded with so sore assay,
    Did grone full grievous underneath the blow,
And trembling with strange feare, did like an earthquake show.

9

As when almightie *Jove* in wrathfull mood,
    To wreake the guilt of mortall sins is bent,
    Hurles forth his thundring dart with deadly food,
    Enrold in flames, and smouldring dreriment,
    Through riven cloudes and molten firmament;
    The fierce threeforked engin making way,
    Both loftie towres and highest trees hath rent,
    And all that might his angrie passage stay,
And shooting in the earth, casts up a mount of clay.

10

His boystrous club, so buried in the ground,
    He could not rearen up againe so light,
    But that the knight him at avantage found,
    And whiles he strove his combred clubbe to quight
    Out of the earth, with blade all burning bright
    He smote off his left arme, which like a blocke
    Did fall to ground, depriv'd of native might;

---

75 *food* fuel
76 *dreriment* destruction
78 *engin* instrument: thunderbolt

    Large streames of bloud out of the truncked stocke
Forth gushed, like fresh water streame from riven rocke.   90

11

Dismaied with so desperate deadly wound,
    And eke impatient of unwonted paine,
    He loudly brayd with beastly yelling sound,
    That all the fields rebellowed againe;
    As great a noyse, as when in Cymbrian plaine
    An heard of Bulles, whom kindly rage doth sting,
    Do for the milkie mothers want complaine,
    And fill the fields with troublous bellowing,
The neighbour woods around with hollow murmur ring.

12

That when his deare *Duessa* heard, and saw   100
    The evill stownd, that daungered her estate,
    Unto his aide she hastily did draw
    Her dreadfull beast, who swolne with bloud of late
    Came ramping forth with proud presumpteous gate,
    And threatned all his heads like flaming brands.
    But him the Squire made quickly to retrate,
    Encountring fierce with single sword in hand,
And twixt him and his Lord did like a bulwarke stand.

13

The proud *Duessa* full of wrathfull spight,
    And fierce disdaine, to be affronted so,   110
    Enforst her purple beast with all her might

---

89 *truncked stocke* hacked-off stump
96 *kindly rage* natural desire
97 *milkie mothers* females; *want* absence
101 *stownd* trouble
104 *gate* pace

    That stop out of the way to overthroe,
    Scorning the let of so unequall foe:
    But nathemore would that courageous swayne
    To her yeeld passage, gainst his Lord to goe,
    But with outrageous strokes did him restraine,
And with his bodie bard the way atwixt them twaine.

14

Then tooke the angrie witch her golden cup,
    Which still she bore, replete with magick artes;
    Death and despeyre did many thereof sup,   120
    And secret poyson through their inner parts,
    Th'eternall bale of heavie wounded harts;
    Which after charmes and some enchauntments said,
    She lightly sprinkled on his weaker parts;
    Therewith his sturdie courage soone was quayd,
And all his senses were with suddeine dread dismayd.

15

So downe he fell before the cruell beast,
    Who on his necke his bloudie clawes did seize,
    That life nigh crusht out of his panting brest:
    No powre he had to stirre, nor will to rize.   130
    That when the carefull knight gan well avise,
    He lightly left the foe, with whom he fought,
    And to the beast gan turne his enterprise;
    For wondrous anguish in his hart it wrought,
To see his loved Squire into such thraldome brought.

16

And high advauncing his bloud-thirstie blade,
    Stroke one of those deformed heads so sore,

116 *outrageous* violent
131 *carefull* observant

That of his puissance proud ensample made;
   His monstrous scalpe downe to his teeth it tore,
   And that misformed shape mis-shaped more:
   A sea of bloud gusht from the gaping wound,
   That her gay garments staynd with filthy gore,
   And overflowed all the field around;
That over shoes in bloud he waded on the ground.

17

Thereat he roared for exceeding paine,
   That to have heard, great horror would have bred,
   And scourging th'emptie ayre with his long traine,
   Through great impatience of his grieved hed
   His gorgeous ryder from her loftie sted
   Would have cast down, and trod in durtie myre,
   Had not the Gyant soone her succoured;
   Who all enrag'd with smart and franticke yre,
Came hurtling in full fierce, and forst the knight retyre.

18

The force, which wont in two to be disperst,
   In one alone left hand he now unites,
   Which is through rage more strong then both were erst;
   With which his hideous club aloft he dites,
   And at his foe with furious rigour smites,
   That strongest Oake might seeme to overthrow:
   The stroke upon his shield so heavie lites,
   That to the ground it doubleth him full low:
What mortall wight could ever beare so monstrous blow?

19

And in his fall his shield, that covered was,
   Did loose his vele by chaunce, and open flew:
   The light whereof, that heavens light did pas,
   Such blazing brightnesse through the aier threw,

That eye mote not the same endure to vew.
Which when the Gyaunt spyde with staring eye,
He downe let fall his arme, and soft withdrew
His weapon huge, that heaved was on hye 170
For to have slaine the man, that on the ground did lye.

20

And eke the fruitfull-headed beast, amaz'd
  At flashing beames of that sunshiny shield,
  Became starke blind, and all his senses daz'd,
  That downe he tumbled on the durtie field,
  And seem'd himselfe as conquered to yield.
  Whom when his maistresse proud perceiv'd to fall,
  Whiles yet his feeble feet for faintnesse reeld,
  Unto the Gyant loudly she gan call,
O helpe *Orgoglio*, helpe, or else we perish all. 180

21

At her so pitteous cry was much amoov'd
  Her champion stout, and for to ayde his frend,
  Againe his wonted angry weapon proov'd:
  But all in vaine: for he has read his end
  In that bright shield, and all their forces spend
  Themselves in vaine: for since that glauncing sight,
  He hath no powre to hurt, nor to defend;
  As where th'Almighties lightning brond does light,
It dimmes the dazed eyen, and daunts the senses quight.

22

Whom when the Prince, to battell new addrest, 190
  And threatning high his dreadfull stroke did see,
  His sparkling blade about his head he blest,

172 *fruitfull-headed* many-headed
192 *blest* waved

    And smote off quite his right leg by the knee,
    That downe he tombled; as an aged tree,
      High growing on the top of rocky clift,
    Whose hartstrings with keene steele nigh hewen be,
    The mightie trunck halfe rent, with ragged rift
Doth roll adowne the rocks, and fall with fearefull drift.

23

Or as a Castle reared high and round,
    By subtile engins and malitious slight
    Is undermined from the lowest ground,
    And her foundation forst, and feebled quight,
    At last downe falles, and with her heaped hight
    Her hastie ruine does more heavie make,
    And yields it selfe unto the victours might;
    Such was this Gyaunts fall, that seemd to shake
The stedfast globe of earth, as it for feare did quake.

24

The knight then lightly leaping to the pray,
    With mortall steele him smot againe so sore,
    That headlesse his unweldy bodie lay,
    All wallowd in his owne fowle bloudy gore,
    Which flowed from his wounds in wondrous store.
    But soone as breath out of his breast did pas,
    That huge great body, which the Gyaunt bore,
    Was vanisht quite, and of that monstrous mas
Was nothing left, but like an emptie bladder was.

25

Whose grievous fall, when false *Duessa* spide,
    Her golden cup she cast unto the ground,
    And crowned mitre rudely threw aside;
    Such percing griefe her stubborne hart did wound,
    That she could not endure that dolefull stound,

But leaving all behind her, fled away:
The light-foot Squire her quickly turnd around,
And by hard meanes enforcing her to stay,
So brought unto his Lord, as his deserved pray.

26

The royall Virgin, which beheld from farre,
In pensive plight, and sad perplexitie,
The whole atchievement of this doubtfull warre,
Came running fast to greet his victorie,
With sober gladnesse, and myld modestie, 230
And with sweet joyous cheare him thus bespake;
Faire braunch of noblesse, flowre of chevalrie,
That with your worth the world amazed make,
How shall I quite the paines, ye suffer for my sake?

27

And you fresh bud of vertue springing fast,
Whom these sad eyes saw nigh unto deaths dore,
What hath poore Virgin for such perill past,
Wherewith you to reward? Accept therefore
My simple selfe, and service evermore;
And he that high does sit, and all things see 240
With equall eyes, their merites to restore,
Behold what ye this day have done for mee,
And what I cannot quite, requite with usuree.

28

But sith the heavens, and your faire handeling
Have made you maister of the field this day,
Your fortune maister eke with governing,
And well begun end all so well, I pray,

234 *quite* repay
244 *handeling* skill in battle

Ne let that wicked woman scape away;
For she it is, that did my Lord bethrall,
My dearest Lord, and deepe in dongeon lay,   250
Where he his better dayes hath wasted all.
O heare, how piteous he to you for ayd does call.

29

Forthwith he gave in charge unto his Squire,
That scarlot whore to keepen carefully;
Whiles he himselfe with greedie great desire
Into the Castle entred forcibly,
Where living creature none he did espye;
Then gan he lowdly through the house to call:
But no man car'd to answere to his crye.
There raignd a solemne silence over all,   260
Nor voice was heard, nor wight was seene in bowre or hall.

30

At last with creeping crooked pace forth came
An old old man, with beard as white as snow,
That on a staffe his feeble steps did frame,
And guide his wearie gate both too and fro:
For his eye sight him failed long ygo,
And on his arme a bounch of keyes he bore,
The which unused rust did overgrow:
Those were the keyes of every inner dore,
But he could not them use, but kept them still in store.   270

31

But very uncouth sight was to behold,
How he did fashion his untoward pace,
For as he forward moov'd his footing old,
So backward still was turnd his wrincled face,
Unlike to men, who ever as they trace,
Both feet and face one way are wont to lead.

This was the auncient keeper of that place,
  And foster father of the Gyant dead;
His name *Ignaro* did his nature right aread.

32

His reverend haires and holy gravitie
  The knight much honord, as beseemed well,
  And gently askt, where all the people bee,
  Which in that stately building wont to dwell.
  Who answerd him full soft, he could not tell.
  Againe he askt, where that same knight was layd,
  Whom great *Orgoglio* with his puissaunce fell
  Had made his caytive thrall; againe he sayde,
He could not tell: ne ever other answere made.

33

Then asked he, which way he in might pas:
  He could not tell, againe he answered.
  Thereat the curteous knight displeased was,
  And said, Old sire, it seemes thou has not red
  How ill it sits with that same silver hed
  In vaine to mocke, or mockt in vaine to bee:
  But if thou be, as thou art pourtrahed
  With natures pen, in ages grave degree,
Aread in graver wise, what I demaund of thee.

34

His answere likewise was, he could not tell.
  Whose sencelesse speach, and doted ignorance
  When as the noble Prince had marked well,
  He ghest his nature by his countenance,

---

279 *Ignaro* Ignorance
295 *pourtrahed* represented
297 *Aread in graver wise* answer more seriously

And calmd his wrath with goodly temperance.
Then to him stepping, from his arme did reach
Those keyes, and made himselfe free enterance.
Each dore he opened without any breach;
There was no barre to stop, nor foe him to empeach.

35

There all within full rich arayd he found,
   With royall arras and resplendent gold.
   And did with store of every thing abound,
   That greatest Princes presence might behold.   310
   But all the floore (too filthy to be told)
   With bloud of guiltlesse babes, and innocents trew,
   Which there were slaine, as sheepe out of the fold,
   Defiled was, that dreadfull was to vew,
And sacred ashes over it was strowed new.

36

And there beside of marble stone was built
   An Altare, carv'd with cunning imagery,
   On which true Christians bloud was often spilt,
   And holy Martyrs often doen to dye,
   With cruell malice and strong tyranny: 320
   Whose blessed sprites from underneath the stone
   To God for vengeance cryde continually,
   And with great griefe were often heard to grone,
That hardest heart would bleede, to heare their piteous mone.

37

Through every rowme he sought, and every bowr,
   But no where could he find that wofull thrall:
   At last he came unto an yron doore,

306 *empeach* hinder

That fast was lockt, but key found not at all
Emongst that bounch, to open it withall;
But in the same a little grate was pight,					330
Through which he sent his voyce, and lowd did call
With all his powre, to weet, if living wight
Were housed therewithin, whom he enlargen might.

38

Therewith an hollow, dreary, murmuring voyce
These piteous plaints and dolours did resound;
O who is that, which brings me happy choyce
Of death, that here lye dying every stound,
Yet live perforce in balefull darkenesse bound?
For now three Moones have changed thrice their hew,
And have beene thrice hid underneath the ground,		340
Since I the heavens chearefull face did vew,
O welcome thou, that doest of death bring tydings trew.

39

Which when that Champion heard, with percing point
Of pitty deare his hart was thrilled sore,
And trembling horrour ran through every joynt,
For ruth of gentle knight so fowle forlore:
Which shaking off, he rent that yron dore,
With furious force, and indignation fell;
Where entred in, his foot could find no flore,
But all a deepe descent, as darke as hell,			350
That breathed ever forth a filthie banefull smell.

40

But neither darkenesse fowle, nor filthy bands,
Nor noyous smell his purpose could withhold,

---

330 *pight* placed
333 *enlargen* free

>   (Entire affection hateth nicer hands)
>   But that with constant zeale, and courage bold,
>   After long paines and labours manifold,
>   He found the meanes that Prisoner up to reare;
>   Whose feeble thighes, unhable to uphold
>   His pined corse, him scarse to light could beare,
> A ruefull spectacle of death and ghastly drere.   360

41

> His sad dull eyes deepe sunck in hollow pits,
>   Could not endure th'unwonted sunne to view;
>   His bare thin cheekes for want of better bits,
>   And empty sides deceived of their dew,
>   Could make a stony hart his hap to rew;
>   His rawbone armes, whose mighty brawned bowrs
>   Were wont to rive steele plates, and helmets hew,
>   Were cleane consum'd, and all his vitall powres
> Decayd, and all his flesh shronk up like withered flowres.

42

> Whom when his Lady saw, to him she ran   370
>   With hasty joy: to see him made her glad,
>   And sad to view his visage pale and wan,
>   Who earst in flowres of freshest youth was clad.
>   Tho when her well of teares she wasted had,
>   She said, Ah dearest Lord, what evill starre
>   On you hath frownd, and pourd his influence bad,
>   That of your selfe ye thus berobbed arre,
> And this misseeming hew your manly looks doth marre?

---

359 *pined corse* starved body
363 *better bits* decent food
364 *deceived of their dew* deprived of proper nourishment
366 *bowrs* muscles

43

But welcome now my Lord, in wele or woe,
    Whose presence I have lackt too long a day;
And fie on Fortune mine avowed foe,
    Whose wrathfull wreakes them selves do now alay.
    And for these wrongs shall treble penaunce pay
    Of treble good: good growes of evils priefe.
    The chearelesse man, whom sorrow did dismay,
    Had no delight to treaten of his griefe;
His long endured famine needed more reliefe.

44

Faire Lady, then said that victorious knight,
    The things, that grievous were to do, or beare,
Them to renew, I wote, breeds no delight;
    Best musicke breeds delight in loathing eare:
    But th'onely good, that growes of passed feare,
    Is to be wise, and ware of like agein.
    This dayes ensample hath this lesson deare
    Deepe written in my heart with yron pen,
That blisse may not abide in state of mortall men.

45

Henceforth sir knight, take to you wonted strength,
    And maister these mishaps with patient might;
Loe where your foe lyes stretcht in monstrous length,
    And loe that wicked woman in your sight,
    The roote of all your care, and wretched plight,
    Now in your powre, to let her live, or dye.
    To do her dye (quoth *Una*) were despight,
    And shame t'avenge so weake an enimy;
But spoile her of her scarlot robe, and let her fly.

---

382 *alay* lessen
384 *priefe* testing

46

So as she bad, that witch they disaraid,
    And robd of royall robes, and purple pall,
    And ornaments that richly were displaid;
    Ne spared they to strip her naked all.
    Then when they had despoild her tire and call,   410
    Such as she was, their eyes might her behold,
    That her misshaped parts did them appall,
    A loathly, wrinckled hag, ill favoured, old,
Whose secret filth good manners biddeth not be told.

43

Her craftie head was altogether bald,
    And as in hate of honorable eld,
    Was overgrowne with scurfe and filthy scald;
    Her teeth out of her rotten gummes were feld,
    And her sowre breath abhominably smeld;
    Her dried dugs, like bladders lacking wind,   420
    Hong downe, and filthy matter from them weld;
    Her wrizled skin as rough, as maple rind,
So scabby was, that would have loathd all womankind.

48

Her neather parts, the shame of all her kind,
    My chaster Muse for shame doth blush to write;
    But at her rompe she growing had behind
    A foxes taile, with dong all fowly dight;
    And eke her feete most monstrous were in sight;
    For one of them was like an Eagles claw,

---

410 *tire and call* robes and head-dress
417 *scald* scabbed
422 *wrizled* wrinkled
426 *rompe* rump

    With griping talaunts armd to greedy fight, 430
        The other like a Beares uneven paw:
More ugly shape yet never living creature saw.

49

Which when the knights beheld, amazd they were,
        And wondred at so fowle deformed wight.
    Such then (said *Una*) as she seemeth here,
        Such is the face of falshood, such the sight
    Of fowle *Duessa*, when her borrowed light
        Is laid away, and counterfesaunce knowne.
    Thus when they had the witch disrobed quight,
        And all her filthy feature open showne, 440
They let her goe at will, and wander wayes unknowne.

50

She flying fast from heavens hated face,
        And from the world that her discovered wide,
    Fled to the wastfull wildernesse apace,
        From living eyes her open shame to hide,
    And lurkt in rocks and caves long unespide.
        But that faire crew of knights, and *Una* faire
    Did in that castle afterwards abide,
        To rest them selves, and weary powres repaire,
Where store they found of all, that dainty was and rare. 450

CANTO ix

His loves and lignage Arthur tells:
    The knights knit friendly bands:
Sir Trevisan flies from Despayre,
    Whom Redcrosse knight withstands.

---

430 *talaunts* talons

1

O Goodly golden chaine, wherewith yfere
    The vertues linked are in lovely wize:
And noble minds of yore allyed were,
In brave poursuit of chevalrous emprize,
That none did others safety despize,
Nor aid envy to him, in need that stands,
But friendly each did others prayse devize
How to advaunce with favourable hands,
As this good Prince redeemd the *Redcrosse* knight from bands.

2

Who when their powres, empaird through labour long,   10
    With dew repast they had recured well
And that weake captive wight now wexed strong,
Them list no lenger there at leasure dwell,
But forward fare, as their adventures fell,
But ere they parted, *Una* faire besought
That straunger knight his name and nation tell;
Least so great good, as he for her had wrought,
Should die unknown, and buried be in thanklesse thought.

3

Faire virgin (said the Prince) ye me require
    A thing without the compas of my wit: 20
For both the lignage and the certain Sire,
From which I sprong, from me are hidden yit.
For all so soone as life did me admit
Into this world, and shewed heavens light,
From mothers pap I taken was unfit:

---

1 *yfere* together
2 *in lovely wize* in a loving manner
25 *pap* breast; *unfit* helpless

And streight delivered to a Faery knight,
To be upbrought in gentle thewes and martiall might.

4

Unto old *Timon* he me brought bylive,
   Old *Timon*, who in youthly yeares hath beene
   In warlike feates th'expertest man alive,
   And is the wisest now on earth I weene;
   His dwelling is low in a valley greene,
   Under the foot of *Rauran* mossy hore,
   From whence the river *Dee* as silver cleene
   His tombling billowes rolls with gentle rore:
There all my dayes he traind me up in vertuous lore.

5

Thither the great Magicien *Merlin* came,
   As was his use, ofttimes to visit me:
   For he had charge my discipline to frame,
   And Tutours nouriture to oversee.
   Him oft and oft I askt in privitie,
   Of what loines and what lignage I did spring:
   Whose aunswere bad me still assured bee,
   That I was sonne and heire unto a king,
As time in her just terme the truth to light should bring.

6

Well worthy impe, said then the Lady gent,
   And Pupill fit for such a Tutours hand.
   But what adventure, or what high intent
   Hath brought you hither into Faery land,
   Aread Prince *Arthur*, crowne of Martiall band?
   Full hard it is (quoth he) to read aright
   The course of heavenly cause, or understand

---

27 *thewes* manners   33 *hore* grey

    The secret meaning of th'eternall might,
That rules mens wayes, and rules the thoughts of living wight.

7

For whither he through fatall deepe foresight
    Me hither sent, for cause to me unghest,
    Or that fresh bleeding wound, which day and night
    Whilome doth rancle in my riven brest,
    With forced fury following his behest,
    Me hither brought by wayes yet never found,   60
    You to have helpt I hold my selfe yet blest.
    Ah curteous knight (quoth she) what secret wound
Could ever find, to grieve the gentlest hart on ground?

8

Deare Dame (quoth he) you sleeping sparkes awake,
    Which troubled once, into huge flames will grow,
    Ne ever will their fervent fury slake,
    Till living moysture into smoke do flow,
    And wasted life do lye in ashes low.
    Yet sithens silence lesseneth not my fire,
    But told it flames, and hidden it does glow,   70
    I will revele, what ye so much desire:
Ah Love, lay downe thy bow, the whiles I may respire.

9

It was in freshest flowre of youthly yeares,
    When courage first does creepe in manly chest,
    Then first the coale of kindly heat appeares
    To kindle love in every living brest;
    But me had warnd old *Timons* wise behest,
    Those creeping flames by reason to subdew,

---

58 *rancle* fester; *riven* pierced
75 *kindly heat* sexual instinct

Before their rage grew to so great unrest,
   As miserable lovers use to rew,
Which still wex old in woe, whiles woe still wexeth new.

10

That idle name of love, and lovers life,
   As losse of time, and vertues enimy
   I ever scornd, and joyd to stirre up strife,
   In middest of their mournfull Tragedy,
   Ay wont to laugh, when them I heard to cry,
   And blow the fire, which them to ashes brent:
   Their God himselfe, griev'd at my libertie,
   Shot many a dart at me with fiers intent,
But I them warded all with wary government.

11

But all in vaine: no fort can be so strong,
   Ne fleshly brest can armed be so sound,
   But will at last be wonne with battrie long,
   Or unawares at disavantage found;
   Nothing is sure, that growes on earthly ground:
   And who most trustes in arme of fleshly might,
   And boasts, in beauties chaine not to be bound,
   Doth soonest fall in disaventrous fight,
And yeeldes his caytive neck to victours most despight.

12

Ensample make of him your haplesse joy,
   And of my selfe now mated, as ye see;
   Whose prouder vaunt that proud avenging boy
   Did soone pluck downe, and curbd my libertie.

81 *wex* grow
88 *Their God* Cupid
90 *government* discretion
98 *disaventrous* ill-omened

  For on a day prickt forth with jollitie
   Of looser life, and heat of hardiment,
   Raunging the forest wide on courser free,
   The fields, the floods, the heavens with one consent
  Did seeme to laugh on me, and favour mine intent.

13

For-wearied with my sports, I did alight
  From loftie steed, and downe to sleepe me layd;   110
  The verdant gras my couch did goodly dight,
  And pillow was my helmet faire displayd:
  Whiles every sence the humour sweet embayd,
  And slombring soft my hart did steale away,
  Me seemed, by my side a royall Mayd
  Her daintie limbes full softly down did lay:
So faire a creature yet saw never sunny day.

14

Most goodly glee and lovely blandishment
  She to me made, and bad me love her deare,
  For dearely sure her love was to me bent,   120
  As when just time expired should appeare.
  But whether dreames delude, or true it were,
  Was never hart so ravisht with delight,
  Ne living man like words did ever heare,
  As she to me delivered all that night;
And at her parting said, She Queene of Faeries hight.

15

When I awoke, and found her place devoyd,
  And nought but pressed gras, where she had lyen,

104–5 *prickt forth . . . hardiment* urged by delight in freedom and physical energy
113 *humour* drowsiness; *embayd* suffused
118 *glee* joy; *lovely blandishment* loving utterance

    I sorrowed all so much, as earst I joyd,
    And washed all her place with watry eyen. 130
    From that day forth I lov'd that face divine;
    From that day forth I cast in carefull mind,
    To seeke her out with labour, and long tyne,
    And never vow to rest, till her I find,
Nine monethes I seeke in vaine yet ni'll that vow unbind.

16

Thus as he spake, his visage wexed pale,
    And chaunge of hew great passion did bewray;
    Yet still he strove to cloke his inward bale,
    And hide the smoke, that did his fire display,
    Till gentle *Una* thus to him gan say; 140
    O happy Queene of Faeries, that hast found
    Mongst many, one that with his prowesse may
    Defend thine honour, and thy foes confound:
True Loves are often sown, but seldom grow on ground.

17

Thine, O then, said the gentle *Redcrosse* knight,
    Next to that Ladies love, shalbe the place,
    Of fairest virgin, full of heavenly light,
    Whose wondrous faith, exceeding earthly race,
    Was firmest fixt in mine extremest case.
    And you, my Lord, the Patrone of my life, 150
    Of that great Queene may well gaine worthy grace:
    For onely worthy you through prowes priefe
Yf living man mote worthy be, to be her liefe.

---

133 *tyne* grief
148 *earthly race* human nature
153 *liefe* beloved

[420-1]

18

So diversly discoursing of their loves,
    The golden Sunne his glistring head gan shew,
    And sad remembraunce now the Prince amoves,
    With fresh desire his voyage to pursew:
    Als *Una* earnd her traveill to renew.
    Then those two knights, fast friendship for to bynd,
    And love establish each to other trew,   160
    Gave goodly gifts, the signes of gratefull mynd,
And eke as pledges firme, right hands together joynd.

19

Prince *Arthur* gave a boxe of Diamond sure,
    Embowd with gold and gorgeous ornament,
    Wherein were closd few drops of liquor pure,
    Of wondrous worth, and vertue excellent,
    That any wound could heale incontinent:
    Which to requite, the *Redcrosse* knight him gave
    A booke, wherein his Saveours testament
    Was writ with golden letters rich and brave;   170
A worke of wondrous grace, and able soules to save.

20

Thus beene they parted, *Arthur* on his way
    To seeke his love, and th'other for to fight
    With *Unaes* foe, that all her realme did pray.
    But she now weighing the decayed plight,
    And shrunken synewes of her chosen knight,
    Would not a while her forward course pursew,
    Ne bring him forth in face of dreadfull fight,

---

158 *earnd* yearned
163 *sure* solid
164 *Embowd* set in
167 *incontinent* at once

204

    Till he recovered had his former hew:
For him to be yet weake and wearie well she knew.   180

21

So as they traveild, lo they gan espy
    An armed knight towards them gallop fast,
    That seemed from some feared foe to fly,
    Or other griesly thing, that him agast.
    Still as he fled, his eye was backward cast,
    As if his feare still followed him behind;
    Als flew his steed, as he his bands had brast,
    And with his winged heeles did tread the wind,
As he had beene a fole of *Pegasus* his kind.

22

Nigh as he drew, they might perceive his head   190
    To be unarmd, and curld uncombed heares
    Upstaring stiffe, dismayd with uncouth dread;
    Nor drop of bloud in all his face appeares
    Nor life in limbe: and to increase his fears,
    In fowle reproch of knighthoods faire degree,
    About his neck an hempen rope he weares,
    That with his glistring armes does ill agree;
But he of rope or armes has now no memoree.

23

The *Redcrosse* knight toward him crossed fast,
    To weet, what mister wight was so dismayd: 200
    There him he finds all sencelesse and aghast,

---

184 *agast* terrified
187 *as he his bands had brast* as if he had broken his reins
189 *As he ... his kind* as if he were descended from the winged horse Pegasus.
192 *uncouth* unknown
200 *what mister wight* what kind of man

That of him selfe he seemd to be afrayd;
Whom hardly he from flying forward stayd,
Till he these wordes to him deliver might;
Sir knight, aread who hath ye thus arayd,
And eke from whom make ye this hasty flight:
For never knight I saw in such misseeming plight.

24

He answerd nought at all, but adding new
   Feare to his first amazment, staring wide
   With stony eyes, and hartlesse hollow hew,
   Astonisht stood, as one that had aspide
   Infernall furies, with their chaines untide.
   Him yet againe, and yet againe bespake
   The gentle knight; who nought to him replide,
   But trembling every joynt did inly quake,
And foltring tongue at last these words seemd forth to shake.

25

For Gods deare love, Sir knight, do me not stay;
   For loe he comes, he comes fast after mee.
   Eft looking backe would faine have runne away;
   But he him forst to stay, and tellen free
   The secret cause of his perplexitie:
   Yet nathemore by his bold hartie speach,
   Could his bloud-frosen hart emboldned bee,
   But through his boldnesse rather feare did reach,
Yet forst, at last he made through silence suddein breach.

26

And am I now in safetie sure (quoth he)
   From him, that would have forced me to dye?

216 *foltring* faltering

And is the point of death now turnd fro mee,
That I may tell this haplesse history?
Feare nought: (quoth he) no daunger now is nye.   230
Then shall I you recount a ruefull cace,
(Said he) the which with this unlucky eye
I late beheld, and had not greater grace
Me reft from it, had bene partaker of the place.

27

I lately chaunst (Would I had never chaunst)
   With a faire knight to keepen companee,
   Sir *Terwin* hight, that well himselfe advaunst
   In all affaires, and was both bold and free,
   But not so happie as mote happie bee:
   He lov'd, as was his lot, a Ladie gent,   240
   That him againe lov'd in the least degree:
   For she was proud, and of too high intent,
And joyd to see her lover languish and lament.

28

From whom returning sad and comfortlesse,
   As on the way together we did fare,
   We met that villen (God from him me blesse)
   That cursed wight, from whom I scapt whyleare,
   A man of hell, that cals himselfe *Despaire*:
   Who first us greets, and after faire areedes
   Of tydings strange, and of adventures rare: 250
   So creeping close, as Snake in hidden weedes,
Inquireth of our states, and of our knightly deedes.

234 *reft* snatched
240 *gent* noble
241 *in the least degree* hardly at all
246 *villen* villain
247 *whyleare* just now

[420-1]

29

Which when he knew, and felt our feeble harts
  Embost with bale, and bitter byting griefe,
  Which love had launched with his deadly darts,
  With wounding words and termes of foule repriefe
  He pluckt from us all hope of due reliefe,
  That earst us held in love of lingring life;
  Then hopelesse hartlesse, gan the cunning thiefe
  Perswade us die, to stint all further strife: 260
To me he lent his rope, to him a rustie knife.

30

With which sad instrument of hastie death,
  That wofull lover, loathing lenger light,
  A wide way made to let forth living breath.
  But I more fearefull, or more luckie wight,
  Dismayd with that deformed dismall sight,
  Fled fast away, halfe dead with dying feare:
  Ne yet assur'd of life by you, Sir knight,
  Whose like infirmitie like chaunce may beare:
But God you never let his charmed speeches heare. 270

31

How may a man (said he) with idle speach
  Be wonne, to spoyle the Castle of his health?
  I wote (quoth he) whom triall late did teach,
  That like would not for all this worldes wealth:
  His subtill tongue, like dropping honny, mealt'th
  Into the hart, and searcheth every vaine,
  That ere one be aware, by secret stealth
  His powre is reft, and weaknesse doth remaine.
O never Sir desire to try his guilefull traine.

254 *Embost with bale* worn out with grief
266 *deformed* disfigured

208

32

Certes (said he) hence shall I never rest,
   Till I that treachours art have heard and tride;
   And you Sir knight, whose name mote I request,
   Of grace do me unto his cabin guide.
   I that hight *Trevisan* (quoth he) will ride
   Against my liking backe, to doe you grace:
   But nor for gold nor glee will I abide
   By you, when ye arrive in that same place;
For lever had I die, then see his deadly face.

33

Ere long they come, where that same wicked wight
   His dwelling has, low in an hollow cave,
   Farre underneath a craggie clift ypight,
   Darke, dolefull, drearie, like a greedie grave,
   That still for carrion carcases doth crave:
   On top whereof aye dwelt the ghastly Owle,
   Shrieking his balefull note, which ever drave
   Farre from that haunt all other chearefull fowle;
And all about it wandring ghostes did waile and howle.

34

And all about old stockes and stubs of trees,
   Whereon nor fruit, nor leafe was ever seene,
   Did hang upon the ragged rocky knees;
   On which had many wretches hanged beene,
   Whose carcases were scattered on the greene,
   And throwne about the cliffs. Arrived there,
   That bare-head knight for dread and dolefull teene,
   Would faine have fled, ne durst approchen neare,
But th'other forst him stay, and comforted in feare.

286 *glee* display
291 *ypight* set

35

That darkesome cave they enter, where they find
    That cursed man, low sitting on the ground,
    Musing full sadly in his sullein mind;
    His griesie lockes, long growen, and unbound,
    Disordred hong about his shoulders round,
    And hid his face; through which his hollow eyne
    Lookt deadly dull, and stared as astound;
    His raw-bone cheekes through penurie and pine,
Were shronke into his jawes, as he did never dine.

36

His garment nought but many ragged clouts,
    With thornes together pind and patched was,
    The which his naked sides he wrapt abouts;
    And him beside there lay upon the gras
    A drearie corse, whose life away did pas,
    All wallowd in his owne yet luke-warme blood,
    That from his wound yet welled fresh alas;
    In which a rustie knife fast fixed stood,
And made an open passage for the gushing flood.

37

Which piteous spectacle, approving trew
    The wofull tale that *Trevisan* had told,
    When as the gentle *Redcrosse* knight did vew,
    With firie zeale he burnt in courage bold,
    Him to avenge, before his bloud were cold,
    And to the villein said, Thou damned wight,
    The author of this fact, we here behold,
    What justice can but judge against thee right,
With thine owne bloud to price his bloud, here shed in sight?

38

What franticke fit (quoth he) hath thus distraught
    Thee, foolish man, so rash a doome to give?
    What justice ever other judgement taught,
    But he should die, who merites not to live?
    None else to death this man despayring drive,
    But his owne guiltie mind deserving death.
    Is then unjust to each his due to give?   340
    Or let him die, that loatheth living breath?
Or let him die at ease, that liveth here uneath?

39

Who travels by the wearie wandring way,
    To come unto his wished home in haste,
    And meetes a flood, that doth his passage stay,
    Is not great grace to helpe him over past,
    Or free his feet, that in the myre sticke fast?
    Most envious man, that grieves at neighbours good,
    And fond, that joyest in the woe thou hast,
    Why wilt not let him passe, that long hath stood   350
Upon the banke, yet wilt thy selfe not passe the flood?

40

He there does now enjoy eternall rest
    And happie ease, which thou doest want and crave,
    And further from it daily wanderest:
    What if some litle paine the passage have,
    That makes fraile flesh to feare the bitter wave?
    Is not short paine well borne, that brings long ease,
    And layes the soule to sleepe in quiet grave?
    Sleepe after toyle, port after stormie seas,
Ease after warre, death after life does greatly please.   360

342 *uneath* uneasily

41

The knight much wondred at his suddeine wit,
   And said, The terme of life is limited,
   Ne may a man prolong, nor shorten it;
   The souldier may not move from watchfull sted,
   Nor leave his stand, untill his Captaine bed.
   Who life did limit by almightie doome,
   (Quoth he) knowes best the termes established;
   And he, that points the Centonell his roome,
Doth license him depart at sound of morning droome.

42

Is not his deed, what ever thing is donne,   370
   In heaven and earth? did not he all create
   To die againe? all ends that was begonne.
   Their times in his eternall booke of fate
   Are written sure, and have their certaine date.
   Who then can strive with strong necessitie,
   That holds the world in his still chaunging state,
   Or shunne the death ordaynd by destinie?
When houre of death is come, let none aske whence, nor why.

43

The lenger life, I wote the greater sin,
   The greater sin, the greater punishment: 380
   All those great battels, which thou boasts to win,
   Through strife, and bloud-shed, and avengement,
   Now praysd, hereafter deare thou shalt repent:
   For life must life, and bloud must bloud repay.
   Is not enough thy evill life forespent?
   For he, that once hath missed the right way,
The further he doth goe, the further he doth stray.

---

368 *Centonell* sentinel; *roome* post
369 *droome* drum

44

Then do no further goe, no further stray,
    But here lie downe, and to thy rest betake,
    Th'ill to prevent, that life ensewen may.
    For what hath life, that may it loved make,
    And gives not rather cause it to forsake?
    Feare, sicknesse, age, losse, labour, sorrow, strife,
    Paine, hunger, cold, that makes the hart to quake;
    And ever fickle fortune rageth rife,
All which, and thousands mo do make a loathsome life.

45

Thou wretched man, of death hast greatest need,
    If in true ballance thou wilt weigh thy state:
    For never knight, that dared warlike deede,
    More lucklesse disaventures did amate:
    Witnesse the dongeon deepe, wherein of late
    Thy life shut up, for death so oft did call;
    And though good lucke prolonged hath thy date,
    Yet death then, would the like mishaps forestall,
Into the which hereafter thou maiest happen fall.

46

Why then doest thou, O man of sin, desire
    To draw thy dayes forth to their last degree?
    Is not the measure of thy sinfull hire
    High heaped up with huge iniquitie,
    Against the day of wrath, to burden thee?
    Is not enough, that to this Ladie milde
    Thou falsed hast thy faith with perjurie,

---

390 *ensewen* pursue
396 *mo* more
400 *amate* overwhelm

And sold thy selfe to serve *Duessa* vilde,
With whom in all abuse thou hast thy selfe defilde?

47

Is not he just, that all this doth behold
    From highest heaven, and beares an equall eye?
    Shall he thy sins up in his knowledge fold,
    And guiltie be of thine impietie?
    Is not his law, Let every sinner die:
    Die shall all flesh? what then must needs be donne,   420
    Is it not better to doe willinglie,
    Then linger, till the glasse be all out ronne?
Death is the end of woes: die soone, O faeries sonne.

48

The knight was much enmoved with his speach,
    That as a swords point through his hart did perse,
    And in his conscience made a secret breach,
    Well knowing true all, that he did reherse,
    And to his fresh remembrance did reverse
    The ugly vew of his deformed crimes,
    That all his manly powres it did disperse,   430
    As he were charmed with inchaunted rimes,
That oftentimes he quakt, and fainted oftentimes.

49

In which amazement, when the Miscreant
    Perceived him to waver weake and fraile,
    Whiles trembling horror did his conscience dant,

---

413 *vilde* vile
429 *deformed* hideous
431 *inchaunted rimes* magical spells
435 *dant* daunt

And hellish anguish did his soule assaile,
To drive him to despaire, and quite to quaile,
He shew'd him painted in a table plaine,
The damned ghosts, that doe in torments waile,
And thousand feends that doe them endlesse paine   440
With fire and brimstone, which for ever shall remaine.

50

The sight whereof so throughly him dismaid,
That nought but death before his eyes he saw,
And ever burning wrath before him laid,
By righteous sentence of th'Almighties law:
Then gan the villein him to overcraw,
And brought unto him swords, ropes, poison, fire,
And all that might him to perdition draw;
And bad him choose, what death he would desire:
For death was due to him, that had provokt Gods ire.   450

51

But when as none of them he saw him take,
He to him raught a dagger sharpe and keene,
And gave it him in hand: his hand did quake,
And tremble like a leafe of Aspin greene,
And troubled bloud through his pale face was seene
To come, and goe with tydings from the hart,
As it a running messenger had beene.
At last resolv'd to worke his finall smart,
He lifted up his hand, that backe againe did start.

52

Which when as *Una* saw, through every vaine   460
The crudled cold ran to her well of life,

446 *overcraw* exult over

As in a swowne: but soon reliv'd againe,
Out of his hand she snatcht the cursed knife,
And threw it to the ground, enraged rife,
And to him said, Fie, fie, faint harted knight,
What meanest thou by this reprochful strife?
Is this the battell, which thou vauntst to fight
With that fire-mouthed Dragon, horrible and bright?

53

Come, come away, fraile, feeble, fleshly wight,
   Ne let vaine words bewitch thy manly hart,   470
   Ne divelish thoughts dismay thy constant spright.
   In heavenly mercies hast thou not a part?
   Why shouldst thou then despeire, that chosen art?
   Where justice growes, there grows eke greater grace,
   The which doth quench the brond of hellish smart,
   And that accurst hand-writing doth deface.
Arise, Sir knight arise, and leave this cursed place.

54

So up he rose, and thence amounted streight.
   Which when the carle beheld, and saw his guest
   Would safe depart, for all his subtill sleight,   480
   He chose an halter from among the rest,
   And with it hung himselfe, unbid unblest.
   But death he could not worke himselfe thereby;
   For thousand times he so himselfe had drest,
   Yet nathelesse it could not doe him die,
Till he should die his last, that is eternally.

479 *carle* wretch
482 *unbid* unprayed for
484 *drest* prepared

[421–2]

CANTO x

Her faithfull knight faire Una brings
to house of Holinesse,
Where he is taught repentance, and
the way to heavenly blesse.

1

What man is he, that boasts of fleshly might,
   And vaine assurance of mortality,
   Which all so soone, as it doth come to fight,
   Against spirituall foes, yeelds by and by,
   Or from the field most cowardly doth fly?
   Ne let the man ascribe it to his skill,
   That thorough grace hath gained victory.
   If any strength we have, it is to ill,
But all the good is Gods, both power and eke will.

2

By that, which lately hapned, *Una* saw,   10
   That this her knight was feeble, and too faint;
   And all his sinews woxen weake and raw,
   Through long enprisonment, and hard constraint,
   Which he endured in his late restraint,
   That yet he was unfit for bloudie fight:
   Therefore to cherish him with diets daint,
   She cast to bring him, where he chearen might,
Till he recovered had his late decayed plight.

---

12 *raw* painful
16 *daint* delicate
17 *chearen might* might recuperate
18 *recovered had* had recovered from

3

There was an auntient house not farre away,
  Renowmd throughout the world for sacred lore,
  And pure unspotted life: so well they say
  It governd was, and guided evermore,
  Through wisedome of a matrone grave and hore;
  Whose onely joy was to relieve the needes
  Of wretched soules, and helpe the helpelesse pore:
  All night she spent in bidding of her bedes,
And all the day in doing good and godly deedes.

4

Dame *Cælia* men did her call, as thought
  From heaven to come, or thither to arise,
  The mother of three daughters, well upbrought
  In goodly thewes, and godly exercise:
  The eldest two most sober, chast, and wise,
  Fidelia and *Speranza* virgins were,
  Though spousd, yet wanting wedlocks solemnize;
  But faire *Charissa* to a lovely fere
Was lincked, and by him had many pledges dere.

5

Arrived there, the dore they find fast lockt;
  For it was warely watched night and day,
  For feare of many foes: but when they knockt,
  The Porter opened unto them streight way:
  He was an aged syre, all hory gray,

20 *lore* doctrine
23 *hore* grey-haired
26 *bidding of her bedes* saying her prayers
28 *Cælia* Heavenly
31 *thewes* manners
33–5 *Fidelia ... Speranza ... Charissa* Faith, Hope, Charity
35 *lovely fere* loving mate

> With lookes full lowly cast, and gate full slow,
> Wont on a staffe his feeble steps to stay,
> Hight *Humiltá*. They passe in stouping low;
> For streight and narrow was the way, which he did show.

6

> Each goodly thing is hardest to begin,
>   But entred in a spacious court they see,
>   Both paine, and pleasant to be walked in,
>   Where them does meete a francklin faire and free,
>   And entertaines with comely courteous glee,
>   His name was *Zele*, that him right well became,
>   For in his speeches and behaviour hee
>   Did labour lively to expresse the same,
> And gladly did them guide, till to the Hall they came.

7

> There fairely them receives a gentle Squire,
>   Of milde demeanure, and rare courtesie,
>   Right cleanly clad in comely sad attire;
>   In word and deede that shew'd great modestie,
>   And knew his good to all of each degree,
>   High *Reverence*. He them with speeches meet
>   Does faire entreat; no courting nicetie,
>   But simple true, and eke unfained sweet,
> As might become a Squire so great persons to greet.

8

> And afterwards them to his Dame he leades,
>   That aged Dame, the Ladie of the place:

---

44 *Humiltá* Humility
49 *francklin* gentleman
57 *sad* sober
61 *courting nicetie* affected manners

Who all this while was busie at her beades:
Which doen, she up arose with seemely grace,
And toward them full matronely did pace.
Where when that fairest *Una* she beheld,
Whom well she knew to spring from heavenly race, 70
Her hart with joy unwonted inly sweld,
As feeling wondrous comfort in her weaker eld.

9

And her embracing said, O happie earth,
Whereon thy innocent feet doe ever tread,
Most vertuous virgin borne of heavenly berth,
That to redeeme thy woefull parents head,
From tyrans rage, and ever-dying dread,
Hast wandred through the world now long a day;
Yet ceasest not thy wearie soles to lead,
What grace hath thee now hither brought this way? 80
Or doen thy feeble feet unweeting hither stray?

10

Strange thing it is an errant knight to see
Here in this place, or any other wight,
That hither turnes his steps. So few there bee,
That chose the narrow path, or seeke the right:
All keepe the broad high way, and take delight
With many rather for to go astray,
And be partakers of their evill plight,
Then with a few to walke the rightest way;
O foolish men, why haste ye to your owne decay? 90

---

72 *weaker eld* weakness of age
79 *soles* feet
82 *errant* on a quest

11

Thy selfe to see, and tyred limbs to rest,
   O matrone sage (quoth she) I hither came,
   And this good knight his way with me addrest,
   Led with thy prayses and broad-blazed fame,
   That up to heaven is blowne. The aunciant Dame
   Him goodly greeted in her modest guise,
   And entertaynd them both, as best became,
   With all the court'sies, that she could devise,
Ne wanted ought, to shew her bounteous or wise.

12

Thus as they gan of sundry things devise,
   Loe two most goodly virgins came in place,
   Ylinked arme in arme in lovely wise,
   With countenance demure, and modest grace,
   They numbred even steps and equall pace:
   Of which the eldest, that *Fidelia* hight,
   Like sunny beames threw from her Christall face,
   That could have dazd the rash beholders sight,
And round about her head did shine like heavens light.

13

She was araied all in lilly white,
   And in her right hand bore a cup of gold,
   With wine and water fild up to the hight,
   In which a Serpent did himselfe enfold,
   That horrour made to all, that did behold;
   But she no whit did chaunge her constant mood:
   And in her other hand she fast did hold
   A booke, that was both signd and seald with blood,
Wherein darke things were writ, hard so be understood.

---

92 *sage* wise
113 *horrour made* roused threateningly

14

Her younger sister, that *Speranza* hight,
    Was clad in blew, that her beseemed well;
    Not all so chearefull seemed she of sight,   120
    As was her sister; whether dread did dwell,
    Or anguish in her hart, is hard to tell:
    Upon her arme a silver anchor lay,
    Whereon she leaned ever, as befell:
    And ever up to heaven, as she did pray,
Her stedfast eyes were bent, ne swarved other way.

15

They seeing *Una*, towards her gan wend,
    Who them encounters with like courtesie;
    Many kind speeches they betwene them spend,
    And greatly joy each other well to see: 130
    Then to the knight with shamefast modestie
    They turne themselves, at *Unaes* meeke request,
    And him salute with well beseeming glee;
    Who faire them quites, as him beseemed best,
And goodly gan discourse of many a noble gest.

16

Then *Una* thus; But she your sister deare;
    The deare *Charissa* where is she become?
    Or wants she health, or busie is elsewhere?
    Ah no, said they, but forth she may not come:
    For she of late is lightned of her wombe,   140
    And hath encreast the world with one sonne more,
    That her to see should be but troublesome.
    Indeede (quoth she) that should her trouble sore,
But thankt be God, and her encrease so evermore.

---

135 *gest* exploit
137 *become* gone

17

Then said the aged *Cælia*, Deare dame,
   And you good Sir, I wote that of your toyle,
   And labours long, through which ye hither came,
   Ye both forwearied be: therefore a whyle
   I read you rest, and to your bowres recoyle.
   Then called she a Groome, that forth him led   150
   Into a goodly lodge, and gan despoile
   Of puissant armes, and laid in easie bed;
His name was meeke *Obedience* rightfully ared.

18

Now when their wearie limbes with kindly rest,
   And bodies were refresht with due repast,
   Faire *Una* gan *Fidelia* faire request,
   To have her knight into her schoolehouse plaste,
   That of her heavenly learning he might taste,
   And heare the wisedome of her words divine.
   She graunted, and that knight so much agraste,   160
   That she him taught celestiall discipline,
And opened his dull eyes, that light mote in them shine.

19

And that her sacred Booke, with bloud ywrit,
   That none could read, except she did them teach,
   She unto him disclosed every whit,
   And heavenly documents thereout did preach,
   That weaker wit of man could never reach,
   Of God, of grace, of justice, of free will,
   That wonder was to heare her goodly speach:

149 *recoyle* retire
153 *ared* understood
160 *agraste* favoured
166 *documents* teaching
167 *weaker wit of man* reason alone

For she was able, with her words to kill, 170
And raise againe to life the hart, that she did thrill.

20

And when she list poure out her larger spright,
  She would commaund the hastie Sunne to stay,
  Or backward turne his course from heavens hight;
  Sometimes great hostes of men she could dismay,
  Dry-shod to passe, she parts the flouds in tway;
  And eke huge mountaines from their native seat
  She would commaund, themselves to beare away,
  And throw in raging sea with roaring threat.
Almightie God her gave such powre, and puissance great. 180

21

The faithfull knight now grew in litle space,
  By hearing her, and by her sisters lore,
  To such perfection of all heavenly grace,
  That wretched world he gan for to abhore,
  And mortall life gan loath, as thing forlore,
  Greev'd with remembrance of his wicked wayes,
  And prickt with anguish of his sinnes so sore,
  That he desirde to end his wretched dayes:
So much the dart of sinfull guilt the soule dismayes.

22

But wise *Speranza* gave him comfort sweet, 190
  And taught him how to take assured hold
  Upon her silver anchor, as was meet;
  Else had his sinnes so great, and manifold

171 *thrill* pierce
176 *in tway* in two
185 *forlore* desolate
190 *comfort* strength

Made him forget all that *Fidelia* told.
In this distressed doubtfull agonie,
When him his dearest *Una* did behold,
Disdeining life, desiring leave to die,
She found her selfe assayld with great perplexitie.

23

And came to *Cælia* to declare her smart,
    Who well acquainted with that commune plight,
    Which sinfull horror workes in wounded hart,
    Her wisely comforted all that she might,
    With goodly counsell and advisement right;
    And streightway sent with carefull diligence,
    To fetch a Leach, the which had great insight
    In that disease of grieved conscience,
And well could cure the same; His name was *Patience*.

24

Who comming to that soule-diseased knight,
    Could hardly him intreat, to tell his griefe:
    Which knowne, and all that noyd his heavie spright
    Well searcht, eftsoones he gan apply reliefe
    Of salves and med'cines, which had passing priefe,
    And thereto added words of wondrous might:
    By which to ease he him recured briefe,
    And much asswag'd the passion of his plight,
That he his paine endur'd, as seeming now more light.

25

But yet the cause and root of all his ill,
    Inward corruption, and infected sin,

---

201 *sinfull horror* horror of sin
210 *noyd* troubled
211 *searcht* examined

    Not purg'd nor heald, behind remained still,
       And festring sore did rankle yet within,   220
       Close creeping twixt the marrow and the skin.
    Which to extirpe, he laid him privily
       Downe in a darkesome lowly place farre in,
       Whereas he meant his corrosives to apply,
And with streight diet tame his stubborne malady.

26

In ashes and sackcloth he did array
       His daintie corse, proud humors to abate,
    And dieted with fasting every day,
       The swelling of his wounds to mitigate,
    And made him pray both earely and eke late: 230
       And ever as superfluous flesh did rot
    Amendment readie still at hand did wayt,
       To pluck it out with pincers firie whot,
That soone in him was left no one corrupted jot.

27

And bitter *Penance* with an yron whip,
       Was wont him once to disple every day:
    And sharpe *Remorse* his hart did pricke and nip,
       That drops of bloud thence like a well did play;
    And sad *Repentance* used to embay
       His bodie in salt water smarting sore,   240
       The filthy blots of sinne to wash away.
    So in short space they did to health restore
The man that would not live, but earst lay at deathes dore.

---

222 *extirpe* root out
225 *streight* strict
236 *disple* discipline
239 *embay* bathe

[421–2]

28

In which his torment often was so great,
    That like a Lyon he would cry and rore,
    And rend his flesh, and his owne synewes eat.
    His owne deare *Una* hearing evermore
    His ruefull shriekes and gronings, often tore
    Her guiltlesse garments, and her golden heare,
    For pitty of his paine and anguish sore;   250
    Yet all with patience wisely she did beare;
For well she wist, his crime could else be never cleare.

29

Whom thus recover'd by wise Patience,
    And trew *Repentance* they to *Una* brought:
    Who joyous of his cured conscience,
    Him dearely kist, and fairely eke besought
    Himselfe to chearish, and consuming thought
    To put away out of his carefull brest.
    By this *Charissa*, late in child-bed brought,
    Was woxen strong, and left her fruitfull nest;   260
To her faire *Una* brought this unacquainted guest.

30

She was a woman in her freshest age,
    Of wondrous beauty, and of bountie rare,
    With goodly grace and comely personage,
    That was on earth not easie to compare;
    Full of great love, but *Cupids* wanton snare
    As hell she hated, chast in worke and will;
    Her necke and breasts were ever open bare,
    That ay thereof her babes might sucke their fill;
The rest was all in yellow robes arayed still.   270

261 *unacquainted* not having been introduced
263 *bountie* goodness

31

A multitude of babes about her hong,
    Playing their sports, that joyd her to behold,
    Whom still she fed, whiles they were weake and young,
    But thrust them forth still, as they wexed old:
    And on her head she wore a tyre of gold,
    Adornd with gemmes and owches wondrous faire,
    Whose passing price uneath was to be told;
    And by her side there sate a gentle paire
Of turtle doves, she sitting in an yvorie chaire.

32

The knight and *Una* entring, faire her greet,   280
    And bid her joy of that her happie brood;
    Who them requites with court'sies seeming meet,
    And entertaines with friendly chearefull mood.
    Then *Una* her besought, to be so good,
    As in her vertuous rules to schoole her knight,
    Now after all his torment well withstood,
    In that sad house of *Penaunce*, where his spright
Had past the paines of hell, and long enduring night.

33

She was right joyous of her just request,
    And taking by the hand that Faeries sonne,   290
    Gan him instruct in every good behest,
    Of love, and righteousnesse, and well to donne,
    And wrath, and hatred warely to shonne,
    That drew on men Gods hatred, and his wrath,
    And many soules in dolours had fordonne:
    In which when him she well instructed hath,
From thence to heaven she teacheth him the ready path.

275 *tyre* head-dress
276 *owches* clasps
292 *well to donne* to do good

[421-2]

34

Wherein his weaker wandring steps to guide,
   An aunciont matrone she to her does call,
   Whose sober lookes her wisedome well descride:
   Her name was *Mercie*, well knowne over all,
   To be both gratious, and eke liberall:
   To whom the carefull charge of him she gave,
   To lead aright, that he should never fall
   In all his wayes through this wide worldes wave,
That Mercy in the end his righteous soule might save.

35

The godly Matrone by the hand him beares
   Forth from her presence, by a narrow way,
   Scattred with bushy thornes, and ragged breares,
   Which still before him she remov'd away,
   That nothing might his ready passage stay:
   And ever when his feet encombred were,
   Or gan to shrinke, or from the right to stray,
   She held him fast, and firmely did upbeare,
As carefull Nourse her child from falling oft does reare.

36

Eftsoones unto an holy Hospitall,
   That was fore by the way, she did him bring,
   In which seven Bead-men that had vowed all
   Their life to service of high heavens king
   Did spend their dayes in doing godly thing:
   Their gates to all were open evermore,
   That by the wearie way were traveiling,
   And one sate wayting ever them before,
To call in commers-by, that needy were and pore.

309 *breares* briars
318 *Bead-men* men of prayer

37

The first of them that eldest was, and best,
  Of all the house had charge and governement,
  As Guardian and Steward of the rest:
  His office was to give entertainement
  And lodging, unto all that came, and went:
  Not unto such, as could him feast againe, 330
  And double quite, for that he on them spent,
  But such, as want of harbour did constraine:
Those for Gods sake his dewty was to entertaine.

38

The second was as Almner of the place,
  His office was, the hungry for to feed,
  And thristy give to drinke, a worke of grace:
  He feard not once him selfe to be in need,
  Ne car'd to hoord for those, whom he did breede:
  The grace of God he layd up still in store,
  Which as a stocke he left unto his seede; 340
  He had enough, what need him care for more?
And had he lesse, yet some he would give to the pore.

39

The third had of their wardrobe custodie,
  In which were not rich tyres, nor garments gay,
  The plumes of pride, and wings of vanitie,
  But clothes meet to keepe keene could away,
  And naked nature seemely to aray;
  With which bare wretched wights he dayly clad,
  The images of God in earthly clay;
  And if that no spare cloths to give he had, 350
His owne coate he would cut, and it distribute glad.

40

The fourth appointed by his office was,
    Poore prisoners to relieve with gratious ayd,
    And captives to redeeme with price of bras,
    From Turkes and Sarazins, which them had stayd;
    And though they faultie were, yet well he wayd,
    That God to us forgiveth every howre
    Much more then that, why they in bands were layd,
    And he that harrowd hell with heavie stowre,
The faultie soules from thence brought to his heavenly bowre.   360

41

The fift had charge sicke persons to attend,
    And comfort those, in point of death which lay;
    For them most needeth comfort in the end,
    When sin, and hell, and death do most dismay
    The feeble soule departing hence away.
    All is but lost, that living we bestow,
    If not well ended at our dying day.
    O man have mind of that last bitter throw;
For as the tree does fall, so lyes it ever low.

42

The sixt had charge of them now being dead,   370
    In seemely sort their corses to engrave,
    And deck with dainty flowres their bridall bed,
    That to their heavenly spouse both sweet and brave
    They might appeare, when he their soules shall save.
    The wondrous workemanship of Gods owne mould,
    Whose face he made, all beasts to feare, and gave

---

354 *redeeme* ransom
359 *stowre* struggle
376 *feare* daunt

[421-2]

    All in his hand, even dead we honour should.
Ah dearest God me graunt, I dead be not defould.

43

The seventh now after death and buriall done,
    Had charge the tender Orphans of the dead
    And widowes ayd, least they should be undone:
    In face of judgement he their right would plead,
    Ne ought the powre of mighty men did dread
    In their defence, nor would for gold or fee
    Be wonne their rightfull causes downe to tread:
    And when they stood in most necessitee,
He did supply their want, and gave them ever free.

44

There when the Elfin knight arrived was,
    The first and chiefest of the seven, whose care
    Was guests to welcome, towardes him did pas:
    Where seeing *Mercie*, that his steps up bare,
    And alwayes led, to her with reverence rare
    He humbly louted in meeke lowlinesse,
    And seemely welcome for her did prepare:
    For of their order she was Patronesse,
Albe *Charissa* were their chiefest founderesse.

45

There she awhile him stayes, him selfe to rest,
    That to the rest more able he might bee:
    During which time, in every good behest
    And godly worke of Almes and charitee
    She him instructed with great industree;

---

378 *defould* defiled
393 *louted* bowed
397 *stayes* keeps

    Shortly therein so perfect he became,
        That from the first unto the last degree,
        His mortall life he learned had to frame
In holy righteousnesse, without rebuke or blame.

46

Thence forward by that painfull way they pas,
    Forth to an hill, that was both steepe and hy;
    On top whereof a sacred chappell was,
    And eke a litle Hermitage thereby,
    Wherein an aged holy man did lye,   410
    That day and night said his devotion,
    Ne other worldly busines did apply;
    His name was heavenly *Contemplation*;
Of God and goodnesse was his meditation.

47

Great grace that old man to him given had;
    For God he often saw from heavens hight,
    All were his earthly eyen both blunt and bad,
    And through great age had lost their kindly sight,
    Yet wondrous quick and persant was his spright,
    As Eagles eye, that can behold the Sunne: 420
    That hill they scale with all their powre and might,
    That his frayle thighes nigh wearie and fordonne
Gan faile, but by her helpe the top at last he wonne.

---

417 *blunt* dull
418 *kindly* natural
419 *persant* penetrating
422 *his* Redcrosse's
423 *her* Mercy's

48

There they do finde that godly aged Sire,
    With snowy lockes adowne his shoulders shed,
    As hoarie frost with spangles doth attire
    The mossy braunches of an Oke halfe ded.
    Each bone might through his body well be red,
    And every sinew seene through his long fast:
    For nought he car'd his carcas long unfed;   430
    His mind was full of spirituall repast,
And pyn'd his flesh, to keepe his body low and chast.

49

Who when these two approching he aspide,
    At their first presence grew agrieved sore,
    That forst him lay his heavenly thoughts aside;
    And had he not that Dame respected more,
    Whom highly he did reverence and adore,
    He would not once have moved for the knight.
    They him saluted standing far afore;
    Who well them greeting, humbly did requight,   440
And asked, to what end they clomb that tedious height.

50

What end (quoth she) should cause us take such paine,
    But that same end, which every living wight
    Should make his marke, high heaven to attaine?
    Is not from hence the way, that leadeth right
    To that most glorious house, that glistreth bright
    With burning starres, and everliving fire,
    Whereof the keyes are to thy hand behight
    By wise *Fidelia*? she doth thee require,
To shew it to this knight, according his desire.   450

432 *pyn'd* starved
439 *afore* before him

51

Thrise happy man, said then the father grave,
   Whose staggering steps thy steady hand doth lead,
   And shewes the way, his sinfull soule to save.
   Who better can the way to heaven aread,
   Then thou thy selfe, that was both borne and bred
   In heavenly throne, where thousand Angels shine?
   Thou doest the prayers of the righteous sead
   Present before the majestie divine,
And his avenging wrath to clemencie incline.

52

Yet since thou bidst, thy pleasure shalbe donne.
   Then come thou man of earth, and see the way,
   That never yet was seene of Faeries sonne,
   That never leads the traveiler astray,
   But after labours long, and sad delay,
   Brings them to joyous rest and endlesse blis.
   But first thou must a season fast and pray,
   Till from her bands the spright assoiled is,
And have her strength recur'd from fraile infirmitis.

53

That done, he leads him to the highest Mount;
   Such one, as that same mighty man of God,
   That bloud-red billowes like a walled front
   On either side disparted with his rod,
   Till that his army dry-foot through them yod,
   Dwelt fortie dayes upon; where writ in stone
   With bloudy letters by the hand of God,
   The bitter doome of death and balefull mone
He did receive, whiles flashing fire about him shone.

457 *sead* said
467 *assoiled* released
473 *yod* went

54

Or like that sacred hill, whose head full hie,
   Adornd with fruitfull Olives all arownd,
   Is, as it were for endlesse memory
   Of that deare Lord, who oft thereon was fownd,
   For ever with a flowring girlond crownd:
   Or like that pleasaunt Mount, that is for ay
   Through famous Poets verse each where renownd,
   On which the thrise three learned Ladies play
Their heavenly notes, and make full many a lovely lay.

55

From thence, far off he unto him did shew
   A litle path, that was both steepe and long,
   Which to a goodly Citie led his vew;
   Whose wals and towres were builded high and strong
   Of perle and precious stone, that earthly tong
   Cannot describe, nor wit of man can tell;
   Too high a ditty for my simple song;
   The Citie of the great king hight it well,
Wherein eternall peace and happinesse doth dwell.

56

As he thereon stood gazing, he might see
   The blessed Angels to and fro descend
   From highest heaven, in gladsome companee,
   And with great joy into that Citie wend,
   As commonly as friend does with his frend.
   Whereat he wondered much, and gan enquere,
   What stately building durst so high extend
   Her loftie towres unto the starry sphere,
And what unknowen nation there empeopled were.

---

493 *ditty* theme
494 *hight it well* it is well named

57

Faire knight (quoth he) *Hierusalem* that is,
    The new *Hierusalem*, that God has built
    For those to dwell in, that are chosen his,
    His chosen people purg'd from sinfull guilt,
    With pretious bloud, which cruelly was spilt
    On cursed tree, of that unspotted lam,   510
    That for the sinnes of all the world was kilt:
    Now are they Saints all in that Citie sam,
More deare unto their God, then younglings to their dam.

58

Till now, said then the knight, I weened well,
    That great *Cleopolis*, where I have beene,
    In which that fairest *Faerie Queene* doth dwell,
    The fairest Citie was, that might be seene;
    And that bright towre all built of christall cleene,
    Panthea, seemd the brightest thing, that was:
    But now by proofe all otherwise I weene;   520
    For this great Citie that does far surpas,
And this bright Angels towre quite dims that towre of glas.

59

Most trew, then said the holy aged man;
    Yet is *Cleopolis* for earthly frame,
    The fairest peece, that eye beholden can:
    And well beseemes all knights of noble name,
    That covet in th'immortall booke of fame
    To be enternized, that same to haunt,
    And doen their service to that soveraigne Dame,
    That glorie does to them for guerdon graunt: 530
For she is heavenly borne, and heaven may justly vaunt.

---

512 *sam* together

60

And thou faire ymp, sprong out from English race,
    How ever now accompted Elfins sonne,
    Well worthy doest thy service for her grace,
    To aide a virgin desolate foredonne.
    But when thou famous victorie hast wonne,
    And high emongst all knights hast hong thy shield,
    Thenceforth the suit of earthly conquest shonne,
    And wash thy hands from guilt of bloudy field:
For bloud can nought but sin, and wars but sorrowes yield.   540

61

Then seeke this path, that I to thee presage,
    Which after all to heaven shall thee send;
    Then peaceably thy painefull pilgrimage
    To yonder same *Hierusalem* do bend,
    Where is for thee ordaind a blessed end:
    For thou emongst those Saints, whom thou doest see,
    Shalt be a Saint, and thine owne nations frend
    And Patrone: thou Saint *George* shalt called bee,
Saint *George* of mery England, the signe of victoree.

62

Unworthy wretch (quoth he) of so great grace,   550
    How dare I thinke such glory to attaine?
    These that have it attaind, were in like cace
    (Quoth he) as wretched, and liv'd in like paine.
    But deeds of armes must I at last be faine,
    And Ladies love to leave so dearely bought?
    What need of armes, where peace doth ay remaine,
    (Said he) and battailes none are to be fought?
As for loose loves are vaine, and vanish into nought.

535 *foredonne* distressed
554–5 *be faine ... to leave* be willing to abandon

63

O let me not (quoth he) then turne againe
    Backe to the world, whose joyes so fruitlesse are;   560
    But let me here for aye in peace remaine,
    Or streight way on that last long voyage fare,
    That nothing may my present hope empare
    That may not be (said he) ne maist thou yit
    Forgo that royall maides bequeathed care,
    Who did her cause into thy hand commit,
Till from her cursed foe thou have her freely quit.

64

Then shall I soone, (quoth he) so God me grace,
    Abet that virgins cause disconsolate,
    And shortly backe returne unto this place,   570
    To walke this way in Pilgrims poore estate.
    But now aread, old father, why of late
    Didst thou behight me borne of English blood,
    Whom all a Faeries sonne doen nominate?
    That word shall I (said he) avouchen good,
Sith to thee is unknowne the cradle of thy brood.

65

For well I wote, thou springst from ancient race
    Of *Saxon* kings, that have with mightie hand
    And many bloudie battailes fought in place
    High reard their royall throne in *Britane* land,   580
    And vanquisht them, unable to withstand:
    From thence a Faerie thee unweeting reft,
    There as thou slepst in tender swadling band,

563 *empare* diminish
565 *bequeathed care* duty entrusted to you
574 *doen nominate* do call
575 *avouchen good* prove well

And her base Elfin brood there for thee left.
Such men do Chaungelings call, so chaungd by Faeries theft.

66

Thence she thee brought into this Faerie lond,
   And in an heaped furrow did thee hyde,
   Where thee a Ploughman all unweeting fond,
   As he his toylesome teme that way did guyde,
   And brought thee up in ploughmans state to byde,   590
   Whereof *Georgos* he thee gave to name;
   Till prickt with courage, and thy forces pryde,
   To Faery court thou cam'st to seeke for fame,
And prove thy puissaunt armes, as seemes thee best became.

67

O holy Sire (quoth he) how shall I quight
   The many favours I with thee have found,
   That hast my name and nation red aright,
   And taught the way that does to heaven bound?
   This said, adowne he looked to the ground,
   To have returnd, but dazed were his eyne,   600
   Through passing brightnesse, which did quite confound
   His feeble sense, and too exceeding shyne.
So darke are earthly things compard to things divine.

68

At last whenas himselfe he gan to find,
   To *Una* back he cast him to retire;
   Who him awaited still with pensive mind.
   Great thankes and goodly meed to that good syre,
   He thence departing gave for his paines hyre.

589 *toylesome* toiling
591 *Georgos* Farmer (Greek)
605 *cast him* resolved

So came to *Una*, who him joyd to see,
And after litle rest, gan him desire,
Of her adventure mindfull for to bee.
So leave they take of *Cœlia*, and her daughters three.

610

CANTO xi

The knight with that old Dragon fights
two dayes incessantly:
The third him overthrowes, and gayns
most glorious victory.

1

High time now gan it wex for *Una* faire,
    To thinke of those her captive Parents deare,
    And their forwasted kingdome to repaire:
    Whereto whenas they now approched neare,
    With hartie words her knight she gan to cheare,
    And in her modest manner thus bespake;
    Deare knight, as deare, as ever knight was deare,
    That all these sorrowes suffer for my sake,
High heaven behold the tedious toyle, ye for me take.

2

Now are we come unto my native soyle,
    And to the place, where all our perils dwell;
    Here haunts that feend, and does his dayly spoyle,
    Therefore henceforth be at your keeping well,
    And ever ready for your foeman fell.
    The sparke of noble courage now awake,
    And strive your excellent selfe to excell;
    That shall ye evermore renowmed make,
Above all knights on earth, that batteill undertake.

10

3 *forwasted* ravaged
5 *hartie* encouraging

3

And pointing forth, lo yonder is (said she)
    The brasen towre in which my parents deare
    For dread of that huge feend emprisond be,
    Whom I from far see on the walles appeare,
    Whose sight my feeble soule doth greatly cheare:
    And on the top of all I do espye
    The watchman wayting tydings glad to heare,
    That O my parents might I happily
Unto you bring, to ease you of your misery.

4

With that they heard a roaring hideous sound,
    That all the ayre with terrour filled wide,
    And seemd uneath to shake the stedfast ground.
    Eftsoones that dreadfull Dragon they espide,
    Where stretcht he lay upon the sunny side
    Of a great hill, himselfe like a great hill.
    But all so soone, as he from far descride
    Those glistring armes, that heaven with light did fill,
He rousd himselfe full blith, and hastned them untill.

5

Then bad the knight his Lady yede aloofe,
    And to an hill her selfe with draw aside,
    From whence she might behold that battailles proof
    And eke be safe from daunger far descryde:
    She him obayd, and turnd a little wyde.
    Now O thou sacred Muse, most learned Dame,

---

20 *brasen* made of brass
30 *uneath* uneasily
36 *untill* towards
37 *yede aloofe* go apart
39 *proof* outcome

>   Faire ympe of *Phœbus*, and his aged bride,
>   The Nourse of time, and everlasting fame,
>   That warlike hands ennoblest with immortall name;

6

> O gently come into my feeble brest,
>   Come gently, but not with that mighty rage,
>   Wherewith the martiall troupes thou doest infest,
>   And harts of great Heroës doest enrage,
>   That nought their kindled courage may aswage, 50
>   Soone as thy dreadfull trompe begins to sownd;
>   The God of warre with his fiers equipage
>   Thou doest awake, sleepe never he so sownd,
> And scared nations doest with horrour sterne astownd.

7

> Faire Goddesse lay that furious fit aside,
>   Till I of warres and bloudy *Mars* do sing,
>   And Briton fields with Sarazin bloud bedyde,
>   Twixt that great faery Queene and Paynim king,
>   That with their horrour heaven and earth did ring,
>   A worke of labour long, and endlesse prayse: 60
>   But now a while let downe that haughtie string,
>   And to my tunes thy second tenor rayse,
> That I this man of God his godly armes may blaze.

8

> By this the dreadfull Beast drew nigh to hand,
>   Halfe flying, and halfe footing in his hast,
>   That with his largenesse measured much land,
>   And made wide shadow under his huge wast;
>   As mountaine doth the valley overcast.

43 *his aged bride* Mnemosyne: memory
48 *infest* assail

[423-4]

    Approching nigh, he reared high afore
        His body monstrous, horrible, and vast,   70
        Which to increase his wondrous greatnesse more,
Was swolne with wrath, and poyson, and with bloudy gore.

9

And over, all with brasen scales was armd,
    Like plated coate of steele, so couched neare,
    That nought mote perce, ne might his corse be harmd
    With dint of sword, nor push of pointed speare;
    Which as an Eagle, seeing pray appeare,
    His aery plumes doth rouze, full rudely dight,
    So shaked he, that horrour was to heare,
    For as the clashing of an Armour bright,   80
Such noyse his rouzed scales did send unto the knight.

10

His flaggy wings when forth he did display,
    Were like two sayles, in which the hollow wynd
    Is gathered full, and worketh speedy way:
    And eke the pennes, that did his pineons bynd,
    Were like mayne-yards, with flying canvas lynd,
    With which whenas him list the ayre to beat,
    And there by force unwonted passage find,
    The cloudes before him fled for terrour great,
And all the heavens stood still amazed with his threat.   90

11

His huge long tayle wound up in hundred foldes,
    Does overspred his long bras-scaly backe,

---

75 *corse* body
78 *rouze* shake; *full rudely dight* with plumage raised in threat
82 *flaggy* folded
85 *the pennes, that did his pineons bynd* the ribs that bore up his wings

[423-4]

Whose wreathed boughts when ever he unfoldes,
And thicke entangled knots adown does slacke,
Bespotted as with shields of red and blacke,
It sweepeth all the land behind him farre,
And of three furlongs does but litle lacke;
And at the point two stings in-fixed arre,
Both deadly sharpe, that sharpest steele exceeden farre.

12

But stings and sharpest steele did far exceed
    The sharpnesse of his cruell rending clawes;
Dead was it sure, as sure as death in deed,
    What ever thing does touch his ravenous pawes,
    Or what within his reach he ever drawes.
But his most hideous head my toung to tell
    Does tremble: for his deepe devouring jawes
Wide gaped, like the griesly mouth of hell,
Through which into his darke abisse all ravin fell.

13

And that more wondrous was, in either jaw
    Threeranckes of yron teeth enraunged were,
In which yet trickling bloud and gobbets raw
    Of late devoured bodies did appeare,
    That sight thereof bred cold congealed feare:
Which to increase, and all atonce to kill,
    A cloud of smoothering smoke and sulphur seare
Out of his stinking gorge forth steemed still,
That all the ayre about with smoke and stench did fill.

93 *boughts* coils
108 *all ravin* all which he devoured

14

His blazing eyes, like two bright shining shields,
    Did burne with wrath, and sparkled living fyre;
    As two broad Beacons, set in open fields,
    Send forth their flames farre off to every shyre,
    And warning give, that enemies conspyre,
    With fire and sword the region to invade;
    So flam'd his eyne with rage and rancorous yre:
    But farre within, as in a hollow glade,
Those glaring lampes were set, that made a dreadfull shade.

15

So dreadfully he towards him did pas,
    Forelifting up aloft his speckled brest,
    And often bounding on the brused gras,
    As for great joyance of his newcome guest.
    Eftsoones he gan advance his haughtie crest,
    As chauffed Bore his bristles doth ypreare,
    And shoke his scales to battell readie drest;
    That made the *Redcrosse* knight nigh quake for feare,
As bidding bold defiance to his foeman neare.

16

The knight gan fairely couch his steadie speare,
    And fiercely ran at him with rigorous might:
    The pointed steele arriving rudely theare,
    His harder hide would neither perce, nor bight,
    But glauncing by forth passed forward right;
    Yet sore amoved with so puissant push,
    The wrathfull beast about him turned light,
    And him so rudely passing by, did brush
With his long tayle, that horse and man to ground did rush.

132 *chauffed* enraged

17

Both horse and man up lightly rose againe,
    And fresh encounter towards him addrest:
    But th'idle stroke yet backe recoyld in vaine,
    And found no place his deadly point to rest.
    Exceeding rage enflam'd the furious beast,
    To be avenged of so great despight;   150
    For never felt his imperceable brest
    So wondrous force, from hand of living wight;
Yet had he prov'd the powre of many a puissant knight.

18

Then with his waving wings displayed wyde,
    Himselfe up high he lifted from the ground,
    And with strong flight did forcibly divide
    The yielding aire, which nigh too feeble found
    Her flitting partes, and element unsound,
    To beare so great a weight: he cutting way
    With his broad sayles, about him soared round: 160
    At last low stouping with unweldie sway,
Snatcht up both horse and man, to beare them quite away.

19

Long he them bore above the subject plaine,
    So farre as Ewghen bow a shaft may send,
    Till struggling strong did him at last constraine,
    To let them downe before his flightes end:
    As hagard hauke presuming to contend
    With hardie fowle, above his hable might,
    His wearie pounces all in vaine doth spend,

158 *Her flitting partes* her unstable nature
164 *Ewghen* yew
167 *hagard* untamed
168 *hardie fowle* formidable game; *hable might* proper strength

>   To trusse the pray too heavie for his flight; 170
> Which comming downe to ground, does free it selfe by fight.

20

> He so disseized of his gryping grosse,
>   The knight his thrillant speare againe assayd
>   In his bras-plated body to embosse,
>   And three mens strength unto the stroke he layd;
>   Wherewith the stiffe beame quaked, as affrayd,
>   And glauncing from his scaly necke, did glyde
>   Close under his left wing, then broad displayd.
>   The percing steele there wrought a wound full wyde,
> That with the uncouth smart the Monster lowdly cryde. 180

21

> He cryde, as raging seas are wont to rore,
>   When wintry storme his wrathfull wreck does threat,
>   The rolling billowes beat the ragged shore,
>   As they the earth would shoulder from her seat,
>   And greedie gulfe does gape, as he would eat
>   His neighbour element in his revenge:
>   Then gin the blustring brethren boldly threat,
>   To move the world from off his stedfast henge,
> And boystrous battell make, each other to avenge.

170 *trusse* seize and carry off
172 *He so disseized of his gryping grosse* his powerful grip being broken in this way
174 *embosse* plunge
180 *uncouth* unfamiliar
186 *His neighbour element* the earth
187 *The blustring brethren* the winds
188 *henge* axis

22

The steely head stucke fast still in his flesh,
    Till with his cruell clawes he snatcht the wood,
    And quite a sunder broke. Forth flowed fresh
    A gushing river of blacke goarie blood,
    That drowned all the land, whereon he stood;
    The streame thereof would drive a water-mill.
    Trebly augmented was his furious mood
    With bitter sense of his deepe rooted ill,
That flames of fire he threw forth from his large nosethrill.

23

His hideous tayle then hurled he about,
    And therewith all enwrapt the nimble thyes
    Of his froth-fomy steed, whose courage stout
    Striving to loose the knot, that fast him tyes,
    Himselfe in streighter bandes too rash implyes,
    That to the ground he is perforce constraynd
    To throw his rider: who can quickly ryse
    From off the earth, with durty bloud distaynd,
For that reprochfull fall right fowly he disdaynd.

24

And fiercely tooke his trenchand blade in hand,
    With which he stroke so furious and so fell,
    That nothing seemd the puissance could withstand:
    Upon his crest the hardned yron fell,
    But his more hardned crest was armd so well,
    That deeper dint therein it would not make;
    Yet so extremely did the buffe him quell,
    That from thenceforth he shund the like to take,
But when he saw them come, he did them still forsake.

198 *nosethrill* nostril
203 *implyes* entangles
208 *trenchand* sharp

25

The knight was wrath to see his stroke beguyld,
   And smote againe with more outrageous might;
   But backe againe the sparckling steele recoyld,
   And left not any marke, where it did light; 220
   As if in Adamant rocke it had bene pight.
   The beast impatient of his smarting wound,
   And of so fierce and forcible despight,
   Thought with his wings to stye above the ground;
But his late wounded wing unserviceable found.

26

Then full of griefe and anguish vehement,
   He lowdly brayd, that like was never heard,
   And from his wide devouring oven sent
   A flake of fire, that flashing in his beard,
   Him all amazd, and almost made affeard: 230
   The scorching flame sore swinged all his face,
   And through his armour all his bodie seard,
   That he could not endure so cruell cace,
But thought his armes to leave, and helmet to unlace.

27

Not that great Champion of the antique world,
   Whom famous Poetes verse so much doth vaunt,
   And hath of twelve huge labours high extold,
   So many furies and sharpe fits did haunt,
   When him the poysoned garment did enchaunt
   With *Centaures* bloud, and bloudie verses charm'd, 240
   As did this knight twelve thousand dolours daunt,

---

217 *beguyld* foiled
221 *Adamant* diamond; *pight* directed
224 *stye* ascend
231 *swinged* singed

Whom fyrie steele now burnt, that earst him arm'd
That erst him goodly arm'd, now most of him harm'd.

28

Faint, wearie, sore, emboyled, grieved, brent
    With heat, toyle, wounds, armes, smart, and inward fire
    That never man such mischiefes did torment;
    Death better were, death did he oft desire,
    But death will never come, when needes require.
    Whom so dismayd when that his foe beheld,
    He cast to suffer him no more respire,
    But gan his sturdie sterne about to weld,
And him so strongly stroke, that to the ground him feld.

29

It fortuned (as faire it then befell)
    Behind his backe unweeting, where he stood,
    Of aunciént time there was a springing well,
    From which fast trickled forth a silver flood,
    Full of great vertues, and for med'cine good.
    Whylome, before that cursed Dragon got
    That happie land, and all with innocent blood
    Defyld those sacred waves, it rightly hot
The well of life, ne yet his vertues had forgot.

30

For unto life the dead it could restore,
    And guilt of sinfull crimes cleane wash away,
    Those that with sicknesse were infected sore,
    It could recure, and aged long decay
    Renew, as one were borne that very day.

251 *sterne* tail
254 *unweeting* unsuspected
260 *hot* was called

Both *Silo* this, and *Jordan* did excell,
And th'English *Bath*, and eke the german *Spau*,
Ne can *Cephise*, nor *Hebrus* match this well:
Into the same the knight backe overthrowen, fell.   270

31

Now gan the golden *Phœbus* for to steepe
    His fierie face in billowes of the west,
    And his faint steedes watred in Ocean deepe,
    Whiles from their journall labours they did rest,
    When that infernall Monster, having kest
    His wearie foe into that living well,
    Can high advance his broad discoloured brest,
    Above his wonted pitch, with countenance fell,
And clapt his yron wings, as victor he did dwell.

32

Which when his pensive Ladie saw from farre,   280
    Great woe and sorrow did her soule assay,
    As weening that the sad end of the warre,
    And gan to highest God entirely pray,
    That feared chance from her to turne away;
    With folded hands and knees full lowly bent
    All night she watcht, ne once adowne would lay
    Her daintie limbs in her sad dreriment,
But praying still did wake, and waking did lament.

33

The morrow next gan early to appeare,
    That *Titan* rose to runne his daily race;   290
    But early ere the morrow next gan reare
    Out of the sea faire *Titans* deawy face,

---

274 *journall* day-time
275 *kest* cast

Up rose the gentle virgin from her place,
And looked all about, if she might spy
Her loved knight to move his manly pace:
For she had great doubt of his safety,
Since late she saw him fall before his enemy.

34

At last she saw, where he upstarted brave
    Out of the well, wherein he drenched lay;
    As Eagle fresh out of the Ocean wave,   300
    Where he hath left his plumes all hoary gray,
    And deckt himselfe with feathers youthly gay,
    Like Eyas hauke up mounts unto the skies,
    His newly budded pineons to assay,
    And marveiles at himselfe, still as he flies:
So new this new-borne knight to battell new did rise.

35

Whom when the damned feend so fresh did spy,
    No wonder if he wondred at the sight,
    And doubted, whether his late enemy
    It were, or other new supplied knight.   310
    He, now to prove his late renewed might,
    High brandishing his bright deaw-burning blade,
    Upon his crested scalpe so sore did smite,
    That to the scull a yawning wound it made:
The deadly dint his dulled senses all dismaid.

36

I wote not whether the revenging steele
    Were hardned with that holy water dew,

---

295 *to move his manly pace* to be stirring
303 *Eyas hauke* young hawk
304 *pineons* flight-feathers

Wherein he fell, or sharper edge did feele,
Or his baptized hands now greater grew;
Or other secret vertue did ensew; 320
Else never could the force of fleshly arme,
Ne molten mettall in his bloud embrew:
For till that stownd could never wight him harme,
By subtilty, nor slight, nor might, nor mighty charme.

37

The cruell wound enraged him so sore,
   That loud he yelled for exceeding paine;
   As hundred ramping Lyons seem'd to rore,
   Whom ravenous hunger did thereto constraine:
   Then gan he tosse aloft his stretched traine,
   And therewith scourge the buxome aire so sore, 330
   That to his force to yeelden it was faine;
   Ne ought his sturdie strokes might stand afore,
That high trees overthrew, and rocks in peeces tore.

38

The same advauncing high above his head,
   With sharpe intended sting so rude him smot,
   That to the earth him drove, as stricken dead,
   Ne living wight would have him life behot:
   The mortall sting his angry needle shot
   Quite through his shield, and in his shoulder seasd,
   Where fast it stucke, ne would there out be got: 340
   The griefe thereof him wondrous sore diseasd,
Ne might his ranckling paine with patience be appeased.

---

329 *traine* tail
330 *buxome* yielding
335 *so rude him smot* struck him so savagely
337 *him life behot* held out hope for his life
339 *seasd* stuck
341 *diseasd* distressed

39

But yet more mindfull of his honour deare,
    Then of the grievous smart, which him did wring,
    From loathed soile he can him lightly reare,
    And strove to loose the farre infixed sting:
    Which when in vaine he tryde with struggeling,
    Inflam'd with wrath, his raging blade he heft,
    And strooke so strongly, that the knotty string
    Of his huge taile he quite a sunder cleft,   350
Five joynts thereof he hewd, and but the stump him left.

40

Hart cannot thinke, what outrage, and what cryes,
    With foule enfouldred smoake and flashing fire,
    The hell-bred beast threw forth unto the skyes,
    That all was covered with darknesse dire:
    Then fraught with rancour, and engorged ire,
    He cast at once him to avenge for all,
    And gathering up himselfe out of the mire,
    With his uneven wings did fiercely fall
Upon his sunne-bright shield, and gript it fast withall.   360

41

Much was the man encombred with his hold,
    In feare to lose his weapon in his paw,
    Ne wist yet, how his talents to unfold;
    Nor harder was from *Cerberus* greedie jaw
    To plucke a bone, then from his cruell claw
    To reave by strength the griped gage away:
    Thrise he assayd it from his foot to draw,
    And thrise in vaine to draw it did assay,
It booted nought to thinke, to robbe him of his pray.

344 *wring* pain
356 *engorged* devouring
366 *reave* snatch; *gage* prize

42

Tho when he saw no power might prevaile, 370
    His trustie sword he cald to his last aid,
    Wherewith he fiercely did his foe assaile,
    And double blowes about him stoutly laid,
    That glauncing fire out of the yron plaid;
    As sparckles from the Andvile use to fly,
    When heavie hammers on the wedge are swaid;
    Therewith at last he forst him to unty
One of his grasping feete, him to defend thereby.

43

The other foot, fast fixed on his shield,
    Whenas no strength, nor stroks mote him constraine 380
    To loose, ne yet the warlike pledge to yield,
    He smot thereat with all his might and maine,
    That nought so wondrous puissance might sustaine;
    Upon the joynt the lucky steele did light,
    And made such way, that hewd it quite in twaine;
    The paw yet missed not his minisht might,
But hong still on the shield, as it at first was pight.

44

For griefe thereof, and divelish despight,
    From his infernall fournace forth he threw
    Huge flames, that dimmed all the heavens light, 390
    Enrold in duskish smoke and brimstone blew;
    As burning *Aetna* from his boyling stew
    Doth belch out flames, and rockes in peeces broke,
    And ragged ribs of mountaines molten new,
    Enwrapt in coleblacke clouds and filthy smoke,
That all the land with stench, and heaven with horror choke.

376 *swaid* struck
386 *minisht* lessened
392 *Aetna* Mount Etna

45

The heate whereof, and harmefull pestilence
    So sore him noyd, that forst him to retire
    A little backward for his best defence,
    To save his bodie from the scorching fire,   400
    Which he from hellish entrailes did expire.
    It chaunst (eternall God that chaunce did guide)
    As he recoyled backward, in the mire
    His nigh forwearied feeble feet did slide,
And downe he fell, with dread of shame sore terrifide.

46

There grew a goodly tree him faire beside,
    Loaden with fruit and apples rosie red,
    As they in pure vermilion had beene dide,
    Whereof great vertues over all were red:
    For happie life to all, which thereon fed,   410
    And life eke everlasting did befall:
    Great God it planted in that blessed sted
    With his almightie hand, and did it call
The tree of life, the crime of our first fathers fall.

47

In all the world like was not to be found,
    Save in that soile, where all good things did grow,
    And freely sprong out of the fruitfull ground,
    As incorrupted Nature did them sow,
    Till that dread Dragon all did overthrow.
    Another like faire tree eke grew thereby,   420
    Whereof who so did eat, eftsoones did know
    Both good and ill: O mornefull memory:
That tree through one mans fault hath doen us all to dy.

---

401 *did expire* breathed out

48

From that first tree forth flowd, as from a well,
    A trickling streame of Balme, most soveraine
    And daintie deare, which on the ground still fell,
    And overflowed all the fertill plaine,
    As it had deawed bene with timely raine:
    Life and long health that gratious ointment gave,
    And deadly woundes could heale, and reare againe   430
    The senselesse corse appointed for the grave.
Into that same he fell: which did from death him save.

49

For nigh thereto the ever damned beast
    Durst not approch, for he was deadly made,
    And all that life preserved, did detest:
    Yet he it oft adventur'd to invade.
    By this the drouping day-light gan to fade,
    And yeeld his roome to sad succeeding night,
    Who with her sable mantle gan to shade
    The face of earth, and wayes of living wight,   440
And high her burning torch set up in heaven bright.

50

When gentle *Una* saw the second fall
    Of her deare knight, who wearie of long fight,
    And faint through losse of bloud, mov'd not at all,
    But lay as in a dreame of deepe delight,
    Besmeard with pretious Balme, whose vertuous might
    Did heale his wounds, and scorching heat alay,
    Againe she stricken was with sore affright,
    And for his safetie gan devoutly pray;
And watch the noyous night, and wait for joyous day.   450

---

426 *daintie deare* exquisitely precious
430 *reare* lift up
441 *her burning torch* the evening star

51

The joyous day gan early to appeare,
    And faire *Aurora* from the deawy bed
    Of aged *Tithone* gan her selfe to reare,
    With rosie cheekes, for shame as blushing red;
    Her golden lockes for haste were loosely shed
    About her eares, when *Una* her did marke
    Clymbe to her charet, all with flowers spred,
    From heaven high to chase the chearelesse darke;
With merry note her loud salutes the mounting larke.

52

Then freshly up arose the doughtie knight,
    All healed of his hurts and woundes wide,
    And did himselfe to battell readie dight;
    Whose early foe awaiting him beside
    To have devourd, so soone as day he spyde,
    When now he saw himselfe so freshly reare,
    As if late fight had nought him damnifyde,
    He woxe dismayd, and gan his fate to feare;
Nathlesse with wonted rage he him advaunced neare.

53

And in his first encounter, gaping wide,
    He thought attonce him to have swallowd quight,
    And rusht upon him with outragious pride;
    Who him r'encountring fierce, as hauke in flight,
    Perforce rebutted backe. The weapon bright
    Taking advantage of his open jaw,
    Ran through his mouth with so importune might,
    That deepe emperst his darksome hollow maw,
And back retyrd, his life bloud forth with all did draw.

---

466 *had nought him damnifyde* had injured him not at all
476 *emperst* pierced

54

So downe he fell, and forth his life did breath,
  That vanisht into smoke and cloudes swift;
So downe he fell, that th'earth him underneath
  Did grone, as feeble so great load to lift;
So downe he fell, as an huge rockie clift,
  Whose false foundation waves have washt away,
  With dreadfull poyse is from the mayneland rift,
  And rolling downe, great *Neptune* doth dismay;
So downe he fell, and like an heaped mountaine lay.

55

The knight himselfe even trembled at his fall,
  So huge and horrible a masse it seem'd;
And his deare Ladie, that beheld it all,
  Durst not approch for dread, which she misdeem'd,
But yet at last, when as the direfull feend
  She saw not stirre, off-shaking vaine affright,
  She nigher drew, and saw that joyous end:
  Then God she praysd, and thankt her faithfull knight,
That had atchiev'd so great a conquest by his might.

CANTO xii

Faire Una to the Redcrosse knight
betrouthed is with joy:
Though false Duessa it to barre
her false sleights doe imploy.

1

Behold I see the haven nigh at hand,
  To which I meane my wearie course to bend;

484 *poyse* weight

Vere the maine shete, and beare up with the land,
The which afore is fairely to be kend,
And seemeth safe from stormes, that may offend;
There this faire virgin wearie of her way
Must landed be, now at her journeyes end:
There eke my feeble barke a while may stay,
Till merry wind and weather call her thence away.

2

Scarsely had *Phœbus* in the glooming East
   Yet harnessed his firie-footed teeme,
   Ne reard above the earth his flaming creast,
   When the last deadly smoke aloft did steeme,
   That signe of last outbreathed life did seeme
   Unto the watchman on the castle wall;
   Who thereby dead that balefull Beast did deeme,
   And to his Lord and Ladie lowd gan call,
To tell, how he had seene the Dragons fatall fall.

3

Uprose with hastie joy, and feeble speed
   That aged Sire, the Lord of all that land,
   And looked forth, to weet, if true indeede
   Those tydings were, as he did understand,
   Which whenas true by tryall he out fond,
   He bad to open wyde his brazen gate,
   Which long time had bene shut, and out of hond
   Proclaymed joy and peace through all his state;
For dead now was their foe, which them forrayed late.

---

3 *Vere* shift; *beare up with* put the helm towards
8 *barke* ship
27 *forrayed* ravaged

4

Then gan triumphant Trompets sound on hie,
    That sent to heaven the ecchoed report
    Of their new joy, and happie victorie   30
    Gainst him, that had them long opprest with tort,
    And fast imprisoned in sieged fort.
    Then all the people, as in solemne feast,
    To him assembled with one full consort,
    Rejoycing at the fall of that great beast,
From whose eternall bondage now they were releast.

5

Forth came that aunicent Lord and aged Queene,
    Arayd in antique robes downe to the ground,
    And sad habiliments right well beseene;
    A noble crew about them waited round   40
    Of sage and sober Peres, all gravely gownd;
    Whom farre before did march a goodly band
    Of tall young men, all hable armes to sownd,
    But now they laurell braunches bore in hand;
Glad signe of victorie and peace in all their land.

6

Unto that doughtie Conquerour they came,
    And him before themselves prostrating low,
    Their Lord and Patrone loud did him proclame,
    And at his feet their laurell boughes did throw.

---

31 *tort* injury
34 *full consort* whole company
38 *antique* in the style of long ago
39 *sad* sober; *habiliments* array
43 *hable armes to sownd* skilled with clashing weapons
44 *laurell braunches* in token of victory
46 *doughtie* redoubtable

Soone after them all dauncing on a row 50
   The comely virgins came, with girlands dight,
   As fresh as flowres in medow greene do grow,
   When morning deaw upon their leaves doth light:
And in their hands sweet Timbrels all upheld on hight.

7

And them before, the fry of children yong
   Their wanton sports and childish mirth did play,
   And to the Maydens sounding tymbrels sung
   In well attuned notes, a joyous lay,
   And made delightfull musicke all the way,
   Until they came, where that faire virgin stood; 60
   As faire *Diana* in fresh sommers day
   Beholds her Nymphes, enraung'd in shadie wood,
Some wrestle, some do run, some bathe in christall flood.

8

So she beheld those maydens meriment
   With chearefull vew; who when to her they came,
   Themselves to ground with gratious humblesse bent,
   And her ador'd by honorable name,
   Lifting to heaven her everlasting fame:
   Then on her head they set a girland greene,
   And crowned her twixt earnest and twixt game; 70
   Who in her selfe-resemblance well beseene,
Did seeme such, as she was, a goodly maiden Queene.

54 *Timbrels* small tambourines
55 *fry* crowd
56 *wanton* carefree

9

And after, all the raskall many ran,
    Heaped together in rude rablement,
    To see the face of that victorious man:
    Whom all admired, as from heaven sent,
    And gazd upon with gaping wonderment.
    But when they came, where that dead Dragon lay,
    Stretcht on the ground in monstrous large extent,
    The sight with idle feare did them dismay,   80
Ne durst approch him nigh, to touch, or once assay.

10

Some feard, and fled; some feard and well it faynd;
    One that would wiser seeme, then all the rest,
    Warnd him not touch, for yet perhaps remaynd
    Some lingring life within his hollow brest,
    Or in his wombe might lurke some hidden nest
    Of many Dragonets, his fruitful seed;
    Another said, that in his eyes did rest
    Yet sparckling fire, and bad thereof take heed;
Another said, he saw him move his eyes indeed.   90

11

One mother, when as her foolehardie chyld
    Did come too neare, and with his talants play,
    Halfe dead through feare, her litle babe revyld,
    And to her gossips gan in counsell say;
    How can I tell, but that his talants may
    Yet scratch my sonne, or rend his tender hand?

73 *the raskall many* the common people
74 *in rude rablement* in a disordered crowd
80 *idle* foolish
82 *faynd* concealed
86 *wombe* belly
87 *Dragonets* baby dragons

93 *revyld* rebuked
94 *gossips* friends

[424–5]

So diversly themselves in vaine they fray;
  Whiles some more bold, to measure him nigh stand,
To prove how many acres he did spread of land.

12

Thus flocked all the folke him round about,   100
  The whiles that hoarie king, with all his traine,
  Being arrived, where that champion stout
  After his foes defeasance did remaine,
  Him goodly greetes, and faire does entertaine,
  With princely gifts of yvorie and gold,
  And thousand thankes him yeelds for all his paine.
  Then when his daughter deare he does behold,
Her dearely doth imbrace, and kisseth manifold.

13

And after to his Pallace he them brings,
  With shaumes, and trompets, and with Clarions sweet;   110
  And all the way the joyous people sings,
  And with their garments strowes the paved street:
  Whence mounting up, they find purveyance meet
  Of all, that royall Princes court became,
  And all the floore was underneath their feet
  Bespred with costly scarlot of great name,
On which they lowly sit, and fitting purpose frame.

14

What needs me tell their feast and goodly guize,
  In which was nothing riotous nor vaine?

103 *defeasance* defeat
108 *manifold* many times
110 *shaumes* instruments related to the oboe; *Clarions* shrill-sounding trumpets
113 *purveyance* provision
116 *of great name* of fine quality
117 *fitting purpose frame* take counsel

What needs of daintie dishes to devize, 120
Of comely services, or courtly trayne?
My narrow leaves cannot in them containe
The large discourse of royall Princes state.
Yet was their manner then but bare and plaine:
For th'antique world excesse and pride did hate;
Such proud luxurious pompe is swollen up but late.

15

Then when with meates and drinkes of every kinde
   Their fervent appetites they quenched had,
   That aunciant Lord gan fit occasion finde,
   Of straunge adventures, and of perils sad, 130
   Which in his travell him befallen had,
   For to demaund of his renowmed guest:
   Who then with utt'rance grave, and count'nance sad,
   From point to point, as is before exprest,
Discourst his voyage long, according his request.

16

Great pleasure mixt with pittifull regard,
   That godly King and Queene did passionate,
   Whiles they his pittifull adventures heard,
   That oft they did lament his lucklesse state,
   And often blame the too importune fate, 140
   That heapd on him so many wrathfull wreakes:
   For never gentle knight, as he of late,
   So tossed was in fortunes cruell freakes;
And all the while salt teares bedeawd the hearers cheaks.

---

121 *trayne* ceremony
125 *antique* ancient
137 *passionate* express
140 *importune* demanding
141 *wreakes* misfortunes

17

Then said that royall Pere in sober wise;
    Deare Sonne, great beene the evils, which ye bore
    From first to last in your late enterprise,
    That I note, whether prayse, or pitty more:
    For never living man, I weene, so sore
    In sea of deadly daungers was distrest;   150
    But since now safe ye seised have the shore,
    And well arrived are, (high God be blest)
Let us devize of ease and everlasting rest.

18

Ah dearest Lord, said then that doughty knight,
    Of ease or rest I may not yet devize;
    For by the faith, which I to armes have plight,
    I bounden am streight after this emprize,
    As that your daughter can ye well advize,
    Backe to returne to that great Faerie Queene,
    And her to serve six yeares in warlike wize,   160
    Gainst that proud Paynim king, that workes her teene:
Therefore I ought crave pardon, till I there have beene.

19

Unhappie falles that hard necessitie,
    (Quoth he) the troubler of my happie peace,
    And vowed foe of my felicitie;
    Ne I against the same can justly preace:
    But since that band ye cannot now release,
    Nor doen undo; (for vowes may not be vaine)
    Soone as the terme of those six yeares shall cease,

---

148 *note* know not
161 *teene* injury
162 *I ought crave pardon* I must excuse myself
166 *preace* object

Ye then shall hither backe returne againe, 170
The marriage to accomplish vowd betwixt you twain.

20

Which for my part I covet to performe,
  In sort as through the world I did proclame,
  That who so kild that monster most deforme,
  And him in hardy battaile overcame,
  Should have mine onely daughter to his Dame,
  And of my kingdome heire apparaunt bee:
  Therefore since now to thee perteines the same,
  By dew desert of noble chevalree,
Both daughter and eke kingdome, lo I yield to thee. 180

21

Then forth he called that his daughter faire,
  The fairest *Un'* his onely daughter deare,
  His onely daughter, and his onely heyre;
  Who forth proceeding with sad sober cheare,
  As bright as doth the morning starre appeare
  Out of the East, with flaming lockes bedight,
  To tell that dawning day is drawing neare,
  And to the world does bring long wishèd light;
So faire and fresh that Lady shewd her selfe in sight.

22

So faire and fresh, as freshest flowre in May; 190
  For she had layd her mournefull stole aside,
  And widow-like sad wimple throwne away,
  Wherewith her heavenly beautie she did hide,

173 *In sort as* just as
174 *deforme* hideous
176 *to his Dame* as his wife;
178 *perteines* belongs
179 *By dew desert* as the reward due to

Whiles on her wearie journey she did ride;
And on her now a garment she did weare,
All lilly white, withoutten spot, or pride,
That seemd like silke and silver woven neare,
But neither silke nor silver therein did appeare.

23

The blazing brightnesse of her beauties beame,
    And glorious light of her sunshyny face
    To tell, were as to strive against the streame.
    My ragged rimes are all too rude and bace,
    Her heavenly lineaments for to enchace.
    Ne wonder; for her owne deare loved knight,
    All were she dayly with himselfe in place,
    Did wonder much at her celestiall sight:
Oft had he seene her faire, but never so faire dight.

24

So fairely dight, when she in presence came,
    She to her Sire made humble reverence,
    And bowed low, that her right well became,
    And added grace unto her excellence:
    Who with great wisedome, and grave eloquence
    Thus gan to say. But eare he thus had said,
    With flying speede, and seeming great pretence,
    Came running in, much like a man dismaid,
A Messenger with letters, which his message said.

25

All in the open hall amazed stood,
    At suddeinnesse of that unwarie sight,

---

202 *rude and bace* rustic and dull
203 *lineaments* features; *enchace* present
214 *pretence* urgency

And wondred at his breathlesse hastie mood.
But he for nought would stay his passage right, 220
Till fast before the king he did alight;
Where falling flat, great humblesse he did make,
And kist the ground, whereon his foot was pight;
Then to his hands that writ he did betake,
Which he disclosing, red thus, as the paper spake.

26

To thee, most mighty king of *Eden* faire,
   Her greeting sends in these sad lines addrest,
   The wofull daughter, and forsaken heire
   Of that great Emperour of all the West;
   And bids thee be advized for the best, 230
   Ere thou thy daughter linck in holy band
   Of wedlocke to that new unknowen guest:
   For he already plighted his right hand
Unto another love, and to another land.

27

To me sad mayd, or rather widow sad,
   He was affiaunced long time before,
   And sacred pledges he both gave, and had,
   False erraunt knight, infamous, and forswore:
   Witnesse the burning Altars, which he swore,
   And guiltie heavens of his bold perjury, 240
   Which though he hath polluted oft of yore,
   Yet I to them for judgement just do fly,
And them conjure t'avenge this shamefull injury.

28

Therefore since mine he is, or free or bond,
   Or false or trew, or living or else dead,

239 *which* on which

Withhold, O soveraine Prince, your hasty hond
  From knitting league with him, I you aread;
  Ne weene my right with strength adowne to tread,
  Through weakenesse of my widowhed, or woe:
  For truth is strong, her rightfull cause to plead, 250
  And shall find friends, if need requireth soe,
So bids thee well to fare, Thy neither friend, nor foe, *Fidessa*.

29

When he these bitter byting words had red,
  The tydings straunge did him abashed make,
  That still he sate long time astonished
  As in great muse, ne word to creature spake.
  At last his solemne silence thus he brake,
  With doubtfull eyes fast fixed on his guest;
  Redoubted knight, that for mine only sake
  Thy life and honour late adventurest, 260
Let nought be hid from me, that ought to be exprest.

30

What meane these bloudy vowes, and idle threats,
  Throwne out from womanish impatient mind?
  What heavens? what altars? what enraged heates
  Here heaped up with termes of love unkind,
  My conscience cleare with guilty bands would bind?
  High God be witnesse, that I guiltlesse ame.
  But if your selfe, Sir knight, ye faultie find,
  Or wrapped be in loves of former Dame,
With crime do not it cover, but disclose the same. 270

247 *aread* warn
248 *Ne weene* think not
256 *muse* thought

31

To whom the *Redcrosse* knight this answere sent,
   My Lord, my King, be nought hereat dismayd,
   Till well ye wote by grave intendiment,
   What woman, and wherefore doth me upbrayd
   With breach of love, and loyalty betrayd.
   It was in my mishaps, as hitherward
   I lately traveild, that unwares I strayd
     Out of my way, through perils straunge and hard;
That day should faile me, ere I had them all declard.

32

There did I find, or rather I was found
   Of this false woman, that *Fidessa* hight,
   Fidessa hight the falsest Dame on ground,
   Most false *Duessa*, royall richly dight,
   That easie was t'invegle weaker sight:
   Who by her wicked arts, and whylie skill,
   Too false and strong for earthly skill or might,
     Unwares me wrought unto her wicked will,
And to my foe betrayd, when least I feared ill.

33

Then stepped forth the goodly royall Mayd,
   And on the ground her selfe prostrating low,
   With sober countenaunce thus to him sayd;
   O pardon me, my soveraigne Lord, to show
   The secret treasons, which of late I know
   To have bene wroght by that false sorceresse.
   She onely she it is, that earst did throw
     This gentle knight into so great distresse,
That death him did awaite in dayly wretchednesse.

---

273 *grave intendiment* careful understanding
284 *t'invegle* to deceive

34

And now it seemes, that she suborned hath
    This craftie messenger with letters vaine,
    To worke new woe and improvided scath,
    By breaking of the band betwixt us twaine;
    Wherein she used hath the practicke paine
    Of this false footman, clokt with simplenesse,
    Whom if ye please for to discover plaine,
    Ye shall him *Archimago* find, I ghesse,
The falsest man alive; who tries shall find no lesse.

35

The king was greatly moved at her speach,
    And all with suddein indignation fraight,
    Bad on that Messenger rude hands to reach.
    Eftsoones the Gard, which on his state did wait,
    Attacht that faitor false, and bound him strait:
    Who seeming sorely chauffed at his band,
    As chained Beare, whom cruell dogs do bait,
    With idle force did faine them to withstand,
And often semblaunce made to scape out of their hand.

36

But they him layd full low in dungeon deepe,
    And bound him hand and foote with yron chains.
    And with continuall watch did warely keepe;

---

298 *suborned* induced
300 *improvided scath* unlooked-for harm
302 *practicke paine* cunning art
303 *clokt* disguised
308 *fraight* moved
309 *rude* rough
311 *faitor* impostor
312 *chauffed* enraged
314 *idle* useless

Who then would thinke, that by his subtile trains
    He could escape fowle death or deadly paines?
Thus when that Princes wrath was pacifide,
    He gan renew the late forbidden banes,
    And to the knight his daughter deare he tyde,
With sacred rites and vowes for ever to abyde.

37

His owne two hands the holy knots did knit,
    That none but death for ever can devide;
His owne two hands, for such a turne most fit,
    The housling fire did kindle and provide,
    And holy water thereon sprinckled wide;
At which the bushy Teade a groome did light,
    And sacred lampe in secret chamber hide,
    Where it should not be quenched day nor night,
For feare of evill fates, but burnen ever bright.

38

Then gan they sprinckle all the posts with wine,
    And made great feast to solemnize that day;
They all perfumde with frankincense divine,
    And precious odours fetcht from far away,
    That all the house did sweat with great aray:
And all the while sweete Musicke did apply
    Her curious skill, the warbling notes to play,
    To drive away the dull Melancholy;
The whiles one sung a song of love and jollity.

---

322 *banes* banns
328 *housling* sacramental
330 *Teade* torch
338 *aray* splendour

39

During the which there was an heavenly noise
    Heard sound through all the Pallace pleasantly,
    Like as it had bene many an Angels voice,
    Singing before th'eternall majesty,
    In their trinall triplicities on hye;
    Yet wist no creature, whence that heavenly sweet
    Proceeded, yet each one felt secretly
    Himselfe thereby reft of his sences meet,
And ravished with rare impression in his sprite.

40

Great joy was made that day of young and old,
    And solemne feast proclaimd throughout the land,
    That their exceeding merth may not be told:
    Suffice it heare by signes to understand
    The usuall joyes at knitting of loves band.
    Thrise happy man the knight himselfe did hold,
    Possessed of his Ladies hart and hand,
    And ever, when his eye did her behold,
His heart did seeme to melt in pleasures manifold.

41

Her joyous presence and sweet company
    In full content he there did long enjoy,
    Ne wicked envie, ne vile gealosy
    His deare delights were able to annoy:
    Yet swimming in that sea of blisfull joy,
    He nought forgot, how he whilome had sworne,
    In case he could that monstrous beast destroy,
    Unto his Farie Queene backe to returne:
The which he shortly did, and *Una* left to mourne.

---

347 *trinall* threefold

42

Now strike your sailes ye jolly Mariners,　　　　　　　　　　370
　　For we be come unto a quiet rode,
　　Where we must land some of our passengers,
　　And light this wearie vessell of her lode.
　　Here she a while may make her safe abode,
　　Till she repaired have her tackles spent,
　　And wants supplide. And then againe abroad
　　On the long voyage whereto she is bent:
Well may she speede and fairely finish her intent.

371 *rode* channel
375 *tackles spent* worn-out gear

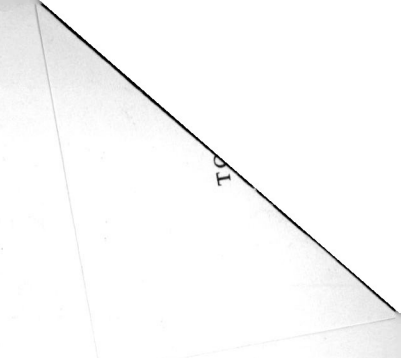

The Faerie Queene: Dedicatory Sonnets

TO THE MOST RENOWMED AND VALIANT LORD,
THE LORD GREY OF WILTON, KNIGHT OF THE
NOBLE ORDER OF THE GARTER, &C.

Most Noble Lord the pillor of my life,
    And Patrone of my Muses pupillage,
    Through whose large bountie poured on me rife,
    In the first season of my feeble age,
I now doe live, bound yours by vassalage:
    Sith nothing ever may redeeme, nor reave
    Out of your endlesse debt so sure a gage,
    Vouchsafe in worth this small guift to receave,
Which in your noble hands for pledge I leave,
    Of all the rest, that I am tyde t'account: 10
    Rude rymes, the which a rustick Muse did weave
    In savadge soyle, far from Parnasso mount,
And roughly wrought in an unlearned Loome:
The which vouchsafe dear Lord your favourable doome.

  3 *rife* abundantly
  6 *Sith* since; *reave* remove
  7 *your endlesse debt* the measureless debt I owe you; *gage* pledge
  8 *Vouchsafe* deign; *in worth* favourably
  9 *pledge* token
 10 *Of all ... t'account* of all else for which I am beholden to you
 11 *Rude* rough
 12 *savadge soyle* barbarous land: Ireland; *Parnasso mount* Parnassus, the haunt of the Muses
 14 *doome* judgement

TO THE RIGHT NOBLE AND VALOROUS KNIGHT, SIR WALTER RALEIGH, LO. WARDEIN OF THE STANNERYES, AND LIEFTENAUNT OF CORNEWAILE

To thee that art the sommers Nightingale,
    Thy soveraine Goddesses most deare delight,
    Why doe I send this rusticke Madrigale,
    That may thy tunefull eare unseason quite?
Thou onely fit this Argument to write,
    In whose high thoughts Pleasure hath built her bowre,
    And dainty love learnd sweetly to endite.
    My rimes I know unsavory and sowre,
To tast the streames, that like a golden showre
    Flow from thy fruitful head, of thy loves praise,   10
    Fitter perhaps to thonder Martiall stowre,
    When so thee list thy lofty Muse to raise:
Yet till that thou thy Poeme wilt make knowne,
    Let thy faire Cinthias praises bee thus rudely showne.

    Stanneryes Stanneries: the mining districts of Devon and Cornwall
3 *rusticke Madrigale* simple song
5 *this Argument to write* to write of this subject
7 *learnd* taught; *endite* write of
9 *To tast* taste of
11 *Martiall stowre* warlike strife
14 *rudely* roughly

TO THE RIGHT HONOURABLE AND MOST
VERTUOUS LADY, THE COUNTESSE OF PENBROKE

Remembraunce of that most Heroicke spirit,
    The hevens pride, the glory of our daies,
    Which now triumpheth through immortall merit
    Of his brave vertues, crowned with lasting baies,
Of hevenlie blis and everlasting praies;
    Who first my Muse did lift out of the flore,
    To sing his sweet delights in lowlie laies;
    Bids me most noble Lady to adore
His goodly image living evermore,
    In the divine resemblaunce of your face;   10
    Which with your vertues ye embellish more,
    And native beauty deck with hevenlie grace:
For his, and for your owne especial sake,
    Vouchsafe from him this token in good worth to take.

Penbroke Pembroke
4 *baies* bays
6 *flore* ground
12 *native* natural
14 *in good worth* graciously

The Faerie Queene: A Letter of the Authors expounding his whole intention in the course of this work

which for that it giveth great light to the Reader, for the better understanding is hereunto annexed

To the Right noble, and Valorous, Sir Walter Raleigh knight, Lo. Wardein of the Stanneryes, and her Majesties liefetenaunt of the County of Cornewayll

Sir knowing how doubtfully all Allegories may be construed, and this booke of mine, which I have entituled the Faery Queene, being a continued Allegory, or darke conceit, I have thought good aswell for avoyding of gealous opinions and misconstructions, as also for your better light in reading thereof, (being so by you commanded,) to discover unto you the general intention and meaning, which in the whole course therof I have fashioned, without expressing of any particular purposes or by-accidents therein occasioned. The generall

---

1 *doubtfully* uncertainly; *construed* interpreted
3 *darke conceit* concept indirectly expressed
6 *discover* make known
7 *expressing* interpreting
8 *by-accidents* incidentals

[426–8]

end therefore of all the booke is to fashion a gentleman or noble person in vertuous and gentle discipline: Which for that I conceived shoulde be most plausible and pleasing, being coloured with an historicall fiction, the which the most part of men delight to read, rather for variety of matter, then for profite of the ensample: I chose the historye of king Arthure, as most fitte for the excellency of his person, being made famous by many mens former workes, and also furthest from the daunger of envy, and suspition of present time. In which I have followed all the antique Poets historicall, first Homere, who in the Persons of Agamemnon and Ulysses hath ensampled a good governour and a vertuous man, the one in his Ilias, the other in his Odysseis: then Virgil, whose like intention was to doe in the person of Aeneas: after him Ariosto comprised them both in his Orlando: and lately Tasso dissevered them againe, and formed both parts in two persons, namely that part which they in Philosophy call Ethice, or vertues of a private man, coloured in his Rinaldo. The other named Politice in his Godfredo. By ensample of which excellente Poets, I labour to pourtraict in Arthure, before he was king, the image of a brave knight, perfected in the twelve private morall vertues, as Aristotle hath devised, the which is the purpose of these first twelve bookes; which if I finde to be well accepted, I may be perhaps encoraged, to frame the other part of polliticke vertues in his person, after that hee came to be king. To some I know this Methode will seeme displeasaunt, which had rather have good discipline delivered plainly in way of precepts, or sermoned at large, as they use, then thus clowdily enwrapped in Allegoricall devises But such, me seeme, should be satisfide with the use of these dayes, seeing all things accounted by their showes, and nothing esteemed of, that is not delightfull and pleasing to commune sence. For this cause is Xenophon preferred before Plato, for that the one in the exquisite depth of his judgement formed a Commune welth such as it should be, but the other in the person of Cyrus and the Persians fashioned a

9 *fashion* portray
10 *gentle* noble
12 *fiction* invention
13 *ensample* example
32 *discipline* teaching
36 *showes* appearances

governement such as might best be: So much more profitable and
gratious is doctrine by ensample, then by rule. So have I laboured to
doe in the person of Arthure: whome I conceive after his long
education by Timon, to whom he was by Merlin delivered to be
brought up, so soone as he was borne of the Lady Igrayne, to have
seene in a dream or vision the Faery Queen, with whose excellent
beauty ravished, he awaking resolved to seeke her out, and so being
by Merlin armed, and by Timon throughly instructed, he went to
seeke her forth in Faerye land. In that Faery Queene I meane glory in
my generall intention, but in my particular I conceive the most
excellent and glorious person of our soveraine the Queene, and her
kingdome in Faery land. And yet in some places els, I doe otherwise
shadow her. For considering she beareth two persons, the one of a
most royall Queene or Empresse, the other of a most vertuous and
beautifull Lady, this latter part in some places I doe express in
Belphœbe, fashioning her name according to your owne excellent
conceipt of Cynthia, (Phœbe and Cynthia being both names of
Diana.) So in the person of Prince Arthure I sette forth magnificence
in particular, which vertue for that (according to Aristotle and the
rest) it is the perfection of all the rest, and conteineth in it them all,
therefore in the whole course I mention the deedes of Arthure apply-
able to that vertue, which I write in that booke. But of the xii. other
vertues, I make xii. other knights the patrones, for the more variety
of the history: Of which these three bookes contayn three. The first
of the knight of the Redcrosse, in whome I express Holynes: The
seconde of Sir Guyon, in whome I sette forth Temperaunce: The
third of Britomartis a Lady knight, in whome I picture Chastity. But
because the beginning of the whole worke seemeth abrupte and as
depending upon other antecedents, it needs that ye know the occa-
sion of these three knights severall adventures. For the Methode of a
Poet historical is not such, as of an Historiographer. For an Histor-
iogapher discourseth of affayres orderly as they were donne,
accounting as well the times as the actions, but a Poet thrusteth into
the middest, even where it most concerneth him, and there recours-

58 *magnificence* magnanimity, 'great-mindedness'
69 *antecedents* earlier events
71 *Historiographer* historian
72 *orderly* in sequence

[426-8]

ing to the thinges forepaste, and divining of thinges to come, maketh a pleasing Analysis of all. The beginning therefore of my history, if it were to be told by an Historiographer, should be the twelfth booke, which is the last, where I devise that the Faery Queene kept her Annuall feaste xii. dayes, uppon which xii. severall dayes, the occasions of the xii. severall adventures hapned, which being undertaken by xii. severall knights, are in these xii books severally handled and discoursed. The first was this. In the beginning of the feast, there presented him selfe a tall clownishe younge man, who falling before the Queen of Faries desired a boone (as the manner then was) which during that feast she might not refuse: which was that hee might have the atchievement of any adventure, which during that feaste should happen, that being graunted, he rested him on the floore, unfitte through his rusticity for a better place. Soone after entred a faire Ladye in mourning weedes, riding on a white Asse, with a dwarfe behind her leading a warlike steed, that bore the Armes of a knight, and his speare in the dwarfes hand. Shee falling before the Queene of Faeries, complayned that her father and mother an ancient King and Queene, had bene by an huge dragon many years shut up in a brasen Castle, who thence suffred them not to yssew: and therefore besought the Faery Queene to assygne her some one of her knights to take on him that exployt. Presently that clownish person upstarting, desired that adventure: whereat the Queene much wondering, and the Lady much gainesaying, yet he earnestly importuned his desire. In the end the Lady told him that unlesse that armour which she brought, would serve him (that is the armour of a Christian man specified by Saint Paul vi. Ephes.) that he could not succeed in that enterprise, which being forthwith put upon him with dewe furnitures thereunto, he seemed the goodliest man in al that company, and was well liked of the Lady. And eftesoones taking on him knighthood, and mounting on that straunge Courser, he went forth with her on that adventure: where beginneth the first booke, vz.

76 *Analysis* arrangement
83 *clownishe* uncouth
89 *weedes* garments
94 *brasen* brass; *yessew* go out
98 *gainesaying* objecting
103 *dewe furnitures* fitting accoutrements

283

[426–8]

A gentle knight was pricking on the playne. &c.

The second day ther came in a Palmer bearing an Infant with bloody hands, whose Parents he complained to have bene slayn by an Enchaunteresse called Acrasia: and therfore craved of the Faery Queene, to appoint him some knight, to performe that adventure, which being assigned to Sir Guyon, he presently went forth with that same Palmer: which is the beginning of the second booke and the whole subject thereof. The third day there came in, a Groome who complained before the Faery Queene, that a vile Enchaunter called Busirane had in hand a most faire Lady called Amoretta, whom he kept in most grievous torment, because she would not yield him the pleasure of her body. Whereupon Sir Scudamour the lover of that Lady presently tooke on him that adventure. But being unable to performe it by reason of the hard Enchauntments, after long sorrow, in the end met with Britomartis, who succoured him, and reskewed his love.

But by occasion hereof, many other adventures are intermedled, but rather as Accidents, then intendments. As the love of Britomart, the overthrow of Marinell, the misery of Florimell, the vertuousnes of Belphœbe, the lasciviousnes of Hellenora, and many the like.

Thus much Sir, I have briefly overronne to direct your understanding to the wel-head of the History, that from thence gathering the whole intention of the conceit, ye may as in a handfull gripe al the discourse, which otherwise may happily seeme tedious and confused. So humbly craving the continuance of your honorable favour towards me, and th' eternall establishment of your happines, I humbly take leave.

> 23 January 1589
> Yours most humbly affectionate
> Ed. Spenser

108 *Palmer* pilgrim
114 *Groome* young man
121 *succoured* helped
124 *Accidents* additions; *intendments* essentials
127 *overronne* gone through
129 *gripe* grasp
130 *happily* by chance

Complaints

MUIOPOTMOS, OR THE FATE OF THE BUTTERFLIE

To the right worthy and vertuous Ladie; the La: *Carey*

Most brave and bountifull La: for so excellent favours as I have received at your sweet handes, to offer these fewe leaves as in recompence, should be as to offer flowers to the Gods for their divine benefites. Therefore I have determined to give my selfe wholy to you, as quite abandoned from my selfe, and absolutely vowed to your services: which in all right is ever held for full recompence of debt or damage to have the person yeelded. My person I wot wel how little worth it is. But the faithfull minde and humble zeale which I beare unto your La: may perhaps be more of price, as may please you to account and use the poore service thereof; which taketh glory to advance your excellent partes and noble vertues, and to spend it selfe in honouring you: not so much for your great bounty to my self, which yet may not be unminded; nor for name or kindreds sake by you vouchsafed, beeing also regardable; as for that honorable name,

---

2 *leaves* pages
11 *partes* qualities
13 *unminded* unremembered

[428–30]

which yee have by your brave deserts purchast to your self, and spred
in the mouths of al men: with which I have also presumed to grace
my verses, and under your name to commend to the world this small
Poëme, the which beseeching your La: to take in worth, and of all
things therein according to your wonted graciousnes to make a
milde construction, I humbly pray for your happines. 20

Your La: ever
humbly;
E.S.

I sing of deadly dolorous debate,
Stir'd up through wrathfull *Nemesis* despight,
Betwixt two mightie ones of great estate,
Drawne into armes, and proofe of mortall fight,
Through prowd ambition, and hartswelling hate,
Whilest neither could the others greater might
And sdeignfull scorne endure; that from small jarre
Their wraths at length broke into open warre.

The roote whereof and tragicall effect,
Vouchsafe, O thou the mournfulst Muse of nyne, 10
That wontst the tragick stage for to direct,
In funerall complaints and waylfull tyne,
Reveale, to me, and all the meanes detect,
Through which sad *Clarion* did at last declyne
To lowest wretchednes; And is there then
Such rancour in the harts of mightie men?

Of all the race of silver-winged Flies
Which doo possesse the Empire of the aire,
Betwixt the centred earth, and azure skies,

18 *take in worth* receive favourably
19–20 *a milde construction* a kindly interpretation
 2 *despight* anger
 4 *proofe* trial
 7 *sdeignfull* disdainful; *jarre* discord
12 *tyne* grief

Was none more favourable, nor more faire, 20
Whilst heaven did favour his felicities,
Then *Clarion*, the eldest sonne and haire
Of *Muscaroll*, and in his fathers sight
Of all alive did seeme the fairest wight.

With fruitfull hope his aged breast he fed
Of future good, which his yong toward yeares,
Full of brave courage and bold hardyhed,
Above th'ensample of his equall peares,
Did largely promise, and to him forered
(Whilst oft his heart did melt in tender teares) 30
That he in time would sure prove such an one,
As should be worthie of his fathers throne.

The fresh yong flie, in whom the kindly fire
Of lustfull youngth began to kindle fast,
Did much disdaine to subject his desire
To loathesome sloth, or houres in ease to wast,
But joy'd to range abroad in fresh attire;
Through the wide compas of the ayrie coast,
And with unwearied wings each part t'inquire
Of the wide rule of his renowmed sire. 40

For he so swift and nimble was of flight,
That from this lower tract he dar'd to stie
Up to the clowdes, and thence with pineons light,
To mount aloft unto the Christall skie,
To vew the workmanship of heavens hight:
Whence downe descending he along would flie

  20 *favourable* favoured
  21 *felicities* happiness
  26 *toward* promising
  28 *equall peares* fellows in rank
  29 *largely* greatly; *forered* foretold
  33 *kindly* natural
  38 *coast* region
  42 *lower tract* journey near the earth's surface; *stie* mount

Upon the streaming rivers, sport to finde;
And oft would dare to tempt the troublous winde.

So on a Summers day, when season milde
With gentle calme the world had quieted, 50
And high in heaven *Hyperions* fierie childe
Ascending, did his beames abroad dispred,
Whiles all the heavens on lower creatures smilde;
Yong *Clarion* with vauntfull lustie head,
After his guize did cast abroad to fare;
And theretoo gan his furnitures prepare.

His breastplate first, that was of substance pure,
Before his noble heart he firmely bound,
That mought his life from yron death assure,
And ward his gentle corpes from cruell wound: 60
For it by arte was framed, to endure
The bit of balefull steele and bitter stownd,
No lesse than that, which *Vulcane* made to shield
Achilles life from fate of *Troyan* field.

And then about his shoulders broad he threw
An hairie hide of some wilde beast, whom hee
In salvage forrest by adventure slew,
And reft the spoyle his ornament to bee:
Which spredding all his backe with dreadfull vew,
Made all that him so horrible did see, 70
Thinke him *Alcides* with the Lyons skin,
When the *Næmean* Conquest he did win.

54 *lustie head* vigour
55 *guize* manner
56 *furnitures* accoutrements
59 *mought* might
60 *gentle corpes* noble body
62 *bit* bite; *balefull* deadly; *stownd* conflict
64 *fate* doom
70 *horrible* hairy

[428–30]

Upon his head his glistering Burganet,
The which was wrought by wonderous device,
And curiously engraven, he did set:
The mettall was of rare and passing price;
Not *Bilbo* steele, nor brasse from *Corinth* fet,
Nor costly *Oricalche* from strange *Phœnice*;
But such as could both *Phœbus* arrowes ward,
And th'hayling darts of heaven beating hard. 80

Therein two deadly weapons fixt he bore,
Strongly outlaunched towards either side,
Like two sharpe speares, his enemies to gore:
Like as a warlike Brigandine, applyde
To fight, layes forth her threatfull pikes afore,
The engines which in them sad death doo hyde:
So did this flie outstretch his fearefull hornes,
Yet so as him their terrour more adornes.

Lastly his shinie wings as silver bright,
Painted with thousand colours, passing farre 90
All Painters skill, he did about him dight:
Not halfe so manie sundrie colours arre
In *Iris* bowe, ne heaven doth shine so bright,
Distinguished with manie a twinckling starre,
Nor *Junoes* Bird in her ey-spotted traine
So manie goodly colours doth containe.

Ne (may it be withouten perill spoken)
The Archer God, the sonne of *Cytheree*,

---

73 *Burganet* helmet
79 *Phoebus arrowes* sunbeams
81 *two deadly weapons* his antennae
84 *Brigandine* a small galley, armed with a ram
91 *dight* arrange
93 *Iris bowe* the rainbow
95 *Junoes Bird* the peacock
98 *The Archer God* Cupid; *Cytheree* Cytherea, Venus

[428-30]

That joyes on wretched lovers to be wroken,
And heaped spoyles of bleeding harts to see, 100
Beares in his wings so manie a changefull token.
Ah my liege Lord, forgive it unto mee,
If ought against thine honour I have tolde;
Yet sure those wings were fairer manifolde.

Full manie a Ladie faire, in Court full oft
Beholding them, him secretly envide,
And wisht that two such fannes, so silken soft,
And golden faire, her Love would her provide;
Or that when them the gorgeous Flie had doft,
Some one that would with grace be gratifide, 110
From him would steale them privily away,
And bring to her so precious a pray.

Report is that dame *Venus* on a day,
In spring when flowres doo clothe the fruitful ground,
Walking abroad with all her Nymphes to play,
Bad her faire damzels flocking her arownd,
To gather flowres, her forhead to array:
Emongst the rest a gentle Nymph was found,
Hight *Astery*, excelling all the crewe
In curteous usage, and unstained hewe. 120

Who being nimbler joynted than the rest,
And more industrious, gathered more store
Of the fields honour, than the others best;
Which they in secret harts envying sore,
Tolde *Venus*, when her as the worthiest
She praised', that *Cupide* (as they heard before)
Did lend her secret aide, in gathering
Into her lap the children of the spring.

99 *to be wroken* to torment
104 *manifolde* many times
110 *with grace be gratifide* be pleased to gain her favour
119 *crewe* company
123 *the fields honour* flowers

[428-30]

Whereof the Goddesse gathering jealous feare,
Not yet unmindfull, how not long agoe 130
Her sonne to *Psyche* secrete love did beare,
And long it close conceal'd, till mickle woe
Thereof arose, and manie a rufull teare;
Reason with sudden rage did overgoe,
And giving hastie credit to th'accuser,
Was led away of them that did abuse her.

Eftsoones that Damzel by her heavenly might,
She turn'd into a winged Butterflie,
In the wide aire to make her wandring flight;
And all those flowres, with which so plenteouslie 140
Her lap she filled had, that bred her spight,
She placed in her wings, for memorie
Of her pretended crime, though crime none were:
Since which that flie them in her wings doth beare.

Thus the fresh *Clarion* being readie dight,
Unto his journey did himselfe addresse,
And with good speed began to take his flight:
Over the fields in his franke lustinesse,
And all the champion he soared light,
And all the countrey wide he did possesse, 150
Feeding upon their pleasures bounteouslie,
That none gainsaid, nor none did him envie.

The woods, the rivers, and the medowes green,
With his aire-cutting wings he measured wide,
Ne did he leave the mountaines bare unseene,
Nor the ranke grassie fennes delights untride.

132 *mickle* much
137 *Eftsoones* at once
141 *spight* distress
143 *pretended* imagined
148 *franke lustinesse* energetic freedom
149 *And all* over all; *champion* countryside

291

[428-30]

But none of these, how ever sweete they beene,
Mote please his fancie, nor him cause t'abide:
His choicefull sense with everie change doth flit.
No common things may please a wavering wit. 160

To the gay gardins his unstaid desire
Him wholly caried, to refresh his sprights:
There lavish Nature in her best attire,
Powres forth sweete odors, and alluring sights;
And Arte with her contending, doth aspire
T'excell the naturall, with made delights:
And all that faire or pleasant may be found,
In riotous excesse doth there abound.

There he arriving, round about doth flie,
From bed to bed, from one to other border, 170
And takes survey with curious busie eye,
Of everie flowre and herbe there set in order;
Now this, now that he tasteth tenderly,
Yet none of them he rudely doth disorder,
Ne with his feete their silken leaves deface;
But pastures on the pleasures of each place.

And evermore with most varietie,
And change of sweetnesse (for all change is sweete)
He casts his glutton sense to satisfie,
Now sucking of the sap of herbe most meete, 180
Or of the deaw, which yet on them does lie,
Now in the same bathing his tender feete:
And then he pearcheth on some braunch thereby,
To weather him, and his moyst wings to dry.

And then againe he turneth to his play,
To spoyle the pleasures of that Paradise:

---

161 *unstaid* unsettled
184 *To weather him* to air himself
186 *spoyle* enjoy

[428–30]

The wholsome Saulge, and Lavender still gray,
Ranke smelling Rue, and Cummin good for eyes,
The Roses raigning in the pride of May,
Sharpe Isope, good for greene wounds remedies,   190
Faire Marigoldes, and Bees alluring Thime,
Sweete Marjoram, and Daysies decking prime.

Coole Violets, and Orpine growing still,
Embathed Balme, and chearfull Galingale,
Fresh Costmarie, and breathfull Camomill,
Dull Poppie, and drink-quickning Setuale,
Veyne-healing Verven, and hed-purging Dill,
Sound Savorie, and Bazill hartie-hale,
Fat Colworts, and comforting Perseline,
Colde Lettuce, and refreshing Rosmarine.   200

And whatso else of vertue good or ill
Grewe in this Gardin, fetcht from farre away,
Of everie one he takes, and tastes at will,
And on their pleasures greedily doth pray.
Then when he hath both plaid, and fed his fill,
In the warme Sunne he doth himselfe embay,
And there him rests in riotous suffisaunce
Of all his gladfulnes, and kingly joyaunce.

What more felicitie can fall to creature,
Than to enjoy delight with libertie,   210

187 *Saulge* sage
190 *Isope* hyssop
192 *prime* spring
193 *Orpine Sedum telephium*, a herbaceous plant
194 *Embathed* fragrant; *Galingale* a kind of mild ginger
195 *Costmarie Chrysanthemum pyrethrum*
196 *Setuale* setwall, zedoary
197 *Verven* vervain, verbena
199 *Colworts* a kind of cabbage; *comforting* strengthening; *Perseline* parsley
200 *Rosmarine* rosemary
201 *vertue* power
206 *embay* bask

And to be Lord of all the workes of Nature,
To raine in th'aire from earth to highest skie,
To feed on flowers, and weeds of glorious feature,
To take what ever thing doth please the eie?
Who rests not pleased with such happines,
Well worthie he to taste of wretchednes.

But what on earth can long abide in state?
Or who can him assure of happie day;
Sith morning faire may bring fowle evening late,
And least mishap the most blisse alter may? 220
For thousand perills lie in close awaite
About us daylie, to worke our decay;
That none, except a God, or God him guide,
May them avoyde, or remedie provide.

And whatso heavens in their secret doome
Ordained have, how can fraile fleshly wight
Forecast, but it must needs to issue come?
The sea, the aire, the fire, the day, the night,
And th'armies of their creatures all and some
Do serve to them, and with importune might 230
Warre against us the vassals of their will.
Who then can save, what they dispose to spill?

Not thou, O *Clarion*, though fairest thou
Of all thy kinde, unhappie happie Flie,
Whose cruell fate is woven even now
Of *Joves* owne hand, to worke thy miserie:
Ne may thee helpe the manie hartie vow,

225 *doome* decree
226 *fleshly wight* mortal being
227 *Forecast* contrive
230 *importune* resistless
232 *dispose to spill* determine to destroy
234 *kinde* race
236 *Joves* Jupiter's
237 *the manie hartie vow* the many heart-felt prayers

[428–30]

Which thy olde Sire with sacred pietie
Hath powred forth for thee, and th'altars sprent:
Nought may thee save from heavens avengement.   240

It fortuned (as heavens had behight)
That in this gardin, where yong *Clarion*
Was wont to solace him, a wicked wight
The foe of faire things, th'author of confusion,
The shame of Nature, the bondslave of spight,
Had lately built his hatefull mansion,
And lurking closely, in awayte now lay,
How he might anie in his trap betray.

But when he spide the joyous Butterflie
In this faire plot dispacing too and fro,   250
Fearless of foes and hidden jeopardie,
Lord how he gan for to bestirre him tho,
And to his wicked worke each part applie:
His heart did earne against his hated foe,
And bowels so with ranckling poyson swelde,
That scarce the skin the strong contagion helde.

The cause why he this Flie so maliced,
Was (as in stories it is written found)
For that his mother which him bore and bred,
The most fine-fingred workwoman on ground,   260
Arachne, by his meanes was vanquished
Of *Pallas*, and in her owne skill confound,

239 *sprent* sprinkled
241 *behight* ordained
247 *awayte* ambush
251 *jeopardie* peril of death
254 *earne* fret
255 *ranckling* corrosive
256 *contagion* corruption
257 *maliced* hated
260 *workwoman* needle-woman

295

[428-30]

When she with her for excellence contended,
That wrought her shame, and sorrow never ended.

For the *Tritonian* Goddesse having hard
Her blazed fame, which all the world had fil'd,
Came downe to prove the truth, and due reward
For her prais-worthie workmanship to yeild
But the presumptuous Damzel rashly dar'd
The Goddesse self to chalenge to the field,   270
And to compare with her in curious skill
Of workes with loome, with needle, and with quill.

Minerva did the chalenge not refuse,
But deign'd with her the paragon to make:
So to their worke they sit, and each doth chuse
What storie she will for her tapet take.
Arachne figur'd how *Jove* did abuse
Europa like a Bull, and on his backe
Her through the sea did beare; so lively seene,
That it true Sea, and true Bull ye would weene.   280

She seem'd still backe unto the land to looke,
And her play-fellowes aide to call, and feare
The dashing of the waves, that up she tooke
Her daintie feete, and garments gathered neare:
But (Lord) how she in everie member shooke,
When as the land she saw no more appeare,
But a wilde wildernes of waters deepe:
Then gan she greatly to lament and weepe.

Before the Bull she pictur'd winged Love,
With his yong brother Sport, light fluttering   290

265 *hard* heard
266 *blazed* acclaimed
272 *quill* bobbin
274 *paragon* rivalry
276 *tapet* tapestry
277 *abuse* deceive

296

[428-30]

Upon the waves, as each had been a Dove;
The one his bowe and shafts, the other Spring
A burning Teade about his head did move,
As in their Syres new love both triumphing:
And manie Nymphes about them flocking round,
And manie *Tritons*, which their hornes did sound.

And round about, her worke she did empale
With a faire border wrought of sundrie flowres,
Enwoven with an Yvie winding trayle:
A goodly worke, full fit for Kingly bowres,   300
Such as Dame *Pallas*, such as Envie pale,
That al good things with venemous tooth devowres,
Could not accuse. Then gan the Goddesse bright
Her selfe likewise unto her worke to dight.

She made the storie of the olde debate,
Which she with *Neptune* did for *Athens* trie:
Twelve Gods doo sit around in royall state,
And *Jove* in midst with awfull Majestie,
To judge the strife betweene them stirred late:
Each of the Gods by his like visnomie   310
Eathe to be knowen; but *Jove* above them all,
By his great lookes and power Imperiall.

Before them stands the God of Seas in place,
Clayming that sea-coast Citie as his right,
And strikes the rockes with his three-forked mace;
Whenceforth issues a warlike steed in sight,

292 *Spring* youth
293 *Teade* torch
294 *Syres* Jupiter's
296 *Tritons* sea deities; *hornes* conches
297 *empale* surround
304 *dight* prepare
306 *Neptune* god of the sea
310 *visnomie* appearance
311 *Eathe* easy

The signe by which he chalengeth the place,
That all the Gods, which saw his wondrous might
Did surely deeme the victorie his due:
But seldome seene, forejudgement proveth true.   320

Then to her selfe she gives her *Aegide* shield,
And steelhed speare, and morion on her hedd,
Such as she oft is seene in warlicke field:
Then sets she forth, how with her weapon dredd
She smote the ground, the which streight foorth did yield
A fruitfull Olyve tree, with berries spredd,
That all the Gods admir'd; then all the storie
She compast with a wreathe of Olyves hoarie.

Emongst those leaves she made a Butterflie,
With excellent device and wondrous slight,   330
Fluttring among the Olives wantonly,
That seem'd to live, so like it was in sight:
The velvet nap which on his wings doth lie,
The silken downe with which his backe is dight,
His broad outstretched hornes, his hayrie thies,
His glorious colours, and his glistering eies.

Which when *Arachne* saw, as overlaid,
And mastered with workmanship so rare,
She stood astonied long, ne ought gainesaid,
And with fast fixed eyes on her did stare,   340
And by her silence, signe of one dismaid,
The victorie did yeeld her as her share:
Yet did she inly fret, and felly burne,
And all her blood to poysonous rancor turne.

320 *seldome seene* it rarely happens
322 *morion* helmet
328 *compast* framed
333 *nap* bloom
337 *overlaid* overcome
343 *felly* fiercely
344 *rancor* bitterness

[428–30]

That shortly from the shape of womanhed
Such as she was, when *Pallas* she attempted,
She grew to hideous shape of dryrihed,
Pined with griefe of follie late repented:
Eftsoones her white streight legs were altered
To crooked crawling shankes, of marrowe empted,   350
And her faire face to fowle and loathsome hewe,
And her fine corpes to a bag of venim grewe.

This cursed creature, mindfull of that olde
Enfestred grudge, the which his mother felt,
So soone as *Clarion* he did beholde,
His heart with vengefull malice inly swelt,
And weaving straight a net with manie a folde
About the cave, in which he lurking dwelt,
With fine small cords about it stretched wide,
So finely sponne, that scarce they could be spide.   360

Not anie damzell, which her vaunteth most
In skilfull knitting of soft silken twyne;
Nor anie weaver, which his worke doth boast
In dieper, in damaske, or in lyne;
Nor anie skil'd in workmanship embost;
Nor anie skil'd in loupes of fingring fine,
Might in their divers cunning ever dare,
With this so curious networke to compare.

Ne doo I thinke, that that same subtil gin,
The which the *Lemnian* God framde craftilie,   370

346 *attempted* challenged
347 *dryrihed* wretchedness
350 *empted* emptied
352 *corpes* body
357 *a net* a cobweb
364 *dieper* fine cloth; *lyne* linen
365 *embost* ornamented
366 *loupes* stitches
369 *gin* snare

Mars sleeping with his wife to compasse in,
That all the Gods with common mockerie
Might laugh at them, and scorne their shamefull sin,
Was like to this. This same he did applie,
For to entrap the careles *Clarion*,
That rang'd each where without suspition.

Suspition of friend, nor feare of foe,
That hazarded his health, had he at all,
But walkt at will, and wandred too and fro,
In the pride of his freedome principall: 380
Litle wist he his fatall future woe,
But was secure, the liker he to fall.
He likest is to fall into mischaunce,
That is regardles of his governaunce.

Yet still *Aragnoll* (so his foe was hight)
Lay lurking covertly him to surprise,
And all his gins that him entangle might,
Drest in good order as he could devise.
At length the foolish Flie without foresight,
As he that did all daunger quite despise, 390
Toward those parts came flying careleslie,
Where hidden was his hatefull enemie.

Who seeing him, with secrete joy therefore
Did tickle inwardly in everie vaine,
And his false hart fraught with all treasons store,
Was fil'd with hope, his purpose to obtaine:
Himselfe he close upgathered more and more
Into his den, that his deceiptfull traine

371 *compasse* trap
381 *wist* knew
384 *governaunce* behaviour
385 *hight* named
394 *tickle* thrill
398 *traine* plot

By his there being might not be bewraid,
Ne anie noyse, ne anie motion made.   400

Like as a wily Foxe, that having spide,
Where on a sunnie banke the Lambes doo play,
Full closely creeping by the hinder side,
Lyes in ambushment of his hoped pray,
Ne stirreth limbe, till seeing readie tide,
He rusheth forth, and snatcheth quite away
One of the litle yonglings unawares:
So to his worke *Aragnoll* him prepares.

Who now shall give unto my heavie eyes
A well of teares, that all may overflow?   410
Or where shall I finde lamentable cryes,
And mournfull tunes enough my griefe to show?
Helpe O thou Tragick Muse, me to devise
Notes sad enough, t'expresse this bitter throw:
For loe, the drerie stownd is now arrived,
That of all happines hath us deprived.

The luckles *Clarion*, whether cruell Fate,
Or wicked Fortune faultles him misled,
Or some ungracious blast out of the gate
Or *Aeoles* raine perforce him drove on hed,   420
Was (O sad hap and howre unfortunate)
With violent swift flight forth caried
Into the cursed cobweb, which his foe
Had framed for his finall overthroe.

There the fond Flie entangled, struggled long,
Himselfe to free thereout; but all in vaine.

403 *hinder* backward
405 *tide* time
414 *throw* turn of fortune
415 *stownd* disaster
420 *Aeoles* Aeolus, god of the winds; *raine* kingdom; *drove on hed* blew him onward
425 *fond* foolish

For striving more, the more in laces strong
Himselfe he tide, and wrapt his winges twaine
In lymie snares the subtill loupes among;
That in the ende he breathelesse did remaine, 430
And all his yougthly forces idly spent,
Him to the mercie of th'avenger lent.

Which when the greisly tyrant did espie,
Like a grimme Lyon rushing with fierce might
Out of his den, he seized greedelie
On the resistles pray, and with fell spight,
Under the left wing stroke his weapon slie
Into his heart, that his deepe groning spright
In bloodie streames foorth fled into the aire,
His bodie left the spectacle of care. 440

VISIONS OF THE WORLDS VANITIE

1

One day, whiles that my daylie cares did sleepe,
My spirit, shaking off her earthly prison,
Began to enter into meditation deepe
Of things exceeding reach of common reason;
  Such as this age, in which all good is geason,
And all that humble is and meane debaced,
Hath brought forth in her last declining season,
Griefe of good mindes, to see goodnesse disgraced.
  On which when as my thought was throghly placed,
Unto my eyes strange showes presented were, 10

427 *laces* bonds
429 *lymie* sticky; *loupes* loops
431 *yougthly* youthful; *idly* uselessly
437 *his weapon* his sting
440 *spectacle of care* emblem of grief
  5 *geason* rare
  6 *debaced* unvalued
  9 *throghly placed* concentrated

[430–3]

Picturing that, which I in minde embraced,
That yet those sights empassion me full nere.
    Such as they were (faire Ladie) take in worth,
    That when time serves, may bring things better forth.

2

    In Summers day, when *Phœbus* fairly shone,
I saw a Bull as white as driven snowe,
With gilden hornes embowed like the Moone,
In a fresh flowring meadow lying lowe:
    Up to his eares the verdant grasse did growe,
And the gay floures did offer to be eaten;   20
But he with fatnes so did overflowe,
That he all wallowed in the weedes downe beaten,
    Ne car'd with them his daintie lips to sweeten:
Till that a Brize, a scorned little creature,
Through his faire hide his angrie sting did threaten,
And vext so sore, that all his goodly feature,
    And all his plenteous pasture nought him pleased:
    So by the small the great is oft diseased.

3

    Beside the fruitfull shore of muddie *Nile*,
Upon a sunnie banke outstretched lay   30
In monstrous length, a mightie Crocodile,
That cram'd with guiltles blood, and greedie pray
    Of wretched people travailing that way,
Thought all things lesse than his disdainfull pride.
I saw a little Bird, cal'd *Tedula*,

  12 *empassion me full nere* move me deeply
  13 *take in worth* receive favourably
  15 *Phoebus* the sun
  17 *embowed* curved
  24 *Brize* gadfly
  25 *threaten* force
  35 *Tedula* Trochilus

[430–3]

The least of thousands which on earth abide,
    That forst this hideous beast to open wide
The greisly gates of his devouring hell,
And let him feede, as Nature doth provide,
Upon his jawes, that with blacke venime swell.   40
    Why then should greatest things the least disdaine,
    Sith that so small so mightie can constraine?

4

The kingly Bird, that beares *Joves* thunder-clap,
One day did scorne the simple Scarabee,
Proud of his highest service, and good hap,
That made all other Foules his thralls to bee:
    The silly Flie, that no redresse did see,
Spide where the Eagle built his towring nest,
And kindling fire within the hollow tree,
Burnt up his yong ones, and himselfe distrest;   50
    Ne suffred him in anie place to rest,
But drove in *Joves* owne lap his egs to lay;
Where gathering also filth him to infest,
Forst with the filth his egs to fling away:
    For which when as the Foule was wroth, said *Jove*,
    Lo how the least the greatest may reprove.

5

Toward the sea turning my troubled eye,
I saw the fish (if fish I may it cleepe)
That makes the sea before his face to flye,

  38 *devouring hell* maw
  43 *The kingly Bird* the eagle; *Joves* Jupiter's
  44 *Scarabee* scarab beetle
  47 *silly* simple
  50 *himselfe* the eagle
  53 *him* Jupiter; *infest* soil
  54 *his* the eagle's
  58 *cleepe* call

[430–3]

And with his flaggie finnes doth seems to sweepe 60
    The fomie waves out of the dreadfull deep,
The huge *Leviathan*, dame Natures wonder,
Making his sport, that manie makes to weep:
A sword-fish small him from the rest did sunder,
    That in his throat him pricking softly under,
His wide Abysse him forced forth to spewe,
That all the sea did roare like heavens thunder,
And all the waves were stain'd with filthie hewe.
    Hereby I learned have, not to despise,
    What ever thing seemes small in common eyes. 70

6

An hideous Dragon, dreadfull to behold,
Whose backe was arm'd against the dint of speare
With shields of brasse, that shone like burnisht golde,
And forkhed sting, that death in it did beare,
    Strove with a Spider, his unequall peare:
And bad defiance to his enemie.
The subtill vermin creeping closely neare,
Did in his drinke shed poyson privilie;
    Which through his entrailes spredding diversly,
Made him to swell, that nigh his bowells brust, 80
And him enforst to yeeld the victorie,
That did so much in his owne greatnesse trust.
    O how great vainnesse is it then to scorne
    The weake, that hath the strong so oft forlorne.

62 *Leviathan* whale
65 *softly* slyly
66 *Abysse* stomach
75 *peare* opposite
78 *privilie* secretly
79 *diversly* everywhere
80 *brust* burst
83 *vainnesse* foolishness
84 *forlorne* distressed

7

    High on a hill a goodly Cedar grewe,
Of wondrous length, and streight proportion,
That farre abroad her daintie odours threwe;
Mongst all the daughters of proud *Libanon*,
    Her match in beautie was not anie one.
Shortly within her inmost pith there bred
A little wicked worme, perceiv'd of none,
That on her sap and vitall moysture fed:
    Thenceforth her garland so much honoured
Began to die, (O great ruth for the same)
And her faire lockes fell from her loftie head,
That shortly balde, and bared she became.
    I, which this sight beheld, was much dismayed,
    To see so goodly thing so soone decayed.

8

    Soone after this I saw an Elephant,
Adorn'd with bells and bosses gorgeouslie,
That on his backe did beare (as batteilant)
A gilden towre, which shone exceedinglie;
    That he himselfe through foolish vanitie,
Both for his rich attire, and goodly forme,
Was puffed up with passing surquedrie,
And shortly gan all other beasts to scorne,
    Till that a little Ant, a silly worme,
Into his nosthrils creeping, so him pained,
That casting downe his towres, he did deforme

---

91 *worme* woodworm
94 *ruth* pity
100 *bosses* metal roundels
101 *as batteilant* as if engaged in battle
105 *surquedrie* pride
107 *silly* simple
108 *nosthrils* nostrils
109 *deforme* spoil

Both borrowed pride, and native beautie stained. 110
    Let therefore nought that great is, therein glorie,
    Sith so small thing his happines may varie.

9

Looking far foorth into the Ocean wide,
A goodly ship with banners bravely dight,
And flag in her top-gallant I espide,
Through the maine sea making her merry flight:
    Faire blew the winde into her bosome right;
And th'heavens looked lovely all the while,
That she did seeme to daunce, as in delight,
And at her owne felicitie did smile. 120
    All sodainely there clove unto her keele
A little fish, that men call *Remora*,
Which stopt her course, and held her by the heele,
That winde nor tide could move her thence away.
    Straunge thing me seemeth, that so small a thing
    Should able be so great an one to wring.

10

A mighty Lyon, Lord of all the wood,
Having his hunger throughly satisfide,
With pray of beasts, and spoyle of living blood,
Safe in his dreadles den him thought to hide: 130
    His sternesse was his prayse, his strength his pride,
And all his glory in his cruell clawes.
I saw a wasp, that fiercely him defide,
And bad him battaile even to his jawes;
    Sore he him stong, that it the blood forth drawes,

112 *varie* change
118 *lovely* favourable
126 *wring* trouble
130 *dreadles* safe
134 *to his jawes* to his face

And his proude heart is fild with fretting ire:
In vaine he threats his teeth, his tayle, his pawes,
And from his bloodie eyes doth sparkle fire;
    That dead himselfe he wisheth for despight.
    So weakest may anoy the most of might.   140

11

What time the Romaine Empire bore the raine
Of all the world, and florisht most in might,
The nations gan their soveraigntie disdaine,
And cast to quitt them from their bondage quight:
    So when all shrouded were in silent night,
The *Galles* were, by corrupting of a mayde,
Possest nigh of the Capitol through slight,
Had not a Goose the treachery bewrayde.
    If then a Goose great *Rome* from ruine stayde,
And *Jove* himselfe, the patron of the place,   150
Preserved from being to his foes betrayde,
Why do vaine men mean things so much deface,
    And in their might repose their most assurance,
    Sith nought on earth can chalenge long endurance?

12

When these sad sights were overpast and gone,
My spright was greatly moved in her rest,

---

137 *threats* threatens with
139 *despight* anger
140 *anoy* harm
141 *raine* rule
143 *soveraigntie* subjection
144 *quitt* rid
146 *Galles* Gauls
147 *nigh* almost; *slight* cunning
148 *bewrayde* made known
152 *deface* despise
156 *spright* spirit

[430–3]

With inward ruth and deare affection,
To see so great things by so small distrest:
   Thenceforth I gan in my engrieved brest
To scorne all difference of great and small,   160
Sith that the greatest often are opprest,
And unawares doe into daunger fall.
   And ye, that read these ruines tragicall
Learne by their losse to love the low degree,
And if that fortune chaunce you up to call
To honours seat, forget not what you be:
   For he that of himselfe is most secure,
   Shall finde his state most fickle and unsure.

---

157 *deare affection* heartfelt passion
163 *ruines tragicall* sad downfalls
164 *losse* failure

Colin Clouts Come Home Againe

To the right worthy and noble Knight Sir *Walter Raleigh*, Captaine of her Majesties Guard, Lord Wardein of the Stanneries, *and Lieutenant of the Countie of Cornwall*

Sir, that you may see that I am not alwaies ydle as yee thinke, though not greatly well occupied, nor altogither undutifull, though not precisely officious, I make you present of this simple pastorall, unworthie of your higher conceipt for the meanesse of the stile, but agreeing with the truth in circumstance and matter. The which I humbly beseech you to accept in part of paiment of the infinite debt in which I acknowledge my selfe bounden unto you, for your singular favours and sundrie good turnes shewed to me at my late being in England, and with your good countenance protect against the malice of evill mouthes, which are alwaies wide open to carpe at and misconstrue my simple meaning. I pray continually for your happinesse. From my house of Kilcolman the 27 of December 1591.

Yours ever humbly
Ed. Sp.

The shepherds boy (best knowen by that name)
That after *Tityrus* first sung his lay,
Laies of sweet love, without rebuke or blame,
Sate (as his custome was) upon a day,

Charming his oaten pipe unto his peres,
The shepheard swaines that did about him play:
Who all the while with greedie listfull cares,
Did stand astonisht at his curious skill,
Like hartlesse deare, dismayd with thunders sound.
At last when as he piped had his fill,
He rested him: and sitting then around,
One of those groomes (a jolly groome was he,
As ever piped on an oaten reed,
And lov'd this shepheard dearest in degree,
Hight *Hobbinol*) gan thus to him areed.

   Colin my liefe, my life, how great a losse
Had all the shepheards nation by thy lacke?
And I poore swaine of many greatest crosse:
That sith thy *Muse* first since thy turning backe
Was heard to sound as she was wont on hye,
Hast made us all so blessed and so blythe.
Whilest thou wast hence, all dead in dole did lie:
The woods were heard to waile full many a sythe,
And all their birds with silence to complaine:
The fields with faded flowers did seem to mourne,
And all their flocks from feeding to refraine:
The running waters wept for thy returne,
And all their fish with languour did lament:
But now both woods and fields, and floods revive,
Sith thou art come, their cause of meriment,
That us late dead, hast made againe alive:
But were it not too painfull to repeat

---

5 *peres* fellows
7 *listfull* attentive
9 *hartlesse* timid
12 *groomes* young men; shepherds
15 *areed* speak
16 *liefe* beloved
17 *nation* society
18 *crosse* suffering
23 *sythe* time
28 *languour* pining

[433–8]

The passed fortunes, which to thee befell
In thy late voyage, we thee would entreat,
Now at thy leisure them to us to tell.
    To whom the shepheard gently answered thus,
Hobbin thou temptest me to that I covet:
For of good passed newly to discus,
By dubble usurie doth twise renew it.
And since I saw that Angels blessed eie, 40
Her worlds bright sun, her heavens fairest light,
My mind full of my thoughts satietie,
Doth feed on sweet contentment of that sight:
Since that same day in nought I take delight,
Ne feeling have in any earthly pleasure,
But in remembrance of that glorious bright,
My lifes sole blisse, my hearts eternall threasure.
Wake then my pipe, my sleepie *Muse* awake,
Till I have told her praises lasting long:
Hobbin desires, thou maist it not forsake, 50
Harke then ye jolly shepheards to my song.
    With that they all gan throng about him neare,
With hungrie eares to heare his harmonie:
The whiles their flocks devoyed of dangers feare,
Did round about them feed at libertie.
    One day (quoth he) I sat, (as was my trade)
Under the foote of *Mole* that mountaine hore,
Keeping my sheepe amongst the cooly shade,
Of the greene alders by the *Mullaes* shore:
There a straunge shepheard chaunst to find me out, 60
Whether allured with my pipes delight,

38 *passed* happening; *discus* recount
42 *satietie* satisfaction
45 *Ne* nor
46 *bright* bright lady
47 *threasure* treasure
50 *forsake* neglect
51 *jolly* merry
58 *cooly* cool

Whose pleasing sound yshrilled far about,
Or thither led by chaunce, I know not right:
Whom when I asked from what place he came,
And how he hight, himselfe he did ycleepe,
The shepheard of the Ocean by name,
And said he came far from the main-sea deepe.
He sitting me beside in that same shade,
Provoked me to plaie some pleasant fit,
And when he heard the musicke which I made,   70
He found himselfe full greatly pleasd at it:
Yet æmuling my pipe, he tooke in hond
My pipe before that æmuled of many,
And plaid theron; (for well that skill he cond)
Himselfe as skilfull in that art as any.
He pip'd, I sung; and when he sung, I piped,
By chaunge of turnes, each making other mery,
Neither envying other, nor envied,
So piped we, until we both were weary.

  There interrupting him, a bonie swaine,   80
That *Cuddy* hight, him thus atweene bespake:
And should it not thy readie course restraine,
I would request thee *Colin*, for my sake,
To tell what thou didst sing, when he did plaie.
For well I weene it worth recounting was,
Whether it were some hymne, or morall laie,
Or carol made to praise thy loved lasse.

  Nor of my love, nor of my losse (quoth he).
I then did sing, as then occasion fell:
For love had me forlorne, forlorne of me,   90

---

62 *yshrilled* resounded
65 *hight* was named; *did ycleepe* did call himself
69 *fit* passage of music or poetry
72 *æmuling* in friendly rivalry
73 *æmuled* envied
80 *bonie swaine* handsome lad
81 *atweene bespake* interposed to say
85 *weene* consider

That made me in that desart chose to dwell.
But of my river *Bregogs* love I soong,
Which to the shiny *Mulla* he did beare,
And yet doth beare, and ever will, so long
As water doth within his bancks appeare.

    Of fellow ship (said then that bony Boy)
Record to us that lovely lay againe:
The staie whereof, shall nought these eares annoy,
Who all that *Colin* makes, do covet faine.

    Heare then (quoth he) the tenor of my tale,   100
In sort as I it to that shepheard told:
No leasing new, nor Grandams fable stale,
But aunciant truth confirm'd with credence old.

    Old father *Mole*, (*Mole* hight that mountain gray
That walls the Northside of *Armulla* dale)
He had a daughter fresh as floure of May,
Which gave that name unto that pleasant vale;
Mulla the daughter of old *Mole*, so hight
The Nimph, which of that water course has charge,
That springing out of *Mole*, doth run downe right   110
To *Buttevant*, where spreading forth at large,
It giveth name unto that aunciant Cittie,
Which *Kilnemullah* cleped is of old:
Whose ragged ruines breed great ruth and pittie,
To travailers, which it from far behold.
Full faine she lov'd, and was belov'd full faine,
Of her owne brother river, *Bregog* hight,

---

 96 *bony* handsome
 97 *Record* relate
 98 *staie* time it takes
 99 *makes* composes; *covet faine* eagerly desire
100 *tenor* import
102 *leasing* falsehood
103 *credence* well-founded belief
108 *hight* named
113 *cleped is* is called
114 *ruth* sorrow
116 *faine* eagerly

So hight because of this deceitfull traine,
Which he with *Mulla* wrought to win delight.
But her old sire more carefull of her good,   120
And meaning her much better to preferre,
Did thinke to match her with the neighbour flood,
Which *Allo* hight, Broad water called farre:
And wrought so well with his continuall paine,
That he that river for his daughter wonne:
The dowre agreed, the day assigned plaine,
The place appointed where it should be doone.
Nath' lesse the Nymph her former liking held;
For love will not be drawne, but must be ledde,
And *Bregog* did so well her fancie weld,   130
That her good will he got her first to wedde.
But for her father sitting still on hie,
Did warily still watch which way she went,
And eke from far observ'd with jealous eie,
Which way his course the wanton *Bregog* bent,
Him to deceive for all his watchfull ward,
The wily lover did devise this slight:
First into many parts of streame he shar'd,
That whilest the one was watcht, the other might
Passe unespide to meete her by the way;   140
And then besides, those little streames so broken
He under ground so closely did convay,
That of their passage doth appeare no token,
Till they into the *Mullaes* water slide.
So secretly did he his love enjoy:
Yet not so secret, but it was descride,
And told her father by a shepheards boy.

118 *traine* trick
121 *preferre* advance
126 *dowre* marriage portion
130 *weld* dominate
136 *ward* vigilance
142 *convay* conduct
146 *descride* observed

[433–8]

Who wondrous wroth for that so foule despight,
In great avenge did roll downe from his hill
Huge mightie stones, the which encomber might 150
His passage, and his water-courses spill.
So of a River, which he was of old,
He none was made, but scattered all to nought,
And lost emong those rocks into him rold,
Did lose his name: so deare his love he bought.

   Which having said, him *Thestylis* bespake,
Now by my life this was a mery lay:
Worthie of *Colin* selfe, that did it make.
But read now eke of friendship I thee pray,
What dittie did that other shepheard sing? 160
For I do covet most the same to heare,
As men use most to covet forreine thing.
That shall I eke (quoth he) to you declare.
His song was all a lamentable lay,
Of great unkindnesse, and of usage hard,
Of *Cynthia* the Ladie of the sea,
Which from her presence faultlesse him debard.
And ever and anon with singults rife,
He cryed out, to make his undersong
Ah my loves queene, and goddesse of my life, 170
Who shall me pittie, when thou doest me wrong?

   Then gan a gentle bony lasse to speake,
That *Marin* hight, Right well he sure did plaine:
That could great *Cynthiaes* sore displeasure breake,
And move to take him to her grace againe.

148 *foule despight* grievous injury
149 *avenge* vengeance
150 *encomber* obstruct
151 *His* Bregog's
162 *forreine* unfamiliar
163 *eke* also
167 *faultlesse* undeservedly; *debard* exiled
168 *singults rife* deep sobs
169 *undersong* accompanying refrain
172 *bony lasse* lovely girl

[433–8]

But tell on further *Colin*, as befell
Twixt him and thee, that thee did hence dissuade.

    When thus our pipes we both had wearied well,
(Quoth he) and each an end of singing made,
He gan to cast great lyking to my lore,   180
And great dislyking to my lucklesse lot:
That banisht had my selfe, like wight forlore,
Into that waste, where I was quite forgot.
The which to leave, thenceforth he counseld mee,
Unmeet for man, in whom was ought regardfull,
And wend with him, his *Cynthia* to see:
Whose grace was great, and bounty most rewardfull.
Besides her peerlesse skill in making well
And all the ornaments of wondrous wit,
Such as all womankynd did far excell: 190
Such as the world admyr'd and praised it:
So what with hope of good, and hate of ill,
He me perswaded forth with him to fare:
Nought tooke I with me, but mine oaten quill:
Small needments else need shepheard to prepare.
So to the sea we came; the sea? that is
A world of waters heaped up on hie,
Rolling like mountaines in wide wildernesse,
Horrible, hideous, roaring with hoarse crie.

    And is the sea (quoth *Coridon*) so fearfull?   200

    Fearful much more (quoth he) then hart can fear:
Thousand wyld beasts with deep mouthes gaping direfull
Therin stil wait poore passengers to teare.
Who life doth loath, and longs death to behold,
Before he die, alreadie dead with feare,
And yet would live with heart halfe stonie cold,

180 *lore* utterance
182 *wight forlore* ruined man
183 *waste* desolate place
186 *wend* go
188 *making well* writing excellent poetry
193 *fare* set out

Let him to sea, and he shall see it there.
And yet as ghastly dreadfull, as it seemes,
Bold men presuming life for gaine to sell,
Dare tempt that gulf, and in those wandring stremes   210
Seek waies unknown, waies leading down to hell.
For as we stood there waiting on the strond,
Behold an huge great vessel to us came,
Dauncing upon the waters back to lond,
As if it scornd the daunger of the same,
Yet was it but a wooden frame and fraile,
Glewed togither with some subtile matter,
Yet had it armes and wings, and head and taile,
And life to move it selfe upon the water.
Strange thing, how bold and swift the monster was,   220
That neither car'd for wynd, nor haile, nor raine,
Nor swelling waves, but thorough them did passe
So proudly, that she made them roare againe.
The same aboord us gently did receave,
And without harme us farre away did beare,
So farre that land our mother us did leave,
And nought but sea and heaven to us appeare.
Then hartlesse quite and full of inward feare,
That shepheard I besought to me to tell,
Under what skie, or in what world we were,   230
In which I saw no living people dwell.
Who me recomforting all that he might,
Told me that that same was the Regiment
Of a great shepheardesse, that *Cynthia* hight,
His liege his Ladie, and his lifes Regent.
If then (quoth I) a shepheardesse she bee,
Where be the flockes and heards, which she doth keep?
And where may I the hills and pastures see,

208 *ghastly* appallingly
209 *presuming* venturing
228 *hartlesse* disheartened
233 *Regiment* realm
235 *Regent* ruler

On which she useth for to feed her sheepe?
These be the hills (quoth he) the surges hie,   240
On which faire *Cynthia* her heards doth feed:
Her heards be thousand fishes with their frie,
Which in the bosome of the billowes breed.
Of them the shepheard which hath charge in chief,
Is *Triton* blowing loud his wreathed horne:
At sound whereof, they all for their relief
Wend too and fro at evening and at morne.
And *Proteus* eke with him does drive his heard
Of stinking Seales and Porcpisces together,
With hoary head and deawy dropping beard,   250
Compelling them which way he list, and whether.
And I among the rest of many least,
Have in the Ocean charge to me assignd:
Where I will live or die at her beheast,
And serve and honour her with faithfull mind.
Besides an hundred Nymphs all heavenly borne,
And of immortall race, doo still attend
To wash faire *Cynthiaes* sheep, when they be shorne,
And fold them up, when they have made an end.
Those be the shepheards which my *Cynthia* serve,   260
At sea, beside a thousand moe at land:
For land and sea my *Cynthia* doth deserve
To have in her commandement at hand.
Thereat I wondred much, till wondring more
And more, at length we land far off descryde:
Which sight much gladed me; for much afore
I feard, least land we never should have eyde:
Thereto our ship her course directly bent,
As if the way she perfectly had knowne.
We *Lunday* passe; by that same name is ment   270

240 *hie* high
249 *Porcpisces* porpoises
251 *list* wishes
261 *moe* more
266 *gladed* cheered

[433–8]

An Island, which the first to west was showne.
From thence another world of land we kend,
Floting amid the sea in jeopardie,
And round about with mightie white rocks hemd,
Against the seas encroching crueltie.
Those same the shepheard told me, were the fields
In which dame *Cynthia* her landheards fed,
Faire goodly fields, then which *Armulla* yields
None fairer, nor more fruitfull to be red.
The first to which we nigh approched, was   280
An high headland thrust far into the sea,
Like to an horne, whereof the name it has,
Yet seemed to be a goodly pleasant lea:
There did a loftie mount at first us greet,
Which did a stately heape of stone upreare,
That seemd amid the surges for to fleet,
Much greater then that frame, which us did beare:
There did our ship her fruitfull wombe unlade,
And put us all ashore on *Cynthias* land.

    What land is that thou meanst (then *Cuddy* sayd)   290
And is there other, then whereon we stand?

    Ah *Cuddy* (then quoth *Colin*) thous a fon,
That hast not seene least part of natures worke:
Much more there is unkend, then thou doest kon,
And much more that does from mens knowledge lurke.
For that same land much larger is then this,
And other men and beasts and birds doth feed:
There fruitfull corne, faire trees, fresh herbage is
And all things else that living creatures need.
Besides most goodly rivers there appeare,   300
No whit inferiour to thy *Funchins* praise,
Or unto *Allo* or to *Mulla* cleare:

---

272 *kend* caught sight of
273 *jeopardie* mortal danger
279 *red* imagined
292 *thous a fon* thou art a fool
294 *unkend* unknown; *kon* know

Nought hast thou foolish boy seene in thy daies.
But if that land be there (quoth he) as here,
And is theyr heaven likewise there all one?
And if like heaven, be heavenly graces there,
Like as in this same world where we do wone?

    Both heaven and heavenly graces do much more
(Quoth he) abound in that same land, then this.
For there all happie peace and plenteous store   310
Conspire in one to make contented blisse:
No wayling there nor wretchednesse is heard,
No bloodie issues nor no leprosies,
No griesly famine, nor no raging sweard,
No nightly bodrags, nor no hue and cries;
The shepheards there abroad may safely lie,
On hills and downes, withouten dread or daunger:
No ravenous wolves the good mans hope destroy,
Nor outlawes fell affray the forest raunger.
There learned arts do florish in great honor,   320
And Poets wits are had in peerlesse price:
Religion hath lay powre to rest upon her,
Advancing vertue and suppressing vice.
For end, all good, all grace there freely growes,
Had people grace it gratefully to use:
For God his gifts there plenteously bestowes,
But gracelesse men them greatly do abuse.

    But say on further, then said *Corylas*,
The rest of thine adventures, that betyded.

    Foorth on our voyage we by land did passe,   330
(Quoth he) as that same shepheard still us guyded,
Untill that we to *Cynthiaes* presence came:
Whose glorie, greater then my simple thought,
I found much greater then the former fame;
Such greatnes I cannot compare to ought:

---

307 *wone* dwell
314 *sweard* sword
315 *bodrags* attacks
322 *Religion hath lay powre to rest upon her* religion has the support of the state

But if I her like ought on earth might read,
I would her lyken to a crowne of lillies,
Upon a virgin brydes adorned head,
With Roses dight and Goolds and Daffadillies;
Or like the circlet of a Turtle true, 340
In which all colours of the rainbow bee;
Or like faire *Phebes* garlond shining new,
In which all pure perfection one may see.
But vaine it is to thinke by paragone
Of earthly things, to judge of things divine:
Her power, her mercy, and her wisedome, none
Can deeme, but who the Godhead can define.
Why then do I base shepheard bold and blind,
Presume the things so sacred to prophane?
More fit it is t'adore with humble mind, 350
The image of the heavens in shape humane.

   With that *Alexis* broke his tale asunder,
Saying, By wondring at thy *Cynthiaes* praise,
Colin, thy selfe thou mak'st us more to wonder,
And her upraising, doest thy selfe upraise.
But let us heare what grace she shewed thee,
And how that shepheard strange, thy cause advanced?

   The shepheard of the Ocean (quoth he)
Unto that Goddesse grace me first enhanced,
And to mine oaten pipe enclin'd her eare, 360
That she thenceforth therein gan take delight,
And it desir'd at timely houres to heare,
All were my notes but rude and roughly dight.
For not by measure of her owne great mynd,
And wondrous worth she mott my simple song,
But joyd that country shepheard ought could fynd

339 *dight* decked; *Goolds* marigolds.
340 *Turtle* turtle-dove
344 *by paragone* by comparison
357 *strange* foreign
363 *rude and roughly dight* simple and unpolished
365 *mott* judged

[433–8]

Worth harkening to, emongst the learned throng.
   Why? (said *Alexis* then) what needeth shee
That is so great a shepheardesse her selfe,
And hath so many shepheards in her fee,   370
To heare thee sing, a simple silly Elfe?
Or be the shepheards which do serve her laesie,
That they list not their mery pipes applie?
Or be their pipes untunable and craesie,
That they cannot her honour worthylie?
   Ah nay (said *Colin*) neither so, nor so:
For better shepheards be not under skie,
Nor better hable, when they list to blow
Their pipes aloud, her name to glorifie.
There is good *Harpalus*, now woxen aged   380
In faithfull service of faire *Cynthia*:
And there is *Corydon* though meanly waged,
Yet hablest wit of most I know this day.
And there is sad *Alcyon* bent to mourne,
Though fit to frame an everlasting dittie,
Whose gentle spright for *Daphnes* death doth tourn
Sweet layes of love to endlesse plaints of pittie.
Ah pensive boy pursue that brave conceipt,
In thy sweet Eglantine of *Meriflure*,
Lift up thy notes unto their wonted height,   390
That may thy *Muse* and mates to mirth allure.
There eke is *Palin* worthie of great praise,
Albe he envie at my rustick quill:
And there is pleasing *Alcon*, could he raise
His tunes from laies to matter of more skill.
And there is old *Palemon* free from spight,

---

370 *fee* service
371 *simple silly Elfe* poor foolish innocent
372 *shepheards* poets
374 *craesie* cracked
378 *hable* capable
388 *conceipt* idea
393 *rustick quill* pastoral poetry

[433-8]

Whose carefull pipe may make the hearer rew:
Yet he himselfe may rewed be more right,
That sung so long untill quite hoarse he grew.
And there is *Alabaster* throughly taught,   400
In all this skill, though knowen yet to few:
Yet were he knowne to *Cynthia* as he ought,
His Eliseïs would be redde anew.
Who lives that can match that heroick song,
Which he hath of that mightie Princesse made?
O dreaded Dread, do not thy selfe that wrong,
To let thy fame lie so in hidden shade:
But call it forth, O call him forth to thee,
To end thy glorie which he hath begun:
That when he finisht hath as it should be,   410
No braver Poeme can be under Sun.
No *Po* nor *Tyburs* swans so much renowned,
Nor all the brood of *Greece* so highly praised,
Can match that *Muse* when it with bayes is crowned,
And to the pitch of her perfection raised.
And there is a new shepheard late up sprong,
The which doth all afore him far surpasse:
Appearing well in that well tuned song,
Which late he sung unto a scornfull lasse.
Yet doth his trembling *Muse* but lowly flie,   420
As daring not too rashly mount on hight,
And doth her tender plumes as yet but trie,
In loves soft laies and looser thoughts delight.
Then rouze thy feathers quickly *Daniell*,
And to what course thou please thy selfe advance:
But most me seemes, thy accent will excell,
In Tragick plaints and passionate mischance.
And there that shepheard of the Ocean is,
That spends his wit in loves consuming smart:
Full sweetly tempred is that *Muse* of his   430

397 *carefull* sorrowful; *rew* pity
412 *swans* poets
414 *that Muse* his talent

[433-8]

That can empierce a Princes mightie hart.
There also is (ah no, he is not now)
But since I said he is, he quite is gone,
Amyntas quite is gone and lies full low,
Having his *Amaryllis* left to mone.
Helpe, O ye shepheards helpe ye all in this,
Helpe *Amaryllis* this her losse to mourne:
Her losse is yours, your losse *Amyntas* is,
Amyntas floure of shepheards pride forlorne:
He whilest he lived was the noblest swaine,   440
That ever piped in an oaten quill:
Both did he other, which could pipe, maintaine,
And eke could pipe himselfe with passing skill.
And there though last not least is *Aetion*,
A gentler shepheard may no where be found:
Whose *Muse* full of high thoughts invention,
Doth like himselfe Heroically sound.
All these, and many others mo remaine,
Now after *Astrofell* is dead and gone:
But while as *Astrofell* did live and raine,   450
Amongst all these was none his Paragone.
All these do florish in their sundry kynd,
And do their *Cynthia* immortall make:
Yet found I lyking in her royall mynd,
Not for my skill, but for that shepheards sake.

   Then spake a lovely lasse, hight *Lucida*,
Shepheard, enough of shepheards thou hast told,
Which favour thee, and honour *Cynthia*:
But of so many Nymphs which she doth hold
In her retinew, thou hast nothing sayd;   460
That seems, with none of them thou favour foundest,
Or art ingratefull to each gentle mayd,
That none of all their due deserts resoundest.
   Ah far be it (quoth *Colin Clout*) fro me,

439 *forlorne* lost
448 *mo* more
451 *Paragone* equal

[433–8]

That I of gentle Mayds should ill deserve:
For that my selfe I do professe to be
Vassall to one, whom all my dayes I serve;
The beame of beautie sparkled from above,
The floure of vertue and pure chastitie,
The blossome of sweet joy and perfect love, 470
The pearle of peerlesse grace and modestie:
To her my thoughts I daily dedicate,
To her my heart I nightly martyrize:
To her my love I lowly do prostrate,
To her my life I wholly sacrifice:
My thought, my heart, my love, my life is shee,
And I hers ever onely, ever one:
One ever I all vowed hers to bee,
One ever I, and others never none.

    Then thus *Melissa* said; Thrise happie Mayd, 480
Whom thou doest so enforce to deifie:
That woods, and hills, and valleyes thou hast made
Her name to eccho unto heaven hie.
But say, who else vouchsafed thee of grace?

    They all (quoth he) me graced goodly well,
That all I praise, but in the highest place,
Vrania, sister unto *Astrofell*,
In whose brave mynd, as in a golden cofer,
All heavenly gifts and riches locked are:
More rich then pearles of *Ynde*, or gold of *Opher*, 490
And in her sex more wonderfull and rare.
Ne lesse praise worthie I *Theana* read,
Whose goodly beames though they be over dight
With mourning stole of carefull wydowhead,
Yet through that darksome vale do glister bright;
She is the well of bountie and brave mynd,
Excelling most in glorie and great light:
She is the ornament of womankind,

---

473 *martyrize* sacrifice
474 *lowly do prostrate* humbly offer
481 *enforce to deifie* strive to render divine

And Courts chief garlond with all vertues dight.
Therefore great *Cynthia* her in chiefest grace 500
Doth hold, and next unto her selfe advance,
Well worthie of so honourable place,
For her great worth and noble governance.
Ne lesse praise worthie is her sister deare,
Faire *Marian,* the *Muses* onely darling:
Whose beautie shyneth as the morning cleare,
With silver deaw upon the roses pearling.
Ne lesse praise worthie is *Mansilia,*
Best knowne by bearing up great *Cynthiaes* traine:
That same is she to whom *Daphnaida* 510
Upon her neeces death I did complaine.
She is the paterne of true womanhead,
And onely mirrhor of feminitie:
Worthie next after *Cynthia* to tread,
As she is next her in nobilitie.
Ne lesse praise worthie *Galathea* seemes,
Then best of all that honourable crew,
Faire *Galathea* with bright shining beames,
Inflaming feeble eyes that her do view.
She there then waited upon *Cynthia,* 520
Yet there is not her won, but here with us
About the borders of our rich *Coshma,*
Now made of *Maa* the Nymph delitious.
Ne lesse praiseworthie faire *Neæra* is,
Neæra ours, not theirs, though there she be,
For of the famous Shure, the Nymph she is,
For high desert, advaunst to that degree.
She is the blosome of grace and curtesie,
Adorned with all honourable parts:
She is the braunch of true nobilitie, 530
Belov'd of high and low with faithfull harts.
Ne lesse praisworthie *Stella* do I read,
Though nought my praises of her needed arre,

499 *dight* adorned
521 *won* dwelling place

Whom verse of noblest shepheard lately dead
Hath prais'd and rais'd above each other starre.
Ne lesse praisworthie are the sisters three,
The honor of the noble familie:
Of which I meanest boast my selfe to be,
And most that unto them I am so nie.
Phyllis, Charillis, and sweet *Amaryllis,* 540
Phillis the faire, is eldest of the three:
The next to her, is bountifull *Charillis.*
But th'youngest is the highest in degree.
Phyllis the floure of rare perfection,
Faire spreading forth her leaves with fresh delight,
That with their beauties amorous reflexion,
Bereave of sence each rash beholders sight.
But sweet *Charillis* is the Paragone
Of peerlesse price, and ornament of praise,
Admyr'd of all, yet envied of none, 550
Through the myld temperance of her goodly raies.
Thrice happie do I hold thee noble swaine,
The which art of so rich a spoile possest,
And it embracing deare without disdaine,
Hast sole possession in so chaste a brest:
Of all the shepheards daughters which there bee,
(And yet there be the fairest under skie,
Or that elsewhere I ever yet did see)
A fairer Nymph yet never saw mine eie:
She is the pride and primrose of the rest, 560
Made by the maker selfe to be admired:
And like a goodly beacon high addrest,
That is with sparks of heavenle beautie fired.
But *Amaryllis,* whether fortunate,
Or else unfortunate may I aread,

537 *honor* glory
548 *Paragone* supreme example
551 *raies* rays
553 *spoile* treasure
554 *it embracing deare without disdaine* cherishing it worthily

[433-8]

That freed is from *Cupids* yoke by fate,
Since which she doth new bands adventure dread.
Shepheard what ever thou hast heard to be
In this or that praysd diversely apart,
In her thou maist them all assembled see, 570
And seald up in the threasure of her hart.
Ne thee lesse worthie gentle *Flavia*,
For thy chaste life and vertue I esteeme:
Ne thee lesse worthie curteous *Candida*,
For thy true love and loyaltie I deeme.
Besides yet many mo that *Cynthia* serve,
Right noble Nymphs, and high to be commended:
But if I all should praise as they deserve,
This sun would faile me ere I halfe had ended.
Therefore in closure of a thankfull mynd, 580
I deeme it best to hold eternally,
Their bounteous deeds and noble favours shrynd,
Then by discourse them to indignifie.

So having said, *Aglaura* him bespake:
Colin, well worthie were those goodly favours
Bestowd on thee, that so of them doest make,
And them requitest with thy thankfull labours.
But of great *Cynthiaes* goodnesse and high grace,
Finish the storie which thou hast begunne.

More eath (quoth he) it is in such a case 590
How to begin, then know how to have donne.
For everie gift and everie goodly meed,
Which she on me bestowed, demaunds a day;
And everie day, in which she did a deed,
Demaunds a yeare it duly to display.
Her words were like a streame of honny fleeting,

567 *new bands* new commitment; *adventure* trial
571 *threasure* treasure
583 *indignifie* belittle
590 *eath* easy
592 *meed* reward
596 *fleeting* flowing

The which doth softly trickle from the hive:
Hable to melt the hearers heart unweeting,
And eke to make the dead againe alive.
Her deeds were like great clusters of ripe grapes, 600
Which load the braunches of the fruitfull vine:
Offring to fall into each mouth that gapes,
And fill the same with store of timely wine.
Her lookes were like beames of the morning Sun,
Forth looking through the windowes of the East:
When first the fleecie cattell have begun
Upon the perled grasse to make their feast.
Her thoughts are like the fume of Franckincence,
Which from a golden Censer forth doth rise:
And throwing forth sweet odours mounts fro thence 610
In rolling globes up to the vauted skies.
There she beholds with high aspiring thought,
The cradle of her owne creation:
Emongst the seats of Angels heavenly wrought,
Much like an Angell in all forme and fashion,
   Colin (said *Cuddy* then) thou hast forgot
Thy selfe, me seemes, too much, to mount so hie:
Such loftie flight, base shepheard seemeth not,
From flocks and fields, to Angels and to skie.
   True (answered he) but her great excellence, 620
Lifts me above the measure of my might:
That being fild with furious insolence,
I feele my selfe like one yrapt in spright.
For when I thinke of her, as oft I ought,
Then want I words to speake it fitly forth:
And when I speake of her what I have thought,
I cannot thinke according to her worth.

---

598 *unweeting* unaware
606 *fleecie cattell* sheep
611 *vauted* vaulted
618 *base* lowly
622 *furious insolence* rage of inspiration
623 *yrapt in spright* caught up in the spirit

Yet will I thinke of her, yet will I speake,
So long as life my limbs doth hold together,
And when as death these vitall bands shall breake,   630
Her name recorded I will leave for ever.
Her name in every tree I will endosse,
That as the trees do grow, her name may grow:
And in the ground each where will it engrosse,
And fill with stones, that all men may it know.
The speaking woods and murmuring waters fall,
Her name Ile teach in knowen termes to frame:
And eke my lambs when for their dams they call,
Ile teach to call for *Cynthia* by name.
And long while after I am dead and rotten: 640
Amongst the shepheards daughters dancing rownd,
My layes made of her shall not be forgotten.
But sung by them with flowry gyrlonds crownd.
And ye, who so ye be, that shall survive:
When as ye heare her memory renewed,
Be witnesse of her bountie here alive,
Which she to *Colin* her poore shepheard shewed.

  Much was the whole assembly of those heards,
Moov'd at his speech, so feelingly he spake:
And stood awhile astonisht at his words,   650
Till *Thestylis* at last their silence brake,
Saying, Why *Colin*, since thou foundst such grace
With *Cynthia* and all her noble crew:
Why didst thou ever leave that happie place,
In which such wealth might unto thee accrew?
And back returnedst to this barrein soyle,
Where cold and care and penury do dwell:
Here to keep sheepe, with hunger and with toyle,
Most wretched he, that is and cannot tell.

  Happie indeed (said *Colin*) I him hold,   660

---

632 *endosse* inscribe
634 *each where* everywhere; *engrosse* write large
638 *eke* also
648 *heards* shepherds

[433–8]

That may that blessed presence still enjoy,
Of fortune and of envy uncomptrold,
Which still are wont most happie states t'annoy:
But I by that which little while I prooved:
Some part of those enormities did see,
The which in Court continually hooved,
And followd those which happie seemd to bee.
Therefore I silly man, whose former dayes
Had in rude fields bene altogether spent,
Durst not adventure such unknowen wayes, 670
Nor trust the guile of fortunes blandishment,
But rather chose back to my sheep to tourne,
Whose utmost hardnesse I before had tryde,
Then having learnd repentance late, to mourne
Emongst those wretches which I there descryde.
 Shepheard (said *Thestylis*) it seemes of spight
Thous speakest thus gainst their felicitie,
Which thou enviest, rather then of right
That ought in them blameworthie thou doest spie.
 Cause have I none (quoth he) of cancred will 680
To quite them ill, that me demeand so well:
But selfe-regard of private good or ill,
Moves me of each, so as I found, to tell,
And eke to warne yong shepheards wandring wit,
Which through report of that lives painted blisse,
Abandon quiet home, to seeke for it,
And leave their lambes to losse, misled amisse.
For sooth to say, it is no sort of life,

662 *uncomptrold* unhindered
663 *t'annoy* to trouble
665 *enormities* abuses
666 *hooved* lay in wait
668 *silly* simple
669 *rude* rustic
671 *blandishment* flattery
680 *cancred* poisoned
681 *quite* repay; *demeand* treated
682 *selfe-regard* first-hand experience; *private* personal

For shepheard fit to lead in that same place,
Where each one seeks with malice and with strife, 690
To thrust downe other into foule disgrace,
Himselfe to raise: and he doth soonest rise
That best can handle his deceitfull wit,
In subtil shifts, and finest sleights devise,
Either by slaundring his well deemed name,
Through leasings lewd, and fained forgerie:
Or else by breeding him some blot of blame,
By creeping close into his secrecie;
To which him needs a guilefull hollow hart,
Masked with faire dissembling curtesie, 700
A filed toung furnisht with tearmes of art,
No art of schoole, but Courtiers schoolery.
For arts of schoole have there small countenance,
Counted but toyes to busie ydle braines,
And there professours find small maintenance,
But to be instruments of others gaines.
Ne is there place for any gentle wit,
Unlesse to please, it selfe it can applie:
But shouldred is, or out of doore quite shit,
As base, or blunt, unmeet for melodie. 710
For each mans worth is measured by his weed,
As harts by hornes, or asses by their eares:
Yet asses been not all whose eares exceed,
Nor yet all harts, that hornes the highest beares.
For highest lookes have not the highest mynd,
Nor haughtie words most full of highest thoughts:

---

695 *well deemed* well-respected
696 *leasings lewd* foul lies; *fained forgerie* slanderous invention
697 *breeding* inventing; *blot of blame* credible scandal
699 *To which* for which
701 *tearmes of art* skills of rhetoric
705 *professours* learned men
707 *Ne* nor; *gentle* noble
709 *shit* shut
711 *weed* clothing
712 *As harts by hornes* as stags by their antlers

[433–8]

But are like bladders blowen up with wynd,
That being prickt do vanish into noughts.
Even such is all their vaunted vanitie,
Nought else but smoke, that fumeth soone away; 720
Such is their glorie that in simple eie
Seeme greatest, when their garments are most gay.
So they themselves for praise of fooles do sell,
And all their wealth for painting on a wall;
With price whereof, they buy a golden bell,
And purchase highest rowmes in bowre and hall:
Whiles single Truth and simple honestie
Do wander up and downe despys'd of all;
Their plaine attire such glorious gallantry
Disdaines so much, that none them in doth call. 730

    Ah *Colin* (then said *Hobbinol*) the blame
Which thou imputest, is too generall,
As if not any gentle wit of name,
Nor honest mynd might there be found at all.
For well I wot, sith I my selfe was there,
To wait on *Lobbin* (*Lobbin* well thou knewest)
Full many worthie ones then waiting were,
As ever else in Princes Court thou vewest.
Of which, among you many yet remaine,
Whose names I cannot readily now ghesse: 740
Those that poore Sutors papers do retaine,
And those that skill of medicine professe.
And those that do to *Cynthia* expound
The ledden of straunge languages in charge:
For *Cynthia* doth in sciences abound,
And gives to their professors stipends large.
Therefore, unjustly thou doest wyte them all,

718 *noughts* nothing
719 *vaunted* boasted
730 *Disdaines* overshadows
741 *Sutors* suitors; *retaine* take proper note of
744 *ledden* speech; *in charge* as their responsibility
745 *sciences* all branches of knowledge
747 *wyte* blame

For that which thou mislikedst in a few.
    Blame is (quoth he) more blamelesse generall,
Then that which private errours doth pursew:
For well I wot, that there amongst them bee,
Full many persons of right worthie parts,
Both for report of spotlesse honestie,
And for profession of all learned arts,
Whose praise hereby no whit impaired is,
Though blame do light on those that faultie bee,
For all the rest do most-what fare amis,
And yet their owne misfaring will not see:
For either they be puffed up with pride,
Or fraught with envie that their galls do swell,
Or they their dayes to ydlenesse divide,
Or drownded lie in pleasures wastefull well,
In which like Moldwarps nousling still they lurke,
Unmyndfull of chiefe parts of manlinesse,
And do themselves for want of other worke,
Vaine votaries of laesie love professe,
Whose service high so basely they ensew,
That *Cupid* selfe of them ashamed is,
Amd mustring all his men in *Venus* vew,
Denies them quite for servitors of his.

    And is love then (said *Corylas*) once knowne
In Court, and his sweet lore professed there?
I weened sure he was our God alone:
And only woond in fields and forests here.

    Not so (quoth he) love most aboundeth there.
For all the walls and windows there are writ,
All full of love, and love, and love my deare,
And all their talke and studie is of it.
Ne any there doth brave or valiant seeme,

---

757 *most-what* for the most part
758 *misfaring* misdeeds
763 *Moldwarps nousling* moles burrowing with their snouts
767 *ensew* follow
774 *woond* dwelt

[433-8]

Unlesse that some gay Mistresse badge he beares: 780
Ne any one himselfe doth ought esteeme,
Unlesse he swim in love up to the eares.
But they of love and of his sacred lere,
(As it should be) all otherwise devise,
Then we poore shepheards are accustomd here,
And him do sue and serve all otherwise.
For with lewd speeches and licentious deeds,
His mightie mysteries they do prophane,
And use his ydle name to other needs,
But as a complement for courting vaine. 790
So him they do not serve as they professe,
But make him serve to them for sordid uses,
Ah my dread Lord, that doest liege hearts possesse,
Avenge thy selfe on them for their abuses.
But we poore shepheards, whether rightly so,
Or through our rudenesse into errour led,
Do make religion how we rashly go,
To serve that God, that is so greatly dred;
For him the greatest of the Gods we deeme,
Borne without Syre or couples, of one kynd, 800
For *Venus* selfe doth soly couples seeme,
Both male and female, through commixture joynd,
So pure and spotlesse *Cupid* forth she brought,
And in the gardens of *Adonis* nurst:
Where growing, he his owne perfection wrought,
And shortly was of all the Gods the first.
Then got he bow and shafts of gold and lead,
In which so fell and puissant he grew,
That *Jove* himselfe his powre began to dread,

780 *badge* love-token
783 *lere* lore
784 *devise* imagine
792 *sordid* debased
793 *Lord* Cupid, Love; *liege* faithful
796 *rudenesse* simplicity
797 *religion* cautious reverence

And taking up to heaven, him godded new. 810
From thence he shootes his arrowes every where
Into the world, at randon as he will,
On us fraile men, his wretched vassals here,
Like as himselfe us pleaseth, save or spill.
So we him worship, so we him adore
With humble hearts to heaven uplifted hie,
That to true loves he may us evermore
Preferre, and of their grace us dignifie:
Ne is there shepheard, ne yet shepheards swaine,
What ever feeds in forest or in field, 820
That dare with evil deed or leasing vaine
Blaspheme his powre, or termes unworthie yield.

   Shepheard it seemes that some celestiall rage
Of love (quoth *Cuddy*) is breath'd into thy brest,
That powreth forth these oracles so sage,
Of that high powre, wherewith thou art possest.
But never wist I till this present day
Albe of love I always humbly deemed,
That he was such an one, as thou doest say,
And so religiously to be esteemed. 830
Well may it seeme by this thy deep insight,
That of that God the Priest thou shouldest bee:
So well thou wot'st the mysterie of his might,
As if his godhead thou didst present see.

   Of loves perfection perfectly to speake,
Or of his nature rightly to define,
Indeed (said *Colin*) passeth reasons reach,
And needs his priest t'expresse his powre divine.
For long before the world he was y'bore
And bred above in *Venus* bosome deare: 840
For by his powre the world was made of yore,

---

810 *godded* deified
812 *at randon* at random
821 *leasing vaine* empty falsehood
822 *termes unworthie yield* speak of him slightingly
823 *celestiall rage* heavenly inspiration

[433-8]

And all that therein wondrous doth appeare.
For how should else things so far from attone
And so great enemies as of them bee,
Be ever drawne together into one,
And taught in such accordance to agree?
Through him the cold began to covet heat,
And water fire; the light to mount on hie,
And th'heavie downe to peize; the hungry t'eat
And voydnesse to seeke full satietie.   850
So being former foes, they wexed friends,
And gan by litle learne to love each other:
So being knit, they brought forth other kynds
Out of the fruitfull wombe of their great mother.
Then first gan heaven out of the darknesse dread
For to appeare, and brought forth chearfull day:
Next gan the earth to shew her naked head,
Out of the deep waters which her drownd alway.
And shortly after, everie living wight
Crept forth like wormes out of her slimie nature,   860
Soone as on them the Suns life giving light,
Had powred kindly heat and formall feature,
Thenceforth they gan each one his like to love,
And like himselfe desire for to beget,
The Lyon chose his mate, the Turtle Dove
Her deare, the Dolphin his owne Dolphinet;
But man that had the sparke of reasons might,
More then the rest to rule his passion,
Chose for his love the fairest in his sight,
Like as himselfe was fairest by creation.   870
For beautie is the bayt which with delight
Doth man allure, for to enlarge his kynd,

843 *attone* unity
844 *of them* among them
849 *peize* weigh
858 *alway* until then
862 *formall feature* recognizable shape
866 *Dolphinet* female dolphin

338

Beautie the burning lamp of heavens light,
Darting her beames into each feeble mynd:
Against whose powre, nor God nor man can fynd,
Defence, ne ward the daunger of the wound,
But being hurt, seeke to be medicynd
Of her that first did stir that mortall stownd.
Then do they cry and call to love apace,
With praiers lowd importuning the skie, 880
Whence he them heares, and when he list shew grace,
Does graunt them grace that otherwise would die.
So love is Lord of all the world by right,
And rules the creatures by his powrfull saw:
All being made the vassalls of his might,
Through secret sence which therto doth them draw.
Thus ought all lovers of their lord to deeme:
And with chaste heart to honor him alway:
But who so else doth otherwise esteeme,
Are outlawes, and his lore do disobay. 890
For their desire is base, and doth not merit,
The name of love, but of disloyall lust:
Ne mongst true lovers they shall place inherit,
But as Exuls out of his court be thrust.

   So having said, *Melissa* spake at will,
Colin, thou now full deeply hast divynd:
Of love and beautie, and with wondrous skill,
Hast *Cupid* selfe depainted in his kynd.
To thee are all true lovers greatly bound,
That doest their cause so mightily defend: 900
But most, all wemen are thy debtors found,
That doest their bountie still so much commend.

   That ill (said *Hobbinol*) they him requite,

---

878 *stir* cause; *stownd* hurt
881 *he* Cupid, Love
884 *saw* decree
894 *Exuls* exiles
898 *in his kynd* according to his nature
902 *bountie* goodness

[433–8]

For having loved ever one most deare:
He is repayd with scorne and foule despite,
That yrkes each gentle heart which it doth heare.
    Indeed (said *Lucid*) I have often heard
Faire *Rosalind* of divers fowly blamed:
For being to that swaine too cruell hard,
That her bright glorie else hath much defamed.   910
But who can tell what cause had that faire Mayd
To use him so that used her so well:
Or who with blame can justly her upbrayd,
For loving not? for who can love compell?
And sooth to say, it is foolhardie thing,
Rashly to wyten creatures so divine,
For demigods they be and first did spring
From heaven, though graft in frailnesse feminine.
And well I wote, that oft I heard it spoken,
How one that fairest *Helene* did revile: 920
Through judgement of the Gods to been ywroken
Lost both his eyes and so remaynd long while,
Till he recanted had his wicked rimes,
And made amends to her with treble praise:
Beware therefore, ye groomes, I read betimes,
How rashly blame of *Rosalind* ye raise.
    Ah shepheards (then said *Colin*) ye ne weet
How great a guilt upon your heads ye draw:
To make so bold a doome with words unmeet,
Of thing celestiall which ye never saw.   930
For she is not like as the other crew
Of shepheards daughters which emongst you bee,

---

913 *upbrayd* reproach
916 *wyten* blame
917 *demigods* half divine
918 *graft in* engrafted in
921 *to been ywroken* to be punished
925 *groomes* young men; *read betimes* now advise
927 *ye ne weet* you do not know
929 *so bold a doome* so rash a judgement

[433–8]

But of divine regard and heavenly hew,
Excelling all that ever ye did see.
Not then to her that scorned thing so base,
But to my selfe the blame that lookt so hie:
So hie her thoughts as she her selfe have place,
And loath each lowly thing with loftie eie.
Yet so much grace let her vouchsafe to grant
To simple swaine, sith her I may not love: 940
Yet that I may her honour paravant,
And praise her worth, though far my wit above.
Such grace shall be some guerdon for the griefe,
And long affliction which I have endured:
Such grace sometimes shall give me some reliefe,
And ease of paine which cannot be recured.
And ye my fellow shepheards which do see
And heare the languours of my too long dying,
Unto the world for ever witnesse bee,
That hers I die, nought to the world denying,   950
This simple trophe of her great conquest.

   So having ended, he from ground did rise,
And after him uprose eke all the rest:
All loth to part, but that the glooming skies
Warnd them to draw their bleating flocks to rest.

---

935 *base* low
940 *sith* since
941 *paravant* above all
943 *guerdon* reward
948 *languours* sorrows

Epithalamion

Ye learned sisters which have oftentimes
Beene to me ayding, others to adorne:
Whom ye thought worthy of your gracefull rymes,
That even the greatest did not greatly scorne
To heare theyr names sung in your simple layes,
But joyed in theyr prayse.
And when ye list your owne mishaps to mourne,
Which death, or love, or fortunes wreck did rayse,
Your string could soone to sadder tenor turne,
And teach the woods and waters to lament   10
Your dolefull dreriment.
Now lay those sorrowfull complaints aside,
And having all your heads with girland crownd,
Helpe me mine owne loves prayses to resound,
Ne let the same of any be envide:
So Orpheus did for his owne bride,
So I unto my selfe alone will sing,
The woods shall to me answer and my Eccho ring.

   1 *learned sisters* the Muses
   2 *Beene to me ayding* have helped me
   8 *wreck* ruin
  11 *dreriment* grief

[438–41]

Early before the worlds light giving lampe,
His golden beame upon the hils doth spred,   20
Having disperst the nights unchearefull dampe,
Doe ye awake, and with fresh lusty hed,
Go to the bowre of my beloved love,
My truest turtle dove,
Bid her awake; for Hymen is awake,
And long since ready forth his maske to move,
With his bright Tead that flames with many a flake,
And many a bachelor to waite on him,
In theyr fresh garments trim.
Bid her awake therefore and soone her dight,   30
For lo the wished day is come at last,
That shall for al the paynes and sorrowes past,
Pay to her usury of long delight:
And whylest she doth her dight,
Doe ye to her of joy and solace sing,
That all the woods may answer and your eccho ring.

Bring with you all the Nymphes that you can heare
Both of the rivers and the forrests greene:
And of the sea that neighbours to her neare,
Al with gay girlands goodly wel beseene.   40
And let them also with them bring in hand,
Another gay girland
For my fayre love of lillyes and of roses,
Bound truelove wize with a blew silke riband.
And let them make great store of bridale poses,
And let them eeke bring store of other flowers

22 *lusty hed* vigour
25 *Hymen* god of marriage
26 *maske* procession
27 *Tead* torch
34 *dight* deck
37 *heare* hear of
40 *beseene* adorned
44 *truelove wize* with a lovers' knot
46 *eeke* also

343

To deck the bridale bowers.
And let the ground whereas her foot shall tread,
For feare the stones her tender foot should wrong
Be strewed with fragrant flowers all along, 50
And diapred lyke the discolored mead.
Which done, doe at her chamber dore awayt,
For she will waken strayt,
The whiles doe ye this song unto her sing,
The woods shall to you answer and your Eccho ring.

Ye Nymphes of Mulla which with carefull heed,
The silver scaly trouts doe tend full well,
And greedy pikes which use therein to feed,
(Those trouts and pikes all others doo excell)
And ye likewise which keepe the rushy lake, 60
Where none doo fishes take,
Bynd up the locks the which hang scatterd light,
And in his waters which your mirror make,
Behold your faces as the christall bright,
That when you come whereas my love doth lie,
No blemish she may spie.
And eke ye lightfoot mayds which keepe the deere,
That on the hoary mountayne use to towre,
And the wylde wolves which seeke them to devoure,
With your steele darts doo chace from comming neer 70
Be also present heere,
To helpe to decke her and to help to sing,
That all the woods may answer and your eccho ring.

Wake, now my love, awake; for it is time,
The Rosy Morne long since left Tithones bed,
All ready to her silver coche to clyme,
And Phœbus gins to shew his glorious hed.

---

51 *diapred* tapestried; *discolored mead* many-coloured meadow
60 *keepe* guard
68 *towre* roam
77 *Phoebus* the sun

Hark how the cheerefull birds do chaunt theyr laies
And carroll of loves praise.
The merry larke hir mattins sings aloft, 80
The thrush replyes, the Mavis descant playes,
The Ouzell shrills, the Ruddock warbles soft,
So goodly all agree with sweet consent,
To this dayes merriment.
Ah my deere love why doe ye sleepe thus long,
When meeter were that ye should now awake,
T'awayt the comming of your joyous make,
And hearken to the birds lovelearned song,
The deawy leaves among.
For they of joy and pleasance to you sing, 90
That all the woods them answer and theyr eccho ring.

My love is now awake out of her dreame,
And her fayre eyes like stars that dimmed were
With darksome cloud, now shew theyr goodly beams
More bright then Hesperus his head doth rere.
Come now ye damzels, daughters of delight,
Helpe quickly her to dight,
But first come ye fayre houres which were begot
In Joves sweet paradice, of Day and Night,
Which doe the seasons of the yeare allot, 100
And al that ever in this world is fayre
Doe make and still repayre.
And ye three handmayds of the Cyprian Queene,
The which doe still adorne her beauties pride,
Helpe to addorne my beautifullest bride:

---

80 *mattins* morning hymn
81 *thrush* song thrush; *Mavis* mavis thrush
82 *Ouzell* blackbird; *Ruddock* robin
83 *agree* are attuned; *consent* harmony
87 *make* mate
95 *Hesperus* the morning (sometimes the evening) star; *rere* raise
98 *fayre houres* the Hours
103 *three handmayds* the Graces; *Cyprian Queene* Venus

And as ye her array, still throw betweene
Some graces to be seene,
And as ye use to Venus, to her sing,
The whiles the woods shal answer and your eccho ring.

Now is my love all ready forth to come, 110
Let all the virgins therefore well awayt,
And ye fresh boyes that tend upon her groome
Prepare your selves; for he is comming strayt.
Set all your things in seemely good aray
Fit for so joyfull day,
The joyfulst day that ever sunne did see.
Faire Sun, shew forth thy favourable ray,
And let thy lifull heat not fervent be
For feare of burning her sunshyny face,
Her beauty to disgrace. 120
O fayrest Phœbus, father of the Muse,
If ever I did honour thee aright,
Or sing the thing, that mote thy mind delight,
Doe not thy servants simple boone refuse,
But let this day let this one day be myne,
Let all the rest be thine.
Then I thy soverayne prayses loud wil sing,
That all the woods shal answer and theyr eccho ring.

Harke how the Minstrels gin to shrill aloud
Their merry Musick that resounds from far, 130
The pipe, the tabor, and the trembling Croud,
That well agree withouten breach or jar.
But most of all the Damzels doe delite,
When they their tymbrels smyte,

---

118 *lifull* life-giving; *fervent* burning
120 *disgrace* mar
123 *mote* might
131 *tabor* small drum; *Croud* viol
132 *agree* harmonize; *jar* discord
134 *tymbrels* small tambourines

And thereunto doe daunce and carrol sweet,
That all the sences they doe ravish quite,
The whyles the boyes run up and downe the street,
Crying aloud with strong confused noyce,
As if it were one voyce.
Hymen io Hymen, Hymen they do shout, 140
That even to the heavens theyr shouting shrill
Doth reach, and all the firmament doth fill,
To which the people standing all about,
As in approvance doe thereto applaud
And loud advaunce her laud,
And evermore they Hymen Hymen sing,
That al the woods them answer and theyr eccho ring.

Loe where she comes along with portly pace
Lyke Phœbe from her chamber of the East,
Arysing forth to run her mighty race, 150
Clad all in white, that seemes a virgin best.
So well it her beseemes that ye would weene
Some angell she had beene.
Her long loose yellow locks lyke golden wyre,
Sprinckled with perle, and perling flowres a tweene,
Doe lyke a golden mantle her attyre,
And being crowned with a girland greene,
Seeme lyke some mayden Queene.
Her modest eyes abashed to behold
So many gazers, as on her do stare, 160
Upon the lowly ground affixed are.
Ne dare lift up her countenance too bold,
But blush to heare her prayses sung so loud,
So farre from being proud.

---

138 *confused* united
145 *advaunce* celebrate; *laud* praise
148 *portly* stately
149 *Phoebe* the Moon
150 *race* journey

Nathlesse doe ye still loud her prayses sing.
That all the woods may answer and your eccho ring.

Tell me ye merchants daughters did ye see
So fayre a creature in your towne before,
So sweet, so lovely, and so mild as she,
Adornd with beautyes grace and vertues store,   170
Her goodly eyes lyke Saphyres shining bright,
Her forehead yvory white,
Her cheekes lyke apples which the sun hath rudded,
Her lips lyke cherryes charming men to byte,
Her brest like to a bowle of creame uncrudded,
Her paps lyke lyllies budded,
Her snowie necke lyke to a marble towre,
And all her body like a pallace fayre,
Ascending uppe with many a stately stayre,
To honors seat and chastities sweet bowre.   180
Why stand ye still ye virgins in amaze,
Upon her so to gaze,
Whiles ye forget your former lay to sing,
To which the woods did answer and your eccho ring.

But if ye saw that which no eyes can see,
The inward beauty of her lively spright,
Garnisht with heavenly guifts of high degree,
Much more then would ye wonder at that sight,
And stand astonisht lyke to those which red
Medusaes mazeful hed.   190
There dwels sweet love and constant chastity,
Unspotted fayth and comely womanhood,
Regard of honour and mild modesty,

---

175 *uncrudded* uncurdled
176 *paps* breasts
186 *lovely spright* living spirit
187 *guifts* gifts
189 *red* saw
190 *mazeful* petrifying

There vertue raynes as Queene in royal throne,
And giveth lawes alone.
The which the base affections doe obay,
And yeeld theyr services unto her will,
Ne thought of thing uncomely ever may
Thereto approch to tempt her mind to ill.
Had ye once seene these her celestial threasures, 200
And unrevealed pleasures,
Then would ye wonder and her prayses sing,
That al the woods should answer and your echo ring.

Open the temple gates unto my love,
Open them wide that she may enter in,
And all the postes adorne as doth behove,
And all the pillours deck with girlands trim,
For to recyve this Saynt with honour dew,
That commeth in to you.
With trembling steps and humble reverence, 210
She commeth in, before th'almighties vew,
Of her ye virgins learne obedience,
When so ye come into those holy places,
To humble your proud faces:
Bring her up to th'high altar, that she may
The sacred ceremonies there partake,
The which do endlesse matrimony make,
And let the roring Organs loudly play
The praises of the Lord in lively notes,
The whiles with hollow throates 220
The Choristers the joyous Antheme sing,
That al the woods may answere and their eccho ring.

Behold whiles she before the altar stands
Hearing the holy priest that to her speakes
And blesseth her with his two happy hands,
How the red roses flush up in her cheekes,

196 *base affections* passions
200 *threasures* treasures

[438–41]

And the pure snow with goodly vermill stayne,
Like crimsin dyde in grayne,
That even th'Angels which continually,
About the sacred Altare doe remaine, 230
Forget their service and about her fly,
Ofte peeping in her face that seemes more fayre,
The more they on it stare.
But her sad eyes still fastened on the ground,
Are governed with goodly modesty,
That suffers not one looke to glaunce awry,
Which may let in a little thought unsownd.
Why blush ye love to give to me your hand,
The pledge of all our band?
Sing ye sweet Angels, Alleluya sing, 240
That all the woods may answere and your eccho ring.

Now al is done; bring home the bride againe,
Bring home the triumph of our victory,
Bring home with you the glory of her gaine,
With joyance bring her and with jollity.
Never had man more joyfull day then this,
Whom heaven would heape with blis.
Make feast therefore now all this live long day,
This day for ever to me holy is,
Poure out the wine without restraint or stay, 250
Poure not by cups but by the belly full,
Poure out to all that wull,
And sprinkle all the postes and wals with wine,
That they may sweat, and drunken be withall.
Crowne ye God Bacchus with a coronall,

227 *vermill* vermillion
228 *in grayne* deeply
231 *service* duty
234 *sad* sober
237 *unsownd* distracting
239 *band* bond
244 *of her gaine* of gaining her
255 *Bacchus* god of wine and ecstasy

350

And Hymen also crowne with wreathes of vine,
And let the Graces daunce unto the rest;
For they can doo it best:
The whiles the maydens doe theyr carroll sing,
To which the woods shal answer and theyr eccho ring. 260

Ring ye the bels, ye yong men of the towne,
And leave your wonted labors for this day:
This day is holy; doe ye write it downe,
That ye for ever it remember may.
This day the sunne is in his chiefest hight,
With Barnaby the bright,
From whence declining daily by degrees,
He somewhat loseth of his heat and light,
When once the Crab behind his back he sees.
But for this time it ill ordained was, 270
To chose the longest day in all the yeare,
And shortest night, when longest fitter weare:
Yet never day so long, but late would passe.
Ring ye the bels, to make it weare away,
And bonefiers make all day,
And daunce about them, and about them sing:
that all the woods may answer, and your eccho ring.

Ah when will this long weary day have end,
And lende me leave to come unto my love?
How slowly do the houres theyr numbers spend? 280
How slowly does sad Time his feathers move?
Hast thee O fayrest Planet to thy home
Within the Westerne fome:
Thy tyred steedes long since have need of rest.
Long though it be, at last I see it gloome,

---

265 *chiefest hight* zenith
266 *Barnaby the bright* St Barnabas' Day
269 *the Crab* Cancer in the Zodiac
275 *bonefiers* bonfires
282 *fayrest Planet* the sun

And the bright evening star with golden creast
Appeare out of the East.
Fayre childe of beauty, glorious lampe of love
That all the host of heaven in rankes doost lead,
And guydest lovers through the nightes dread, 290
How chearefully thou lookest from above,
And seemst to laugh atweene thy twinkling light
As joying in the sight
Of these glad many which for joy doe sing,
That all the woods them answer and their echo ring.

Now ceasse ye damsels your delights forepast;
Enough is it, that all the day was youres:
Now day is doen, and night is nighing fast:
Now bring the Bryde into the brydall boures.
Now night is come, now soone her disaray, 300
And in her bed her lay;
Lay her in lillies and in violets,
And silken courteins over her display,
And odourd sheetes, and Arras coverlets.
Behold how goodly my faire love does ly
In proud humility;
Like unto Maia, when as Jove her tooke,
In Tempe, lying on the flowry gras,
Twixt sleepe and wake, after she weary was,
With bathing in the Acidalian brooke. 310
Now it is night, ye damsels may be gon,
And leave my love alone,
And leave likewise your former lay to sing:
The woods no more shal answere, nor your echo ring.

Now welcome night, thou night so long expected,
That long daies labour doest at last defray,

---

292 *atweene* between
300 *disaray* undress
303 *Arras* precious tapestry
316 *defray* repay

And all my cares, which cruell love collected,
Hast sumd in one, and cancelled for aye:
Spread thy broad wing over my love and me,
That no man may us see, 320
And in thy sable mantle us enwrap,
From feare of perrill and foule horror free.
Let no false treason seeke us to entrap,
Nor any dread disquiet once annoy
The safety of our joy:
But let the night be calme and quietsome,
Without tempestuous storms or sad afray:
Lyke as when Jove with fayre Alcmena lay,
When he begot the great Tirynthian groome:
Or lyke as when he with thy selfe did lie, 330
And begot Majesty.
And let the mayds and yongmen cease to sing:
Ne let the woods them answer, nor theyr eccho ring.

Let no lamenting cryes, nor dolefull teares,
Be heard all night within nor yet without:
Ne let false whispers, breeding hidden feares,
Breake gentle sleepe with misconceived dout.
Let no deluding dreames, nor dreadful sights
Make sudden sad affrights;
Ne let housefyres, nor lightnings helpelesse harmes, 340
Ne let the Pouke, nor other evill sprights,
Ne let mischivous witches with theyr charmes,
Ne let hob Goblins, names whose sence we see not,
Fray us with things that be not.
Let not the shriech Oule, nor the Storke be heard:
Nor the night Raven that still deadly yels,
Nor damned ghosts cald up with mightly spels,
Nor griesly vultures make us once affeard:
Ne let th'unpleasant Quyre of Frogs still croking

340 *helplesse* unavoidable
341 *the Pouke* evil spirit
342 *mischivous* wicked

Make us to wish theyr choking. 350
Let none of these theyr drery accents sing;
Ne let the woods them answer, nor theyr eccho ring.

But let stil Silence trew night watches keepe,
That sacred peace may in assurance rayne,
And tymely sleep, when it is tyme to sleepe,
May poure his limbs forth on your pleasant playne,
The whiles an hundred little winged loves,
Like divers fethered doves,
Shall fly and flutter round about your bed,
And in the secret darke, that none reproves, 360
Their prety stealthes shal worke, and snares shal spread
To filch away sweet snatches of delight,
Conceald through covert night.
Ye sonnes of Venus, play your sports at will,
For greedy pleasure, carelesse of your toyes,
Thinks more upon her paradise of joyes,
Then what ye do, albe it good or ill.
All night therefore attend your merry play,
For it will soone be day:
Now none doth hinder you, that say or sing, 370
Ne will the woods now answer, nor your Eccho ring.

Who is the same, which at my window peepes?
Or whose is that faire face, that shines so bright,
Is it not Cinthia, she that never sleepes,
But walkes about high heaven al the night?
O fayrest goddesse, do thou not envy
My love with me to spy:
For thou likewise didst love, though now unthought,
And for a fleece of woll, which privily,
The Latmian shephard once unto thee brought, 380
His pleasures with thee wrought.
Therefore to us be favorable now;

363 *covert* sheltering
374 *Cinthia* the moon

And sith of wemens labours thou hast charge,
And generation goodly dost enlarge,
Encline thy will t'effect our wishfull vow,
And the chast wombe informe with timely seed,
That may our comfort breed:
Till which we cease our hopefull hap to sing,
Ne let the woods us answere, nor our Eccho ring.

And thou great Juno, which with awful might 390
The lawes of wedlock still dost patronize,
And the religion of the faith first plight
With sacred rites hast taught to solemnize:
And eeke for comfort often called art
Of women in their smart,
Eternally bind thou this lovely band,
And all thy blessings unto us impart.
And thou glad Genius, in whose gentle hand,
The bridale bowre and geniall bed remaine,
Without blemish or staine, 400
And the sweet pleasures of theyr loves delight
With secret ayde doest succour and supply,
Till they bring forth the fruitfull progeny,
Send us the timely fruit of this same night.
And thou fayre Hebe, and thou Hymen free,
Grant that it may so be.
Til which we cease your further prayse to sing,
Ne any woods shal answer, nor your Eccho ring.

And ye high heavens, the temple of the gods,
In which a thousand torches flaming bright 410

---

384 *enlarge* set free
386 *informe* animate
392 *religion* bond
395 *smart* child-birth
396 *lovely* loving
399 *geniall* procreative
410 *torches* stars and planets

Doe burne, that to us wretched earthly clods,
In dreadful darknesse lend desired light;
And all ye powers which in the same remayne,
More then we men can fayne,
Poure out your blessing on us plentiously,
And happy influence upon us raine,
That we may raise a large posterity,
Which from the earth, which they may long possesse,
With lasting happinesse,
Up to your haughty pallaces may mount,   420
And for the guerdon of theyr glorious merit
May heavenly tabernacles there inherit,
Of blessed Saints for to increase the count.
So let us rest, sweet love, in hope of this,
And cease till then our tymely joyes to sing,
The woods no more us answer, nor our eccho ring.

Song made in lieu of many ornaments,
With which my love should duly have bene dect,
Which cutting off through hasty accidents,
Ye would not stay your dew time to expect,   430
But promist both to recompens,
Be unto her a goodly ornament,
And for short time an endlesse moniment.

---

413 *powers* planetary deities
421 *guerdon* reward
427 *in lieu* in place of
428 *dect* decked

Prothalamion

Or

A Spousall Verse made by
Edm. Spenser
in Honour of the Double mariage of the two Honorable and vertuous *Ladies, the Ladie* Elizabeth *and the Ladie* Katherine Somerset, Daughters to the Right Honourable the Earle of *Worcester* and espoused to the two worthie Gentlemen M. *Henry Gilford,* and M. *William Peter* Esquyers

1

Calme was the day, and through the trembling ayre,
  Sweete breathing *Zephyrus* did softly play
A gentle spirit, that lightly did delay
Hot *Titans* beames, which then did glyster fayre:
When I whom sullein care,
Through discontent of my long fruitlesse stay

---

2 *Zephyrus* the west wind
3 *spirit* breath; *delay* cool
4 *Titans* the sun's

[441-3]

In Princes Court, and expectation vayne
Of idle hopes, which still doe fly away,
Like empty shaddowes, did aflict my brayne,
Walkt forth to ease my payne
Along the shoare of silver streaming *Themmes*,
Whose rutty Bancke, the which his River hemmes,
Was paynted all with variable flowers,
And all the meades adornd with daintie gemmes,
Fit to decke maydens bowres,
And Crowne their Paramours,
Against the Brydale day, which is not long:
    Sweete *Themmes* runne softly, till I end my Song.

2

There, in a Meadow, by the Rivers side,
A Flocke of *Nymphes* I chaunced to espy,
All lovely Daughters of the Flood thereby,
With goodly greenish locks all loose untyde,
As each had bene a Bryde,
And each one had a little wicker basket,
Made of fine twigs entrayled curiously,
In which they gathered flowers to fill their flasket:
And with fine Fingers, cropt full feateously
The tender stalkes on hye.
Of every sort, which in that Meadow grew,
They gathered some; the Violet pallid blew,
The little Dazie, that at evening closes,
The virgin Lillie, and the Primrose trew,

11 *Themmes* Thames
12 *rutty* uneven
13 *variable* varicoloured
16 *Paramours* lovers
21 *the Flood* the Thames
25 *entrayled curiously* woven intricately
26 *flasket* flower-basket
27 *feateously* neatly

With store of vermeil Roses,
To decke their Bridegromes posies,
Against the Brydale day, which was not long:
    Sweete *Themmes* runne softly, till I end my Song.

3

With that, I saw two Swannes of goodly hewe,
Come softly swimming downe along the Lee;
Two fairer Birds I yet did never see:
The snow which doth the top of *Pindus* strew,   40
Did never whiter shew,
Nor *Jove* himselfe when he a Swan would be
For love of *Leda*, whiter did appeare:
Yet *Leda* was they say as white as he,
Yet not so white as these, nor nothing neare;
So purely white they were,
That even the gentle streame, the which them bare,
Seem'd foule to them, and bad his billowes spare
To wet their silken feathers, least they might
Soyle their fayre plumes with water not so fayre,   50
And marre their beauties bright,
That shone as heavens light,
Against their Brydale day, which was not long:
    Sweete *Themmes* runne softly, till I end my Song.

4

Eftsoones the *Nymphes*, which now had Flowers their fill,
Ran all in haste, to see that silver brood,
As they came floating on the Christal Flood.
Whom when they sawe, they stood amazed still,
Their wondring eyes to fill,
Them seem'd they never saw a sight so fayre,   60

---

33 *vermeil* vermillion
55 *Eftsoones* at once

[441-3]

Of Fowles so lovely, that they sure did deeme
Them heavenly borne, or to be that same payre
Which through the Skie draw *Venus* silver Teeme,
For sure they did not seeme
To be begot of any earthly Seede,
But rather Angels or of Angels breede:
Yet were they bred of *Somers-heat* they say,
In sweetest Season, when each Flower and weede
The earth did fresh aray,
So fresh they seem'd as day, 70
Even as their Brydale day, which was not long:
   Sweete *Themmes* runne softly, till I end my Song.

5

Then forth they all out of their baskets drew,
Great store of Flowers, the honour of the field,
That to the sense did fragrant odours yeild,
All which upon those goodly Birds they threw,
And all the Waves did strew,
That like old *Peneus* Waters they did seeme,
When downe along the pleasant *Tempes* shore
Scattered with Flowres, through *Thessaly* they streeme, 80
That they appear through Lillies plenteous store,
Like a Brydes Chamber flore:
Two of those *Nymphes*, meane while, two Garlands bound,
Of freshest Flowres which in that Mead they found,
The which presenting all in trim Array,
Their snowie Foreheads therewithall they crownd,
Whil'st one did sing this Lay,
Prepar'd against that Day,
Against their Brydale day, which was not long:
   Sweete *Themmes* runne softly, till I end my Song. 90

63 *Teeme* chariot
86 *Their* the two brides'

360

6

Ye gentle Birdes, the worlds faire ornament,
And heavens glorie, whom this happie hower
Doth leade unto your lovers blisfull bower,
Joy may you have and gentle hearts content
Of your loves couplement:
And let faire *Venus*, that is Queene of love,
With her heart-quelling Sonne upon you smile,
Whose smile they say, hath vertue to remove
All Loves dislike, and friendships faultie guile
For ever to assoile.   100
Let endlesse Peace your steadfast hearts accord,
And blessed Plentie wait upon your bord,
And let your bed with pleasures chast abound,
That fruitfull issue may to you afford,
Which may your foes confound,
And make your joyes redound,
Upon your Brydale day, which is not long:
    Sweete *Themmes* run softlie, till I end my Song.

7

So ended she; and all the rest around
To her redoubled that her undersong,   110
Which said, their bridale daye should not be long.
And gentle Eccho from the neighbour ground,
Their accents did resound.
So forth those joyous Birdes did passe along,
Adowne the Lee, that to them murmurde low,
As he would speake, but that he lackt a tong

  96 *Venus* goddess of love
  97 *heart-quelling* heart-conquering; *her...Sonne* Cupid
  98 *vertue* power
 100 *assoile* dispel
 102 *bord* table
 110 *undersong* refrain
 112 *neighbour* nearby

[441-3]

Yeat did by signes his glad affection show,
Making his streame run slow.
And all the foule which in his flood did dwell
Gan flock about these twaine, that did excell   120
The rest, so far, as *Cynthia* doth shend
The lesser starres. So they enranged well,
Did on those two attend,
And their best service lend,
Against their wedding day, which was not long:
    Sweete *Themmes* run softly, till I end my song.

8

At length they all to mery *London* came,
To mery London, my most kyndly Nurse,
That to me gave this Life first native sourse:
Though from another place I take my name,   130
An house of aunciaent fame.
There when they came, whereas those bricky towres,
The which on *Themmes* brode aged backe doe ryde,
Where now the studious Lawyers have their bowers,
There whylome wont the Templer Knights to byde,
Till they decayd through pride:
Next whereunto there standes a stately place,
Where oft I gayned giftes and goodly grace
Of that great Lord, which therein wont to dwell,
Whose want too well now feeles my freendles case: 140
But Ah here fits not well
Olde woes but joyes to tell
Against the bridale daye, which is not long:
    Sweete *Themmes* runne softly, till I end my Song.

119 *foule* waterfowl
121 *Cynthia* the moon; *shend* shame
122 *enranged* ordered
124 *service* duty
134 *bowers* chambers
135 *whylome* formerly
139 *that great Lord* the Earl of Leicester, d.1588

9

Yet therein now doth lodge a noble Peer,
Great *Englands* glory and the Worlds wide wonder,
Whose dreadfull name, late through all *Spaine* did thunder,
And *Hercules* two pillors standing neere,
Did make to quake and feare:
Faire branch of Honor, flower of Chevalrie,   150
That fillest *England* with thy triumphs fame,
Joy have thou of thy noble victorie,
And endlesse happinesse of thine owne name
That promiseth the same:
That through thy prowesse and victorious armes,
Thy country may be freed from forraine harmes:
And great *Elisaes* glorious name may ring
Through al the world, fil'd with thy wide Alarmes,
Which some brave muse may sing
To ages following,   160
Upon the Brydale day, which is not long:
    Sweete *Themmes* runne softly, till I end my Song.

10

From those high Towers, this noble Lord issuing,
Like Radiant *Hesper* when his golden hayre
In th'*Ocean* billowes he hath Bathed fayre,
Descended to the Rivers open vewing,
With a great traine ensuing.
Above the rest were goodly to bee seene
Two gentle Knights of lovely face and feature

145 *a noble Peer* the Earl of Essex
157 *Elisaes* Queen Elizabeth I's
158 *Alarmes* calls to arms
159 *brave muse* inspired epic poet
164 *Hesper* the morning (sometimes the evening) star
166 *the Rivers open vewing* the watergate
167 *ensuing* following
169 *Two gentle Knights* the bridegrooms

Beseeming well the bower of anie Queene, 170
With gifts of wit and ornaments of nature,
Fit for so goodly stature:
That like the twins of *Jove* they seem'd in sight,
Which decke the Bauldricke of the Heavens bright.
They two forth pacing to the Rivers side,
Received those two faire Brides, their Loves delight,
Which at th'appointed tyde,
Each one did make his Bryde,
Against their Brydale day, which is not long:
    Sweete *Themmes* runne softly, till I end my Song. 180

174 *Bauldricke* shoulder-belt: the Zodiac

Two Cantos of Mutabilitie

Which, both for Forme and Matter, appeare to be parcell of some following Booke of the Faerie Queene, under the Legend of *Constancie* Never before imprinted

CANTO vi

*Proud Change (not pleasd, in mortall things,
beneath the Moone, to raigne)
Pretends, as well of Gods, as Men,
to be the Soveraine.*

1

What man that sees the ever-whirling wheele
    Of *Change*, the which all mortall things doth sway,
    But that therby doth find, and plainly feele,

parcell part
Legend title
2 *sway* rule

[443–8]

How *MUTABILITY* in them doth play
Her cruell sports, to many mens decay?
Which that to all may better yet appeare,
I will rehearse that whylome I heard say,
How she at first her selfe began to reare,
Gainst all the Gods, and th'empire sought from them to beare.

2

But first, here falleth fittest to unfold
   Her antique race and linage ancient,
   As I have found it registred of old,
   In *Faery* Land mongst records permanent:
   She was, to weet, a daughter by descent
   Of those old *Titans*, that did whylome strive
   With *Saturnes* sonne for heavens regiment.
   Whom, though high *Jove* of kingdome did deprive,
Yet many of their stemme long after did survive.

3

And many of them, afterwards obtain'd
   Great power of *Jove*, and high authority;
   As *Hecaté*, in whose almighty hand,
   He plac't all rule and principality,
   To be by her disposed diversly,
   To Gods, and men, as she them list divide:
   And drad *Bellona*, that doth sound on hie
   Warres and allarums unto Nations wide,
That makes both heaven and earth to tremble at her pride.

7 *whylome* formerly
9 *th'empire* sovereignty
11 *antique* ancient
14 *to weet* indeed
16 *heavens regiment* rule of the heavens
18 *stemme* race
20 *of* from
26 *allarums* calls to battle

4

So likewise did this *Titanesse* aspire,
  Rule and dominion to her selfe to gaine;
  That as a Goddesse, men might her admire,
  And heavenly honours yield, as to them twaine.
  At first, on earth she sought it to obtaine;
  Where she such proofe and sad examples shewed
  Of her great power, to many ones great paine
  That not men onely (whom she soone subdewed)
But eke all other creatures, her bad dooings rewed.

5

For, she the face of earthly things so changed,
  That all which Nature had establisht first
  In good estate, and in meet order ranged,
  She did pervert, and all their statutes burst:
  And all the worlds faire frame (which none yet durst
  Of Gods or men to alter or misguide)
  She alter'd quite, and made them all accurst
  That God had blest; and did at first provide
In that still happy state for ever to abide.

6

Ne shee the lawes of Nature onely brake,
  But eke of Justice, and of Policie;
  And wrong of right, and bad of good did make,
  And death for life exchanged foolishlie:
  Since which, all living wights have learn'd to die,
  And all this world is woxen daily worse.

36 *rewed* regretted
39 *meet* proper
40 *statutes* laws
41 *frame* structure
44 *at first* in the beginning
51 *woxen* become

[443–8]

    O pittious worke of *MUTABILITIE*!
    By which, we all are subject to that curse,
And death in stead of life have sucked from our Nurse.

7

And now, when all the earth she thus had brought
    To her behest, and thralled to her might,
    She gan to cast in her ambitious thought,
    T'attempt the empire of the heavens hight,
    And *Jove* himselfe to shoulder from his right.
    And first, she past the region of the ayre,   60
    And of the fire, whose substance thin and slight,
    Made no resistance, ne could her contraire,
But ready passage to her pleasure did prepaire.

8

Thence, to the Circle of the Moone she clambe,
    Where *Cynthia* raignes in everlasting glory,
    To whose bright shining palace straight she came,
    All fairely deckt with heavens goodly story;
    Whose silver gates (by which there sate an hory
    Old aged Sire, with hower-glasse in hand,
    Hight *Tyme*) she entred, were he liefe or sory: 70
    Ne staide till she the highest stage had scand,
Where *Cynthia* did sit, that never still did stand.

56 *thralled* enslaved
57 *gan* began
62 *contraire* oppose
63 *to her pleasure did prepaire* opened at her wish
64 *Circle* sphere
65 *Cynthia* the moon
67 *heavens...story* the history of the gods
70 *were he liefe or sory* whether he wished it or not
71 *stage* level; *scand* ascended

368

9

Her sitting on an Ivory throne shee found,
    Drawne of two steeds, th'one black, the other white,
    Environd with tenne thousand starres around,
    That duly her attended day and night;
    And by her side, there ran her Page, that hight
    Vesper, whom we the Evening-starre intend:
    That with his Torche, still twinkling like twylight,
    Her lightened all the way where she should wend,   80
And joy to weary wandring travailers did lend:

10

That when the hardy *Titanesse* beheld
    The goodly building of her Palace bright,
    Made of the heavens substance, and up-held
    With thousand Crystall pillors of huge hight,
    Shee gan to burne in her ambitious spright,
    And t'envie her that in such glorie raigned.
    Eftsoones she cast by force and tortious might,
    Her to displace; and to her selfe to have gained
The kingdome of the Night, and waters by her wained.   90

11

Boldly she bid the Goddesse downe descend,
    And let her selfe into that Ivory throne;
    For, shee her selfe more worthy thereof wend,
    And better able it to guide alone:
    Whether to men, whose fall she did bemone,
    Or unto Gods, whose state she did maligne,
    Or to th'infernal Powers, her need give lone

---

78 *intend* name
90 *wained* moved
96 *maligne* envy
97 *her need give lone* she must lend

Of her faire light, and bounty most benigne,
Her selfe of all that rule shee deemed most condigne.

12

But shee that had to her that soveraigne seat
   By highest *Jove* assign'd, therein to beare
   Nights burning lamp, regarded not her threat,
   Ne yielded ought for favour or for feare;
   But with sterne countenaunce and disdainfull cheare,
   Bending her horned browes, did put her back:
   And boldly blaming her for comming there,
   Bade her attonce from leavens coast to pack,
Or at her perill bide the wrathfull Thunders wrack.

13

Yet nathemore the *Giantesse* forbare:
   But boldly preacing-on, raught forth her hand
   To pluck her downe perforce from off her chaire;
   And there-with lifting up her golden wand,
   Threatened to strike her if she did with-stand.
   Where-at the starres, which round about her blazed,
   And eke the Moones bright wagon, still did stand,
   All beeing with so bold attempt amazed,
And on her uncouth habit and sterne looke still gazed.

14

Meane-while, the lower World, which nothing knew
   Of all that chaunced here, was darkened quite;
   And eke the heavens, and all the heavenly crew

---

99 *condigne* worthy
110 *preacing-on* advancing; *raught* stretched
118 *lower World* the earth
120 *heavenly crew* planetary spirits

[443–8]

Of happy wights, now unpurvaide of light,
Were much afraid, and wondred at that sight;
Fearing least *Chaos* broken had his chaine,
And brought againe on them eternal night:
But chiefely *Mercury*, that next doth raigne,
Ran forth in haste, unto the king of Gods to plaine.

15

All ran together with a great out-cry,
   To *Joves* faire Palace, fixt in heavens hight;
And beating at his gates full earnestly,
   Gan call to him aloud with all their might,   130
   To know what meant that suddaine lack of light.
The father of the Gods when this he heard,
   Was troubled much at their so strange affright,
   Doubting least *Typhon* were againe uprear'd,
Or other his old foes, that once him sorely fear'd.

16

Eftsoones the sonne of Maia forth he sent
   Downe to the Circle of the Moone, to knowe
The cause of this so strange astonishment,
   And why shee did her wonted course forslowe;
   And if that any were on earth belowe   140
That did with charmes or Magick her molest,
   Him to attache, and downe to hell to throwe:
   But, if from heaven it were, then to arrest
The Author, and him bring before his presence prest.

---

121 *unpurvaide of* unprovided with
134 *least* lest
135 *fear'd* terrified
136 *Eftsoones* at once; *the sonne of Maia* Mercury
139 *forslowe* delay
142 *attache* arrest
144 *Author* perpetrator; *prest* at once

[443–8]

17

The winged-foot God, so fast his plumes did beat,
   That soone he came where-as the *Titanesse*
   Was striving with faire *Cynthia* for her seat:
   At whose strange sight, and haughty hardinesse,
   He wondered much, and feared her no lesse.
   Yet laying feare aside to doe his charge,   150
   At last, he bade her (with bold stedfastnesse)
   Ceasse to molest the Moone to walke at large,
Or come before high *Jove*, her dooings to discharge.

18

And there-with-all, he on her shoulder laid
   His snaky-wreathed Mace, whose awfull power
   Doth make both Gods and hellish fiends affraid:
   Where-at the *Titanesse* did sternely lower,
   And stoutly answer'd, that in evill hower
   He from his *Jove* such message to her brought,
   To bid her leave faire *Cynthias* silver bower;   160
   Sith shee his *Jove* and him esteemed nought,
No more the *Cynthia's* selfe; but all their kingdoms sought.

19

The Heavens Herald staid not to reply,
   But past away, his doings to relate
   Unto his Lord; who now in th'highest sky,
   Was placed in his principall Estate,

---

145 *The wingd-foot God* Mercury
152 *molest* hinder
153 *discharge* defend
155 *snaky-wreathed Mace* the caduccus
157 *lower* frown
164 *past* went
165 *th'highest sky* the sphere of Jupiter
166 *principall Estate* royal spendour

[443-8]

    With all the Gods about him congregate:
    To whom when *Hermes* had his message told,
    It did them all exceedingly amate,
       Save *Jove*; who, changing nought his count'nance bold,   170
Did unto them at length these speeches wise unfold;

20

Harken to mee awhile yee heavenly Powers;
    Ye may remember since th'Earths cursed seed
    Sought to assaile the heavens eternall towers,
    And to us all exceeding feare did breed:
    But how we then defeated all their deed,
    Yee all doe knowe, and them destroied quite;
    Yet not so quite, but that there did succeed
    An off-spring of their bloud, which did alite
Upon the fruitfull earth, which doth us yet despite.   180

21

Of that bad seed is this bold woman bred,
    That now with bold presumption doth aspire
    To thrust faire *Phœbe* from her silver bed,
    And eke our selves from heavens high Empire,
    If that her might were match to her desire:
    Wherefore, it now behoves us to advise
    What way is best to drive her to retire;
    Whether by open force, or counsell wise,
Areed ye sonnes of God, as best ye can devise.

167 *Gods* planetary gods; *congregate* gathered
168 *Hermes* Mercury
169 *amate* amaze
183 *Phoebe* the moon
189 *Areed* advise

22

So having said, he ceast; and with his brow 190
   (His black eye-brow, whose doomefull dreaded beck
   Is wont to wield the world unto his vow,
   And even the highest Powers of heaven to check)
   Made signe to them in their degrees to speake:
   Who straight gan cast their counsell grave and wise.
   Meane-while, th'Earths daughter, thogh she nought did reck
   Of *Hermes* message; yet gan now advise,
What course were best to take in this hot bold emprize.

23

Eftsoones she thus resolv'd; that whil'st the Gods
   (After returne of *Hermes* Embassie) 200
   Were troubled, and amongst themselves at ods,
   Before they could new counsels re-allie,
   To set upon them in that extasie;
   And take what fortune time and place would lend:
   So, forth she rose, and through the purest sky
   To *Joves* high Palace straight cast to ascend,
To prosecute her plot: Good on-set boads good end.

24

Shee there arriving, boldly in did pass:
   Where all the Gods she found in counsell close,
   All quite unarm'd, as then their manner was. 210
   At sight of her they suddaine all arose,
   In great amaze, ne wist what way to chose.

---

192 *vow* will
196 *nought did reck* cared nothing
198 *emprize* enterprise
202 *re-allie* formulate
203 *extasie* bewilderment
212 *amaze* confusion; *ne wist* nor knew

But *Jove*, all fearelesse, forc't them to aby;
And in his soveraine throne, gan straight dispose
Himselfe more full of grace and Majestie,
That mote encheare his friends, and foes mote terrifie.

25

That, when the haughty *Titanesse* beheld,
 All were she fraught with pride and impudence,
 Yet with the sight thereof was almost queld;
 And inly quaking, seem'd as reft of sense,
 And voyd of speech in that drad audience;
 Untill that *Jove* himselfe, her selfe bespake:
 Speake thou fraile woman, speake with confidence,
 Whence art thou, and what doost thou here now make?
What idle errand hast thou, earths mansion to forsake?

26

Shee, halfe confused with his great commaund,
 Yet gathering spirit of her natures pride,
 Him boldly answer'd thus to his demaund:
 I am a daughter, by the mothers side,
 Of her that is Grand-mother magnifide
 Of all the Gods, great *Earth*, great *Chaos* child:
 But by the fathers (be it not envide)
 I greater am in bloud (whereon I build)
Then all the Gods, though wrongfully from heaven exil'd.

27

For, *Titan* (as ye all acknowledge must)
 Was *Saturnes* elder brother by birth-right;
 Both, sonnes of *Uranus*: but by unjust

---

216 *encheare* hearten
221 *drad audience* dread presence
224 *make* do

[443–8]

    And guilefull meanes, through *Corybantes* slight,
      The younger thrust the elder for his right:
    Since which, thou *Jove*, injuriously hast held   240
      The Heavens rule from *Titans* sonnes by might;
      And them to hellish dungeons downe hast feld:
Witnesse ye Heavens the truth of all that I have teld.

28

Whil'st she thus spake, the Gods that gave good eare
    To her bold words, and marked well her grace,
    Beeing of stature tall as any there
    Of all the Gods, and beautiful of face,
    As any of the Goddesses in place,
    Stood all astonied, like a sort of Steeres;
    Mongst whom, some beast of strange and forraine race,   250
    Unwares is chaunc't, far straying from his peeres:
So did their ghastly gaze bewray their hidden feares.

29

Till having pauz'd awhile, *Jove* thus bespake;
    Will never mortall thoughts ceasse to aspire,
    In this bold sort, to Heaven claime to make,
    And touch celestiall seates with earthly mire?
    I would have thought, that bold *Procrustes* hire,
    Or *Typhons* fall, or proud *Ixions* paine;
    Or great *Prometheus*, tasting of our ire,
    Would have suffiz'd, the rest for to restraine;   260
And warn'd all men by their example to refraine:

---

238 *slight* trickery
242 *hellish dungeons* Hades
243 *teld* told
249 *sort* herd; *Steeres* cattle
252 *ghastly* terrified

30

But now, this off-scum of that cursed fry,
    Dare to renew the like bold enterprize,
    And chalenge th'heritage of this our skie;
    Whom what should hinder, but that we likewise
    Should handle as the rest of her allies,
    And thunder-drive to hell? With that, he shooke
    His Nectar-deawed locks, with which the skyes
    And all the world beneath for terror quooke,
And eft his burning levin-brond in hand he tooke.   270

31

But, when he looked on her lovely face,
    In which, faire beames of beauty did appeare,
    That could the greatest wrath soone turne to grace
    (Such sway doth beauty even in Heaven beare)
    He staide his hand: and having chang'd his cheare,
    He thus againe in milder wise began;
    But ah! if Gods should strive with flesh yfere,
    Then shortly should the progeny of Man
Be rooted out, if *Jove* should doe still what he can:

32

But thee faire *Titans* child, I rather weene,   280
    Through some vaine errour or inducement light,
    To see that mortall eyes have never seene;
    Or through ensample of thy sisters might,
    Bellona; whose great glory thou doost spight,
    Since thou hast seene her dreadfull power belowe,
    Mongst wretched men (dismaide with her affright)

---

270 *levin-brond* thunder-bolt
275 *cheare* mood
277 *yfere* on equal terms
286 *affright* terrifying appearance

[443–8]

    To bandie Crownes, and Kingdomes to bestowe:
And sure thy worth, no lesse than hers doth seem to showe.

33

But wote thou this, thou hardy *Titanesse*,
    That not the worth of any living wight   290
    May challenge ought in Heavens interesse;
    Much lesse the Title of old *Titans* Right:
    For, we by Conquest of our soveraine might,
    And by eternal doome of Fates decree,
    Have wonne the Empire of the Heavens bright;
    Which to our selves we hold, and to whom wee
Shall worthy deeme partakers of our blisse to bee.

34

Then ceasse thy idle claime thou foolish gerle,
    And seeke by grace and goodnesse to obtaine
    That place from which by folly *Titan* fell;   300
    There-to thou maist perhaps, if so thou faine
    Have *Jove* thy gratious Lord and Soveraigne.
    So, having said, she thus to him replide;
    Ceasse *Saturnes* sonne, to seeke by proffers vaine
    Of idle hopes t'allure mee to thy side,
For to betray my Right, before I have it tride.

35

But thee, O *Jove*, no equall Judge I deeme
    Of my desert, or of my dewfull Right;
    That in thine owne behalfe maist partiall seeme:
    But to the highest him, that is behight   310
    Father of Gods and men by equall might;
    To weet, the God of Nature, I appeale.

---

294 *doome* judgement
297 *partakers* sharers

There-at *Jove* wexed wroth, and in his spright
   Did inly grudge, yet did it well conceale;
And bade *Dan Phœbus* Scribe her Appellation seale.

36

Eftsoones the time and place appointed were,
   Where all, both heavenly Powers and earthly wights,
   Before great Natures presence should appeare,
   For triall of their Titles and best Rights:
   That was, to weet, upon the highest hights   320
   Of *Arlo-hill* (Who knowes not *Arlo-hill*?)
   That is the highest head (in all mens sights)
   Of my old father *Mole*, whom Shepheards quill
Renowmed hath with hymnes fit for a rurall skill.

37

And, were it not ill fitting for this file,
   To sing of hilles and woods, mongst warres and Knights,
   I would abate the sternenesse of my stile,
   Mongst these sterne stounds to mingle soft delights;
   And tell how *Arlo* through *Dianaes* spights
   (Beeing of old the best and fairest Hill   330
   That was in all this holy-Islands hights)
   Was made the most unpleasant, and most ill.
Meane while, O *Clio*, lend *Calliope* thy quill.

38

Whylome, when IRELAND florished in fame
   Of wealths and goodnesse, far above the rest
   Of all that beare the *British* Islands name,

315 *Dan Pheobus* 'Master' Apollo; *Appellation* appeal
325 *file* account
331 *this holy-Islands* Ireland's
333 *Clio* muse of history; *Calliope* muse of epic

[*443–8*]

    The Gods then us'd (for pleasure and for rest)
        Oft to resort there-to, when seem'd them best:
        But none of all there-in more pleasure found,
        Then *Cynthia*; that is soveraine Queene profest   340
        Of woods and forrests, which therein abound,
Sprinkled with wholsom waters, more then most on ground.

39

But mongst them all, as fittest for her game,
    Either for chace of beasts with hound or boawe,
    Or for to shroude in shade from *Phœbus* flame,
    Or bathe in fountaines that doe freshly flowe,
    Or from high hilles, or from the dales belowe,
    She chose this *Arlo*; where shee did resort
    With all her Nymphes enranged on a rowe,
    With whom the woody Gods did oft consort: 350
For, with the Nymphes, the Satyres love to play and sport.

40

Amongst the which, there was a Nymph that hight
    Molanna; daughter of old father *Mole*,
    And sister unto *Mulla*, faire and bright:
    Unto whose bed false *Bregog* whylome stole,
    That Shepherd *Colin* dearely did condole,
    And made her lucklesse loves well knowne to be.
    But this *Molanna*, were she not so shole,
    Were no lesse faire and beautifull then shee:
Yet as she is, a fairer flood may no man see.   360

---

344 *boawe* bow
345 *Phœbus* Apollo: the sun
356 *condole* lament
358 *shole* shallow

41

For, first, she springs out of two marble Rocks,
    On which, a grove of Oakes high mounted growes,
    That as a girlond seemes to deck the locks
    Of som faire Bride, brought forth with pompous showes
    Out of her bowre, that many flowers strowes:
    So, through the flowry Dales she tumbling downe,
    Through many woods, and shady coverts flowes
    (That on each side her silver channell crowne)
Till to the Plaine she come, whose Valleyes shee doth drowne.

42

In her sweet streames, *Diana* used oft 370
    (After her sweatie chace and toilesome play)
    To bathe her selfe; and after, on the soft
    And downy grasse, her dainty limbes to lay
    In covert shade, where none behold her may:
    For, much she hated sight of living eye.
    Foolish God *Faunus*, though full many a day
    He saw her clad, yet longed foolishly
To see her naked mongst her Nymphes in privity.

43

No way he found to compasse his desire,
    But to corrupt *Molanna*, this her maid, 380
    Her to discover for some secret hire:
    So, her with flattering words he first assaid;
    And after, pleasing gifts for her purvaid,
    Queene-apples, and red Cherries from the tree,
    With which he her allured and betraid,

---

364 *pompous* splendid
374 *covert* concealing
384 *Queene-apples* quinces
385 *betraid* induced

To tell what time he might her Lady see
When she her selfe did bathe, that he might secret bee.

44

There-to hee promist, if shee would him pleasure
   With this small boone, to quit her with a better;
   To weet, that where-as shee had out of measure   390
   Long lov'd the *Fanchin*, who by nought did set her,
   That he would undertake, for this to get her
   To be his Love, and of him liked well:
   Besides all which, he vow'd to be her debter
   For many moe good turnes then he would tell;
The least of which, this little pleasure should excell.

45

The simple maid did yield to him anone;
   And eft him placed where he close might view
   That never any saw, save onely one;
   Who, for his hire to so foole-hardy dew,   400
   Was of his hounds devour'd in Hunters hew.
   Tho, as her manner was on sunny day,
   Diana, with her Nymphes about her, drew
   To this sweet spring; where, doffing her array,
She bath'd her lovely limbes, for *Jove* a likely pray.

46

There *Faunus* saw that pleased much his eye,
   And made his hart to tickle in his brest,
   That for great joy of some-what he did spy,
   He could him not containe in silent rest;
   But breaking forth in laughter, loud profest   410
   His foolish thought. A foolish *Faune* indeed,
That couldst not hold they selfe so hidden blest,

397 *anone* soon

But wouldest needs thine owne conceit areed.
Babblers unworthy been of so divine a meed.

47

The Goddesse, all abashed with that noise,
   In haste forth started from the guilty brooke;
   And running straight where-as she heard his voice,
   Enclos'd the bush about, and there him tooke,
   Like darred Larke; not daring up to looke
   On her whose sight before so much he sought.   420
   Thence, forth they drew him by the hornes, and shooke
   Nigh all to peeces, that they left him nought;
And then into the open light they forth him brought.

48

Like as an huswife, that with busie care
   Thinks for her Dairie to make wondrous gaine,
   Finding where-as some wicked beast unware
   That breakes into her Dayr'house, there doth draine
   Her creaming pannes, and frustrate all her paine;
   Hath in some snare or gin set close behind,
   Entrapped him, and caught into her traine,   430
   Then thinkes what punishment were best assign'd,
And thousand deathes deviseth in her vengefull mind:

49

So did *Diana* and her maydens all
   Use silly *Faunus*, now within their baile:
   They mocke and scorne him, and him foule miscall;
   Some by the nose him pluckt, some by the taile,
   And by his goatish beard some did him haile:

414 *meed* reward
419 *darred* terrified

Yet he (poore soule) with patience all did beare;
For, nought against their wills might countervaile:
Ne ought he said what ever he did heare;   440
But hanging downe his head, did like a Mome appeare.

50

At length, when they had flouted him their fill,
  They gan to cast what penaunce him to give.
  Some would have gelt him, but that same would spill
  The Wood-gods breed, which must for ever live:
  Others would through the river him have drive,
  And ducked deepe: but that seem'd penaunce light;
  But most agreed and did this sentence give,
  Him in Deares skin to clad; and in that plight,
To hunt him with their hounds, him selfe save how hee might.   450

51

But *Cynthia's* selfe, more angry then the rest,
  Thought not enough, to punish him in sport,
  And of her shame to make a gamesome jest;
  But gan examine him in straighter sort,
  Which of her Nymphes, or other close consort,
  Him thither brought, and her to him betraid?
  He, much affeard, to her confessed short,
  That 'twas *Molanna* which her so bewraid.
Then all attonce their hands upon *Molanna* laid.

439 *countervaile* oppose
441 *Mome* fool
442 *flouted* mocked
444 *gelt* gelded; *spill* destroy
455 *consort* company
458 *bewraid* disclosed

52

But him (according as they had decreed)   460
    With a Deeres-skin they covered, and then chast
    With all their hounds that after him did speed;
    But he more speedy, from them fled more fast
    Then any Deere: so sore him dread aghast.
    They after follow'd all with shrill out-cry,
    Shouting as they the heavens would have brast:
    That all the woods and dales where he did flie,
Did ring againe, and loud reeccho to the skie.

53

So they him follow'd till they weary were;
    When, back returning to *Molann'* againe,   470
    They, by commaund'ment of *Diana*, there
    Her whelm'd with stones. Yet *Faunus* (for her paine)
    Of her beloved *Fanchin* did obtaine,
    That her he would receive unto his bed.
    So now her waves passe through a pleasant Plaine,
    Till with the *Fanchin* she her selfe doe wed,
And (both combin'd) themselves in one faire river spred.

54

Nath'lesse, *Diana*, full of indignation,
    Thence-forth abandoned her delicious brooke;
    In whose sweet streame, before that bad occasion,   480
    So much delight to bathe her limbes she tooke:
    Ne onely her, but also quite forsooke
    All those faire forrests about *Arlo* hid,
    And all that Mountaine, which doth over-looke
    The richest champian that may else be rid,
And the faire *Shure*, in which are thousand Salmons bred.

---

464 *aghast* terrified
485 *champian* open country

55

Them all, and all that she so deare did way,
   Thence-forth she left; and parting from the place,
   There-on an heavy haplesse curse did lay,
   To weet, that Wolves, where she was wont to space,   490
   Should harbour'd be, and all those Woods deface,
   And Thieves should rob and spoile that Coast around.
   Since which, those Woods, and all that goodly Chase,
   Doth to this day with Wolves and Thieves abound:
Which too-too true that lands in-dwellers since have found.

CANTO vii

Pealing, from Jove, to Natur's *Bar,*
bold Alteration *pleades*
Large Evidence: but Nature *soone*
her righteous Doome areads.

1

Ah! whither doost thou now thou greater Muse
   Me from these woods and pleasing forrests bring?
   And my fraile spirit (that dooth oft refuse
   This too high flight, unfit for her weake wing)
   Lift up aloft, to tell of heavens King
   Thy soveraine Sire) his fortunate successe,
   And victory, in bigger noates to sing,
   Which he obtain'd against that *Titanesse*,
That him of heavens Empire sought to dispossesse.

2

Yet sith I needs must follow thy behest,   10
   Doe thou my weaker wit with skill inspire,
   Fit for this turne; and in my feeble brest

---

493 *Chase* countryside

[448-52]

    Kindle fresh sparks of that immortall fire,
    Which learned minds inflameth with desire
    Of heavenly things: for, who but thou alone,
    That art yborne of heaven and heavenly Sire,
    Can tell things doen in heaven so long ygone;
So farre past memory of man that may be knowne.

3

Now, at the time that was before agreed,
    The Gods assembled all on *Arlo* hill;   20
    As well those that are sprung of heavenly seed,
    As those that all the other world doe fill,
    And rule both sea and land unto their will:
    Onely th'infernall Powers might not appeare;
    Aswell for horror of their count'naunce ill,
    As for th'unruly fiends which they did feare;
Yet *Pluto* and *Proserpina* were present there.

4

And thither also came all other creatures,
    What-ever life or motion doe retaine,
    According to their sundry kinds of features;   30
    That *Arlo* scarsly could them all containe;
    So full they filled every hill and Plaine:
    And had not *Natures* Sergeant (that is *Order*)
    Them well disposed by his busie paine,
    And raunged farre abroad in every border,
They would have caused much confusion and disorder.

5

Then forth issewed (great goddesse) great dame *Nature*,
    With goodly port and gracious Majesty;

17 *ygone* ago   38 *port* bearing
26 *feare* accompany

> Being far greater and more tall of stature
> Then any of the gods or Powers on hie: 40
> Yet certes by her face and physnomy,
> Whether she man or woman inly were,
> That could not any creature well descry:
> For, with a veile that wimpled every where,
> Her head and face was hid, that mote to none appeare.

6

> That some doe say was so by skill devised,
> To hide the terror of her uncouth hew,
> From mortall eyes that should be sore agrized;
> For that her face did like a Lion shew,
> That eye of wight could not indure to view: 50
> But others tell that it so beautious was,
> And round about such beames of spendor threw,
> That it the Sunne a thousand times did pass,
> Ne could be seene, but like an image in a glass.

7

> That well may seemen true: for, well I weene
> That this same day, when she on *Arlo* sat,
> Her garment was so bright and wondrous sheene,
> That my fraile wit cannot devize to what
> It to compare, nor finde like stuffe to that,
> As those three sacred *Saints*, though else most wise,   60
> Yet on mount *Thabor* quite their wits forgat,
> When they their glorious Lord in strange disguise
> Transfigur'd sawe; his garments so did daze their eyes.

---

41 *certes* certainly; *physnomy* features
44 *wimpled* was pleated
48 *agrized* horrified

8

In a fayre Plaine upon an equall Hill,
    She placed was in a pavilion;
    Not such as Craftes-men by their idle skill
    Are wont for Princes states to fashion:
    But th'earth her self of her owne motion,
    Out of her fruitfull bosome made to growe
    Most dainty trees; that, shooting up anon,   70
    Did seeme to bow their bloosming heads full lowe,
For homage unto her, and like a throne did shew.

9

So hard it is for any living wight,
    All her array and vestiments to tell,
    That old *Dan Geffrey* (in whose gentle spright
    The pure well head of Poesie did dwell)
    In his *Foules parley* durst not with it mel,
    But it transferd to *Alane*, who he thought
    Had in his *Plaint of kindes* describ'd it well:
    Which who will read set forth so as it ought,   80
Go seek he out that *Alane* where he may be sought.

10

And all the earth far underneath her feete
    Was dight with flowres, that voluntary grew
    Out of the ground, and sent forth odours sweet;
    Tenne thousand more of sundry sent and hew,
    That might delight the smell, or please the view:
    The which, the Nymphes, from all the brooks thereby
    Had gathered, which they at her foot-stoole threw;
    That richer seem'd then any tapestry,
That Princes bowres adorne with painted imagery.   90

70 *anon* at once
77 *mel* meddle

11

And *Mole* himselfe, to honour her the more,
   Did deck himself in freshest faire attire,
   And his high head, that seemeth alwaies hore
   With hardned fronts of former winters ire,
   He with an Oaken girlond now did tire,
   As if the love of some new Nymph late seene,
   Had in him kindled youthfull fresh desire,
   And made him change his gray attire to greene;
Ah gentle *Mole*! such joyance hath thee well bescene.

12

Was never so great joyance since the day, 100
   That all the gods whylome assembled were,
   On *Hæmus* hill in their divine array,
   To celebrate the solemne bridall cheare,
   Twixt *Peleus*, and dame *Thetis* pointed there;
   Where *Phœbus* self, that god of Poets hight,
   They say did sing the spousall hymne full cleere,
   That all the gods were ravisht with delight
Of his celestriall song, and Musicks wondrous might.

13

This great Grandmother of all creatures bred
   Great *Nature*, ever young yet full of eld, 110
   Still mooving, yet unmoved from her sted;
   Unseene of any, yet of all beheld;
   Thus sitting in her throne as I have teld,
   Before her came dame *Mutabilitie*;
   And being lowe before her presence feld,

   95 *tire* dress
   99 *bescene* befitted
   110 *eld* age
   111 *sted* place

390

[448–52]

With meek obaysance and humilitie,
Thus gan her plaintif Plea, with words to amplifie;

14

To thee O greatest goddesse, onely great,
    An humble suppliant loe, I lowely fly
    Seeking for Right, which I of thee entreat;   120
    Who Right to all dost deale indifferently,
    Damning all Wrong and tortious Injurie,
    Which any of they creatures doe to other
    (Oppressing them with power, unequally)
    Sith of them all thou art the equall mother,
And knittest each to each, as brother unto brother.

15

To thee therefore of this same *Jove* I plaine,
    And of his fellow gods that faine to be,
    That challenge to themselves the whole worlds raign;
    Of which, the greatest part is due to me,   130
    And heaven it selfe by heritage in Fee:
    For, heaven and earth I both alike do deeme,
    Sith heaven and earth are both alike to thee;
    And, gods no more then men thou doest esteeme:
For, even the gods to thee, as men to gods do seeme.

16

Then weigh, O soveraigne goddesse, by what right
    These gods do claime the worlds whole soverainty;
    And that is onely dew unto thy might
    Arrogate to themselves ambitiously:

---

121 *indifferently* impartially
122 *Damning* condemning; *tortious* wicked
131 *Fee* tenure
138 *that is* what is

    As for the gods owne principality,   140
    Which *Jove* usurpes unjustly; that to be
    My heritage, *Jove*'s self cannot deny,
    From my great Grandsire *Titan*, unto mee,
Deriv'd by dew descent; as is well knowen to thee.

                            17

Yet mauger *Jove*, and all his gods beside,
    I do possess the worlds most regiment;
    As, if ye please it into parts divide,
    And every parts inholders to convent,
    Shall to your eyes appeare incontinent.
    And first, the Earth (great mother of us all)   150
    That only seems unmov'd and permanent,
    And unto *Mutability* not thrall;
Yet is she chang'd in part, and eeke in generall.

                            18

For, all that from her springs, and is ybredde,
    How-ever fayre it flourish for a time,
    Yet see we soone decay; and, being dead,
    To turne again unto their earthly slime:
    Yet, out of their decay and mortall crime,
    We daily see new creatures to arize;
    And of their Winter spring another Prime,   160
    Unlike in forme, and chang'd by strange disguise:
Se turne they still about, and change in restlesse wise.

---

145 *mauger* inspite of
146 *regiment* rule
148 *inholders* tenants; *convent* call together
149 *incontinent* immediately
154 *ybredde* bred
160 *Prime* spring

19

As for her tenants; that is, man and beasts,
   The beasts we daily see massacred dy,
   As thralls and vassalls unto mens beheasts:
   And men themselves doe change continually,
   From youth to eld, from wealth to poverty,
   From good to bad, from bad to worst of all.
   Ne doe their bodies only flit and fly:
   But eeke their minds (which they immortall call)   170
Still change and vary thoughts, as new occasions fall.

20

Ne is the water in more constant case;
   Whether those same on high, or these belowe.
   For th'Ocean moveth stil, from place to place;
   And every River still doth ebbe and flowe:
   Ne any Lake, that seems most still and slowe,
   Ne Poole so small, that can his smoothnesse holde,
   When any winde doth under heaven blowe;
   With which, the clouds are also tost and roll'd;
Now like great Hills; and, streight, like sluces, then unfold.   180

21

So likewise are all watry living wights
   Still tost, and turned, with continuall change,
   Never abyding in their stedfast plights.
   The fish still floting, doe at randon range,
   And never rest; but evermore exchange
   Their dwelling places, as the streames them carrie:
   Ne have the watry foules a certaine grange,

---

164 *dy* die
165 *beheasts* commands
169 *flit* alter
187 *grange* dwelling-place

Wherein to rest, ne in one stead do tarry;
But flitting still doe flie, and still their places vary.

22

Next is the Ayre: which who feeles not by sense
    For, of all sense it is the middle meane)
    To flit still? and, with subtill influence
    Of his thin spirit, all creatures to maintaine,
    In state of life? O weake life! that does leane
    On thing so tickle as th'unsteady ayre;
    Which every howre is chang'd, and altred cleane
    With every blast that bloweth fowle or faire:
The faire doth it prolong; the fowle doth it impaire.

23

Therein the changes infinite beholde,
    Which to her creatures every minute chaunce;
    Now boyling hot: streight, friezing deadly cold:
    Now, faire sun-shine, that makes all skip and daunce:
    Streight, bitter storms and balefull countenance,
    That makes them all to shiver and to shake:
    Rayne, hayle, and snowe do pay them sad penance,
    And dreadfull thunder-claps (that make them quake)
With flames and flashing lights that thousand changes make.

24

Last is the fire: which, though it live for ever,
    Ne can be quenched quite; yet, every day,
    Wee see his parts, so soone as they do sever,
    To lose their heat, and shortly to decay;
    So, makes himself his owne consuming pray.
    Ne any living creatures doth he breed:
    But all, that are of others bredd, doth slay;

---

195 *tickle* unstable
198 *it* life

And, with their death, his cruell life doth feed;
Nought leaving, but their barren ashes, without seede.

25

Thus, all these fower (the which the ground-work bee
    Of all the world and of all living wights)
    To thousand sorts of *Change* we subject see:
    Yet are they chang'd (by other wondrous slights)   220
    Into themselves, and lose their native mights;
    The Fire to Aire, and th'Ayre to Water sheere,
    And Water into Earth: yet Water fights
    With Fire, and Aire with Earth approaching neere:
Yet all are in one body, and as one appeare.

26

So, in them all raignes *Mutabilitie*;
    How-ever these, that Gods themselves do call,
    Of them doe claime the rule and soveraity:
    As, *Vesta*, of the fire æthereall;
    Vulcan, of this, with us so usuall;   230
    Ops, of the earth; and *Juno* of the Ayre;
    Neptune, of Seas; and Nymphes, of Rivers all.
    For, all those Rivers to me subject are:
And all the rest, which they usurp, be all my share.

27

Which to approven true, as I have told,
    Vouchsafe, O goddesse, to thy presence call
    The rest which doe the world in being hold:
    As, times and seasons of the yeare that fall:
    Of all the which, demand in generall,
    Or judge thy selfe, by verdit of thine eye,   240
    Whether to me they are not subject all.
    Nature did yeeld thereto; and by-and-by,
Bade *Order* call them all, before her Majesty.

28

So, forth issew'd the Seasons of the yeare;
　First, lusty *Spring*, all dight in leaves of flowres
　That freshly budded and new bloosmes did beare
　(In which a thousand birds had built their bowres
　That sweetly sung, to call forth Paramours):
　And in his hand a javelin he did beare,
　And on his head (as fit for warlike stoures)　　　　　　　　　　250
　A guilt engraven morion he did weare;
That as some did him love, so others did him feare.

29

Then came the jolly *Sommer*, being dight
　In a thin silken cassock coloured greene,
　That was unlyned all, to be more light:
　And on his head a girlond well beseene
　He wore, from which as he had chauffed been
　The sweat did drop; and in his hand he bore
　A boawe and shaftes, as he in forrest greene
　Had hunted late the Libbard or the Bore,　　　　　　　　　　　260
And now would bathe his limbes, with labor heated sore.

30

Then came the *Autumne* all in yellow clad,
　As though he joyed in his plentious store,
　Laden with fruits that made him laugh, full glad
　That he had banisht hunger, which to-fore
　Had by the belly oft him pinched sore.
　Upon his head a wreath that was enrold

248 *Paramours* lovers
250 *stoures* conflict
251 *morion* helmet
257 *chauffed* heated
260 *Libbard* leopard
267 *enrold* entwined

With eares of corne, of every sort he bore:
    And in his hand a sickle he did holde,
To reape the ripened fruits the which the earth had yold. 270

31

Lastly, came *Winter* cloathed all in frize,
    Chattering his teeth for cold that did him chill,
    Whil'st on his hoary beard his breath did freese;
    And the dull drops that from his purpled bill
    As from a limbeck did adown distill.
    In his right hand a tipped staffe he held,
    With which his feeble steps he stayed still:
    For, he was faint with cold, and weak with eld;
That scarse his loosed limbes he hable was to weld.

32

These, marching softly, thus in order went, 280
    And after them, the Monthes all riding came;
    First, sturdy *March* with brows full sternly bent,
    And armed strongly, rode upon a Ram,
    The same which over *Hellespontus* swam:
    Yet in his hand a spade he also hent,
    And in a bag all sorts of seeds ysame,
    Which on the earth he strowed as he went,
And fild her womb with fruitfull hope of nourishment.

33

Next came fresh *Aprill* full of lustyhed,
    And wanton as a Kid whose horne new buds: 290
    Upon a Bull he rode, the same which led

270 *yold* yielded
274 *bill* nose
283 *Ram* Aries
285 *hent* carried
286 *ysame* together
289 *lustyhed* vigour
291 *Bull* Taurus

Europa floting through th'*Argolick* fluds:
His hornes were gilden all with golden studs
And garnished with garlonds goodly dight
Of all the fairest flowres and freshest buds
Which th'earth brings forth, and wet he seem'd in sight
With waves, through which he waded for his loves delight.

34

Then came faire *May*, the fayrest mayd on ground,
   Deckt all with dainties of her seasons pryde,
   And throwing flowres out of her lap around: 300
   Upon two brethrens shoulders she did ride,
   The twinnes of *Leda*; which on eyther side
   Supported her like to their soveraine Queene.
   Lord! how all creatures laught, when her they spide,
   And leapt and daunc't as they had ravisht beene!
And *Cupid* selfe about her fluttred all in greene.

35

And after her, came jolly *June*, arrayd
   Al in greene leaves, as he a Player were;
   Yet in his time, he wrought as well as playd,
   That by his plough-yrons mote right well appeare;   310
   Upon a Crab he rode, that him did beare
   With crooked crawling steps an uncouth pase,
   And backward yode, as Bargemen wont to fare
Bending their force contrary to their face,
Like that ungracious crew which faines demurest grace.

---

301 *two brethrens* Gemini
305 *ravisht* rapt
308 *a Player* an actor
311 *Crab* Cancer
312 *uncouth pase* curious gait
313 *yode* went
315 *ungracious crew* hypocrites

36

Then came hot *July* boyling like to fire,
  That all his garments he had cast away:
  Upon a Lyon raging yet with ire
  He boldly rode and made him to obay:
  It was the beast that whylome did forray   320
  The Nemæan forrest, till th'*Amphytrionide*
  Him slew, and with his hide did him array;
  Behinde his back a sithe, and by his side
Under his belt he bore a sickle circling wide.

37

The sixt was *August*, being rich arrayd
  In garment all of gold downe to the ground:
  Yet rode he not, but led a lovely Mayd
  Forth by the lilly hand, the which was cround
  With eares of corne, and full her hand was found;
  That was the righteous Virgin, which of old   330
  Liv'd here on earth, and plenty made abound;
  But, after Wrong was lov'd and Justice solde,
She left th'unrighteous world and was to heaven extold.

38

Next him, *September* marched eeke on foote;
  Yet was he heavy laden with the spoyle
  Of harvests riches, which he made his boot,
  And him enricht with bounty of the soyle:

318 *Lyon* Leo
320 *forray* ravage
321 *th'Amphytrionide* Hercules
322 *array* dress
327 *a lovely Mayd* Virgo
333 *extold* raised
334 *eeke* also
336 *boot* gain

    In his one hand, as fit for harvests toyle,
    He held a knife-hook; and in th'other hand
    A paire of waights, with which he did assoyle   340
    Both more and lesse, where it in doubt did stand,
And equall gave to each as Justice duly scann'd.

39

Then came *October* full of merry glee:
    For, yet his noule was totty of the must,
    Which he was treading in the wine-fats see,
    And of the joyous oyle, whose gentle gust
    Made him so frollick and so full of lust:
    Upon a dreadfull Scorpion he did ride,
    The same which by *Dianaes* doom unjust
    Slew great *Orion*: and eeke by his side   350
He had his ploughing share, and coulter ready tyde.

40

Next was *November*, he full grosse and fat,
    As fed with lard, and that right well might seeme;
    For, he had been a fatting hogs of late,
    That yet his browes with sweat, did reek and steem,
    And yet the season was full sharp and breem;
    In planting eeke he took no small delight:
    Whereon he rode, not easie was to deeme;
    For it a dreadful *Centaure* was in sight,
The seed of *Saturne*, and faire *Nais*, *Chiron* hight.   360

---

340 *A paire of waights* Libra; *assoyle* determine
342 *scann'd* perceived
344 *noule* head; *totty of the must* reeling with new wine
345 *wine-fats* vats of wine; *see* flood
346 *gentle gust* delicious taste
348 *Scorpion* Scorpio
356 *breem* chill
359 *Centaure* Sagittarius

41

And after him, came next the chill *December*:
  Yet he through merry feasting which he made,
  And great bonfires, did not the cold remember;
  His Saviours birth his mind so much did glad:
    Upon a shaggy-bearded Goat he rode,
    The same wherewith *Dan Jove* in tender yeares,
    They say, was nourisht by th'*Idæan* mayd;
    And in his hand a broad deepe boawle he beares;
Of which, he freely drinks an health to all his peeres.

42

Then came old *January*, wrapped well
  In many weeds to keep the cold away;
  Yet did he quake and quiver like to quell,
  And blowe his nayles to warme them if he may:
    For, they were numbd with holding all the day
    An hatchet keene, with which he felled wood,
    And from the trees did lop the needlesse spray:
    Upon an huge great Earth-pot steane he stood;
From whose wide mouth, there flowed forth the Romane floud.

43

And lastly, came cold *February*, sitting
  In an old wagon, for he could not ride;
  Drawne of two fishes for the season fitting,
  Which through the flood before did softly slyde
    And swim away: yet had he by his side
    His plough and harnesse fit to till the ground,

---

364 *His Saviours birth* Christmas
365 *Goat* Capricorn
371 *weeds* clothes
377 *Earth-pot steane* pottery urn; Aquarius
381 *two fishes* Pisces

[448–52]

    And tooles to prune the trees, before the pride
    Of hasting Prime did make them burgein round:
So past the twelve Months forth, and their dew places found.

44

And after these, there came the *Day*, and *Night*,
    Riding together both with equall pase,
    Th'one on a Palfrey blacke, the other white;   390
    But *Night* had covered her uncomely face
    With a blacke veile, and held in hand a mace,
    On top whereof the moon and stars were pight,
    And sleep and darknesse round about did trace:
    But *Day* did beare, upon his scepters hight,
The goodly Sun, encompast all with beames bright.

45

Then came the *Howres*, faire daughters of high *Jove*,
    And timely *Night*, the which were all endewed
    With wondrous beauty fit to kindle love;
    But they were Virgins all, and love eschewed,   400
    That might forslack the charge to them fore shewed
    By mighty *Jove*; who did them Porters make
    Of heavens gate (whence all the gods issued)
    Which they did dayly watch, and nightly wake
By even turnes, ne ever did their charge forsake.

46

And after all came *Life*, and lastly *Death*;
    Death with most grim and griesly visage seene,

---

386 *burgein* bud
389 *pase* pace
394 *trace* move
400 *eschewed* rejected
401 *forslack* hinder; *fore shewed* ordained

402

Yet is he nought but parting of the breath;
Ne ought to see, but like a shade to weene,
Unbodied, unsoul'd, unheard, unseene. 410
But *Life* was like a faire young lusty boy,
Such as they faine *Dan Cupid* to have beene,
Full of delightfull health and lively joy,
Deckt all with flowres, and wings of gold fit to employ.

47

When these were past, thus gan the *Titanesse*;
Lo, mighty mother, now be judge and say,
Whether in all thy creatures more or lesse
CHANGE doth not raign and beare the greatest sway:
For, who sees not, that *Time* on all doth pray?
But *Times* do change and move continually. 420
So nothing here long standeth in one stay:
Wherefore, this lower world who can deny
But to be subject still to *Mutabilitie*?

48

Then thus gan *Jove*; Right true it is, that these
And all things else that under heaven dwell
Are chaung'd of *Time*, who doth them all disseise
Of being: But, who is it (to me tell)
That *Time* himselfe doth move and still compell
To keepe his course? Is not that namely wee
Which poure that vertue from our heavenly cell, 430
That moves them all, and makes them changed be?
So them we gods doe rule, and in them also thee.

---

409 *to weene* to think of
414 *employ* use
426 *disseise* deprive
430 *that vertue* planetary influence

49

To whom, thus *Mutability*: The things
    Which we see not how they are mov'd and swayd,
    Ye may attribute to your selves as Kings,
    And say they by your secret powre are made:
    But what we see not, who shall us perswade?
    But were they so, as ye them faine to be,
    Mov'd by your might, and ordred by your ayde;
    Yet what if I can prove, that even yee   440
Your selves are likewise chang'd, and subject unto mee?

50

And first, concerning her that is the first,
    Even you faire *Cynthia*, whom so much ye make
    Joves dearest darling, she was bred and nurst
    On *Cynthus* hill, whence she her name did take:
    Then is she mortall borne, how-so ye crake;
    Besides, her face and countenance every day
    We changed see, and sundry forms partake,
    Now hornd, now round, now bright, now brown and gray:
So that *as changefull as the Moone* men use to say.   450

51

Next, *Mercury*, who though he lesse appeare
    To change his hew, and alwayes seeme as one;
    Yet he his course doth altar every yeare,
    And is of late far out of order gone:
    So *Venus* eeke, that goodly Paragone,
    Though faire all night, yet is she darke all day;
    And Phœbus self, who lightsome is alone,
    Yet is he oft eclipsed by the way,
And fills the darkned world with terror and dismay.

---

438 *faine* pretend
446 *crake* boast
455 *Paragone* pattern of excellence

52

Now *Mars* that valiant man is changed most:
    For, he some times so far runs out of square,
    That he his way doth seem quite to have lost,
    And cleane without his usuall sphere to fare;
    That even these Star-gazers stonisht are
    At sight thereof, and damne their lying bookes:
    So likewise, grim Sir *Saturne* oft doth spare
    His sterne aspect, and calme his crabbed lookes:
So many turning cranks these have, so many crookes.

53

But you *Dan Jove*, that only constant are,
    And King of all the rest, as ye do clame,
    Are you not subject eeke to this misfare?
    Then let me aske you this withouten blame,
    Where were ye borne? some say in *Crete* by name,
    Others in *Thebes*, and others other-where;
    But wheresoever they comment the same,
    They all consent that ye begotten were,
And borne here in this world, ne other can appeare.

54

Then are ye mortall borne, and thrall to me,
    Unlesse the kingdome of the sky yee make
    Immortall, and unchangeable to bee;
    Besides, that power and vertue which ye spake,
    That ye here worke, doth many changes take,
    And your owne natures change: for, each of you
    That vertue have, or this, or that to make,
    Is checkt and changed from his nature trew,
By others opposition or obliquid view.

465 *damne* condemn
468 *cranks* windings; *crookes* shifts
486 *obliquid* directed obliquely

[448–52]

55

Besides, the sundry motions of your Spheares,
    So sundry waies and fashions as clerkes faine,
    Some in short space, and some in longer yeares;
    What is the same but alteration plaine?   490
    Onely the starrie skie doth still remaine:
    Yet do the Starres and Signes therein still move,
    And even it self is mov'd, as wizards saine.
    But all that moveth, doth mutation love:
Therefore both you and them to me I subject prove.

56

Then since within this wide great *Universe*
    Nothing doth firme and permanent appeare,
    But all things tost and turned by transverse:
    What then should let, but I aloft should reare
    My Trophee, and from all, the triumph beare?   500
    Now judge then (O thou greatest goddesse trew!)
    According as thy selfe doest see and heare,
    And unto me addoom that is my dew;
That is the rule of all, all being rul'd by you.

57

So having ended, silence long ensewed,
    Ne *Nature* to or fro spake for a space,
    But with firme eyes affixt, the ground still viewed.
    Meane while, all creatures, looking in her face,

---

488 *clerkes* scholars
492 *Signes* of the Zodiac
493 *wizards* wise men; *saine* say
494 *mutation* change
498 *by tranverse* haphazardly
503 *addoom* award
506 *to or fro* for or against

>   [448–52]

            Expecting th'end of this so doubtfull case,
            Did hang in long suspence what would ensew,   510
            To whether side should fall the soveraigne place:
            At length, she looked up with chearefull view,
        The silence brake, and gave her doome in speeches few.

                                58

        I well consider all that ye have sayd,
            And find that all things stedfastnes doe hate
            And changed be: yet being rightly wayd
            They are not changed from their first estate;
            But by their change their being doe dilate:
            And turning to themselves at length againe,
            Doe worke their owne perfection so by fate: 520
            Then over them Change doth not rule and raigne;
        But they raigne over change, and doe their states maintaine.

                                59

        Cease therefore daughter further to aspire,
            And thee content thus to be rul'd by me:
            For thy decay thou seekst by they desire;
            But time shall come that all shall changed bee,
            And from thence forth, none no more change shall see.
            So was the *Titaness* put downe and whist,
            And *Jove* confirm'd in his imperiall see.
            Then was that whole assembly quite dismist,   530
        And *Natur's* selfe did vanish, whither no man wist.

    510 *ensew* follow
    511 *To whether* to which
    518 *dilate* expand
    528 *whist* silenced
    529 *see* throne
    531 *wist* knew

CANTO viii 'UNPERFITE'

1

When I bethinke me on that speech whyleare,
   Of *Mutability*, and well it way:
   Me seemes, that though she all unworthy were
   Of the Heav'ns Rule; yet very sooth to say,
   In all things else she beares the greatest sway.
   Which makes me loath this state of life so tickle,
   And love of things so vaine to cast away;
   Whose flowring pride, so fading and so fickle,
Short *Time* shall soon cut down with his consuming sickle.

2

Then gin I thinke on that which Nature sayd,   10
   Of that same time when no more *Change* shall be,
   But stedfast rest of all things firmely stayd
   Upon the pillours of Eternity,
   That is contrayr to *Mutabilitie*:
   For, all that moveth, doth in *Change* delight:
   But thence-forth all shall rest eternally
   With Him that is the God of Sabbaoth hight:
O that great Sabbaoth God, graunt me that Sabaoths sight.

---

1 *whyleare* lately heard
2 *way* weigh
3 *Me seemes* it seems to me
6 *tickle* unstable
14 *contrayr to* the opposite

Notes

The Shepheardes Calender

To select from a work as richly integrated as this is hard. 'June' and 'October' have been chosen for their scope and technical variety and also their bearing on Spenser's view of his own poetic vocation. The woodcuts, emblems and E.K.'s *Glosse* are included for their own interest and as integral to the format of the poem.

In 'June' Colin appears in person, as he does in only four of the twelve eclogues: the introductory and closing monologues, 'Januarie' and 'December', and 'November', where his lament for Dido expresses human grief transcended by heavenly realization. In 'June', as the lover, who is also the poet, his sacred voice and vision are fully established. The intricate fluidity of the verse form allows the delicate interplay of wit, celebration, complaint and self-deprecation in the opening dialogue to give way to the grave plangency of the closing lament, where Colin's grief for the faithlessness of Rosalind also expresses that of Christ for the intransigence of mankind.

Colin's presence is felt throughout. His songs are sung reverently by other of the shepherds in 'Aprill' and 'August', and he is referred to constantly as the type of the poet, divinely inspired, both suffering and privileged in the hard practice of his art. In 'October', where the central theme is poetry itself, and in particular the state of poetry in England at the time, his name is a touchstone; a reminder of true and universal potential. The subject of this eclogue invites variety of style by way of example and argument. Lyric grace, satiric parody and epic reach are all indicated, stretching the pastoral form without ever breaking it.

JUNE

Text

Subtitle   *Ægloga sexta* the sixth eclogue.
          Hobbinol Gabriel Harvey recognized himself in the shepherd Hobbinol, who in *SC* represents steadfast friendship and maturity.

10   *whych Adam lost* Colin's reference to the Redemption expands the allegory of the eclogue to take in the theological level.

24   *elvish ghosts* 'elvish' here implies 'malicious'. The sinister association of at least some categories of Faery beings with the restless dead is common in folklore at this time. See also *Epith.* 341–8 and n.

68   *that Pan with Phoebus strove* E.K. summarizes the account of this contest as given by Ovid, *Metamorphoses* XI. 146ff. Colin takes Pan and Phoebus Apollo as the patrons of pastoral and epic poetry respectively.

81   *Tityrus* Tityrus is Virgil's own persona in his pastoral work. In *SC* Spenser uses the name generally for Chaucer, as E.K. notes, implying his parity with Virgil in the English poetic tradition. In 'October' 55 Virgil is 'the Romish *Tityrus*'.

Glosse

127   *in scripture called Eden* E.K.'s geographical placing of Eden agrees with learned opinion of the time.

162–3   *for Guelfes and Gibelines, we say Elfes and Goblins* This is the first recorded instance of this false but persistent etymology.

172   *Musaeus* Musaeus was a Greek poet, writing in the late fifth century BC. Marlowe's poem *Hero and Leander*, *c.*1597, was inspired by his most famous work.

174   *his Pageaunts* See Introduction, n.8.

181   *Ipse ego ... mala* Virgil, *Eclogues* II. 51: 'Let me gather pale apples with soft bloom.'

187   *Clarion* E.K. is mistaken. See gloss to text.

196   *Tullie* Writers of this period often refer familiarly to the great Roman orator and stylist Marcus Tullius Cicero as Tullie or Tully.

208–9   *Anchora speme* there is still hope.

OCTOBER

Text

Subtitle *Ægolga decima* the tenth ecologue.
Cuddie Pierce (Piers) and Cuddie both appear elsewhere in *SC*. In 'Maye' Piers is the shepherd as priest: the Protestant minister in contention with Palinode, a Catholic. His agruments for sober vigilance and pastoral responsibility by implication prevail over those of his worldly opponent. In 'October' his detachment, and concern with the nature and function of the poetic vocation rather than its tangible rewards, is consistent with his earlier characterization, despite the shift in register. Cuddie's self-involvement in 'October' is recognizable from his appearance in 'Februarie', where he expresses the contempt of heedless and short-sighted youth for the wisdom of age. In 'August' he is judge in a singing-contest between two other shepherds, before singing a song 'That Colin made'. The mention made in the argument of Spenser's 'booke called the English Poete', now lost, suggests that the shepherds' exchanges in 'October' may have been intended as complementary to a prose analysis of the same topic. A number of attempts have been made to identify both Pierce and Cuddie with various of Spenser's contemporaries, but without real success.

5 *bydding base* a game, in which the players challenge each other to run from the 'base': home. It may here be used metaphorically of singing contests of the kind which Cuddie himself judges in 'August'.

8 *Oten reedes* a pipe of oat-straw; Lat. *avena*, see *Glosse*. Virgil uses the phrase to characterize pastoral Poetry; *Eclogues* I. 2.

11 *the Grashopper* Aesop's fable of the grasshopper, who sang all summer and, unlike the industrious ant, made no provision for the winter, was proverbial at this time and earlier.

28 *The shepheard* The poet Orpheus won back his dead wife, Eurydice, from Pluto, king of the underworld, but lost her again when he broke the condition that he should not look back at her until they had arrived back in the world of the living.

32 *Argus* E.K. summarizes the story of Argus as told by Ovid, *Metamorphoses* I. 601ff.

45 *Elisa* Elisa is Spenser's pastoral name for Elizabeth I here and in 'April'. E.K. is cautious about naming the Earl of Leicester as 'the worthy whome shee loveth best', but the mention of the 'white beare', his personal badge, makes the identification certain. Spenser

55	*the Romish Tityrus* Virgil, see 'June' 81n. Maecenas, a Roman noble high in the favour of the Emperor Augustus, was Virgil's patron, as he was also of Horace among others. Cuddie here summarizes Virgil's poetic career: the pastoral *Eclogues*, the *Georgics*, concerned with husbandry, and his epic, the *Aeneid*.
76	*rolle ... rybaudrye* Spenser is here parodying the alliterative fashion of the time as he does also in *TM*. E.K. derides it similarly in his dedicatory Epistle to *SC*, and indeed extends his disapproval to Piers and Cuddie themselves. See *Glosse*.
Embleme	*(Est Deus in nobis), agitante calescimus illo* '(God is within us), we are inflamed by his urging.' Ovid, *Fasti* VI. 5. It is possible that the first part of this line was intended as Piers's emblem, given by way of a reply '*Epiphonematicos*' as E.K. says; that is, in agreement, as a summing up. See *Glosse*.

Glosse

128	*Mantuane* Mantuanus: Johannes Baptista Spagnola, 1448–1516, a Carmelite monk of Mantua, was the author of a number of strongly moral Latin ecologues. *SC* is considerably influenced by his work.
215	*a most eloquent Oration of Tullies* Cicero, *Pro Archia* 10.24.
216	*a sonet* Petrarch, 187 in Carducci's edition. E.K. paraphrases and cites the opening. This story with the further instances given of the esteem in which poets may be held are all commonplaces of Renaissance criticism.
223	*Ennius* a Latin poet who lived 239–169 BC.
225	*Pindarus* Pindar was one of the greatest of Greek lyric poets. He lived 518–438 BC.
230	*Darius* king of Persia, who was defeated by Alexander the Great in 330 BC.
251	*The silver swanne* These lines do not appear in any of Spenser's surviving work, but a similar image occurs in *Ruines of Time* 589–600.
254	*Petrachs saying* Petrarch, Sonnet 38 in *Vita*: 'It enabled my weak talent to blossom in its shade, and grow among sorrows.'
261	*Mantuanes saying* 'Divine matters demand a mind free from anxiety.' The wording is not Mantuan's, but a similar thought occurs in his *Eclogues* V.
263	*that comen verse* Horace, *Epistles* I.v.19: 'What eloquence have flowing goblets not induced.'
275–6	*as is said in Virgile ... and the like in Horace* Virgil, *Eclogues* VIII.10:

	'Your songs alone are worthy of the buskin of Sophocles' (That is, to be compared with the work of the greatest of the Greek tragedians); Horace, *Ars Poetica* 280: 'to speak grandly, and to wear the buskin'.
278	*Bellona* The identification of Bellona with Pallas Athene is found only in Renaissance mythography.
289	*as Ovid sayth* This is not an exact quotation, though it is reminiscent of several lines in both Ovid and Virgil referring to the power of verse: 'Or if by songs ...'.

The Faerie Queene: Book I

In the First Book the reader is introduced to the scope and methodology of the whole poem. Spenser's original readers would have become very quickly acclimatized in Faerie Land. Their descendants in this century have more difficulty, since the signposts provided are themselves no longer generally familiar. The Critical Commentary to this selection may in part at least help to overcome this initial barrier, and so allow the guidelines Spenser has himself given to be perceptible. Certain patterns that operate throughout the poem are clearly established in Book I: negative vision precedes positive, as the House of Pride is seen before that of Holiness; the fall of night is ominous and daybreak brings clarity of mind as well as sight. The hero's function of Everyman invites the reader to identify with him in the intimacy of continuous narrative. At ix. 18–20, this function is effectively transferred to Prince Arthur. The rhythm of contact, of guidance, extending over the whole poem as we have it, becomes wider, less insistent, to be maintained by the reader's own exploratory energy, but the heavenly goal ultimately to be sought, and which transcends even Gloriana's Cleopolis, is proposed in the last three Cantos of Book I, in the vision and triumph of its titular hero.

PROEM

16	*Tanaquill* Tanaquil is Spenser's other name for his Faerie Queene, Gloriana. In the legendary period of Roman history Tanaquil is a redoubtable queen, the wife of Tarquin Priscus. A number of authors cite her as a type of noble royalty.

CANTO i

69–81	*The sayling pine ...* Tree-lists of this kind appear in a number of classical writings, but Spenser's immediate source was probably

Chaucer's *Parliament of Fowls* 176–82. The epithets given to the trees refer to their various properties: emblematic (laurel, willow); natural (fir, myrrh, olive, plane, maple); useful (yew, birch, sallow [pussy willow] holm-oak); proverbial (beech, ash).

123 *the ugly monster* The emblematic description of Errour is the first of its kind in the poem: the reader is made to visualize her, detail by detail, and at the same time to interpret her nature through his own reactions.

181 *old father Nilus* The belief in the spontaneous generation of frogs, snakes and even mice fom the mud left after the inundation of the Nile is mentioned by many classical and later authorities.

328 *blacke Plutoes griesly Dame* Proserpina is often identified by the mythographers with Hecate, patroness of witchcraft and of deceptive dreams; see I.i.43. 'Gorgon' is here a contracted form of 'Demogorgon'; a deity of the underworld taken by later writers to represent the first stirrings of the creation, amorphous and terrifying. See I.v.22.

345 *Morpheus* Spenser's immediate source for this passage is Chaucer's *Book of the Duchess* 132–95. Morpheus, 'the Shaper', is the god of sleep and dreams.

384 *Archimago* This is the first time that the necromantic adversary is named.

393 *The Yvorie dore* The ivory gate is that by which false dreams leave the underworld: true dreams come through the transparent gate of horn. In Virgil, *Aeneid* VI. 893–8, Aeneas returns to the upper world through the gate of ivory.

405 *Una* This is the first occurrence of Una's name: 'one', in the sense of pure and undivided.

425 *Faire Venus* This passage parodies the joyous celebration of true love consummated. Compare *Epith.* 92–110.

CANTO ii

56 *Tithones* Tithonus is the mortal, ever-ageing, lover of Aurora, the goddess of the dawn.

85 *Proteus* The sea god Proteus has the power to change his shape. He is taken by the mythographers to represent chaos as it first emerges into form. Spenser makes use of this tradition in the episode of the Cave of Proteus; IV.xi.3–4; 9ff.

99 *Saint George* Archimago may be aware of Redcrosse's real name; certainly his present disguise is a parodic image of Christian

chivalry. The mention of 'The true *Saint George*' (101) prepares the reader for Redcrosse's own discovery of his true identity in I.x.61.

198 *Tiberis* The 'Emperour' is the Pope, identified with Antichrist. As his daughter Duessa here recalls 'the great whore, that sitteth upon many waters', Revelations 17:1, which are specified here as being those of the river Tiber in Rome.

270ff. *gory bloud* the principal source for this motif is Virgil. *Aeneid* III.20ff. The main outlines of Fradubio's story are derived from Ariosto, *Orlando Furioso* VI.

355–64 *Prime* The most usual meanings are given in the gloss to the text. The first day of the new moon is associated with Hecate; see I.i.37n. The tradition of a penance undergone by witches generally refers to the end of December: the turn of the year at the winter solstice, and *Prime* here may indicate the new moon immediately following. Fradubio's horrible discovery anticipates that of I.viii.46–9, when at Una's command Duessa is stripped of her disguise.

CANTO iii

136–7 *Aldeboran ... Cassiopeias chaire* The changing positions of the stars marks the course of the night. Aldeboran is a bright star in the constellation of Taurus.

139ff. *One knocked* The episode of Kirkrapine, Abessa and Corceca is examined in section (ii) of the Critical Commentary.

185 *that long wandring Greeke* Ulysses, whose wanderings delayed his return home after the Trojan War by ten years. In the course of his adventures he stayed for a year with Circe and for seven with Calypso, both of divine descent.

CANTO iv

41 *flit* This description recalls the house built on sand, Matthew 7:25–6.

60 *Persia* Descriptions of the Persian Court in Herodotus and Xenophon especially made Persia a synonym for luxurious pomp. See also I.ii.13.

73 *fairest child* Phaeton, the son of Apollo, tried to drive the sun-chariot of his father and fell in flaming ruin: a type of the fall of the angels.

95	*Jove* Jupiter stands here for Almighty God, as Pluto and Proserpina do for the powers of darkness.
100	*Lucifera* Lucifera's name is derived from that of Lucifer: 'Bearer of Light', Isaiah 14:12.
153	*Argus* See 'October' 32n.
369	*renverst* To carry or display a coat of arms reversed is in heraldry a mark of ignominy.
432	*Stygian shores* The unburied (here the vengeful) dead wander for a hundred years on the shores of the Styx, unable to cross to their place among the dead. See Virgil, *Aeneid* VI.295ff.

CANTO v

172	*Night* Night is called 'the mother of the gods' by many writers of the classical period. Hesiod calls her the daughter of Chaos. Spenser, refining upon this through later mythographical concepts, says she was 'begot in *Daemororgons* hall', I.v.18: see I.i.37n. His description combines the traditional attributes of Night – her chariot, her black horses and her dusky robes, I.v.20 – with those of Hecate – the dogs that howl at her approach, the owl and the wolf, I.v.30. Night here personifies the perilous obscurity of actual darkness and also darkness of the spirit, as these are consistently manifested in the action of the whole poem.
273	*Avernus* Avernus is one of the entrances to Hades, the classical underworld. Spenser's description – the avenging Furies; the rivers; Cerberus, the guardian hound at the gate; the damned and their torments – all derive ultimately from Virgil's presentation of Hades in *Aeneid* VI. Tantalus appears again, in company with Pilate, in the same setting as seen by Guyon, knight of temperance, II.vii.59–62.
324	*Hippolytus* Hippolytus, whose story is summarized in I.v.36–9, was only one of those whom Æsculapius, son of Apollo, brought back to life through his healing powers. Accounts of his punishment vary. Generally it is because of the complaints of Pluto, god of the dead, that Jupiter strikes him with thunder.
415–32	*king of Babylon* Nebuchadnezzar: Daniel 4. Spenser relates the story of his transformation literally. Lists of this kind are common in late medieval and Renaissance writing, bringing together figures from classical and biblical history to exemplify a moral, as here, against pride. 'That mightie Monarch', I.v.48, is

Alexander the Great: Ammon is a name given to Jupiter in Libya. Medieval and Renaissance writers vary in their attitude to Alexander. To some he is a type of chivalric virtue and to others, as here, of sinful ambition. The proverbially wealthy Croesus, king of Lydia, is a type of worldly pride; Antiochus IV, king of Syria, destroyed Jerusalem, and is his spiritual counterpart, Nimrod, 'the mighty hunter before the Lord', Genesis 10:9, and Ninus, the king of Assyria who is said to be the founder of Nineveh, exemplify pride in conquest.

436 *the Romaines fall* Fallen Rome is for Spenser and for his period generally a supreme type of the transience of human glory. As such it provides the central image both of *The Ruines of Rome* and *The Ruines of Time*. The names listed here encapsulate the history of Rome up to the time of Augustus: Romulus, with his brother Remus, founded the city; Tarquinius Superbus ('the proud') was the last of its kings, driven into exile after his rape of Lucretia and her suicide; Lentulus is most probably Lentulus Sura, who was executed for his part in Cataline's conspiracy; Scipio and Hannibal were the generals commanding the Roman and Carthaginian forces respectively during the Second Punic War; the struggles of Marius and Sulla for supreme power in Rome led to a bloody civil war, which was followed by that between Pompey and Julius Caesar. Marcus Antonius was the lover of Cleopatra, queen of Egypt, see I.v.50. Their attempt to sieze the Roman Empire ended with Augustus' naval victory at Actium. Both committed suicide.

442 *wemen* Spenser presents his own type of female pride in the figure of the Amazon queen Radigund, V.v,vii. Here his historical examples show the same essential qualities of unbridled passion and rebellion against natural and social order. Semiramis was a legendary warrior queen of Assyria; the wife of Ninus. See I.v.48. She was famous for her ferocity and her licentiousness, and was said to have been killed by her son, defending himself from her incestuous advances. Sthenoboea was a queen of Argos. She tried to seduce her husband's guest, Bellerophon, and when he rejected her she accused him of attempted rape. The version given here, that she hanged herself, may be due to conflation with the very similar story of Hippolytus and his stepmother, Phaedra. See I.v.37. Cleopatra, the last queen of Egypt, committed suicide by snake-bite rather than submit to Augustus. The interpretations of her character and actions that fit her for the present context are derived from Roman accounts.

CANTO vi

61-153 *Faunes* Fauns and satyrs are rural deities: the latter reappear, VI.x, when Hellenore decides to live with them, sharing their sensual delight though not their innocence. Silvanus is also a god of the countryside. His name is often interchangeable with those of Pan and Faunus, as here: Dryope was Faunus' wife, and Phloe his mistress. Silvanus carries a staff of cypress in memory of his love for Cyparissus, a lovely boy who was changed into a cypress tree by Apollo.

129 *Cybeles* Cybele was a mother goddess whose rites were atavistic, ecstatic and terrifying to the onlooker, accompanied by drums and cymbals.

154 *Hamadryades* The Hamadryads are the nymphs of the trees, as the Naiads are those of springs, rivers and fountains.

184 *Thyamis* Thyamis' name seems to be derived from a Greek word for passion, as Labryde's is from one meaning greedy, uncontrolled. Therion means a wild beast. Thyamis' relationship with the Satyr anticipates that of Hellenore with his tribe in III.x, but makes almost an opposite point. Hellenore reverts to an instinctual existence; Thyamis is held captive by it, by her own passions but against her will. After Satyrane's birth she returns to human society. Satyrane's education lies first in the control of the passions, figured by the various beasts he subdues, and later in their direction, in undertaking 'straunge adventures', I.vi.29. His meeting with Una is a crux in his growth towards chivalric maturity, a process which is seen to continue through Books III and IV.

CANTO vii

32 *the fountaine* Springs and fountains whose waters have curious properties are frequently mentioned by writers of this time concerned with natural history and geography. The causal myth told by Spenser is his own, derived from analogous passages in Ovid (*Metamorphoses* IV.285.ff.; XV.317ff.) and later poets.

74 *his boasted sire* Spenser has adapted the traditional descent of the giants from Heaven and Earth to suit the allegorical character of Orgoglio.

136 *Duessa* Duessa here appears in the full Apocalyptic panoply of the Whore of Babylon as she is described in Revelations 17:1-6.

Spenser likens the Beast upon which she sits to 'that renowmed Snake': the Lernean Hydra slaine by Alcides, Hercules, who is often taken by the later mythographers as a type of Christ overcoming the works of the Devil. In the following Canto I.viii.16-20, Duessa's Beast is defeated by Prince Arthur who in this episode is also a type of Christ as the Deliverer.

254 *A goodly knight* This is Arthur's first appearance in the poem.

285 *Selinis* Selinus is a city in Sicily. Marlowe's adaptation of this simile in *Tamburlaine the Great* 4096-101, is the most famous of several passages which relate the play to *FQ* I. *Tamburlaine* was written and acted c.1587, but not printed until 1590. Spenser may have seen it, but Abraham Fraunce quotes from *FQ* II in his *Arcadian Rhetoricke*, 1588, and it is likely that Marlowe saw some part of Spenser's work in the manuscripts which were evidently circulating at the time.

289 *His warlike shield* Arthur's marvellous shield is derived from that of Ariosto's Atlanta. *Orlando Furioso* II.55ff.

319 *Merlin* This passage is discussed in the Critical Commentary, section (ii). Arthur relates Merlin's part in his upbringing in I.ix.5.

381-96 *a King and Queene* Una's parents are Adam and Eve as the progenitors of mankind: their kingdom is Eden, with three of its four rivers named as in Genesis 2:10-14. The Dragon is the Devil's malice, bred in hell (Tartary, Tartarus), by which the Paradise which is Una's rightful heritage is laid waste. The beleaguered castle recalls Orgoglio's dungeons: both refer to the hell harrowed by Christ. The four years' duration of the siege stands for the four thousand years said by biblical commentators to have elapsed between the Fall and the Redemption.

412 *Cleopolis* Cleopolis, 'city of glory', is mirrored historically in the London of Elizabeth's time as her court and rule are in those of Gloriana.

CANTO viii

23 *an horne* Horns with magical properties are common in romance.
100 *his deare Duessa* see I.vii.16n.
359 *pined corse* There is dreadful similarity between this description and Spenser's eye-witness account in the *Veue* of the famine following Lord Grey's brutal suppression of the Munster Rebellion in 1581; 'They [the Irish] weare broughte to soe wonderfull wretchednes as that anie stonie harte would have rewed the same

> ... they Came Crepinge forthe uppon theire handes for theire Legges Coulde not beare them, they lokes like Anotomies of deathe, they spoke like ghostes Crying out of theire graves.'

406 *that witch* Duessa, despoiled of her gorgeous trappings, appears as old and monstrously deformed. Spenser has elaborated on Ariosto's description of Alcina, when her true nature is magically revealed, *Orlando Furioso* VII.71ff.; also see I.ii.40–1n.

CANTO ix

22 *from me are hidden yit* Arthur's name is known, but not his lineage. See Critical Commentary, section (ii).

28 *Timon* Merlin's care for the infant Arthur is traditional, as is the delegation of his upbringing to a foster-father. In Malory he is entrusted to Sir Ector. Timon is Spenser's own name, intended to recall the Greek τιμεῖν 'honour'. The hill by which he lives, Rauran, is Rauran-Vaur, in Merionethshire: an ancestral seat of the Penmynydd branch of the Tudors.

161 *goodly gifts* The exchange of gifts between the knights indicates a shift of focus: from this point in the poem Prince Arthur takes on the function of Everyman. The 'liquor pure' with its healing powers is a motif found often in romance. Its particular significance here is the power of the state to strengthen and protect the church. The 'Booke' he receives from Redcrosse is the Bible. Queen Elizabeth was presented with an English Bible by a figure representing Truth in one of the allegorical pageants that took place along the route as she went to her Coronation, and she, her brother Edward VI and her father are often pictured receiving copies of the Bible in translations they have authorized.

369 *morning droome* Redcrosse refutes Despair's arguments in their own terms, those of self-indulgence. The last lines of the verse clinch his rebuttal with a classical tag to be found in a number of writers including Plato. In the verse following he takes the point further: death is no more to be feared than sought. The phrase 'their certaine date' has been taken as deterministic, but in context implies only that a man's destiny is in God's hands, not his own. In the next four verses despair shifts his ground, taking up this last point and playing on Recrosse's awareness of guilt and very recent failure to undermine his trust in God's mercy (of which Una reminds him, I.ix.53), in order to bring him into his own state: the despair which is mortal sin. The final suicide of

Despair, I.ix.54, encapsulates his essential nature.

473 *that chosen art* This phrase has again been taken as implying Spenser's belief in determinism, even in predestination. Even were Redcrosse a specific individual he might, like any ruler or indeed any poet, have been born with a certain role to fulfil. But Redcrosse not only represents Everyman: he also figures the true church (of England), whose share in the divine triumph over its persecutors at the end of created time is described by St John, Revelations 20.

CANTO x

19 *an auntient house* The plan and conduct of the House of Holiness like that of its opposite, the House of Pride (I.iv), derives from two closely related allegorical traditions, the courtly and the theological. For a discussion and summary of Spenser's possible sources in both, see the *Variorum* edition of Spenser's *Works*, FQ I, 1932, pp. 404–21.

28 *Caelia* Caelia is Heavenly Grace which alone makes the three theological Virtues, Faith Hope and Charity, accessible to man. Faith and Hope are virgins because they look for fulfilment in heaven; Charity manifests heaven in this world and is 'the greatest of these'. See I Corinthians 13.

110 *a cup of gold* The most usual attribute of Faith is 'the sword of the Spirit, which is the word of God', Ephesians 6:17. The cup with the serpent is generally associated with St John. It signifies both the power of faith to overcome evil and the terrifying mysteries of faith itself: wine and water are mingled in it as in the Communion chalice, and the book she carries is the Bible, sealed with Christ's blood and to be understood only by the faithful. Spenser's use of the cup here recalls and corrects the Apocalyptic image of Duessa, I.viii.14. Hope's anchor is traditional.

167 *weaker wit* Reason is man's highest natural faculty, and cannot attain to faith, hope or charity without the intervention of grace. Through Faith's teaching comes understanding, and she has power to transcend the natural order in accordance with God's will. The instances given are recorded in her Book: the sun stood still at Joshua's command until his victory was complete. Joshua 10:12; the shadow on the dial returned backwards ten degrees as a sign to King Hezekiah that he would be healed, II Kings 10:11; Gideon put his enemies to flight by an inspired strategem, Judges 7; the Israelites passed dry-shod

	through the Red Sea, Exodus 14:21-31; Christ spoke of the power of faith to move mountains, Matthew 21:21.
190	*comfort sweet* This whole passage, down to I.x.29, provides a close psychological analysis of the events described in the previous Canto: Redcrosse's temptation by Despair and his rescue by Una.
225	*streight diet* The imagery used to express Redcrosse's painful cure derives both from penitential tradition and from contemporary medical theory and practice.
259	*Charissa* Charity is usually depicted as here, with her many children. Spenser has her crowned and enthroned as a queen. Doves are sacred to Venus, who represented the power of generation in the created world and is a a related expression of God's love. She appears as such in IV.x. Turtle doves are specifically emblematic of marital fidelity. Charity is love raised to its highest, heavenly, power.
318	*seven Bead-men* The Bead-men represent the seven corporal works of mercy.
469	*the highest Mount* This is the same mountain to which St John was carried in the spirit and from which, like Redcrosse, he held the heavenly city, Revelations 21. Spenser's comparisons for it give an ascending scale: it is like Mount Sinai, where Moses received the Ten Commandments, Exodus 2; like the Mount of Olives, where Christ taught his disciples, Matthew 24:3, and like Parnassus, haunt of the nine Muses, who here stand for the inspiration by which the poet may communicate divine vision.
519	*Panthea* The name of Gloriana's palace, Panthea, is derived from the Pantheon in Rome, the temple of all the gods. In Faerie Land it was built by Elfant, II.x.73. It has been identified with a number of Elizabeth's royal palaces: most convincingly with Greenwich, which had expansive window-space. The concept probably comes from Chaucer's House of Fame 'that shoone ful lyghter than a glas', *House of Fame* 1289.
532	*English race* The significance of Redcrosse's Saxon lineage is discussed in section (ii) of the Critical Commentary.
585	*Faeries theft* A similar account is given of Artegall's infancy in III.iii.26. The belief in changelings is a commonplace of the time and is the only such motif used in *FQ* where Spenser retains the sinister overtones of folklore tradition concerning Faerie.

CANTO xi

2 *her captive Parents* See I.vii.43n.

56 *of warres* Spenser is here looking ahead to *FQ* V. See Critical Commentary, section (ii). There the 'great Faery Queene' is Elizabeth I, and the 'Paynim king' Philip of Spain, and the epic content that of marital endeavour. Here Spenser is presenting spiritual heroism, and he asks the muse to qualify her style accordingly.

107 *the griesly mouth of hell* In medieval and Renaissance drama the mouth of hell was generally represented as the open jaws of a dragon.

120 *two broad Beacons* FQ I may well have been completed before the Armada of 1588; this is probably a reference to the warning beacons which were being prepared in anticipation of a Spanish invasion.

235 *that great Champion* The significance of this comparison between Redcrosse and Hercules, which is carried through in the reference to Cerberus, the three-headed watch-dog of Hades, I.xi.41, is discussed in the Critical Commentary, section (iii).

261 *The well of life* The well of life is the water of baptism. The whole episode of the dragon-fight is a refocusing and recapitulation of the preceding action. Redcrosse first enters the poem wearing 'the whole armour of God' (Ephesians 6:13); here his progress to salvation is shown in full. The well cleanses him of original sin, and he rises from it in the dawn following 'As Eagle fresh out of the Ocean wave' (I.xi.34). The ageing eagle was said by late classical and medieval authorities to fly up to the sun, until its feathers were burned. Then it plunged into the sea, or a fountain, and flew up again young and newly fledged. This is taken traditionally as an image of baptism, by which 'the old Adam' is cast off, and spiritual life renewed.

269 *this well* The virtues of the waters of baptism are defined by a series of comparisons. They surpass that of Silo (Siloam), in which Jesus commanded a blind man to bathe his eyes that his sight might be restored (John 9:7) because they give spiritual vision; that of Jordan, in which Christ himself was baptized (Matthew 3:13-17) because all water then became a sacramental element; those of Bath and 'the german *Spau*' because those heal only the ills of the body; that of Cephissus in Boeotia because, according to Pliny (*Natural History* II.126), it whitens the fleeces of sheep, whereas baptism purifies the flocks of Christ; those of Hebrus, in Thrace, into which the head of Orpheus was thrown after his death at the hands of the Maenads,

because Orpheus is only a type of Christ, to whose salvation baptism gives access.

392 *Aetna* The volcano of Etna, in Sicily, was dramatically active in the sixteenth century. A number of poets in Italy and England derive images from its eruptions.

414 *The tree of life* The tree of life grew in Eden beside the forbidden tree of knowledge, Genesis 3:22 ('Another like faire tree', I.xi.47). It was taken by the Christian commentators to represent the cross: Christ is its fruit, his body and blood the bread and wine of the Eucharist. Here it is 'the crime of our first fathers fall' because it was the Fall of Adam and Eve which made necessary the sacrificial Redemption of Christ. The Anglican catechism recognizes as essential only two of the seven sacraments of the Roman Church: 'Two only, as generally necessary to salvation, that is to say, Baptism and the Supper of the Lord.' Spenser, who as a Protestant did not believe in transubstantiation, is careful in his development of the traditional image of the tree: it is the healing balm flowing from it, I.xi.48, that has marvellous virtue, not its fruit. Redcrosse has now partaken of both 'necessary' sacraments, and on the third morning of the battle arises to certain victory, I.xi.52.

CANTO xii

32 *in sieged fort* The royal procession that welcomes St George after his victory is mentioned in many versions of his legend, and appears frequently in art. Spenser uses it to point a number of allegorical levels. Una's parents are Adam and Eve, released with the patriarchs, the prophets and the innocent from bondage to Satan when Christ descended into hell and harrowed it. See I.vii.43n. Their age, and their 'antique' style of dress is a reminder of historical perspective; they belong to the Old Dispensation, the time of the Old Testament, now superseded by the New. The triumph of Redcrosse figures that of Christ. As Everyman, fully entered into the sacramental life of the church, and as the church in England restored to its original purity, Redcrosse has overcome sin, corruption and temptation. The welcome he enjoys anticipates his marriage to Una, itself a type of heavenly blessedness. As the parents of Una, truth, the king and queen also represent the power of pure doctrine, freed from diabolic inhibition at the Reformation. Redcrosse has gained strong support as well as gratitude; see I.xii.25–36.

161 *her teene* The historical allegory here refers immediately to the threat posed by Philip of Spain to Elizabeth's England and her church. See I.xi.7n. The 'six yeares' of Redcrosse's duty probably represent an Apocalyptic computation. Six hundred years from Spenser's time takes history into the second millennium. St John says that after the shattering of world order and the fall of Babylon there will follow the thousand-year triumph of the true church, after which Satan will be loosed again for the final struggle that is to precede the Day of Judgement and the making of all things new, Revelations 20-1. Learned opinion generally held that the Creation would end around AD 4000. See I.vii.43n, and Critical Commentary, section (ii).

195 *a garment* See Revelations 19:7-8, and also the Song of Songs 4:7, taken as referring to the church as the bride of Christ.

229 *Emperour of all the West* See I.ii.22n.

320 *deadly paines* Archimago's escape is recounted in II.i.1.

324 *sacred rites* The marriage ceremonies are elaborated from those of the classical period. Many of the details recur figuratively in *Epith.* 241-60.

347 *trinall triplicities* The verse number here points the reference to the ninefold angelic hierarchy, whose song is heard as in Revelations 19:6-7.

The Faerie Queene: Dedicatory Sonnets

The three sonnets given here are selected for interest as well as quality. Spenser's finest sonnets comprise the great sequence *Amoretti* which was printed with *Epith.* in 1595. Its structure is both complex and delicate, to a point where selection would verge on misrepresentation. None of the seventeen Dedicatory Sonnets which Spenser published with Books I-III of *FQ* in 1590 has the lyric subtlety of *Amoretti*; their occasion demands another, more public voice. They are remarkable in other ways however. Their range indicates Spenser's sense of the importance of his new work as much as or more than any hope of patronage. Burghley, for example, to whom he addresses his second sonnet, was no friend of his and unlikely to be won over by mere compliment, and Grey remained in royal disfavour after his recall from Ireland. Essex, a great noble and a rising star at Court, is, like Raleigh, addressed as a maker of poetry as well as being potentially its epic subject. The Countess of Pembroke, Sir Philip Sidney's sister, is honoured in her dead brother's name as well as her own. In these sonnets Spenser is taking Cleopolis as his standpoint from which to address Elizabeth's Court, marking both contrast and alignment.

TO LORD GREY

10   *Of all the rest* The career of Artegall, patron of justice, *FQ*, V, is largely based on that of Grey. See Introduction, section (i), and Critical Commentary, section (ii).

TO SIR WALTER RALEIGH

2   *Thy soveraine Goddesses* Queen Elizabeth's.
12   *thy lofty Muse* Calliope, muse of epic poetry.
13   *thy poem* Raleigh addressed a number of poems to the queen. Here Spenser probably has in mind *The Oceans Love to Cynthia*, of which only Book XI and the opening of Book XII are extant. It makes overt reference to *FQ*: see *Letter* 50n.

TO THE COUNTESSE OF PENBROKE

1   *that most Heroicke spirit* Sir Philip Sidney, the Countess's brother.
4   *baies* Poets are crowned with bay or laurel: trees sacred to Apollo.
7   *his sweet delights* Spenser here refers to himself elliptically as having been inspired by the muse under Sidney's influence. The 'lowlie laies' are his earliest pastoral writing: *SC*, dedicated to Sidney.

The Faerie Queene: A Letter of the Authors to Sir Walter Raleigh

Some of the kinds of light thrown on *FQ* by the *Letter* are discussed in the Introduction, and in the Critical Commentary, section (ii). It is an 'open letter', on the one hand clarifying obscurities and anticipating objections and on the other laying out the future perspective of the poem as a whole as Spenser conceived it at this time. It is clear that, while he had a number of developments and indeed specific episodes clearly planned, their structural presentation was still fluid. See Notes. The *Letter* does not provide a rigid blueprint. It rather represents a crucial stage in the organic growth of the work: a flexible guideline towards the point where it would finally be abandoned with the poem itself. See Critical Commentary, section (iv).

14   *king Arthure* The implications of Spenser's choice of Arthur as his hero are discussed in the Introduction and Critical Commentary, most fully in section (ii).

18	*Agamemnon* king of Mycenae; in Homer's *Iliad*, the leader of the Greeks in the Trojan War.
	Ulysses Odysseus, hero of Homer's *Odyssey*.
21	*Aeneas* The hero of Virgil's *Aeneid*.
	Orlando The principal character of Ariosto's *Orlando Furioso*, 1532.
22	*Tasso* Rinaldo and Godfredo are central characters in Tasso's *Gerusalemme Liberata*, 1576, 1581.
28	*as Aristotle hath devised* Many ingenious efforts have been made to relate Spenser's presentation of the virtues to that of Aristotle. His influence is great, but any kind of exact equation is nullified by Spenser's Christianity alone. It is likely that what he means in the *Letter* is that his conception of the virtues as interdependent and complementary is comparable to that of Aristotle.
41	*as might best be* Spenser sees the difference between Plato's *Republic* and Xenophon's *Cyropaedia* as being essentially that between theory and practice.
43	*whome I conceive* See *FQ* I.ix.3–15 and n.
52	*in Faerye land* See *FQ* I.ix.13–15, and Critical Commentary, section (iv).
53	*she beareth two persons* Gloriana, Tanaquil, the Faerie Queene herself, and Belphoebe, the virgin huntress, are only two of the queen's mirrors in the poem. Spenser instances them here as referring to Elizabeth's regal and private virtues respectively: also because he has followed Raleigh in choosing a name for the queen derived from the titles of the moon goddess Diana. In *The Ocean's Love to Cynthia* Raleigh returns the compliment, saying of his estrangement from Elizabeth's favour: 'A Queen shee was to mee, no more Belphebe' (327), referring to *FQ* III and IV. See Critical Commentary, section (ii).
98	*much gainesaying* This is a motif common in romance writers including Malory in the tale of Gareth and Lynet: the lady objects to the escort assigned her on the grounds that he seems to be of base birth. Una's reasons are other: only a Christian knight can succeed in this quest, and the armour of God she brings with her transforms him. The war-horse led by her dwarf is 'strange', new to Redcrosse as he now is: the image of horse and rider stands for the passions directed by the will. As appears in *FQ* I.i.1 and in the action following, Redcrosse's control is still uncertain.
108	*a Palmer* Spenser's outline for Book XII, the starting point for the narratives of Books I–III etc., is indicative merely. Guyon and the Palmer find the 'Infant with bloody hands', II.i.35: he is an orphan,

his father having died through Acrasia's treachery and his mother having stabbed herself. She only lives long enough to tell their story. The baby's hands are dabbled in her blood. Acrasia is Guyon's opposite, and this is his first direct encounter with her power and its effects.

118-19 *the lover of that Lady* Britomart comes on the despairing Scudamour, III.xi, and successfully undertakes the rescue of Amoret. The story and its psychological developments are slightly recast in the second part of *FQ*: at IV.i.1-3 Amoret is said to have been stolen by Busirane on the day of her wedding to Scudamour and in IV.x. Scudamour tells how he won her from the Temple of Venus.

124 *the love of Britomart* Britomart's quest for her future husband, Artegall, is recounted in *FQ* III and IV.

125 *the overthrow of Marinell* Marinell is overthrown by Britomart and grievously wounded, III,iv.

the misery of Florimell Florimel's adventures occur chiefly in *FQ* III and IV.

126 *Belphœbe* Belphœbe first appears in *FQ* II.iii: later in *FQ* III and IV.
the lasciviousnes of Hellenora See *FQ* III.ix-x.

Complaints

Complaints. Containing sundrie small Poemes of the Worlds Vanitie appeared early in 1591, following the publication of Books I-III of *FQ*. The circumstances, and the relation of some of its contents to Spenser's 'lost poems', are considered in the Introduction. The collection includes earlier poems, some of which Spenser almost certainly revised and even rewrote, together with recent work. Both are represented here. The prevailing tone of the volume is indicated by the title. Taken together, despite great variety of form, tone and register, the contents maintain the poetic stance of ironic moral detachment which Mantuanus' *Eclogues* had established as a rhetorical tradition in the previous century. See 'October', 127n. It is recognizable in the work of many of Spenser's contemporaries, notably Fulke Greville and Sir John Davies.

MUIOPOTMOS

This is one of the *Complaints* probably written while Spenser was in London in 1590, shortly before its publication. The original title-page has the date 1590, which may mean that it was published separately before inclusion in the collection. It is dedicated to Lady Carey, and refers delicately to her distant kinship with the poet: one of the sonnets appended to *FQ* I–III is also dedicated to her. It is among the most delightful and original of Spenser's works: exquisitely witty, richly inventive in its handling of classical mythology and its exploitation of the mock-heroic register to carry a fine satiric edge. The insect characterization was probably suggested by his earlier adaptation of the Virgilian *Culex*: *VG*, also included in *Complaints*.

1   *I sing* The opening lines parody those of the *Iliad*: 'I sing of the wrath of Achilles ...'. Nemesis here, as in the Latin rather than the Greek poets, stands for vengeful anger.

9   *tragicall effect* Spenser has in mind the medieval concept of tragedy as a fall from fortune. Melpomene is the muse of tragedy.

51   *Hyperions fierie childe* The Sun, and Moon and the Dawn according to Hesiod, were children of the Titan Hyperion, *Theogony* 134f., 371ff. Spenser is probably referring to Ovid, who calls the Sun 'born of Hyperion' *Metamorphoses* IV. 192.

63   *which Vulcane made* The butterfly's chitinous carapace is described as if it were seen under a magnifying glass, in terms of fantastic armour. Vulcan (identified with the Greek Hephaestus) was the smith of the gods, who made Achilles' marvellous shield, *Iliad* XVIII.

71   *Alcides* The down appearing on the butterfly's thorax is compared to the hide of the Nemean lion worn by Hercules.

77   *not Bilbo steele* In Spenser's time Bilbao was famous for the quality of its swords. In the classical period Corinth produced fine brass, of which orichalcum was a kind especially prized. That it came from Phoenicia seems to be Spenser's own exotic touch. Mention of it in this context is meant to recall Virgil's description of the arming of Turnus, whose corselet was wrought of it, *Aeneid* XIII.xii.87–9. See 438n.

95   *Juñoes Bird* Juno's bird is the peacock. From the description as a whole it is likely that Spenser was thinking of a peacock butterfly.

113   *Report is* This story is Spenser's own, invented to complement the Ovidian tale of Arachne. See 260–352 and nn.

131   *Psyche* The tale of Cupid's love for Psyche, their trials and eventual happiness is told as an allegorical episode by Apuleius in *The Golden Ass* V–VI, c. AD 170.

186   *that Paradise* The garden is planted with medicinal herbs and sweet spices, exactly described. Spenser may have had a specific garden in mind, see 425n. It represents the Court, and also Eden, in both of which malice lies in wait for careless innocence.

245 *the bondslave of spight* Aragnoll, like the serpent in Eden, is a noxious intruder. The epithets here applied to him indicate that despite the miniature focus of the action his motivation is to be taken seriously, as a type of diabolic malevolence.

258 *it is written found* Spenser had adapted the story of Arachne's fatal challenge to Pallas, or Minerva, divine patroness of needlework from Ovid, *Metamorphoses* VI.1–145. He describes only one of the twenty-one subjects said by Ovid to have been depicted by Arachne: the story of Europa, for which he draws on the fuller account given by Ovid, *Metamorphoses* II.846–75 among other sources.

265 *Tritonian Goddesse* Tritonia is a title of Minerva.

305 *the olde debate* As in Ovid, the goddess chooses as her subject the contest between herself and Neptune for the patronage of Athens, that privilege to belong to whichever deity should provide the greatest benefit for mankind. Neptune produced the horse, but Pallas Athene's olive tree gave her the victory. The butterfly which gives the final touch to the work is Spenser's own invention. It perfectly integrates this apparent digression with the structure of the whole poem.

321 *her Aegide shield* The Aegis was Jupiter's shield, which he gave to his daughter Pallas, Minerva.

345 *from the shape of womanhed* In Ovid's account Arachne attempts to hang herself, and is turned by the goddess into a spider.

369 *subtil gin* The story of the net forged by Vulcan to trap his wife, Venus, in bed with her lover, Mars, first appears in the *Odyssey* VIII.266–369, but Spenser's immediate source is probably Ovid, *Metamorphoses* IV.176–89.

425 *strugled long* This passage so exactly describes the behaviour of a hunting spider as to make it likely that Spenser had actually seen a butterfly caught in this way.

438 *his deepe groning spright* Clarion's death recalls that of Turnus in the last line of the *Aeneid* XII.952: 'Groaning, his indignant spirit fled beneath the shades.' See 77n.

VISIONS OF THE WORLDS VANITIE

The connection between this group of twelve sonnets, the 'lost' *Dreames* and the *Visions* of Petrarch and du Bellay is discussed in the Introduction. This is an early work, at least in conception. It uses the very concise sonnet form which Spenser developed for himself, and which finds its richest exploitation in *Amoretti*. This may indicate that the work was revised before publication, though a lack of technical fluency rather suggests that these sonnets may themselves have been formally experimental. Like the translated *Visions*, these are emblem poems. From the first publication of Alciati's *Emblemata* in 1531 this was an enormously popular form, consisting properly of three parts: a picture accompanied by a motto; a proverb or quotation such as the emblems given to the shepherds in *SC*, and an interpretative verse. Spenser, writing to Hervey before 1580, says that he hopes to publish his *Dreames* in the same format as *SC*: with illustrations and gloss. What he has done here is to evoke each time two contrasting images: a type of worldly security followed by its reversal, before pointing the moral. As in the emblem books themselves most of the examples or their close analogues are well known: art and originality are to be recognized in their application and expression.

1   *One day* This and the last sonnet set the work as a whole in its philosophical and moral context: a technique developed from the medieval dream-framework.

7   *declining season* The belief that since the Fall the world and its inhabitants had been in a state of gradual decay was widely held at this time. Spenser makes frequent reference to it, e.g. 'October' 61ff.

13   *(faire ladie)* The lady to whom Spenser addresses his sequence has not been satisfactorily identified.

16   *a Bull* This fable appears in some versions of Aesop and elsewhere. The opening image comes from Virgil's description of Taurus in the Zodiac, *Georgics* I.218: 'Taurus with gilded horns opens the year.' Spenser may here by inference be pre-empting Mutabilitie's argument that the heavens themselves are subject to alteration. See *Mutabilitie* vii.55.

35   *Tedula* 'Tedula' seems to be derived from a feminine form of trochilus: a small bird which happily picks leeches and other parasites from between the crocodile's teeth as described by Pliny, *Natural History* VIII.25 [XXXVII.2].

38   *devouring hell* See *FQ* I.xi.12n.

44   *Scarabee* The fable of the eagle, bearer of Jupiter's thunderbolts, and the scarab, or dung-beetle, occurs in both Aesop and Alciati. Spenser's 'Scarabee' burns the eagle's nest: earthly fire against celestial lightening. More usually it breaks the eggs.

47   *Flie* 'Fly' is at this time a generic term for any insect. See e.g. *Muio.* 425.

54   *to fling away* Over-compression here has confused the syntax. The scarab heaps filth on the eagle's eggs lying in Jupiter's lap, forcing him to throw away the eggs as well.

62	*Leviathan* 'Leviathan' is often used for 'whale', and is so glossed in both the Geneva and Bishops' Bibles. The description of Leviathan, Job 41, together with the story of Jonah's whale, led the commentators to take sea-monsters generally as types of hell.
64	*sword-fish* Descriptions of fights between sword-fish and killer whales in particular occur from the classical period on, and are apparently based on fact.
66	*Abysse* See 38n and 62n.
71	*Dragon* Compare this description with that of Redcrosse's enemy, *FQ* I.xi.8–14.
75	*Spider* Spiders were generally believed to be venomous.
85	*Cedar* The *Visions* of Petrarch and of du Bellay both include a great tree in decay: a laurel struck by lightning emblematic of Laura's death (Petrarch 3) and the '*Dodonian* tree' (Bellay 5) representing classical civilization. Spenser's is the cedar of Lebanon, believed to be immune from parasites. The paradox may have been suggested by Petrarch: the laurel was thought to be impervious to lightning. The similarity of this description to that of the mighty oak in decay, 'Februarie' 102ff., suggests that here also Spenser may be presenting the church in its state of unnatural corruption under Rome.
91	*worme* 'Worm' is at this time used generically for any creeping thing or insect.
99	*Elephant* This is a variation on Aesop's fable of the elephant and the mouse.
102	*gilden towre* Spenser has in mind the heraldic 'Elephant and Castle', caparisoned for war, as shown from the time of the Crusades.
107	*worme* See 91n.
122	*Remora* The remora, or sucker-fish, attaches itself to larger creatures such as sharks and is carried with them to share their food-supply. That it can bring a ship to a halt is an exaggeration going back to classical times. Pliny has it, with Spenser's own moral: 'Alas for human vanity!', *Natural History* XXXII.1.
127	*Lyon* This is a variation on Aesop's fable of the lion tormented by flies; the lion has a single enemy, consistent with Spenser's patterning of the whole work. See 47n.
141	*the Romaine Empire* The invasion of Italy by a Gallic army under Brennus took place *c.*390 BC: long before Rome was more than a city state. Rome was taken, and the Capitol beseiged: the warning given by the geese kept there prevented its fall as Spenser

	describes, though he gives the credit to one goose only. See 127n.
146	*a mayde* Spenser has conflated two stories here. Tarpeiea's treachery belongs to the legendary history of the Sabine Wars in the time of Romulus, mythical co-founder of Rome with his brother, Remus.
150	*patron of the place* The great Temple of Jupiter Capitolinus stood on the Capitoline Hill.
163	*ruines tragicall* The variety and interplay of sympathies evoked by Spenser's chosen examples show his primary concern to be the vulnerability of any worldly achievement, whether good or evil in itself.

Colin Clouts Come Home Againe

The structure of *CCCHA*, its historical context and thematic coherence are discussed in the Critical Commentary, section (ii). It was written between 1591, the date of the Dedication to Raleigh, and 1595, when it was published: a number of contemporary references show that it cannot have been finished before that year. See 369 n. Its final unity is highly sophisticated; arrived at experientially, but not simply the result of opportune interpolation and addition. It is in no way a sequel to *SC*: its alignment is rather with *FQ*. The range and rhetorical fluidity of the pastoral convention in which it is based allows of its providing a complementary vision to that of chivalric epic already offered in *FQ* I-III, as well as guiding Spenser's objective exploration of his own poetic vocation in terms that look forward to Colin's appearance and interpretative function in *FQ* VI.x.

Dedication	*not precisely officious* Spenser is here referring to his poetry: he does not neglect it, but neither is it his sole preoccupation.
	evill mouthes Evidently Spenser felt that Raleigh had defended his work against wilful misconstruction, of the kind to which any long-term supporter of Leicester's policies, and more recently Grey's, might have been liable but to which he was deeply sensitive. See also *Letter* 14-15.
	1591 This indicates that Spenser began work on the poem soon after his return from England and may even have completed a preliminary draft very rapidly.
1	*that name* The success of *SC* led Spenser to retain the persona of 'Colin Clout' throughout his career, and other poets most frequently refer to him by this name. Here as in *SC* he claims poetic descent from Chaucer. See 'June' 81: *Glosse* and n.
15	*Hobbinol* In *SC* Hobbinol represents Hervey, see 'June' note to

	subtitle; the Irish location makes that identification unlikely here, though no certain alternative has been suggested.
40	*that Angels* Elizabeth's
57	*Mole* 'Mole' is Spenser's name for the mountains to the north of his estate at Kilcolman: the Ballahoura Mountains and the Galties, of which the highest peak is Galtymore. 'Mulla' is the Awbeg; a tributary of the Blackwater, which runs to the east and south of his lands. See *Mutabilitie* vi.40ff.; *Epith.* 56.
60	*straunge shepheard* Raleigh, called 'the shepheard of the Ocean' in reference both to his exploits at sea and to the title of his poem addressed to Elizabeth, *The Oceans Love to Cynthia.*
81	*Cuddy* Cuddy appears more than once in *SC*; see 'October' note to subtitle. His present identity among Spenser's neighbouring land-holders in Ireland has not been clearly established.
92	*my river Bregogs* The river Bregoge runs through Spenser's lands to join the Awbeg. The Irish name means 'deceitful', and the story of his clandestine love for 'Mulla' has many analogues in myth and folklore. It is likely to have been derived from local topographical tradition.
111	*Buttevant* Buttevant stands on the Cork–Limerick road, near Kilcolman. Kilnemullah is its old name, now again in use.
123	*Allo* 'Allo' is Spenser's name for the Blackwater river, then known as the Broadwater.
156	*Thestylis* Thestylis may be identified with Lodovick Bryskett. See Introduction (p. 13). He is the only one of the Irish shepherds who can be named with any certainty.
166	*Cynthia* Raleigh's name for Elizabeth. See 60n.
173	*Marin* No precise identification can now be given to any of the Irish shepherdesses. Marin's name suggests only that she lived near the sea.
188	*in making well* The queen's poetic talents are praised elsewhere by Spenser (*TM* 576–7), as well as by other writers, often extravagantly. Such of her poems as survive with any certainty of authorship are vigorous and somewhat old-fashioned in style. Spenser's consistent use of 'peerlesse' in this connection clearly verges on flattery, but their quality certainly matches up to that of a number of compositions by poets highly praised later in *CCCHA*. See 369n.
197	*a world of waters* Spenser's description of the crossing of the Irish Sea has a triple function. A first reading takes the register as mock-heroic, with a graceful transition to the imperial conceit of Cynthia as shepherdess of the ocean's creatures. Once land is sighted (265) the journey is seen as a progression, political and elemental, from terrify-

ing instability towards the central order of her Court. The 'deep waters' (858), which in Colin's concluding praise of Love, represent the chaotic origins of the creation striving towards form, in retrospect overlays the journey and its monstrous terrors with the same significance.

239   *her sheepe* This conceit is adapted from Apollonius Rhodius, *Argonautica* I.570ff., where Orpheus sings of the sea as the pastoral domain of the moon goddess Artemis.

245   *Triton* Triton is a sea god: here also possibly the Lord High Admiral, Lord Howard.

248   *Proteus* Proteus is a sea god, with the power to change his shape. The mythographers take him as a type of form still emergent from chaos. As such he appears in *FQ* IV 3-4, 9, xi. and see 197n above.

301   *Funchins* The Funcheon is another river near Kilcolman.

312   *no wayling there* Spenser here contrasts the comparative peace of England with the wretchedness of Ireland, seen here, as in *Mutabilitie* vii.55, as typifying the most grievous consequenmces of the Fall. See also *FQ* I.viii.40n.

337   *I would her lyken* Spenser has three exquisite similes for Elizabeth: a bridal wreath, a dove's iridescent collar and the rare moon-rainbow. All three are circles, images of perfection and eternity.

370   *So many shepherds* The only poets of Cynthia's pastoral Court to have been certainly identified, besides Raleigh, and Alabaster and Daniel who are given their own names, are Alcyon: Sir Arthur Gorges, for whose wife Spenser wrote an elegy, *Daphnaida*, 1591; Amyntas: the Earl of Derby, who died in 1594; and Astrophel: Sir Philip Sidney. Drayton, Sir Edward Dyer, Watson, Constable, Thomas Sackville, Lord Buckhurst, Sir John Davies and Sir John Harrington are likely to be among those mentioned either specifically or as being among the 'many others mo' who might to readers in any period seem worthy of this kind of attention. However, the metaphysical contortions of Alabaster and the dullness of his Latin Eliseis are reminders that tastes change, and that this may easily affect our interpretation of the few hints that Spenser offers. Thomas Churchyard, whose prolific writings seem now very unremarkable, may well have been right to see himself as Palemon.

412   *swans* The 'swans' of the river Po in North Italy are Ariosto, Tasso and Virgil, who was born in Mantua; his epic celebration of Rome gives him claim also to the Tiber. See 'October' 90.

435   *Amaryllis* See 536n.

459   *so many Nymphs* All but two of the ladies of the Court, Flavia and

Candida, can be credibly identified. Urania is Sidney's sister, Mary, Countess of Pembroke, to whom Spenser dedicated *The Ruines of Time*. Theana is the widowed Countess of Warwick, and Marian, her sister, the Countess of Cumberland. Spenser was to dedicate his *Fowre Hymnes* to them jointly in 1596. Mansilia is the Marchioness of Northampton, aunt by marriage of Sir Arthur Gorges: Spenser dedicated *Daphnaida* to her. See 370n. Galathea is most probably Lady Kildare, whose jointure included lands in Coshma and to whose father Spenser addressed one of the Dedicatory Sonnets published with *FQ* I–III. She had by this time left Ireland. The Countess of Ormonde is likely to be Neæra. Her husband's estates were in the Suir (Shure) valley; another of the Dedicatory Sonnets is addressed to him. Stella raises a problem of tact as well as identity. Sidney's 'Stella' was generally thought to be Lady Rich, but his wife was Frances Walsingham, now Lady Essex. Spenser has taken pains, both in placing and expression, to leave this delicate question open even for his contemporaries.

536 *the sisters three* Phyllis, Charillis and Amaryllis are daughters of Sir John Spencer of Althorpe, with whose family Spenser claimed distant kinship, as he says here. See Introduction (p. 2). Phyllis, the eldest, is Lady Carey, to whom he dedicated *Muio.*; Charillis is Lady Compton and Mounteagle, to whom he dedicated *MHT*; Amaryllis is Lady Strange, recently widowed by the death of the Earl of Derby, whom Spenser lamented as Amyntas, for whom she is earlier seen to mourn. Spenser dedicated *TM* to her.

560 *primrose* The primrose is at this time an image of excellence rather than modesty.

589 *Finish the storie* Spenser's eulogy of the queen carries strong biblical overtones, drawing especially on the Song of Songs. This Book was generally taken by the commentators to refer to the love of God for his church. Spenser is including the queen's government of the true church (of England) in his praise, at the same time raising the pastoral idiom to its highest, Edenic level of inspiration. Compare Cranmer's speech at Elizabeth's christening in Shakespeare's *Henry VIII* V.5.

628 *yet will I speake* This passage combines the descent from ecstasy to the familiar conventions expressing love as permeating the moral lover's world and his perceptions of it with the poet's counter-claim of immortality for his own creation.

631 *her name* The conceit of carving a name in the bark of a tree, so that the letters will enlarge with the tree's growth, is common in Latin love poetry. The corresponding image, of letters dug into the turf

and picked out with stones, seems to be Spenser's own. He may have had in mind descriptions of such prehistoric chalk outlines as that of the White Horse in Berkshire.

665 *those enormities* Spenser had earlier shown the vices of the Court and its hangers-on uncompromisingly and with deep personal feeling (*MHT* 581-942: *TM* 61-97). Attacks in this kind are a literary commonplace: Skelton's *Bouge of Court* written under Henry VII is a notable instance. It is the juxtapostion of this passage with what has gone before that makes it remarkable. It is frequently read as being simply subversive. Certainly it offers the same warning to youthful self-confidence as does *Muio.*, and in direct terms. In the structure of the whole work, however, it has two further functions. It provides motive for the poet's withdrawal and with it a new perspective: the Court itself appears as a universal microcosm, divinely stable at its centre, ruinously self-destructive at its perimeter. Second, Spenser's final concentration of attack on the courtly abuse of love provides a thematic transition into the concluding movement of the poem.

736 *Lobbin* Lobbin is the Earl of Leicester, who had died in 1588. See Introduction (pp. 9-10). Hobbinol's comments regain the positive standpoint from which the poem takes its conclusion.

799 *the greatest of the Gods* The philosophical concept of love as the creator of the world is to be found in many classical writers, and above all in the *Symposium* of Plato. The later Christian Neoplatonist mythographers had elaborated on it. Spenser develops the same theme in his *HL* and *HB*, recasting it in terms of Christian theology in the complementary Hymnes *HHL* and *HHB*.

802 *both male and female* The androgynous Venus appears in classical writings. Spenser so presents her statue in her temple: *FQ* IV.x.40-1.

804 *gardens of Adonis* Spenser substitutes his own Garden of Adonis, *FQ* III.vi.29-50, for Plato's garden of Zeus, *Symposium* 202. See *Epith.* 99 and n.

807 *gold and lead* Cupid's gold and leaden arrows bring happy or unhappy love.

844 *so great enemies* The elements, fire and water, earth and air, are naturally at war. The power of love is seen as binding them in harmony, and so as being itself the force opposing chaos and instability throughout the creation. See *HL* 71-91.

863 *his like to love* See the Hymn to Venus, *FQ* IV.x.44-7.

908 *Faire Rosalind* At this late date, and very close to his second marriage, celebrated in *Epith.*, Spenser is hardly likely to have in mind the same human correlative for his ideal and unattainable inspiration as in *SC.*

She appears again, unnamed, *FQ* VI.x, as the 'Shepheards lass' dancing in the midst of the Graces for whom Colin pipes.

920 *fairest Helene* The story is told of Stesichorus, and is commonly refered to in the Renaissance. Plato alludes to it briefly, *Phaedrus* 243.

954 *the glooming skies* The dispersal of the shepherds with their flocks at nightfall provides a conventional ending to an eclogue. Virgil uses it, and see 'June' 117-20.

Epithalamion

Spenser wrote this poem for his marriage to Elizabeth Boyle on 11 June 1594. See Introduction (p. 15). It was published in 1595, together with *Amoretti*, the great sonnet sequence which reflects the progress and vicissitudes of his courtship. See Introduction, n. 33. In this volume he fulfils his promise made to Elizabeth in sonnet LXXV:

> let baser things devise
> to dy in dust, but you shall live by fame:
> my verse your vertues rare shall eternize,
> and in the hevens write your glorious name.
> Where whenas death shall all the world subdew,
> Our love shall live, and later life renew.

A number of Epithalamia (wedding songs) were written at this time and later: those by Donne and Herrick are perhaps the best known. Like them Spenser follows classical models, in particular Catullus (61): his poem opens with an invocation, and then traces the day through its every stage of ceremony and festival to nightfall. This poem is unique, however, in that Spenser is celebrating his own marriage, which he sees as being itself a divinely sanctioned type of God's creative love; see Critical Commentary, section (ii). As poet and bridegroom his standpoint and perceptions are alike privileged, and the poem divides itself accordingly. The daylight hours are given to the public celebrations of the wedding, sacramental and social; those of darkness to its private mystery, marked by the change in the refrain from 315, and expressed through allusive mythological patterning. The richly inventive verse form is his own. For many readers this poem represents Spenser's most marvellous achievement.

9 *sadder tenor* It is possible that by this phrase Spenser means specifically 'a minor key'; he may be referring more generally to the subject matter of *Complaints* and to *Daphnaida*.

16 *Orpheus* It is said of Orpheus that his songs tamed wild beasts, caused rivers to slow and trees to move. He was also founder or initiate of

many of the Mystery religions of the ancient world. He is the type of
the poet whose inspiration extends to the divine mysteries of nature.
His bride was Eurydice, whom he failed through human weakness to
bring back from death. His descent into Hades is taken by many
commentators as figuring that of Christ into hell, as his power to
tame nature recalls Adam in Eden and Christ as the good shepherd.
In relating himself to Orpheus Spenser is activating all these
concepts; at the same time the reference to Eurydice is a reminder of
mortality as correlative to temporal existence. The idea of Orpheus
singing his own marriage song is derived from Ovid, *Metamorphoses*
X.1-3, where Hymen, god of marriage, 'Is called by the voice of
Orpheus, though in vain'.

25   *Hymen* Hymen is the god of marriage: his torch is carried in the groomsmen's procession to the bride's house. If it burns brightly, as here, the omens are good.

37   *Nymphes* The bride has her own procession in ancient as in modern times. By calling on the nymphs of the rivers and forests nearby to attend her awakening Spenser extends the implications of the action into the natural order, so that through imagery and invocation can be perceived a re-enactment of the creation: *Epith.* 19-128: Genesis 1:1-27.

45   *bridale poses* The very precision of these lines describing the preparations made by Elizabeth Boyle's bridesmaids for her ceremonial adornment gives definition to their fuller meaning, as also below, 299-304.

56   *Mulla* See *CCCHA* 57n.

75   *Tithones bed* Tithonus was the mortal lover of Aurora, goddess of the dawn. He asked her for unending life, but forgot he would grow old. See 98n and 421n.

81   *descant* A melody sung extempore upon a ground or bass.

98   *fayre houres* The Hours, who personify the flow of time through the seasons, are the daughters of Jupiter and Themis ('Order'). Spenser sees the creation as a temporal as well as a physical structure. They attend upon the bride as upon the occasion of marriage to which they have brought her. The Graces, handmaids of Venus, are manifest in Elizabeth Boyle's mortal beauty. See also *CCCHA* 804n and *FQ* VI.x.

140   *Hymen* This is the invocation to Hymen sung by the boys in the bride's procession as she leaves her house. Spenser is overlaying the customs of his own time with classical reminiscence as he does in 25-9 and 253-7. See also *FQ* I.xii.36 and n.

154   *loose* At this time brides wore their hair unbraided. Queen Elizabeth appears with her hair loose in her coronation portrait.

170   *Adornd* The description of the bride shows her beauty as manifesting that of the whole natural order: the macrocosm. God's extended image. Like Eve she is, with Adam, that same image contracted: the microcosm.

190   *Medusaes mazeful hed* The sight of the snaky-haired head of the Gorgon Medusa turned the beholders to stone. She was killed by Perseus, who gave the terrible head to Athene, who bore it on her shield. Gorgon heads were often pictured to frighten off evil influences, and to warn off interlopers from private or sacred ground. All who see her may wonder at the bride's outward loveliness; knowledge of her 'inward beauty' is privileged: only to be hinted at.

266   *Barnaby the bright* At this time, before the Gregorian reform of the calendar adopted in England in 1752, midsummer came on St Barnabas' Day, 11 June.

307   *Maia* Maia was the mother of Hermes, Mercury; he is the messenger of the gods: see *Mutabilitie* vi.16-19. As such he also conducts the spirits of the dead to judgement, and acts as guide to candidates entering the Mysteries. The 'Acidalian brooke' is a fountain sacred to Venus into whose Mysteries Spenser and his bride seek initiation.

315   *welcome night* This is the only passage in Spenser's work where night is welcome. Darkness, here as elsewhere, is ominous and threatening, but it is Night herself whom he invokes, protective and concealing, from whom, in the classical as the Christian cosmology, Light first came. See *FQ* I.v.20n.

328   *Alcmena* the mother of Hercules, 'the great Tirynthian groome', taken by many mythographers as a type of Christ and of Christian heroism. See *FQ* I.xi.27n.

330   *with thy selfe* This is generally taken to be Spenser's own invented myth. My own opinion is that Spenser had in mind Latona, one meaning of whose name is 'night', on whom Jupiter fathered Apollo and Diana, the sun and moon.

334   *Let no ...* Danger, malice and ill omen are banished, with their human and spiritual agents, the latter in terms of contemporary folklore. See Critical Commentary, section (iii).

349   *Frogs* This is likely to be an amusing reference to actual frogs croaking nearby on summer nights; it may also refer to the peasants who insulted Latona and were turned into frogs, and so to human insensitivity. Wedding festivities at this time were riotous and prolonged. See 330n.

380	*The Latmian shephard* Endymion was a shepherd beloved by the moon, who visited him in dreams on Mount Latmos.
383	*thou hast charge* The moon goddess was invoked under the name of Lucina for help and protection in childbirth.
390	*Juno* wife of Jupiter and queen of the gods; she is the patroness of marriage, its ceremonies, rights and duties.
398	*Genius* Genius is the power presiding over procreation: the generative continuum of the creation. As such he appears in the Garden of Adonis, *FQ* III.vi.31-3.
405	*Hebe* goddess of youth and renewal.
421	*guerdon* Spenser here looks forward along and out of time to the heavenly reward to be earned by future generations of his descendants. These lines give a positive dimension to mortality, of which Eurydice suggested an introductory reminder and Tithonus the false antithesis. See 16n and 75n.
427	*many ornaments* The envoi has produced much critical speculation. The 'hasty accidents' may imply that the original date of the wedding was brought forward, and the preparations hurried. The actual date seems not to have been chosen casually, however. Whatever Spenser might have wished to give his bride, this he did, for her delight and secular immortality.

Prothalamion

This was the last of Spenser's works to be published in his lifetime. It was written in 1596, while he was in England; see Introduction (p. 15). The reference to Essex's exploits in Cadiz, 147-9, means that it must have been written after his return in mid-August. The title-page describes the poem as 'A Spousall Verse': it celebrates a formal meeting between Lady Elizabeth and Lady Katherine, daughters of Edward Somerset, Fourth Earl of Worcester, and their future husbands, Henry (later Sir Henry) Guildford and William Petre, later Baron Petre. This may actually have been the occasion of their betrothal: Fidelia and Speranza are described as being 'Though spousd, yet wanting wedlock's solemnize', *FQ* I.x.4, and the two states, though equally binding, were distinct. The double wedding itself, to which the poem looks forward, took place, on 8 November in the same year, also at Essex House. It is not known whether Spenser wrote the poem unprompted or by request. In it he is an onlooker, not a participant, and he takes advantage of the fact to shift focus, attention and imagery through a series of deliberately subjective transitions, lyric, elegaic and nationally heroic, always playing subtly on the theme of promise expressed in the delicate refrain.

6	*fruitlesse stay* If Spenser had entertained hopes of at last obtaining preferment at Court during his time in England he had certainly been disappointed. His stated mood at the opening of the poem places him as an observer, isolated and detached, and the summary of his vain hopes as 'empty shaddowes' throws the description following into vivid relief.
23	*a Bryde* See *Epith.* 154n. The nymphs, daughters of the river, express the self-renewing fertility of the natural order as in the marriage procession of the Thames and the Medway, *FQ* IV.xi. The flowers they gather belong to no one season: here Eden is recalled, and the everlasting spring of the Golden Age. A similar point is made by the choice of flowers brought to honour 'Eliza' in 'Aprill', *SC*.
37	*two Swannes* The swans flocking on the Thames were famous at this time. Spenser first sees the ladies at a distance; as their barges move towards him they appear as swans, pure and stately.
38	*The Lee* The Lee is a tributary of the Thames at Greenwich, but the setting of the poem, in the City, makes this very unlikely here. It is more probable that the phrase 'downe along the Lee', which Spenser echoes at 115, and which he uses elsewhere, means 'passing alongside the meadow' (lea): the flowery banks already described.
40	*Pindus* a mountain in Greece, sacred to Apollo and the Muses.
43	*Leda* Jupiter took the form of a swan to seduce Leda, and from her two eggs were born two sets of twins: Clytemnestra and Helen of Troy; Castor and Pollux. See 173 and 169n.
63	*silver Teeme* Swans, like doves and sparrows, are sacred to Venus, and often draw her chariot. 'Teeme' here seems to stand for the chariot. 'Teame' here seems to stand for the chariot itself, rather than the birds harnessed to it.
67	*Somers-heat* word-play on 'Somerset', their family name.
78	*Peneus* a river running through the Vale of Tempe in Greece.
110	*undersong* The undersong is the refrain, by which the 'Lay' is integrated into the poem as a whole: it is taken up by the other nymphs, in the style of a madrigal. It is possible that the exquisite pastoral fancy of the description overlays the sight of an actual entertainment devised to welcome the ladies as they made their progress into London.
127	*London* The biographical importance of these lines is discussed in the Introduction (p. 2).
132	*bricky towres* The Inner and Middle Temple had been leased to students of the Common Law since before the Dissolution of the Monasteries.

137 *a stately place* Spenser had known the great mansion, standing in what had been the Outer Temple, when Leicester lived there: the 'great Lord', who had died in 1588. This personal expression of sorrow and gratitude is a reminder of fame lastingly earned as well as of mortality.

145 *a noble Peer* Spenser sees Essex as England's hero in epic succession to Leicester, and the sack of Cadiz, where Essex commanded the land forces, as a catalyst for both national and poetic triumph.

168 *Above the rest* The bridegrooms appear pre-eminent in Essex's train as he welcomes their ladies, having an assured place in the heroic context defined by his exploits. The public glory just evoked reflects on their own present and future rejoicing. The stellar imagery expresses this brilliance and expansion of vision. Essex himself is compared to the morning star: the bridegrooms to the warrior twins, Gemini in the Zodiac. See 43n.

174 *Bauldricke* See *FQ* I.vii.29–30; Arthur's 'bauldrick brave' is itself an image of the Zodiac.

176 *Brides* Probably Spenser here intends a play on words between 'Bride' and 'bird'. As the ladies leave their barges and come into close view on land the beauty of the swans is assimilated into that of women.

Two Cantos of Mutabilitie

The thematic relation of the Cantos to *FQ* I–VI is discussed in the Critical Commentary, section (iv). The question of their integrity with Spenser's plan for the whole poem remains specifically problematic. Internal and stylistic evidence dates their composition as taking place certainly after 1591, and most probably considerably later. See 323n. They first appeared in the folio of 1609, ten years after Spenser's death. The opinion of the publisher, Matthew Lowndes, that 'both for Forme and Matter' they 'appeare to be parcell of some following Booke of the *Faerie Queene*' is natural; nowhere else does Spenser use the 'Spenserian' stanza. It also implies that 'Booke VII' is an arbitrary convenience. Even the numbering given to the Cantos: vi, vii and Canto viii 'unperfite', might have been chosen at random, since clearly the Cantos could neither begin nor end any Book. That in no extant Book is there an allegorical interruption so varied, strenuous or sustained is a cogent argument for the Cantos being taken as an entirely independent work; it is in itself inconclusive only in that major innovations do in fact occur in every successive Book. A crucial passage occurs at vi.37: the only indication given in the Cantos of an assumed chivalric context. See 326n. This has frequently been cited as evidence that the Cantos are, as Lowndes thought, part of the later Book of which the rest is lost, or which was never completed, and of which he took the thematic virtue to have been 'Constancie'. I see these lines rather as pointing purposeful shifts of register, indicated by the Muses presently to be addressed. The Cantos themselves I take to be an Epilogue to *FQ*, at once retrospective and corollary, intended to follow on directly from the concluding disillusionment of Book VI. The 'Constancie', or stability, by which this is finally to be transcended, being apprehensible only in the nature of God, cannot by definition find expression in the active life into which Redcrosse was sent from Contemplation's Mount, *FQ* I.x.63. There are indications elsewhere that Spenser came increasingly to see the poet's vocation as contemplative in itself, see Headnote to *CCCHA*. The perspective in which the Cantos end is that established in the *Hymnes* of *Heavenly Love* and *Beautie*:

> Ah ceasse to gaze on matter of thy grief.
>
> And looke at last up to that soveraine light,
> From whose pure beams al perfect beauty springs,
> That kindleth love in every godly spright,
> Even the love of God, which loathing brings
> Of this vile world, and these gay seeming things;
> With whose sweete pleasures being so possest,
> Thy straying thoughts henceforth for ever rest.
>
> (*HHB* 296–301)

CANTO vi

5	*many mens decay* At the close of *FQ* VI Spenser laments that since his imprisonment by Calidore the Blatant Beast (vicious slander) had 'got into the world at liberty againe', where now he 'rends without regard of person or of time' (VI.xii.38–40). Here he proposes a universal analysis of the malaise to which the Beast is specifically contributory.
13	*records permanent* These are also consulted by Arthur and Guyon, *FQ* II.x. See Critical Commentary, section (ii).
15	*Titans* The Titans are the children of Uranus (the sky) and Gaea (earth), who rebelled against Jupiter, Saturn's son.
21	*Hecaté* Hecate, generally seen as a power of the underworld and the patroness witchcraft, as at *FQ* I.i.43, has also far wider powers. In Hesiod's account of her, on which later mythographers draw, 'She had honour also in starry heaven, and is greatly revered by the

immortal Gods' (*Theogony* 411ff.). Like Diana and Proserpina she is an aspect of the moon.

25 *Bellona* Bellona is the Roman goddess of war: see *SC* 'October' 114 and 267n. In *The Visions of Bellay* xv she is '*Typhoeus* sister', and therefore a giantess. Spenser does not always distinguish clearly between the Titans and the giants. This is almost certainly deliberate. Their conflation leaves the impression of a single rebellion against Jupiter; a clearer analogue with the fall of the angels. See 109n.

38 *Nature* Nature, whom we are presently to meet in person, is the creative aspect of the divine will. See 312n.

58 *the heavens hight* Spenser's universe is terracentric, on the Ptolemaic system. Mutabilitie passes through the elemental spheres of air and fire enclosing the globe to the planetary spheres beyond. The first of these is that of the moon. The effects of the Fall were believed to be sublunary only: Mutabilitie aspires higher.

66 *palace* Mutabilitie's progress through the planetary spheres is elaborated from Ovid's account of Phaeton's fatal career, *Metamorphoses* II.1ff. See *FQ* I.iv.9n.

109 *Giantesse* Mutabilitie is referred to both as Titaness and giantess. See 25n.

123 *Chaos* According to poets of the classical period the world was formed out of chaos: a pre-existent state of darkness and confusion. Spenser follows later mythographers in seeing chaos as the raw material of the creation, the continuum of which draws on it for 'The substances of natures fruitfull progenyes', *FQ* III.vi.36. In HL it is love which brings the order out of Chaos:

> Ayre hated earth, and water hated fire,
> Till Love relented their rebellious yre

when these opposites were 'Together linkt with Adamantine chaines' (83–9). This is the chain, one link of which snapped when the Blatant Beast 'broke his yron chaine', *FQ* VI.xii.38, whose final disintegration is feared when Mutabilitie casts the moon into eclipse.

125 *that next* In the Ptolemaic system the sphere of Mercury is the next beyond that of the moon. In ascending to the sphere of Jupiter he would pass through those of Venus, the sun and Mars.

134 *Typhon* one of the giants who rebelled against Jupiter.

141 *or Magick* Writers in the classical period refer frequently to witches as having the power to cause eclipses.

167 *congregate* Spenser's description of the assembly of the gods recalls

Ovid's account of their debating the rebellion of the giants, *Metamorphoses* XI.167ff.

173   *th'Earths cursed seed* The Titans and giants, both of whom rebelled against Jupiter. See 25n.

228   *boldly answer'd* For Mutabilitie's dismissive account of Jupiter's claim to divine rule Spenser has drawn on the synthesis provided by Natalis Comes (Natale Conti), c.1520–82: the mythographer to whom generally he is most specifically indebted. Saturn's elder brother, Titan, agreed to abdicate the throne of heaven on condition that Saturn would not found a dynasty of his own: Saturn therefore devoured his children. Jupiter escaped as in other versions of the myth, on which Spenser has drawn for the Corybantes. These were originally priests of Cybele, famous for their wild music and convulsive dancing. They became identified with the Curetes: Cretan priests to whom Jupiter's mother, Rhea, entrusted him as an infant. Their shouts and the clashing of their cymbals drowned his cries, and Saturn remained ignorant of his birth. Mutabilitie states that Jupiter's reign invalidates the pact his father made with Titan, since he rules as Saturn's son. She bases her own claim on primogeniture; she is Titan's direct descendant.

261   *their example* Jupiter cites a range of the impious who have suffered due punishment. Procrustes was a sadistic brigand who preyed on helpless travellers. He was killed by Theseus. In each of the other instances Jupiter administered justice directly. Typhon was a rebellious giant, cast down by a thunderbolt: his monstrous shape makes him now one of the terrors of the underworld. Ixion was a mortal, a king who betrayed hospitality on earth and as guest of the gods: he is bound on a wheel in Hades. Prometheus was a Titan: he went against Jupiter's edict and brought down fire from heaven to men. He was chained to a mountain in the Caucasus, where an eagle was to prey on him, devouring his liver, for 30,000 years; later he was rescued by Hercules.

262   *that cursed fry* the descendants of the Titans and giants.

277   *should strive* Spenser here echoes Genesis 6:3 and Psalms 78:79: a reminder that Mutabilitie's nature is primarily evident in human behaviour. See *Mutabilitie* vi.6.

294   *Fates decree* By 'Fates decree' Spenser implies the divine purpose in the creation, of which Jupiter and his fellow deities are designated agents. As planetary gods their powers are neither random nor independent but delegated. In angelogical terms planetary spirits belong to the order of thrones; third down in the ninefold hierarchy. See *FQ* I.xii.39.

312	*the God of Nature* Mutabilitie appeals to God Almighty whose 'decree' Jupiter has invoked. See 294n.
315	*Dan Phoebus* Spenser makes Apollo, the sun, act as scribe to the gods; perhaps as an extension of his patronage of poetry and so of the written word.
321	*Arlo-hill* Arlo-hill is Galtymore, the highest mountain in the Galties. Spenser's primary reasons for this choice of setting are considered in the Critical Commentary, section (iv). In Spenser's time the Vale of Aherlow at the foot of the range was a refuge and vantage point for Irish rebels. See *Mutabilitie* vi.55. Galtymore is also the setting for a number of legends concerning the Irish gods and heroes, of which Spenser would have known: a range of association which he transposes according to his own purposes.
323	*Shepheards quill* Spenser had earlier recounted the story of Mulla, Molanna's sister-river. See *CCCHA* 100ff. and 57n. This reference places the date of the Cantos as being certainly not earlier than 1591: see headnote to *CCCHA*.
326	*warres and Knights* This phrase is taken by some critics to indicate that the Cantos are in fact part of a later Book of *FQ*. They may, however, indicate a decisive shift from the chivalric continuum of that poem, which Spenser sees as being the province of Clio, muse of history: see *FQ* I Proem 2 and Critical Commentary, section (ii). As Colin, *FQ* VI.x.28, Spenser offers a comparable apology to the queen for his having interrupted the epic register of his work to express the nature of the Graces through his own experience of love.
333	*thy quill* At first sight the story of Molanna seems to be a pastoral intermission between Clio's shaping of the poet's inspiration and that of Calliope. The point of the story emerges, however, as fully epic in its conclusion. It is possible that the successive ranges of register perceptible from this point up to the opening of the Canto following are intended to be recognized as eluding the pre-planned schema here indicated.
337	*The Gods* See 321n. The tale of Molanna has classical sources in the stories of Actaeon and Arethusa. A number of legends connected with the landscape around the Galties also provide analogues that Spenser may well have found suggestive: see *Variorum*, FQ VI and VII, appendix I, pp. 424–7.
356	*did condole* See 323n.
358	*Molanna* Spenser's name for the Behanna.
376	*Faunus* The 'foolish' country god Faunus is given Actaeon's role in Spenser's story, which has no human participants.

391   *Fanchin* the river Funcheon. See *CCCHA* 301n.
399   *onely one* Actaeon, whose terrible fate Spenser has transposed into surface comedy. Faunus escapes the tragic consequences of Diana's anger, as the land she therefore curses and abandons does not.

CANTO vii

1   *greater Muse* This muse may be Calliope, invoked earlier. See *Mutabilitie* vi.37 and n. The phrase 'bigger notes' is one Spenser uses elsewhere of epic writing: see 'October' 46. His astonished obedience to her direction, however, suggests that his inspiration may have been overtaken by a yet greater muse: Urania, whose classical province was astronomy, but whose vision is shown in *TM* to extend from the nature of the physical heavens to that of their creator:

> The Starres pure light, the Spheres swift movement,
> The Spirites and Intelligences fayre,
> And Angels waiting on th'Almighties chayre.
>
> And there, with humble mind and high insight
> Th'eternall Makers majestie we viewe.
>
> (508–12)

24   *th'infernall powers* Pluto and Proserpina are present as rulers of the underworld, but such ministers of eternal punishment as the Furies are excluded.
37   *great dame Nature* Nature is the creative aspect of the divine will, conceived of as feminine. Her appearance in the poem is itself both a sacred mystery and its revelatory exposition. For her powers, attributes and appearance Spenser has drawn on a long and complex tradition, some of the principal sources for which are cited in the notes following.
44   *a veile* The statue of Venus is also veiled, *FQ* IV.x.40. As the generative principle in the created continuum Venus expresses one facet of Nature's inclusive mystery. The motif derives from Plutarch's description of the statue of Isis, *De Iside*, chapter 9.
49   *like a Lion* This image may have been suggested by Alanus' description of Nature's diadem, one blazing jewel of which was shaped like a lion. See 78n.
54   *in a glass* This phrase is an echo of I Corinthians 12.
60   *those three sacred Saints* Peter, James and John 'were sore afraid'

when they saw Christ transfigured: Mark 9:6. The account given in Matthew 17:2 otherwise provides a closer parallel: the glory of Christ's face is there compared to the sun, and the whiteness of his garments simply to 'the light'. The Geneva translation, with which Spenser would have been most familiar, here glosses the mountain as 'Tabor'.

75 *Dan Geffrey* In his *Parliament of Fowls* Chaucer describes Nature's beauty as outshining the sun, and she is seen enthroned on a flowery hill (295-322). Spenser would have recognized in this description the classical figure of the Great Mother as described particularly by Apollonius Rhodius, where she is also said to be superior to Jupiter and all other gods; she is to be invoked on a wooded hill-top, and at her approach the wild beasts gather in welcome, flowers spring up and the trees put out fresh leaves (*Argonautica* I.1092-150).

78 *Alane* Alanus de Insulis, a writer of the twelfth century. Spenser follows Chaucer in directing the reader to his enormously detailed and elaborate description of Nature in *De Planctu Naturae* ('Plaint of Kindes'). It is not known whether Spenser himself had read Alanus' work; the parallels that exist may be derived from other sources that they had in common or be coincidental. See 49n.

91 *Mole* See *CCCHA* 57n.

103 *bridall cheare* Peleus himself is often associated with Mount Haemus, but his marriage to the sea goddess Thetis is generally said to have taken place on Mount Pelion, for example by Catullus in Carmen LXIV, from whom Spenser has taken the telling detail that Apollo sang the 'spousall hymne'. It was this wedding which was interrupted by Ate, Discord, who threw among the assembled goddesses a golden apple, inscribed 'for the fairest'. Their ensuing quarrel led to the fatal Judgement of Paris and so to the Trojan War. At *FQ* II.vii.53-5 Guyon sees the tree on which the apple grew in Hades, in Proserpina's garden. Elsewhere Spenser sees marriage as expressing the original concord of the creation; see *Epith.* 37n. Here by association the myth extends to include the Fall, with its consquence of Mutabilitie's sublunary power.

109 *great Grandmother* Spenser has in mind her ancient title, *Mater Deum* 'Mother of the Gods'. For him she expresses that loving aspect of the divine will which calls form and ordered continuity out of chaos. See *Mutabilitie* vi.123n.

111	*yet unmoved* This paradox derives from Boethius' concept of the deity. See *CCCHA* Head note and 665n.
143	*Titan* See *Mutabilitie* vi.228n.
217	*these fower* See *Mutabilitie* vi.123n.
229	*As, Vesta* Vesta, in whose shrine in Rome sacred fire burned perpetually, is identified with celestial fire, belonging to the highest of the elemental spheres below the moon: Vulcan, the smith of the gods, with fire in its daily uses. Ops, the wife of Saturn and mother of the Olympian gods, presided over the powers of earth. Juno, as queen of heaven has the air as her dominion. These attributions are common in classical and later mythography.
243	*Order* Order is Nature's 'Sergeant'; his operation is inherent in the cosmos the sequence and continuity of which Mutabilitie presents as anarchic. He has already appeared by human analogy as the marshall of Mercilla's Court, where regal mirrors divine justice, *FQ* V.ix.23.
244	*the Seasons* Personification of the seasons with their attributes is common in classical and later art and literature. Spenser may have elaborated his description from Ovid, *Metamorphoses* II.23-30, where the months and seasons appear to the left and right of Apollo's throne.
281	*the Monthes* March here leads the procession of the months, according to the usual dating of the time from which Spenser departed in *SC*, where his plan demanded the central placing of June and July. See Critical Commentary, section (iii). His descriptions of the individual months combine their traditional 'occupations', familiar from Books of Hours, misericords and the decorative arts generally, with their Zodiacal signs, glossed mythologically. Aries is the Ram of the Golden Fleece; Taurus is Europa's bull as described in *Muio.* 77-300; the heavenly twins are Leda's sons as in *Proth.* 42-3, 173-4. Cancer, like Pisces, has no mythological associations surviving in the classical tradition. Leo is the Nemean lion killed by Hercules; Virgo is Astraea, goddess of justice, whose flight from the world Spenser recalls also at the opening of *MHT*. Libra was in origin Egyptian; the balance in which the hearts of the dead are weighed against the feather of truth. Scorpio is the scorpion which was sent to kill Orion. Spenser evidently has in mind the version of the story which shows the goddess as merely spiteful. Sagittarius is the centaur Chiron, tutor of Achilles and famous for his healing skills.

Capricornus was originally a foster-brother of Jupiter. He is often confused, as here, with Amalthea's goat, whose milk nourished the infant god, and which in the stars is properly Capella. January stands upon the water-pot of Aquarius, often identified as Ganymede. The reference to 'the Romane floud' remains obscure unless by association between Jupiter's eagle, which carried Ganymede to heaven, and the Roman eagle.

388 *Day, and Night* Spenser has elaborated these figures from a number of sources.

397 *the Howres* See *Epith.* 98-100. Ovid also makes them heaven's porters, *Fasti*, I.125.

435 *your selves* Mutabilitie's attack on the planetary gods takes two principal directions: the mythological and the astronomical. The moon goddess Diana takes her title of Cynthia from Mount Cynthus in Delos, where she was born on earth; (by Greek word-play it means also goddess of the waves; see *CCCHA* passim). The conflicting stories of Jupiter's birth and upbringing are likewise used against him. The evidence Mutabilitie draws from astronomy is of special interest as showing Spenser's intelligent awareness of contemporary findings and the questions they were posing. The phases of Mercury and the eclipses were nothing new, but the erratic orbit of Mars and the apparent eccentricity of Mercury were virtually inexplicable by the Ptolemaic system.

466 *Saturne* Saturn should properly follow Jupiter, who is left for the last, clinching assault. In his case Mutabilitie has neither myth nor astronomy to draw upon: she can only point out that his astrological influence varies in the degree of its malignancy.

493 *it self is mov'd* Mutabilitie refers here not only to the apparent movement of the Zodiac, but more tellingly to the precession of the equinoxes, by which the signs have slipped from the positions noted by Ptolemy. She is using for her own argument the same observations as Spenser cited in the Proem to *FQ* V as indicating change and decline in the cosmic order 'toward his dissolution'. Both passages indicate a state of imaginative and intellectual unease similar to that expressed about fifteen years later by Donne in *The First Anniversary*:

> The Sun is lost, and th'earth, and no mans wit
> Can well direct him where to look for it.
>
> (207-8)

517 *They are not changed* The creation is temporal as well as physical: in Nature's plan fulfilment itself necessitates change. A number of

critics have found sources for Spenser's philosophy as here expressed in Lucretius, Boethius and the Neoplatonists. Put at its simplest Nature's doctrine is the same as lies behind Queen Elizabeth's favourite emblem of the moon glossed by the motto *semper eadem*: always the same. The changes of the moon, being cyclic, are constant also. Mutabilitie's dependence on the times and seasons for support was short-sighted and mistaken, since even the precession of the equinoxes will finally bring the stars back to their original stations.

525 *thy decay* The fulfilment of Mutabilitie's ambition would mean a return to chaos, in which change has no place or meaning.

526 *time shall come* The final change will be at the general Resurrection, when the 'perfection' attained through temporal experience shall become immutable and eternal. Nature's words are an echo of I Corinthians 15:51–4.

CANTO viii 'UNPERFITE'

17 *the God of Sabbaoth* The God of Hosts, or of Armies, as in Romans 9:29: 'Lord of Sabaoth'.

18 *that Sabaoths sight* Spenser evidently here intends a play on the Hebrew words *Sabaoth* 'armies' and *Sabbath* 'rest, time of rest', here used in the same sense as in Abelard's hymn:

> O quanta qualia
> Sunt illa Sabbata

('How great and marvellous are those Sabbaths'), referring to the state of the Blessed.

Critical commentary

(i) CRITICAL PERSPECTIVES

Something of the critical climate in which Spenser was writing and of his intimacy with it has been already indicated. The range of response to his work in his own lifetime makes interesting comparison with that evoked for example by Shakespeare. Both poets excite spontaneous, even apparently casual praise. Francis Meres for one includes them in a general comment, equating the literary achievements of his own age with those of the classical past: 'So the English tongue is mightily enriched and georgouslie invested in rare ornaments and resplendent abiliments by *Sir Philip Sidney, Spencer, Daniel, Drayton, Warner, Shakespeare, Marlow* and *Chapman.*' Until the middle of the seventeenth century, one of the adjectives most frequently applied to Spenser, or to 'Colin', is 'learned', the connotations of which extend beyond literary appreciation. Over this period scholars draw widely on his work by way of argument, confirmation and example in history, iconography, theology, psychology and geography among other disciplines. Even in his own lifetime his works took on referential authority, such as those of Homer and Virgil themselves had carried for centuries. They retained this status as long as citation of this kind remained general scholarly practice; that is, effectively until the founding of the Royal Society in 1662, when it was overtaken by new methodologies having their own counterparts in literary criticism.

Spenser makes his own attitudes to his work and to himself as poet apparent throughout his writing. From his time at Cambridge onward he assumes explicitly a poetic stance both challenging and centrally provocative. E.K.'s prefatory Epistle to *SC* sets that poem in linear descent from Theocritus and Virgil through Petrarch and the modern Europeans: 'So finally flyeth this our new Poete, as a bird, whose principals [flight-feathers] be scarce grown out, but yet as that in time shall be hable to keep wing with the best.' In the *Letter* Spenser claims in *FQ* similarly to have 'followed all the antique Poets historically'. He is operating on known critical ground, in full cognizance of its parameters as his contemporaries conceived of them, and anticipating their response accordingly.

For *SC*, a pastoral poem, however wide-ranging or innovatory, there existed formulae sufficiently clear-cut to allow of detailed analysis, at least by comparison, as Webbe's point-for-point juxtaposition with the *Ecologues* of Virgil shows. *FQ*, however, proved at once too radically experimental and too inclusive of apparently contradictory precedent for such treatment. No critical tools were available for anything like its full analysis; indeed, despite the very different kinds of particular perception shown most notably by Sir Kenelm Digby and by Spenser's editors John Hughes and John Upton, it could be argued that only in this century have they begun to be shaped for real efficiency. Drayton's comment, that 'To particularise the Lawes of this Poeme, were to teach the making of a Poeme; a Worke for a Volume, not an Epistle' outlines this dilemma as one distinct from that of his readers' comprehension or perception of Spenser's achievement. Meres's praise is exact in terms of Spenser's central aim:

> As *Achilles* had the advantage of *Hector*, because it was his fortune to be extolled and renowned by the heavenly verse of *Homer*: so *Spenser's Elisa* the *Fairy Queen* hath the advantage of all the Queens in the world, to be eternized by so devine a poete.

A recurrent phrase, used here by Richard Barnfield, may well encapsulate a profounder response to the poem than any now readily accessible:

> Live *Spenser* ever in thy *Fairy Queene*.
> Whose like (for deep Conceit) was never seene.

In particular the level of historical allusion in the poem was to Spenser's contemporaries both perceptible and immediately exciting, as a number of surviving marginalia indicate.

Spenser's own sensitivity to his critical ambience appears in the special care he took to pre-empt disparagement of two specific aspects of his work: his use of archaisms and dialect in *SC*, minutely defended in E.K.'s Epistle, and of romance narrative and motif in *FQ*, discussed in the *Letter*. Both come under attack at once, Sidney's dislike of the 'olde rusticke language' of *SC* is echoed, inclusive of *FQ*, from Ben Jonson to Pope. Daniel, writing in 1599, complains:

> Why do you seeke for fained *Pallidins*
> Out of the smoke of idle vanitie,
> That mayst give glorie to the true dissignes
> Of *Bourchier, Talbot, Nevile, Willoughby*?
> Why should not you strive to fill up your lines
> With wonders of your own, with veritie?

From the mid seventeenth century objections in this kind take an unforeseen edge from the neoclassical demand for precise historicity in epic, so that Spenser's own authorities are condemned with him. Fanshawe's comment is extreme, but not atypical: 'For (to name no more) the *Greek* HOMER, the *Latin* VIRGIL, *our Spencer*, and even the *Italian* TASSO (who had a *true*, a *great*, and *no obsolete story*, to work upon) are in effect wholly *fabulous*.'

Spenser knowingly laid himself open to both these lines of attack. His reasons for so doing, with some of their consequences, are discussed in the Introduction, section (i), p. 9 and section (ii). Neither, however, in his own time or later, impinge seriously on the assumed greatness of his achievement, though his use of a 'fabulous' narrative in particular comes to contribute very strongly to the growing question of exactly in what that greatness might consist.

Camden relates that Spenser was buried 'at *Westminster* neere *Chaucer* ... all Poets carrying his body to Church, and casting their doleful Verses, and Pens too into his grave'. Whatever the truth of this tradition, there survive a significant number of obituary poems, indicative of his standing and reputation among contemporary writers, many of them younger than himself. Elegiac reference to him persists into the second decade of the seventeenth century: in the work particularly of his avowed disciples evocations of their lost Colin are coloured by sentiment rather than by any strong sense of emulation. Their writing, even that of William Browne or Phineas Fletcher, the best of the 'Spenserians', is in general slight, their capacity not extending for the most part beyond charm and elegance. The newer writers of the metaphysical school are both more forceful and more interesting in themselves, to their contemporaries as to us. A sufficient indication of this appears from a reading of *Justa Eduardo King*, the collection of memorial verse written by Edward King's Cambridge contemporaries, to which Milton contributed *Lycidas*, 1638. The English and even the Latin and Greek contributions tend with one exception towards the fashionably conceited. The exception is *Lycidas* itself. Milton is no poet's disciple, but his lifelong debt to Spenser is great and pervasive, recognizable now as to his contemporaries. Dryden calls him, 'The Poetical Son of *Spenser*', and certainly he is presently called to account by the neoclassical critics on similar grounds: the use of archaisms, as in Richard Bentley's double-edged comment: 'Nay even *Oppian* himself, who took the allow'd privilege of using antiquated Words (as among Us *Spencer* and *Milton* did, though a little more sparingly) could not be understood in his own Town, except by the learned', and the use of allegory, as in the episode concerning the origin of Sin and Death, in *Paradise Lost* Book II, 649–889; Addison remarked that: 'Such allegories rather savour of the Spirit of *Spencer* and *Ariosto*, than of *Homer and Virgil*.' Spenser had been already established by Thomas Rhymer and his successors as having been corrupted by Ariosto; Milton is now seen as having been led astray in his turn. Despite the 'irregularity' of his writing, however, Spenser's genius is hardly questioned, merely its imperfect expression. Samuel Wesley's comment typifies this paradox: 'This however must be granted, the Design was noble, and required such a comprehensive Genius as his, but to draw the first sketch of it.'

The objections of the neoclassical critics originated from disappointed expectation. In the work of a poet acceptedly great they looked for what in Spenser's case was finally irrelevant. Sir Kenelm Digby, in his extraordinary and brilliant analysis of the notorious 'arithmetical' stanza, *FQ* II.ix.22, 1628, is the first Spenserian critic seriously to consider what might have been the poet's actual intentions until John Upton, more than a century later. Addison, who admits of Spenser's allegories that he 'had an admirable Talent in Representations of this kind', in some ways initiates evasion of the critical impasse, recognizing it as such at least by implicaton. He and his successors read, and admire where they can: once the question of epic propriety is waived the allegories generally receive particular commendation. As a critical approach it is in itself deconstructive. At its worst it becomes no more than the subjective appreciation of accidental beauties, to which Hazlitt's notorious reassurance to Spenser's readers that 'if [they] do not meddle with the allegory, the allegory will not meddle with them' is the logical conclusion. Matthew Prior, writing in about 1708, indicates, though still hypothetically, a more positive approach when he says of *FQ*: 'The Whole would have been an *Heroic* Poem, but in another Cast and Figure, than any that had ever been written before.' John Hughes, in his edition of the *Works*, 1715, takes this initiative somewhat further. In his view *FQ* is a 'Poem of a particular kind, describing in a Series of Allegorical Adventures or Episodes the most noted Virtues and Vices', though he does not go on to consider of what particular kind. His treatment of the poem depends on his essentially neoclassical judgement as to its 'Beauties and ... Blemishes', and concludes with a catalogue of the former, chosen with a fine ear and nice perception by moral as well as aesthetic criteria. Hughes's great and original contribution to Spenserian scholarship was in his use of the historic method. His attempts to relate the poem to its sixteenth-century context of manners, taste and critical influence was of seminal importance. It opened up possibilities to be enlarged upon by his immediate successors and hardly exhausted even today. His sensitivity to tone extends to the minor poems, in particular *Amoretti*, in which he finds 'natural Tenderness, Simplicity and Correctness'.

Dr John Jortin's *Remarks on Spenser's Poems*, which first appeared anonymously in 1734, expanded considerably on Spenser's known sources, and offered several emendations to the text, some of which have been generally accepted since. He was also the first to put forward the need for a thorough collation of the text. This suggestion was taken up by John Upton in his edition of *The Faerie Queene*, 1758, which is also the first annotated edition.

Hughes's emphasis on Spenser's historical context had since been paralleled by Lewis Theobald in his studies of Shakespeare, in 1728 and 1733, after which the learning essential for such exploration had come to be accepted as a qualification prerequisite in any editor, It was one that Upton possessed to a high degree. He identifies many of Spenser's sources through the mythographers, in particular Comes and Boccaccio, showing his awareness of their importance to a sixteenth-century readership. He is familiar with Spenser's Italian authors. His sensitivity to Spenser's use of biblical and especially of Apocalyptic material is remarkable, and goes far beyond the mere placing of references. He also identifies some of the most important of Spenser's authorities in natural history. His inclusion of Digby's *Observations*, which had not been reprinted since 1644, is an indication of his critical sensibility, complemented by his own original essays in emblematic interpretation. He also explores the British Chronicles, but is least happy when dealing with Spenser's debt to medieval literature. Here his slight sympathy is the corollary of his own firmly classical assumptions. It comes naturally to him to categorize his strong sense of the poem's unity as 'Homeric', and by the same analogy to justify his liking for Spenser's archaisms. His work still offers guidelines for research, and excites a profound regret that his death in 1760 prevented his intention of producing a complete annotated edition of the *Works*.

Thomas Warton's *Observations on the Faerie Queene*, 1754 and 1762, is of special importance as exemplifying changes in the critical climate which were becoming general during the pre-Romantic period. So he states very fairly that 'it is absurd to think of judging Ariosto or Spenser by precepts which they did not attend to'. This is in keeping with prevailing critical attitudes, to Shakespeare in particular. Warton follows Upton in his approaches to source material and to the interpretation of specific passages, paying attention especially to the influences of the visual and spectacular arts as well as literature. He suggests that *FQ* 'may be equally an HISTORICAL or POLITICAL poem', but he is no more able than Hughes to discover an all-over view of the poem. Having postulated that Spenser might have done better to have kept Arthur as his single hero or, alternatively, to have omitted him altogether, the kind of delight which he actually finds in the poet's 'warm imagination and ... strong sensibility' supplies his final criterion. He concludes that the work has no plan, and that none was intended; that in its composition 'little labour or art was applied', and that this is even to its credit:

> If there be any poem, whose graces please, because they are situated beyond the reach of art, and where the force and faculties of creative imagination delight, because they are unassisted and unrestrained by those of deliberate judgement, it is this. In reading Spenser if the critic is not satisfied, yet the reader is transported.

This passage might stand as representative of Spenser's reputation among intelligent readers well into the nineteenth century. The penetrating distinction offered by Richard Hurd between the respective demands of the Grecian and Gothic aesthetics of design, considered as alternatives equally valid, was not taken up by his immediate successors. J. Aikin, whose edition of the *Works* appeared in 1802, is in general agreement with Warton. He believes that *FQ* will 'probably not often be *read through*, nor will the plan or precise meaning of its "mysteries and historical allusions" receive much attention'. In this, as in his somewhat dismissive treatment of the minor poems, he reflects one range of contemporary taste, as H.J. Todd, editor of the first Variorum *Spenser* (1805), does another by his emphasis on the 'piety and morality' of his author.

As this dichotomy expanded, taste became critical idiom. Spenser's allegories, to which his neoclassical readers had responded almost despite themselves, were now out of fashion. Coleridge's statement of the interrelation of 'the allegorical and epic activity' of *FQ* had no present effect. More influential was his comment on Spenser's descriptions as being 'composed of a wondrous series of images, as in our dreams'. James Russell Lowell, writing in 1875, and his opponent, Edward Dowden, replying in 1884, crystallize the polarity inherent in Spenserian criticism from the early Romantic period. Each propounds his standpoint with perception, learning and often with extraordinary sensibility; it has even been suggested that together they provide the starting-point for any useful consideration of later Spenserian criticism, at least until the 1960s.

Lowell's fine ear, acute awareness of literary and historic influence and delicate verbal sense lead him finally to the conclusion that 'To read Spenser is like dreaming awake.' Like Macaulay before him he finds the allegory frankly boring. 'No man', he says, 'can read *The Faerie Queene* and be anything but the better for it', as for a healing and delicious anodyne: 'Whoever wishes to be rid of thought and let the busy anvils of the brain be silent for a time, let him read in *The Faerie Queene.*'

Dowden's counter-attack expands thematically from Milton's comment in *Areopagitica*: 'Our sage and serious Poet *Spencer*, whom I dare be known to think a better teacher than *Scotus* or *Aquinas* ...'. He aligns Spenser's primary intention with Wordsworth's wish 'either to be considered a teacher or else nothing'. His perspective allows him clear and often original vision. He is aware of variations of tone, as well as moral subtleties in the allegorical characterization, concluding that: 'It is the heresy of modern art that only useless things should be made beautiful.... In elder days the armour of a knight was as beautiful as sunlight, or as flowers.' The positions assumed by Lowell and Dowden effectively bracket the central area of Spenserian criticism until the appearance of the *Variorum*

Spenser, edited by Edwin Greenlaw, C.G. Osgood and F.M. Padleford from 1932 and indeed later. Greenlaw's work is supported by immense learning and by a strongly investigative approach to Tudor history. He sees Spenser as being 'From the first a student of theories of government', and as seeing his own poetic vocation as directly complementing the immediate involvement of Leicester, Sidney and later Raleigh in government policy at home and abroad. By this reading the Fifth Book of *FQ* 'shows the poet's art at its zenith': praise it will scarcely bear by any other. Conversely, his fellow-editor, Osgood, reads *FQ* entirely subjectively, so that Redcrosse's career in Book I becomes 'almost autobiographical', with the allegory of the work overall encapsulating 'the moral issues of the poet'; his personal struggles with ambition, lust, anger, disillusionment.

W.L. Renwick, writing in 1925, cleared a new perspective from which a number of paths were later seen to lead and to subdivide. He states that the Renaissance, in contradistinction to the later medieval period, saw man 'as a whole, indivisible, mind and body and soul together', and that Spenser was typical of his time in following no single philosophical or ethical school: 'The character of his thought, here as elsewhere, can be appreciated better through a rough grasp of his peculiar mixture of sources than by a complete study of one.'

The homogeneity of thought here postulated comes to be assumed generally by scholars in the period, not by Spenserians only. Paradoxically this leads in the first instance to the breakdown of Renwick's initial distinction between medieval and Renaissance categories, as appears, for example, in B.E.C. Davis's view of Spenser's relation to Malory in particular, and most influentially in the chapter dealing with Spenser in C.S. Lewis's *Allegory of Love*.

More recent work on the Renaissance has operated increasingly on this basis of inclusiveness. Such specialist subjects as art history, iconography, historiography or numerology are taken as foci of areas essentially interrelated, as in the work of Edgar Wind, Frances A. Yates and Alastair Fowler. Spenser's writing constitutes such a focus in its own composite right, capable of a wide range of particular scrutiny. What this is beginning to reveal relates perhaps more excitingly to Spenser's structural methodology. By Kent Hieatt's numerological and Thomas P. Roche's iconographical approaches especially, this is shown to be not only marvellously and subtly allusive in its complexities but also indisputably 'strict beyond all modern expectations'.

E. de Selincourt, in the preface to his edition of Spenser's *Works*, 1912, said that 'A full interpretation of his genius, worthy of its theme, is yet to be written', and this remains true. Spenser's work provides its own best introduction, however its critics may help to improve acquaintance.

(ii) HISTORY AND RELIGION

Spenser's imagination is rooted in history, in his awareness of event and experience as contributing to an inclusive continuum, from whatever angle or distance this may be apprehended at a given moment. It provides the human perspective for all his work. It may confirm a universal insight, as does the glimpse of Rome's past glory offered in *VWV* 11, or itself direct structure and focus. Historical event, change and development are not, as Spenser sees them, conclusive in themselves. Their context is eternal: their general end and that of their every contributor lies outside temporal flux, 'when no more *Change* shall be' (*Mutabilitie* viii.2). *SC*, *Epith.*, *CCCHA* and *FQ* in their different ways operate consistently within the whole context of created time, for which specific historic reference provides delineation. In these works, and in *FQ* in particular, Spenser's use of historical reference is both pervasive and self-illuminating.

The outermost temporal schema of *SC* operates from the Fall to the Last Days. Colin Clout, as shepherd and inspired poet, is aligned with Adam cast out of Eden in 'Januarie'. Christ's Incarnation was believed to have taken place at the mid-point of time, and is figured accordingly in the imagery of 'June' and 'Julye': Colin speaks for 'the truest shepheard', Christ, in 'June'. In 'December' he recalls Everyman, in expectation of final judgement as subsequent to his review of human experience from youth through to old age. Throughout the poem historical reference and moral vision alike coincide with this overriding pattern and its breakdown into Old and New Testament correlation: in 'Aprill' the praise of Elizabeth's rule in terms of the Golden Age parallels the Messianic prophecies of Isaiah, and in 'Maye' the kid, trapped by the devilish fox has no hope of rescue. In 'September' by deliberate contrast the narrative line recalls that of the parable of the Prodigal Son. The new dispensation operates to allow of salvation through repentance, while 'Roffy's' good exercise of his pastoral responsibility refers immediately to the Bishop of Rochester, Spenser's employer at the time he was completing the poem, as a contemporary type of the 'good shepherd' of the Christian priesthood.

In 'October' historic reference carries the theme of universal decay, as the world moves towards its winter, and this is centred on poetry. Virgil and his patrons are long dead: their successors in Spenser's own time frustrated or simply unworthy. Piers' suggestion that epic inspiration may be found in contemporary history, in 'fayre *Elisa*' or in the exploits of Leicester, 'the worthy whome she loveth best' gives hope of renewal, the fulfilment of which lies outside the secondary creation of a pastoral world as eternity does outside the continuum of which this is a mirror.

In *Epith.* the marriage day and its measured division by time and ceremony reflect the same inclusive pattern. It is Midsummer Day when 'the sunne is in his chiefest hight', type of the coming of Christ as the Sun of Righteousness at the zenith of created time. Coincidentally the marriage itself expresses Edenic concord re-enacted, allowing a nexus from which the Creator's intention may be seen and experienced along all its radii from the first light to final triumph in eternity. The very precision with which the occasion is set in its actual time, place and historical circumstance enhances its figurative validity.

The structure of *CCCHA* derives from contemporary history and circumstance, and appears at first reading to be deceptively casual. The occasion and subject of the poem is Spenser's friendship with Raleigh in Ireland towards the end of 1589, their voyage together to England and to the Court, Spenser's presentation to the queen and her gracious reception of *FQ* I-III, his impressions of the Court itself, favourable and otherwise, and his return to Ireland, where he recounts his adventures. This outline suggests a linear progression. In fact the effect of the poem is cumulative, with contemporary historical reference its controlling focus. Raleigh returns to the Court as from exile: he is Spenser's guide through the perils of the voyage, deliberately exaggerated. The Court, or rather the royal presence, is at once goal and reward, hard-won. The queen herself is celebrated as a type of divine glory: 'The image of the heavens in shape humane' (351), and the celestial perspective is sustained through the praise then given to the 'shepherds' and 'nymphs' attendant on the queen under names witty, graceful or fanciful. These are her courtiers, poets and noble ladies, many of whom are identifiable. Through the pastoral idiom Spenser is showing the reader a living type of universal order, against which the negative evocation of the 'enormities' of 'that same place' (665, 689) appears the more harshly by contrast: the fallen world seen next to Eden. The relation of the two derives from Boethius: instability increases with distance from the divine poise of the centre, here the queen's own person, her immediate circle. Spenser's condemnation of the corruption that spreads around and outward culminates in his attack on the courtly degradation of love itself, 'That *Cupid* selfe of them ashamed is' (768), and to the corrective praise of love as the principle of creation and generation. The poem ends with Spenser's praise of his own love, Rosalind, whose 'divine regard and heavenly hew' (933) recalls the celestial vision of the queen, aligning human with divine, individual with universal grace.

In *FQ* I a universal and eternal context is again proposed, to be contingent on the poem as a whole. Una's parents are Adam and Eve: the dragon that lays waste their land that Apocalyptic old serpent, the Devil himself. Redcrosse in his final triumph is at one level Christ; the three days' battle his harrowing of hell by which Adam and Eve were released from prison, as are Una's parents. Redcrosse's marriage to Una is a type of the Marriage of the Lamb, not to be consummated until the end of time and the descent to the new heaven and earth of the New Jerusalem glimpsed earlier by Redcrosse from Contemplation's Mount. Spenser may well have intended to adumbrate this eternal fulfilment again in Book XII, where the reciprocal triumph of Arthur's union with Gloriana might have brought the eschatological imagery full circle. It is likely that Spenser's deployment of historical reference throughout *FQ* derives its methodology from that of Apocalyptic exegesis, which from the twelfth century into Spenser's own day applied the text not only to the end of time but also to events along its entire continuum.

The action of *FQ* relates to time, as do the responses of its readers, contingent as both must be on eternal consequence. History, in a more specific sense than has yet been considered, gives to that action both definition and perspective. Its importance is at once indicated. In the Proem to Book I Spenser invokes the Muse: 'Helpe then, O holy Virgin chiefe of nine.' This is Clio, muse of history, whom Spenser elsewhere calls the 'eldest Sister of the crew' (*TM* 53). It is she who will,

> Lay forth out of thine everlasting scryne
> The antique rolls which there lye hidden still,
> Of Faerie knights and fairest *Tanaquil*.

This emphasis was clearly perceptible to Spenser's contemporaries. The antiquary Richard Carew for example, writing in 1595, equates Spenser with Lucan as he does Surrey with Virgil, Daniel with Ovid. *FQ* is not, of course, a historical poem even in so direct a sense as Lucan's *Pharsalia*. Rather it makes use of history to confirm and illuminate its multivalent structure. Duration in Faerie Land is contingent on human experience, abolishing anachronism and inconsistency. Prince Arthur, before his historical reign, when the Saxons were invading foes, can meet Redcrosse, by birth a Saxon prince of a later dynasty and generation, without falsification of role or probability on either side.

Both Arthur and Redcrosse have their place and origins in history. Arthur has come into Faerie Land, following his vision of its queen: Redcrosse was taken there 'unweeting', as an infant. Both motifs recur: the warrior maiden Britomart, patroness of chastity, is a British (Welsh) princess, come into Faerie Land to seek her destined husband, Artegall, knight of justice, who like Redcrosse was himself 'stolne away' from 'infant cradle' (Artegall III.iii.26): the young Tristram, who has his future place in Arthur's reign, was sent as a child,

> Into the land of *Faerie*, where no wight
> Should weet of me, nor worke me any wrong.

(VI.ii.30)

Spenser's use of historical reference directs the reader's attention outside Faerie Land to the continuum of his own known world. In general such reference is of two kinds, to the past and to the present, though the nature of temporal perception in Faerie Land allows of the interaction of the two with each other and even with their hoped-for outcome.

Spenser's historical material was familiar to his readers, his use of historical reference and recapitulation obviously distinct from romance. This is no longer so. Even from the late seventeenth century the categories become confused, and now at a casual reading they may appear almost indistinguishable, and consequently inoperative. One reason for this is that a whole range of modern historical fantasy, the direct descendant of the prose romances of Spenser's day, takes as source material the very chronicles he read as history, in particular the twelfth-century *Historia Regum Britanniae* of Geoffrey of Monmouth. The Arthurian tetralogy of Mary Stewart is a notable example. The distinction between romance and chronicle material is a vital factor in the structural balance of the poem as a whole. A crucial instance is the first point of contact between the two in the poem. Prince Arthur enters the action at I.vii.29. His consolation of Una and his rescue of Redcrosse from Orgoglio's dungeon express his function of champion and deliverer, prefiguring Redcrosse's later alignment with Christ in his defeat of the dragon. In the aftermath of victory Una addresses him by name for the first time, and the whole episode assumes new perspective: it illuminates and interprets history,

> But what adventure, or what high intent
> Hath brought you hither into Faery land,
> Aread Prince *Arthur*, crowne of Martiall band?

(I.ix.6)

Henry VII had claimed Tudor descent from early British royalty in support of his own very dubious right to the throne, and had even named his eldest son Arthur, for the 'once and future king'. The prince's early death as well as the first serious questionings of Arthur's historicity by Polydore Vergil from 1534 halted the process of Arthurian propaganda for a generation. Under Elizabeth, however, it revived. The chivalric idiom developed and was exploited through Court spectacle and compliment as well as literature. The Earl of Leicester centred his extravagant entertainment on the queen of Kenilworth in 1575 on the Arthurian tradition, so angled as to constitute a proposal of marriage as public as it was unsuccessful. Spenser refers to this occasion in 'Aprill' (at the queen's approach she had been met by the Lady of the Lake, whom her presence had released from long enchantment and captivity):

> And whither rennes this bevie of Ladies bright,
>   raunged in a rowe?
> They beene all Ladyes of the lake behight,
>   that unto her goe.

The question of Arthur's historicity remained long unresolved, indeed some aspects of the debate may still be considered open. Certainly Milton in 1638 was taking the tradition seriously enough to consider a range of Arthurian topics as possible subject-matter for his proposed epic (*Mansus* 80-4).

Spenser used a number of chronicle sources besides Geoffrey, of which Holinshed, 1577 and 1587; Hardyng, 1543; and Stow, 1580 and 1584 are among the most important. Evidently he collated his sources with care, often drawing on two or more accounts for a single reference or episode. *FQ* I makes no extended use of such material. The mention of Arthur's name would excite the reader's memory of his historical context, so directing an informed response to Una's question and to the prince's answer. In Book I the focus is on the foreground setting, Faerie Land itself, establishing its nature, condition and potential, of which Arthur's vision and quest are the exemplary complement to Redcrosse's trials and eventual spiritual triumph. The reader's response to both should initiate his conscious interaction with Spenser's purposeful 'fashioning' of noble character, as set out in the *Letter*. Redcrosse himself is given origin, but no precisely genealogical context:

> thou springst from ancient race
> Of *Saxon* kings
>
> (*FQ* I.x.65)

As Holinesse, Redcrosse's Saxon birth is generic, not individual. The antiquarian interest of Elizabeth's reign was directed by English theologians to the discovery in the Anglo-Saxon period of pure Christian doctrine, untainted by the later corruption of Rome. Archbishop Parker in particular made a systematic collection of Anglo-Saxon manuscripts in his search for evidence to support this claim in commentaries, glosses and homilies: these he bequeathed to the library of his college, Corpus Christi, Cambridge, on his death in 1575. Spenser would have known of this, and of the argument by which the Church of England had at the Reformation returned to the truth from which Rome had deviated. The separation of Redcrosse from Una, his deception by Duessa, his imprisonment and rescue, their reunion, his education and the knowledge given to him of his own identity in the House of Holiness mirror this historical process in terms of its spiritual significance.

The interplay between world history and event in Faerie Land, indicated at key intersections in Book I, is maintained and diversified as the poem continues. The function of memory in particular, first called into play with the mention of Arthur's name, is formalized in Book II. Arthur and Guyon, knight of temperance, visit the House of Alma, an allegory of the temperate human body inhabited by the virtuous soul. The library of the House is the memory, and there each knight finds the book that concerns himself. While Guyon reads one 'That hight *Antiquitie of Faerie* lond,' Arthur takes 'An auncient booke, hight *Briton moniments*' (II.ix.59,60). This gives a detailed summary of the chronicle history of Britain from primeval barbarism, through the founding of the kingdom by Brutus, Aeneas' grandson, to the time when,

> *Uther,* which *Pendragon* hight
> Succeeding There abruptly did it end.

(II.x.68)

The reader's own memory is again called into play to supply the continuation: Arthur's own reign when he shall have returned from Faerie Land to his recorded place in history. The mother of all the Muses, of whom Clio is the eldest, is Mnemosyne, memory, so that the reader is being drawn into the poem as an active participant. His own temporal relationship to what is here recalled has been implied by Spenser's introductory address to Elizabeth:

> Thy name, O soveraine Queene, thy realme and race,
> From this renowmed prince derived are.

(II.x.4)

Elizabeth's reign is the end toward which the continuum of history is directed from any standpoint in Faerie Land. Arthur's discoveries are retrospective, since he has yet to contribute what the reader knows as his own part. In terms of the poem Arthur's part in history is by no means confined to his reign, its time and place as encapsulated in chronicle, though these, or rather knowledge and memory of them, are naturally prerequisite: his further potential for such interaction derives from them. There is no account given of Arthur's historical exploits in *FQ*. The reader's knowledge is here taken for granted as a focus for what takes place in Faerie Land, but the period of his actual reign is left open, indefinite, between the firm, literal bracketing of retrospect and prophecy. Later, when Britomart comes to Merlin's cave for counsel, she is told:

> The man whom heavens have ordaynd to bee
> The spouse of *Britomart,* is *Arthegall,*

who is,

> the sonne of *Gorlois,*
> And the brother unto *Cador,* Cornish king.

(III.iii.26,27)

Artegall appears in some of the chronicles as a knight of the Round Table: Cador is often named as Duke of Cornwall though only once as Gorlois' son. That Artegall was his brother and therefore, like him, Arthur's half-brother, appears to be Spenser's own modification, though he may well have used chronicle sources as yet undiscovered. Artegall's future union with the Welsh princess, Britomart, who has no recognizable place in chronicle at all, enables Spenser to give double force to Merlin's prophecy in its conclusion. Having told Britomart of her destiny and of the part to be played in history by her immediate descendants, he traces her line on through the times of Saxon, Danish and Norman supremacy, until:

> Tho when the time is full accomplishid,
> There shall a sparke of fire, which hath longwhile
> Bene in his ashes raked up, and hid,
> Be freshly kindled in the fruitfull Ile
> Of *Mona*, where it lurked in exile;
> Which shall breake forth into bright burning flame,
> And reach into the house, that beares the stile
> Of royal majesty and soveraigne name;
> So shall the Briton bloud their crowne againe reclaime,

that is, the accession of the Tudors. Merlin stops short in his account of the reign of 'the royall virgin', Elizabeth: 'But yet the end is not' (III.iii.48–50). Just as Arthur's reading of *Briton moniments* broke off at Uther's succession, so here again prophecy intersects with its continuation in history.

Spenser only once again makes extended use of chronicle material in the poem as we have it: at III.ix.23–51. In this passage present and future perspectives combine to focus on the present. Paridell, a false and lecherous knight, is temporarily reconciled with Britomart. Both are enjoying the reluctant hospitality of Malbecco. Paridell's highly emotive recital of his descent from Paris by his first love, the nymph Oenone, is a move in his seduction of Malbecco's young and flirtatious wife, Hellenore, but it serves to remind Britomart of her own legitimate Trojan ancestry,

> from whose race of old
> She heard, that she was lineally extract:
> For noble *Britons* sprong from *Trojans* bold,
> And *Troynovant* was built of old *Troyes* ashes cold.

At her request Paridell recalls the story of Aeneas, and the eventual founding of Rome. Here Britomart interposes: in Rome '*Troy* againe out of her dust was reard', but,

>   a third kingdom yet is to arise
> Out of the *Trojans* scattered of-spring,
> That in all glory and great enterprise,
> Both first and second *Troy* shall dare to equalise.
>
> It *Troynovant* is hight, that with the waves
> Of wealthy *Thamis* washed is along.

This is London, called by its learned and evocative title much in use by poets throughout the Tudor period. Paridell joins in her praise of the exploits of '*Trojan Brute*', ending:

> His worke great *Troynovant*, his worke is eke
> Faire *Lincolne*, both renowmed far away,
> That who from East to West will endlong seeke,
> Cannot two fairer Cities find this day,
> Except *Cleopolis*: so heard I say
> Old *Mnemon*.

Mnemon is again memory, or its function: 'the remembrancer', whose authority for Brutus' founding of Troynovant first aligns it by name with the London of Spenser's own time and then relates it to Cleopolis, Gloriana's city in Faerie Land: a comparison which operates along all its history.

Some indication of Spenser's handling of historical allegory has already been given in the discussion of Redcrosse and in particular of his relationship with Una. A great deal of work has been done on the precise details of contemporary reference and comment in *FQ* and elsewhere in Spenser's work. Here I shall discuss only a few examples, and those whose meanings are relatively undisputed.

Book I introduces the historical level of the poem's allegorical structure, and displays its method, which is both general, even absolute, and particular. In the Proem Spenser refers to 'The argument of mine afflicted stile', Gloriana, 'fairest *Tanaquil*', as 'that true glorious type' of Elizabeth. In the *Letter* he says:

> In that Faery Queene I meane glory in my generall intention, but in

469

> my particular I conceive the most excellent and glorious person of our soveraine the Queene and her kingdome in Faery land. And yet in some places els, I doe otherwise shadow her.

In Spenser's own time Gloriana is aligned with his own queen, but any period should provide its own instance of inspiring rulership of which Gloriana remains the valid type. Similarly Una, truth, 'otherwise' shadows the queen: as head of the church in England Elizabeth manifests that spiritual truth by which holiness is rightly guided. Spenser would not question in principle the realignment in our own day of these absolutes with Elizabeth II. It would unfortunately be as easy, though more tendentious, to find negative equivalents also. Spiritual corruption and deceit are figured in Archimago. For Spenser these qualities were manifested above all in the Roman Church of his day, hence Archimago's monkish discourse and false piety (*FQ* I.i.35). Duessa's potential for evil complements that of Archimago. Her beauty is both false and perilous. In *FQ* I.viii she appears in her archetypal guise, the Whore of Babylon, riding the seven-headed beast, as in the Apocalyptic vision in Revelations 17. As such she might appear in any age: treachery and lust are never absent from the world. For Spenser Mary Queen of Scots was Duessa's immediate correlative: a Catholic, believed to have been privy to the murder of her second husband, and for all her seventeen years in England a focus for treasonous conspiracy. Duessa's part through *FQ* can be related to Mary's career in some detail, up to her trial at the Court of Mercilla, her reluctant condemnation by that figure of Elizabeth's Royal Justice, and her eventual execution (*FQ* V.ix-x). The qualities which in the poem make up her being are themselves indestructible, but as their agent she is not. The great opposites to the virtues of each Book are overcome, but the only one to be destroyed is the dragon, killed by Redcrosse. St John had seen 'the great dragon ... called the Devil and Satan' (Revelations 12:9) defeated outside and before time. Redcrosse's victory is a reminder that though he still fights viciously, claiming casualties in every generation, it is a battle he has already lost.

His defeat informs the eternal context of the poem and of history, but in either or both there can be no triumph to give respite. Archimago escapes from the dungeons of Una's father to wreak new harm (II.i.1); Calidore's loathsome adversary, the Blatant Beast, at last has

>   broke his iron chaine,
> And got into the world at liberty againe.
>
> (VI.xii.38)

Guyon's enemy, Acrasia, and Britomart's, Busirane, are led away captive, not killed. Evil can be annulled by virtue, but weakness, sin or folly can reactivate it at any time.

The narrative idiom of Faerie Land is that of romance: the adventurous quest. By his subtle and evocative use of motifs belonging to this genre Spenser is able to indicate and to interpret historical event, even in some specific detail, without losing the general in the particular. The episode of Una's sojourn with Corceca and Abessa is a case in point (I.iii.10-23). It refers to the state of monasticism in Pre-Reformation England, as Spenser saw it. Spiritual blindness produces a false ideal of celibate devotion, both corrupt and parasitic. Abessa is 'fed fat' with Kirkrapine's booty; wealth and sacred offerings diverted from their right use. The names and imagery used make the point clear, but the motif of ogreish lust and greed is familiar in its own right. The evil qualities depicted are not in themselves dependent on a given historical situation, much less confined to it. Similarly Braggadocchio's inept advances to Belphoebe and her devastating response (II.iii) refer to the suit of the Duke of Anjou for Elizabeth's hand, and Spenser's opinion of the proposed match is clearly indicated by a vividly realized portrayal of lustful impertinence justly rebuked by virginal disdain that can be itself relevant in any society, at any of its levels.

These examples are typical of Spenser's handling of historical reference in that they present contemporary or near-contemporary issues in such a way as to shape the reader's opinion and response, general, even universal as well as specific. For the greater part of *FQ* as we have it historical correlation of this kind is occasional, not continuous. Even where a narrative line of some complexity is developed, as in the account of the relationship between Belphoebe and Timias (*FQ* III, IV), which delicately 'shadows' that between Elizabeth and Raleigh, the story is interwoven with others and with other ranges entirely. Book V, of justice, is the exception, in that though Spenser varies his referential methods significantly, historic event, in particular Lord Grey's administration in Ireland and the English campaigns on the Continent, provide narrative, theme and example at a consistently and often painfully close range throughout the Book.

Of all the virtues justice is the only one that in Eden would have been neither necessary nor recognizable, though in the world as it is none of those others can flourish in its absence. For this reason justice is 'Most sacred vertue ... of all the rest' (*FQ* V.Proem), essential in a ruler: in any age it is the means by which disorder, endemic in an imperfect world, is to be rectified, restored, extirpated. But while the nature of justice in the abstract may be agreed upon from one age or one society to another, this is hardly true of what may be thought at any time to constitute just action. For a twentieth-century reader Spenser's view of justice seems as terrifying in its severity as the laxity of our own would be to Spenser. It is even possible that Spenser anticipated this problem as one inherent in any specific treatment of the subject. If so, he faced it head-on, even in his own time.

In the episode of the giant with the false balance, in which he claims 'That all the world he would weigh equally' (V.ii.30), Spenser presents an emblematic paradigm of justice which, whether or not it relates to the extremist tenets of the German Anabaptists of the previous generation, hardly admits of argument in its own terms. It provides for the concrete examples given in the narrative of the Book a perspective which is complementary rather than corrective. The harshness of Lord Grey's policy had led to his peremptory recall from Ireland in 1582; in choosing him as his principal contemporary correlative to Artegall, knight of justice, Spenser is quite deliberately taking up a position to be defended: his own viewpoint and no common consensus. To present Grey to the queen as the exemplary agent of her royal justice is both a challenge and an appeal:

> Pardon the boldnesse of thy basest thrall,
> That dare discourse of so divine a read,
> As thy great justice praysed over all:
> The instrument whereof loe here thy *Arthegall*.
>
> (V.Proem)

Prince Arthur has a greater part to play in the action of Book V than in that of any other: the very closeness of that action to the happenings of Spenser's own time makes this appropriate. His quest in Faerie Land educates him for his part in known history, and in doing so provides both mirror and example for English heroic achievement in any age. The subject-matter of Book V allows Spenser to concentrate this focus on his own time, on which the historical perspectives already indicated earlier in the poem have been seen to converge.

Prince Arthur has no single correlative in Elizabethan England. Sidney and Raleigh catch light from him from time to time, as well as being figured more intimately in Calidore, knight of courtesy, and in Timias, Arthur's own squire. So do Essex, and, above all, Leicester, in whom Spenser saw Arthur's most constant image. Leicester died in 1588, two years before the appearance of *FQ* I–III. By diversifying Arthur's reflection in his own time Spenser makes of Leicester's original place in the poem not so much a memorial as a goal, a potential realization of noble identity, accessible in any age:

> It *Merlin* was, which whylome did excell
> All living wightes in might of magicke spell:
> Both shield, and sword, and armour all he wrought
> For this young Prince, when first to armes he fell;
> But when he dyde, the Faerie Queene it brought
> To Faerie lond, where yet it may be seene, if sought.
>
> (I.vii.36)

(iii) ALLEGORY, MYTHOLOGY AND ICONOGRAPHY

In the *Letter* Spenser describes *FQ* as being 'a continued Allegory, or darke conceit'. He goes on to state his purpose in writing the poem, 'to fashion a gentleman or noble person in vertuous and gentle discipline', and to outline some part of its content and meaning. Of allegory itself, its nature and methods, he says little, taking his reader's familiarity with these for granted. His contemporary, Sir John Harington, is more specific. In his *Brief Apology for Poetry*, prefatory to his translation of Ariosto's *Orlando Furioso*, 1591, he says:

> The ancient Poets have indeed wrapped as it were in their writings divers and sundry meanings, which they call the senses or mysteries thereof. First of all for the litterall sence (as it were the utmost barke or ryne) they set downe in manner of an historie the acts and notable exploits of some persons worthy memorie: then in the same fiction, as a second rine and somewhat moe fine, as it were nearer to the pith and marrow, they place the Morall sence profitable for the active life of

man, approving vertuous actions and condemning the contrarie. Manie times also under the selfsame words they comprehend some true understanding of natural Philosophie, or sometimes of politicke government, and now and then of divinitie: and these same senses that comprehend so excellent knowledge we call the Allegorie, which *Plutarch* defineth to be when one thing is told, and by that another is understood.

This summary applies better to Spenser than to Ariosto, whose *Orlando Furioso*, though it has allegorical insertions, was not conceived originally as a 'continued Allegory', though Harington and Spenser himself were not unusual in reading it as such. The 'senses' here listed may clearly be perceived in *FQ* I.

'The litterall sense': this is the fable, the narrative line by which the exploits of Arthur, the hero of the whole poem, interact with those of the knightly representatives of virtue in each Book; here Redcrosse.

'The Morall sence': Redcrosse is 'Holinesse', and by the very nature of his quest he is also Everyman, for whose fall, recovery, restoration and eventual blessedness the parable of the Prodigal Son (Luke 15) had set the pattern.

'Of natural Philosophie': that is, the facts of natural history or natural science. This 'sense' contributes to the allegory of the Deadly Sins as they appear in Lucifera's Triumph, *FQ* I.iv.16–37. Each suffers from the diseases to which anyone indulging in the vice he embodies might be expected to be vulnerable, whether as cause or effect. According to the medical theory of Spenser's time a person whose constitution was dominated by the choleric humour would be easily enraged. He would be specially liable also to certain physical ills. Spenser's Wrath suffers accordingly from,

> The swelling Splene, and Frenzy raging rife,
> The shaking Palsey, and Saint *Fraunces* fire.

The sexual appetite does not of itself undermine the physical constitution as does uncontrolled rage, but its indiscriminating indulgence has correspondingly hideous dangers. Lechery is syphilitic. He has actively invited his disease:

> Which lewdnesse fild him with reprochfull paine
> Of that fowle evill, which all men reprove,
> That rots the marrow, and consumes the braine.

The physical corruption of the Sins mirrors their spiritual nature with medical exactness.

'Of Politicke government': This 'sense' is generally referred to as historical allegory. It is exploited most fully in *FQ* V. In *FQ* I the episode of Corceca, Abessa and Kirkrapine (iii.12-23) is to be so applied in its reference to the Dissolution of the Monasteries.

'Now and then of divinitie': this 'sense' is properly subdivided into spiritual and mystical allegory. The first expresses human experience as relating directly to salvation: for example, Redcrosse's education in the House of Holiness, *FQ* I.x. The second elucidates the relation of God to man by reference to the events of Christ's incarnation, to the sacraments of the church and to the eschatological context of the creation. In Book I, the Book of Holiness, this range of allegory is naturally more evident than elsewhere in the poem, culminating in Cantos xi-xii. Read according to the spiritual allegory, Redcrosse's battle with the dragon is that lifelong struggle with Satan for which the individual has the help of the two sacraments admitted by the English church after the Reformation: Baptism ('the well of life', xi.29-34), and the Eucharist ('the tree of life', xi.46-52). According to the mystical allegory the three-day battle presents Christ's harrowing of hell, from which he rose the third day.

These 'senses' apply elsewhere in Spenser's work. In *SC* the pastoral convention provides its own special subtleties. The word 'shepherd' has different connotations according to the kind of reading to be applied. The literal sense is expressed in the setting as it changes through the year. It is defined by precise descriptive touches, and by the use of rustic and proverbial language characterizing the shepherds themselves as belonging to it: 'The grassy ground with daintye Daysies dight' ('June'); 'I beate the bush, the byrds to them do flye' ('October'). On the moral level Colin Clout himself stands for Everyman. He is established in this position in 'Januarie', through the correlation of his wintery regret for lost joy with the situation of Adam cast out of Eden. As the poem develops he appears and is referred to particularly as the lover, whose unhappiness exemplifies the generality of experience in an imperfect world, as the priest ('pastor') exhorting and inspiring his hearers, and as the poet, by whose art the creation is itself augmented as well as reproved or celebrated. All three aspects are variously diffused through other characters as they are introduced and interact: for example Hobbinol expresses friendship in 'June', and Cuddie poetic ambition in 'October'. Specific ranges of theological and ecclesiatical dispute and concern are singled out for commentary and analysis in the dialogues of 'Maye', 'Julye' and 'September': their predominant 'sense' relates to church government. The two latter in particular, with their references to Algrin (Archbishop Grindal) and Roffyn (the Bishop of Rochester, *Roffinensis*), were almost certainly completed during the time of Spenser's service with Rochester himself. The spiritual level of allegory is also operative in these eclogues, by virtue of their subject-matter; the conduct of the church and its shepherds directly concerns the spiritual well-being of their congregations, their flocks, in this world and the next. His standpoint as poet allows Colin himself also the use of mystical allegory. In 'November' his marvellous lament for Dido concludes with an insight into heaven, here evoked in the classical terms appropriate to the pastoral convention of the whole work:

> There lives shee with the blessed Gods in blisse,
> There drincks she *Nectar* with *Ambrosia* mixt,
> And joyes enjoyes, that mortall men doe misse.

In *SC* this passage serves the same function as does Redcrosse's vision of the Heavenly City, seen from Contemplation's Mount, in *FQ* (I.x.55-7); it offers a glimpse through and beyond the temporal structures and concerns mirrored in either poem to their eternal context and goal. Colin's voice here is both prophetic and revelatory, recalling that of St John in the Apocalypse, just as in 'June' his lover's grief for the loss of his Rosalind transposes into the voice of Christ himself, the 'truest shepheard', lamenting the faithlessness of mankind, as readily as that of the forsaken Hosea expresses God's reproaches to Israel (Hosea 2).

In *SC* all allegorical levels work through the pastoral convention, to which other kinds of referential imagery are subordinated. In *FQ* the idiom is chivalric. Elsewhere generally there is no such predominant voice; response and understanding are evoked and controlled by various means. One of these is tone: the structure of *CCCHA* in particular depends strongly on the interplay of shifting rhetorical registers: *Muio.* takes point from its mock-heroic presentation. Another is context. In *Epith.* Spenser invokes the 'Nymphes of Mulla' and the classical deities concerned with the celebration, delights and fruitfulness of marriage; these are themselves terms of definition for hope and blessedness. He banishes fear of malice and ill-fortune colloquially, through the familiar folklore of his own time: 'the Pouke ... mischivous witches ... hob

Goblins ... damned ghosts cald up with mightly spels'. This distinction has here a particular effect of clarity and emphasis, and it occurs nowhere else in Spenser's work. In *SC* as in Faerie Land the classical and native appellations are juxtaposed and somrtimes even interchangeable; for example in 'June' Hobbinol tells Colin that:

> frendly Faeries, met with many Graces,
> And lightfote Nymphes can chace the lingring night,
> With Heydeguyes, and trimly trodden traces.

The Bible and classical mythology are the most important and versatile of Spenser's referential sources. Some of the principal ways in which he makes use of the former have already been discussed, here and in the second section of the Critical Commentary. A reading of *FQ* I in isolation would suggest that biblical reference is of predominant importance in Spenser's work: an emphasis which is in natural keeping with the subject of this Book rather than being a characteristic of his writing generally. Classical mythology provides a referential system of equal potential, with its own very different methodology. For Spenser, as for his educated contemporaries, mythology is a subtly developed language, apt for precise expression at any allegorical level. Harington in fact illustrates his discussion of allegory by mythological example: an analysis of the story of Perseus and the Gorgon Medusa according to each of the 'senses' he has just outlined.

Spenser and even Milton inherited a long tradition of mythological exegesis which since the late seventeenth century has lost almost all currency. Even in the classical period there are writers who variously interpret the myths of their own world. Some commentators unpack literal meanings: Plutarch in the first century AD relates the Osiris myth to the seasonal inundation of the Nile; Euhumerus in the second-century BC took the gods to have been great rulers or sages, the memory of whose wisdom and benificence had caused them to be remembered as divine. This theory remained influential, and has been periodically revived from the eighteenth century on: Spenser himself uses it only in *FQ* V, citing Hercules and Bacchus as Artegall's peers (i.2), and Isis and Osiris as supremely just rulers now honoured as gods for their 'divine' virtue (vii.1–3). Other interpretations are figurative: Lucretius, an Epicurean and hence an atheist, opens his great poem *De Natura Rerum* ('Of the Nature of Things') with a hymn to Venus as the personification of the principle of generation in the natural order. Spenser's adaptation of this passage occurs at *FQ* IV.x.44–7, sung before Venus in her temple: Spenser's Venus figures the same principle as does Lucretius', except that Spenser sees this as an aspect of God's creative love. Virgil in Eclogue IV and Horace in the Epode project the myth of the Golden Age into the near future as an image of peace and glory shortly to be achieved under Augustus: Spenser, among many others, sees Elizabeth's rule in the same terms, particularly in 'Aprill'. Eclogue IV was seen from the early Christian era as prophesying Christ's birth, so extending the potential of mythological reference to include mystical allegory.

A great number of the classical myths exist in variant forms, and this in itself would suggest the possibility of handling such material creatively. Plato himself had invented myths, or figurative allegories, to express abstract or psychological concepts. Apuleius may well have derived his story of Cupid and Psyche from folklore, but it first appears in the second century AD in his *Golden Ass* as an allegory of the trials of the soul in its quest for union with the divine through initiation into the Mysteries of Isis.

The early Christian fathers therefore had available to them a number of viable approaches to pagan literature and its mythological content. Their attitude to both was naturally ambivalent. St Jerome, translator of the Bible into Latin, aptly exemplifies this state of mind: he constantly condemns the pagan authors, deploring their themes and influence, while at the same time echoing them, phrase by allusive phrase. The educational syllabus of the late classical world was based on the works of the great pagan authors in all branches of knowledge, and though later authorities came to be added during the early and later medieval periods they still held their central place in Spenser's time and later. Mythography, the interpretation of myths according to their supposed origins and allegorical meanings, developed in subtlety and learning over this period, culminating in such elaborate syntheses as those of Boccaccio (*Genealogiae Deorum* 'The Genealogies of the Gods', written 1350–75) and Natalis Comes (Natale Conti: *Mythologiae* 'Mythologies', 1551), to name two of the most influential of such works certainly used by Spenser, and known to his readership.

Spenser's use of myth is typical of his time in its range and seriousness: extraordinary in its richness and inventive fluency. It is never purely decorative. The 'Nymphes of Mulla' are evoked in *Epith.* not simply as a witty touch of classical charm, but because, as Natalis says, nymphs: 'Are to be thought of as representing the vital qualities of moisture' (V.xii), by which fertility is initiated and sustained throughout nature. Their presence is prerequisite to the prayer that concludes the poem: 'Send us the timely fruit of this same night.' Precision of this kind characterizes Spenser's use of mythological material whether as here by direct reference, or in simile. The description of Contemplation's Mount provides an instance where Spenser's juxtaposition of mythological with biblical reference has seemed to some readers to be incongruous (*FQ* I.x.53–4). The 'highest Mount' is likened in succession to Mount Sinai, where Moses received the tables of the Law; to the Mount of Olives, associated with Christ, the prince of peace, who 'oft thereon was fownd'; to Mount Helicon,

> On which the thrise three learned Ladies play
> Their heavenly notes, and make full many a lovely lay.

The Old and New Testaments provide each a sacred perspective. It is from this double standpoint that the poet can perceive the true vision of holiness, but only through the inspiration he receives from heaven itself can this be expressed and so communicated.

Two ranges of mythological reference are of special importance in *FQ* since their consistent use contributes to the reader's awareness of structure and progression in the poem. Both also exemplify Spenser's inventive fluency in the handling of such material.

The sight of the New Jerusalem which Spenser allows us to share with Redcrosse has no infernal counterpart in the poem as we have it. Nowhere does Spenser present hell and its torments in terms of the bottomless pit of the Apocalypse. The dragon embodies hell, but hell as it invaded the creation at the Fall, capable of repulsion by the individual Christian soul; not as it exists outside time and space, however it has there been defeated in another sense. Hell is shown and explored however: the classical geography of Hades provides a setting and precedent for both; an idiom as flexible and identifiable as that of pastoral in *SC*. It is introduced in Archimago's demonic invocation, *FQ* I.i.37. He 'bad awake blacke *Plutoes* griesly Dame' in her aspect of Hecate (i.43) who is queen of witches and, as Natalis says (*Mythologiae* III.15), has power over dreams and phantasmata. That in spite of the classical names this is a rite damnable in Christian terms is made explicit. Archimago,

> cursed heaven, and spake reprochfull shame
> Of highest God, the Lord of life and light.

This insight into the means by which Redcrosse is to be deceived is the reader's alone. When Duessa descends into Hades in Night's chariot (*FQ* I.v.), bearing the moribund Sansjoy to Aesculapius for healing, the reader's perception is double: he follows what is said and done, but both are by definition alien to his humanity. When Duessa returns to the House of Pride Redcrosse has already departed: during the very time that the reader has passed in Hades with its native inhabitants the Dwarf has seen into its nature with human eyes, and brought Redcrosse to share his insight. Beneath the House is 'a dongeon deepe',

> Where ... huge members lay
> Of cative wretched thrals, that wayled night and day.
>
> (*FQ* I.v.45)

These are the damned, victims of Pride herself and of the Sins in her train. Those who are cited, men and women both, belong all to the pre-Christian world, and include not only names proverbially associated with specific sins, as Croesus with avarice and Tarquin with lust, but also others with more ambiguous, even with positive connotations: 'Great *Romulus*'; 'Stout *Scipio*, and stubborne *Hanniball*'; 'High *Caesar*'. The image of the prison dungeon is recalled when Arthur rescues Redcrosse himself from the 'darkenesse fowle' under Orgoglio's castle (I.viii), and again when the defeat of the dragon releases Una's parents from their long confinement 'fast imprisoned in seiged fort' (I.xii.4): by tradition Adam and Eve were released from hell at its harrowing, and others with them: from that time damnation has been the consequence of sin, not merely of the human condition. Redcrosse sees Pride's dungeon as it exists before Christ's descent into hell, which in the narrative sequence of the poem he has yet to express by defeating the dragon. The dual perspective on hell provided by Duessa's errand in Hades (itself a proleptic parody of Christ's descent) and by Redcrosse's horrified realization of its human implications is maintained as the poem develops through the later Books. In *FQ* II.vii Guyon, the knight of temperance, enters the Cave of Mammon.

> Through which a beaten broad high way did trace,
> That streight did lead to *Plutoes* griesly raine.

Guyon's exploration is reminiscent of that of Virgil's Aeneas (*Aeneid* VI), but the correlation of the classically familiar Hades around him with hell itself is carefully maintained. Spenser places the tree from which came the golden apple which Ate, goddess of discord, used to provoke the Trojan War, in Proserpina's garden, shadowing the tree of knowledge and the consequences of the Fall in human history. Standing by the 'blacke flood' of Cocytus, Guyon sees the damned in torment. Only two are named: Tantalus and Pilate, representative of both the old and the new dispensations. Dante had also conflated classical with biblical material in *Inferno*, and to place sinners of the Christian period in Hades, so making it, as here, a figure of hell was not an unusual device in itself, but Spenser's handling of multidimensional allegory gives him extraordinarily precise control over its application. Having once overlaid the image of Hades with that of the dungeon beneath Lucifera's house he can combine these images with their corresponding viewpoints, as in the episode of the Cave of Mammon, or evoke either in the context of the other. Malengin's cave, of which, 'some say, it goeth down to hell' (*FQ* V.ix.6), and the Cave of the Brigands from which Calidore rescues his Pastorella, recalling both Orpheus and Christ, 'That long had lyen dead, and made againe alive' (VI.xi.50), are examples which occur later in the poem, and which gain force from accumulating resonance. The concept of darkness is concentrated by the images of Hades, prison and cave, and especially by the personification of Night in *FQ* I.v.30, where the howling dogs and the presence of wolves and owls are defining attributes, those of Hecate. Night in *FQ* is moral and spiritual darkness, not as in *Epith.*, the darkness of privacy and sacred mystery. Her personified appearance confirms a pattern that began to emerge in *FQ* I.i: the alternating associations of night as negative and day as positive; of nightfall with gloom and danger, and dawn with the renewal of hope and joy.

The second frame of mythological reference to be considered elucidates a complementary dichotomy, of true light against false glitter, natural against usurped splendour. In *FQ* I.iv.8, Lucifera first appears: 'A mayden Queene, that shone as *Titans* ray', in richness that

> Exceeding shone, like *Phœbus* fairest childe,
>   That did presume his father's firie wayne ...

that is, like Phaeton who tried to drive the chariot of the sun and fell in flaming ruin. The simile at once recalls Lucifer's fall from heaven. The comparison of Lucifera's brightness to that of '*Titans* ray' now takes on added meaning: Lucifera's shining is pretended and false as was that of Phaeton. 'Titan' is a title of Apollo as 'Titania' is of his sister Diana, and Spenser elsewhere uses 'Titan' for the sun, as, for example, in the lovely description of dawn in *FQ* I.ii.7: 'And the high hils *Titan* discovered.' In the present context, however, it is likely that the term carries a further overtone, even a play on the word itself. The Titans, children of Heaven and Earth, made war on the Olympian gods and were defeated by them. Spenser makes Lucifera the daughter of Pluto and Proserpina, in conformity with his use of the classical idiom of Hades, and adds in *FQ* I.iv.11:

> Yet did she thinke her peareless worth to pas
> That parentage, with pride so did she swell,
> And thundering *Jove*, that high in heaven doth dwell,
> And wield the world, she claymed for her syre,
> Or if that any else did *Jove* excell:
> For to the highest she did still aspyre,
> Or if ought higher were then that, did it desyre.

Mutabilitie will advance her claim in terms very close to this. She is a Titaness,

> a daughter by descent
> Of those old *Titans*, that did whylome strive
> With *Saturnes* son for heavens regiment,
>
> (*Mutabilitie* vi.2)

and so by mythological analogy close kin to Lucifera herself.

Spenser is here using the Titans as a figure for the rebellious angels. Mutabilitie herself expresses change: the prime effect of the Fall. He appears to have made little distinction between the Titans and the giants, who sprang from the Earth when Chronus' blood fell on her, and who also rebelled against Olympus: on at least one occasion he uses the terms interchangeably. Argante is 'a Geauntesse' and also 'a daughter of the *Titans*' (*FQ* III.vii.47). This is less likely to be confusion than deliberate conflation. Both rebelled against heaven, and both suffered defeat. They and their putative descendants aptly express the fallen angels and the effects of man's own subsequent fall: a concept Milton was to develop in *PL* in the allegory of Sin and Death; *PL* 649–889. The giants have also a biblical correlative: the giants who were offspring of mortal women by 'the sons of God', Genesis 6:4, and who perished in the Flood. The 'sons of God' were generally taken to be fallen angels. The classical and biblical connotations of the term 'giant' together combine the concept of Satanic rebellion with that of sin as being recognizably derived from the union of spiritual evil with human fallibility. Orgoglio, Argante and the giant overthrown by Artegall, *FQ* V.ii, all exemplify this fusion of associations, each with specific emphasis.

The description of Lucifera herself and of her house has also a secondary, thematic function. It provides the culmination of a process by which the criteria, even the vocabulary, of true and pretended brightness come to be reliably distinguished from this point in the poem onward. A brief analysis will also exemplify some of the ways in which Spenser is able to handle recurrent imagery so as to manipulate the responses of his reader.

The pattern is initiated by Duessa's first entrance, *FQ* I.ii.13, 'in scarlot red', hung with jewels; already suggesting the full panoply of the Whore of Babylon (Revelations 17) in which she is to appear before Orgoglio's castle. The over-richness of her garments is itself a warning. This is underlined by the memory of Una's gracious simplicity of dress and bearing, though as yet this is muted. Her face has been veiled. Duessa's blatant charms are at once apparent; her garishness contrasted with Una's sober modesty.

In the next Canto the terms of this contrast shift radically. Una, wandering in search of Redcrosse, pauses to rest in the 'secret shadow' of the woods (I.iii.4):

> From her faire head her fillet she undight.
> And laid her stole aside. Her angels face
> As the great eye of heaven shyned bright,
> And made a sunshine in the shadie place;
> Did never mortall eye behold such heavenly grace.

Una's radiance is her own. Its revelation throws Duessa's specious glitter into focus, accurate and distasteful. The juxtaposition of these two passages is the first major instance of a technique which operates over the whole poem. A negative is introduced before its positive: the House of Pride before the House of Holiness (I.x); Acrasia's Bower, corrupt and enervating (II.xii) before the exquisite vitality of the Garden of Adonis (III.vi). This pattern is educative as well as aesthetic: revulsion from what is false strengthens, even initiates, right longing.

Una's beauty and Lucifera's 'gorgeous array' are both compared to the sun, but the similes carry opposite meaning. Una's radiance is of the same nature as sunlight; Lucifera's only appears so. Lucifera's house is the extension of its mistress. It is

> A stately Pallace built of squared bricke,
> Which cunningly was without mortar laid,
> Whose wals were high, but nothing strong, not thick,
> And golden foile all over them displad.
>
> (*FQ* I.iv.4)

Its eventual fall is inevitable: like the doomed house in the parable it is built 'on a sandy hill that still did flit' (Matthew 7:26-7). Its apparent splendour is mere paint and gilding. Here Duessa finds surroundings that entirely suit her, and where she is a welcome and familiar guest. So Una will presently appear in the House of Holiness.

This is the 'spiritual house' of I Peter 2:5-9. In it Redcrosse acquires both identity and spiritual awareness. Una, secure in her own nature, has no need of that strenuous discipline. Her kinship is with the rewards it brings through grace. The Theological Virtues, Faith, Hope and Charity, welcome her as their beloved equal, 'of heavenly birth'. The 'sunny beames' of Fidelia's beauty reflect her own. The Virtues have each their attribute: Fidelia's Bible and chalice with the coiled serpent, signifying either sacred wisdom or evil contained; Speranza's silver anchor and presently Charissa's turtle-doves and 'multitude of babes'. Una partakes of the nature of all three. They hold up a triple mirror to truth, Una, one and indivisible, and also to the queen as upholder of spiritual truth in Spenser's own England. Spenser is here using an emblematic device not uncommon at the time, one aptly coinciding with his address to the queen in the Proem to Book I as 'Mirrour of grace and Majestie divine'. The title-page of the first issue of the Bishops' Bible printed in 1568, for example, has a portrait of the queen set between Faith, holding her book and the cross, and Charity with her twin babes. A presentation copy, richly bound, was in the royal library. (It is now in the Folger Shakespeare Library.) On opening it anyone would see the queen as Hope: specifically as the hope given by her rule for the church in England. She herself would take the same meaning, but from a mirror-image.

The figures of Lucifero, the sins and the Theological Virtues exemplify one technique of personification. The qualities they represent are expressed through formal description, including traditional attributes such as Gluttony's 'yvie girland' and Speranza's anchor, and extending to the setting in which they are presented. Figures of this kind do not recur, though the qualities they represent may do so: their purpose is referential as well as expository. Image and meaning are fixed in the reader's mind and understanding.

Una, Redcrosse and Duessa are realized very differently. They belong to the narrative line of the poem. The qualities they represent are apprehended not at once but by degrees, through action as well as by description at each stage. They do not appear always the same. When Una puts aside her veil, or Redcrosse emerges from Orgoglio's dungeon, 'A ruefull spectacle of death and ghastly drere' (I.viii.40), something is added to the reader's growing understanding of truth or of spiritual peril.

A third technique which combines these two is used when a key figure is introduced who is to play a recurrent but occasional part in the narrative. The description of Prince Arthur as his enters the poem armed in solar splendour is the most elaborate instance. His appearance expresses his nature and his role: startling radiance and emblematic definition of detail are fixed not in detachment from the action but in the reader's memory and expectation. As the poem continues, the entry of Arthur into each Book takes on its own shining rhythm: nothing is added to the introductory description, which is reactivated simply by the recurrence of his name. Later in the poem the introductory descriptions of Belphœbe (II.iii.20-31) and Florimell (III.i.15-16) serve a similar function.

The fullness and deliberation of these passages allows the imagery in each case to be precisely expanded by a number of descriptive and allusive techniques. One of these is the elaborated image, dilating on a particular quality or insight. Spenser says of Arthur's diamond shield that,

> so exceeding shone his glistring ray,
> That *Phœbus* golden face it did attaint,
> As when a cloud his beames doth over-lay;
> And silver *Cynthia* wexed pale and faint,
> As when her face is staynd with magicke arts constraint.

(I.vii.34)

Arthur's shield is faith (Ephesians 6:16). Its light is that of the godhead itself, outshining even the purest of created brilliance. The same technique is often used to point the course of the narrative, as when

Orgoglio falls like a ruined castle, his 'unweldy' body bleeding hugely from the wounds Prince Arthur has inflicted, but as he dies'

> That huge great body, which the Gyaunt bore,
> Was vanisht quite, and of that monstrous mas
> Was nothing left, but like an emptie bladder was.

(I.viii.24)

The collapse of style from the epic simile to brief factual statement and of grand to dismissive image expresses Orgoglio's nature as much as his mere extinction. A very different example occurs at the beginning of *Proth.*: the long and exquisite introduction of the noble brides as swans, attended by joyful nymphs singing and scattering flowers, 'softly swimming downe along the Lee' to their forthcoming marriage in London. Then as now there were swans on the Thames: 'purely white' and also sacred to Venus, their feathers 'silken' as bridal robes. The suggestion of realism only clarifies the perspective offered. The technique of such passages is very close to that of the emblem, where a picture is shown, actually or through description to be activated by the mind's eye, and then interpreted to the reader. The sonnets of *VWV* are emblem poems of this formal kind, thematically related, but each complete in itself.

Simile, by which a particular facet of the whole is caught into focus, provides a different range of perceptions. Prince Arthur's armour for example,

> shined farre away
> Like glauncing light of *Phœbus* brightest ray,

while his baldrick,

> shynd, like twinkling stars, with stones most precious rare.

(*FQ* I.vii.29)

The brightness evoked includes the entire physical heavens. Elsewhere Spenser uses simile, often in extended form, to encapsulate a moment of action, and to project its meaning. An intricate and versatile example occurs in the description of the dragon-fight, *FQ* I.xi.27. In the course of the first day Redcrosse is scorched by 'a flake of fire'; that is, by the heat of lust, original sin of the flesh. His agony is compared to that of Hercules poisoned by the shirt of Nessus:

> Not that great Champions of the antique world,
>   Whom famous Poëtes verse so much doth vaunt,
>   And hath of twelve huge labours high extold,
>   So many furies and sharpe fits did haunt,
>   When him the poysoned garment did enchaunt
>   With *Centaures* bloud, and bloudie verses charm'd,
> As did this knight twelve thousand dolours daunt.

The conclusion of Hercules' career can be interpreted morally: the poisoned garment is the lustful flesh; even the noblest of men may be corrupted by desire. Driven mad by his pain, Hercules commanded a pyre to be lit on which he cast himself and was burned to death, when he was received among the gods and given Hebe, Youth, as his wife. The whole episode can be read spiritually: the fires of Purgatory (for a Protestant reader, penitence), consume the gross heat of bodily sin, and the purified soul attains blessedness and is renewed. It has also a mystical application. Hercules is often taken as a mythological type of Christ, and his labours applied to the events of incarnation. The shirt of Nessus inflicts the agony of the Passion, suffered in the flesh for the sin and corruption of mankind. The descent into hell itself is seen as figured in Hercules' labour of dragging Cerberus from Hades. Spenser reminds us of this reading a few verses later (I.xi.41) when, on the second day of the battle, the dragon clutches the knight's shield, and,

> Nor harder was from *Cerberus* greedie jaw
> To plucke a bone, then from his cruell claw
> To reave by strength the griped gage away.

The comparison to Hercules applies on the literal, moral, spiritual and mystical levels of the action, sharpening the reader's attention and bringing them into focus with each other.

Simile presents a mirror-image, seen from a specifically revealing angle. It is essentially selective. When Nature herself descends to Arlo Hill to judge Mutabilitie's claim (*Mutabilitie* vii), Spenser says of her radiant garment that he

>   cannot divize to what
> It to compare, nor find like stuffe to that,

though in his impotence he is

> And those three sacred *Saints*, though else most wise,
> Yet on mount Thabor quite their wits forgat,
> When they their glorious Lord in strange disguise
> Transfigur'd saw; his garments so did daze their eyes.

The light of Nature herself, God's creative power,

> the Sunne a thousand times did pass,
> Ne could be seen, but like an image in a glass.

Nature's own mirror is the entire creation: once fragmented by comparison and cross-reference it can be only self-revealing. The poets have in different ways provided an alternative: the mirror of art, by which Nature herself is perceived and augmented. Spenser refers his reader to a famous and apt example, the twelfth-century *De Planctu Naturae* ('Plaint of Kindes') of Alain de Lille (Alanus de Insulis, Spenser's Alane) (*Mutabilitie* vii.9). In this work the poet describes Nature as she appeared to him in a vision, crowned with the stars, glorious in every feature, into whose robes were woven the skies, the forests, meadows and mountains, the rivers and seas, all with their inhabitants, all in painstaking detail. It was, to Spenser's generation as to Chaucer's a reference well enough known to recall the passage to any educated reader, and clearly enough for him to notice one telling discrepancy. Unlike Alain's Nature, Spenser's is veiled:

> For, with a veile that wimpled every where,
> Her hoad and face was hid, that mote to none appeare.
>
> (*Mutabilitie* vii.5)

Unlike Alain, Spenser does not attempt to translate the divine into directly comprehensible terms, however inclusive. His own mirror of art is *FQ* itself. Throughout it nature is reflected, 'but like an image in a glass' (*Mutabilitie* vii.6). Even here, in her very presence, this final mystery remains. Nature's veil is the divine counterpart of the 'continued Allegory, or darke conceit' (*Letter* 3) of the poem he himself has made.

(iv) FAERIE LAND

In the Proem to *FQ* II Spenser calls detailed attention to a radical shift he has made in handling the romance convention through which the action of his poems is expressed. Equivocally, but point for point, he directs retrospective attention to Book I in terms of questions to be raised and answered. He starts from general assumptions as to the nature of romance itself, 'historicall fiction', as he terms it in the *Letter*:

> Right well I wote most mighty Soveraine,
>   That all this famous antique history,
>   Of some th' aboundance of an idle braine
>   Will judged be, and painted forgery,
>   Rather then matter of just memory.

Such an objection, applicable to the genre of romance writing, has been already subverted in the the Proem to Book I, where Spenser invokes Clio, muse of history:

> Helpe then, O holy Virgin chiefe of nine,
>   Thy weaker Novice to performe thy will,
>   Lay forth out of thine everlasting scryne
>   The antique rolles which there lye hidden still,
>   Of Faerie knights and fairest *Tanaquill*,
>   Whom that most noble Briton Prince so long
>   Sought through the world.

FQ is not a romance, by definition, though it uses the idiom of romance narrative. It is introduced as history, but by the end of Book I it is clear that this is not directly referrable to any range of the chronicle history to which Arthur elsewhere belongs:

> Sith none, that breatheth living aire, can know,
> Where is that happy land of Faery,
> Which I so much do vaunt, but no where show,
> But vouch antiquities, which nobody can know.
>
> (II.Proem 1)

Here and throughout this passage Spenser is being wittily disingenuous: any reader will have recognized the poem as being an allegory from the first verse, when Redcrosse appears for all his inexperience arrayed in the battered armour of God that has been scarred by fifteen centuries of conflict in His name. The historical 'sense' is equally perceptible, certainly from the episode of Corceca and Abessa in the third Canto. Spenser is

489

calling attention not to the content of his poem so much as to its setting. At *FQ* I.i.3 Spenser says of Redcrosse:

> Upon a great adventure he was bond,
>   That greatest *Gloriana* to him gave,
>   The greatest Glorious Queene of *Faerie* lond:

that is, his quest does not merely take him into Faerie Land. It began and will end there.

By centring the action of his poem in Faerie Land itself Spenser has inverted a primary convention of romance narrative structure; one recognizable from Homer through to the present day. However the action may lead by choice or accident into another continuum distinct from our own, Faery or Circe's Isle, it will conclude in the known context of human society: Ithaca, Camelot, Spenser's Faerie Land is accessible from human history as Prince Arthur's quest indicates. Once it has been fulfilled he must return for that history to continue. When he does so he will in one sense only be absent from Faerie Land. There history is perceived tangentially, detached from the continuum of the poem but accessible at any point, either in Spenser's lifetime or our own.

The temporal and thematic structure of the poem depends on this detachment being kept in balance. Faerie Land lies in a particular relation to the human world; it is not merely an extension of it. Spenser continues the Proem to Book II with a dismissive hypothesis:

> But let that man with better sence advize,
>   That of the world least part to us is red:
>   And dayly how through hardy enterprize,
>   Many great Regions are discovered,
>   Which to late age were never mentioned.
>   Who ever heard of th'Indian *Peru*?
>   Or who in venturous vessell measured
>   The *Amazon*'s huge river now found trew?
> Or fruitfullest *Virginia* who did ever vew?

No reader is likely to have considered the possibility of a distant voyager coming at last within sight of the shining towers of Cleopolis, but another and important point is here implied. The very nature of Faerie Land is distinct and of itself. It is not simply characterized by the prevalence of curious and exotic marvels such as might be drawn from travellers' tales of 'th'Indian *Peru*'. It is a place of discovery, not mere astonishment, which further distinguishes it from certain ranges of popular romance as such. Spenser's next point refers obliquely to just such a discovery:

> Yet all these were, when no man did them know,
> Yet have from wisest ages hidden beene:
> And later times things more unknowne shall show.
> Why then should witlesse man so much misweene
> That nothing is, but that which he hath seene?

Certainly one of Spenser's means to his end of fashioning 'a gentleman or noble person in vertuous and gentle discipline' is to show his readers things unknown to them previously. The poem is not a fantasy, nor is it science fiction of a kind known even in the classical world and receiving new popularity in Spenser's time as a vehicle usually of satiric comedy:

> What if within the Moones faire shining spheare?
> What if in every other starre unseene
> Of other worldes he happily should heare?
> He wonder would much more: yet such to some appeare.

This passage works throughout by negatives. It implies what Faerie Land is not. To understand the poem the reader must discover what it is. This he must do for himself, though not unaided:

> Of Faerie lond yet if he more inquire,
> By certaine signes here set in sundry place
> He may it find.

Some of these 'signes' have been already indicated in the course of Book I. One purpose of the Proem to Book II is to give the reader pause, to let him reconsider what has gone before if not to dismiss any of the erroneous possibilities here outlined. In Canto I the setting was named and part at least of its nature established. The quest assigned to Redcrosse would be at once recognizable in terms of the chivalric *Perigrinatio Vitae*, the allegorical Pilgrimage of Life, for which the French *Conte du Graal* is the outstanding precedent. Similarly the historical 'sense' of the allegory would be clearly distinguishable as it came to the surface of the narrative. This very familiarity might well inhibit wider perception: holiness is the subject only of the first Book, though it proposes the context for them all, and what is learned in the course of reading it is relevant elsewhere. Some of the patterns of structure and imagery initiated in Book I have been already discussed, and there are others that become evident as the poem develops.

There are, however, two points of special importance that a reading of the Proem to Book II should bring to mind. Both are recalled by the passage itself, which continues:

> And thou, O fairest Princesse under sky,
> In this faire mirrhour maist behold thy face,
> And thine owne realmes in lond of Faery,
> And in this antique Image thy great auncestry.

In Proem I the queen was addressed as 'Mirrour of grace and Majestie divine', an image given special definition by the iconography of Una and the virtues in the House of Holiness (*FQ* I.x). Here the poem itself is to provide a mirror for the queen, specifically in the figure of Belphoebe who first appears in the third Canto. But in *FQ* I the reader has already been offered a mirror of another kind; Redcrosse as Everyman exemplifies the universal condition of the Christian life. The queen herself is shown the lovely reflection of her own private virtue only in Book II, the subject of which is temperance, most rational and so most characteristically human of the virtues and the prerequisite to the right exercise of them all. Somewhere in Faerie Land any reader may discover his own mirror for himself.

The queen is told also that both her kingdom and her ancestry may be seen in Faerie Land. The reader, being reminded of the part so far played by Prince Arthur, as well as of his historical place in the Tudor descent, should also recall his own involuntary entry into the poem when at the first mention of the prince's name memory supplied both knowledge and prophecy of his lineage and reign. Both these are 'signes' taken up and made explicit in *FQ* II, ix and x.

In the House of Alma Guyon and Arthur each meet their own feminine nature; their complementary mirror-image. Guyon encounters a lovely lady, robed in blue, who can hardly answer him for bashfulness. Alma explains:

> She is the fountaine of your modestee;
> You shamefast are, but *Shamefastnesse* itself is shee.

Arthur seeks out a lady of great dignity, but sad and thoughtful, robed in purple and gold. She knows him and his quest without being told, for she shares his nature. Her name is Prays-desire. In Jungian terms each knight comes to know his *anima*. The concept was familiar to Spenser and his contemporaries; it is a psychological commonplace of Hermetic imagery. It also gives a contributory 'sense' to the whole presentation of Britomart's quest for Artegall, her destined husband, which runs through Books III–V: the interpretation of her dream in Isis' temple shows her to be 'clemence', the feminine complement to Artegall's 'just endever': Isis to his Osiris (*FQ* V.vii.22).

The mirror-image, recurrent literally and metaphorically throughout the poem, relates to self-knowledge, to subjective awareness of the individual as the microcosm, the contracted image of the Creator as this is to be discovered in Faerie Land. When Arthur and Guyon explore Alma's house they are learning their own physical and emotional humanity. The Chambers of the Brain display the faculties of the mind. In the Chamber of the Memory Arthur finds the book *Briton moniments*. While he is reading it Guyon takes up another.

> That hight *Antiquitie* of *Faerie* lond,
> In which when as he greedily did looke,
> Th'off-spring of Elves and Faries there he fond,
> As it delivered was from hond to hond.

There he discovers that the native inhabitants of Faerie Land, himself among them, are descended from a man, Elfe, created by Prometheus. The mythographers interpreted the myth of Prometheus' creation of man as referring to civilization, by which the barbarism of natural, primitive humanity is refashioned. The history of faerie royalty which Guyon reads is the chronicle of human civilization: their achievements emblematic milestones of progress in government and the arts. Only the last four named relate exactly to human history in England: Elficleos, Elferon and Oberon are Henry VII, his eldest son, Arthur and Henry VIII, whose daughter is Tanaquil, Gloriana herself.

It is this continuum which the reader enters at the first moment of recognition, and from which he can at any time see his own. Faerie Land is both mirror and perspective. To enter it is to be educated, in the highest sense. Guyon's reading finally makes it clear what Faerie Land is. What its effect can be is discovered only as it is explored further.

Once Redcrosse has expressed the universal paradigm of salvation his function of Everyman is taken over by Prince Arthur in terms of individual self-fulfilment. The reader follows the same progression as the prince: he is educated in the same virtues and in the ranges of awareness to which each in turn gives access. Faerie Land itself, which never appeared alien, comes to acquire another kind of familiarity. Almost it becomes transparent, though never shadowy. Names and contours from the experiential world slip recognizably into the landscape. This process is initiated at the end of Book IV with the naming of the rivers of the world which meet in Proteus' cave to celebrate the marriage of the Thames and the Medway, the '*Amazons* huge river' among them. In Book V the closeness of Artegall's career to contemporary history maintains this effect. In Book VI Colin Clout, the mirror of the poet himself, pipes to the Graces and expounds the meaning of their dance to the reader as to Calidore (*FQ* VI.x). The grassy spaces, the rich woodlands through which Calidore's quest has led him, are as perilous as any other reach of Faerie Land. Before the end of the Book the Valley of the Shepherds will have been ravaged, and the choice it seemed to offer of contemplative retirement invalidated. But there is Acidale, and there Spenser chooses to propound the quintessential doctrine of Faerie Land, 'which skill men call Civility'.

For the reader will never come to Cleopolis, never see Gloriana for himself, face to face. Not at least in *FQ*. Possibly in *CCCHA* there is a sight of her, serene in divine splendour, attended not by armoured knights but by shepherds, her poets, and nymphs as gracious as they are fair, while the darkness of malice and greed laps too closely at their radiance and stability.

The Mutabilitie Cantos stand a little outside the six complete Books. They offer a retrospect, conclusive in itself, and a renewal of the eternal context assumed in *FQ* I. Spenser himself has come to the very edge of Faerie Land. On its border he turns to look back, not unchanged. His new voice rises above that of Colin Clout as this final vision transcends that even of the Graces. He is inspired now by Urania herself, muse of sacred song:

> Ah! whither doost thou now thou greater Muse
>   Me from these woods and pleasing forrests bring?
>   And my fraile spirit (that dooth oft refuse
>   This too high flight, unfit for her weake wing)
>   Lift up aloft, to tell of heavens King

> (Thy soveraine Sire) his fortunate successe,
> And victory, in bigger noates to sing,
> Which he obtain'd against that *Titanesse*,
> That him of heavens Empire sought to dispossesse.
>
> (*Mutabilitie* vii.1)

In *Mutabilitie* the site chosen for Nature's decision on the Titaness's claim to universal dominion will be '*Arlo-hill* (who knows not *Arlo-hill*?)'. Hardly any one of Spenser's readers would have done so till he named it. It is his name for Mount Galtymore in Ireland, the highest peak of the Ballahoura Mountains, near his own estate of Kilcolman. Spenser's deep love for the beauty of the Irish countryside filters through into the landscape of Faerie Land time and again. So does his loathing of the brutal and vicious barbarism which he saw as characterizing its inhabitants. Arlo-hill is the setting for Nature's judgment because it is of Spenser's own familiar knowledge set in a scene of Mutabilitie's most hideous work:

> Ne shee the lawes of Nature onely brake,
> But eke of Justice, and of Policie;
> And wrong of right, and bad of good did make.
>
> (*Mutabilitie* vi.6)

Kilcolman itself was very shortly to share the fate of the shepherds' valley. Faerie Land coincides finally with the human world through their mutual vulnerability. The last hard lesson offered in Faerie Land itself is learned by Calidore not on Acidale but in the bloody fighting at the cave-door of Pastorella's prison.

There is no way of knowing what kind of decision Spenser made to end his poem here. Paul Alpers has suggested in a recent lecture that he was becoming increasingly interested in experimenting with 'large lyric forms', as in *Epith.* and *Proth.* Perhaps simply he could see his own way no further. Certainly what is learned in Faerie Land must in any age be put into practice outside of it. Only so can its history be extended. The continuum of Faerie Land is, to this extent, interdependent with our own:

> But *Guyon* all this while his booke did read,
> Ne yet has ended.
>
> (*FQ* II.x.70)

Select bibliography

The titles listed below are grouped for convenience according to the subheadings of the Introduction and Critical Commentary. Comprehensive bibliographies to Spenser's work are:

Atkinson, Dorothy F., *Edmund Spenser: A Bibliographical Supplement*, London and Baltimore, 1937-72.

Carpenter, Frederic Ives, *A Reference Guide to Edmund Spenser*, Chicago, 1923.

McNier, Waldo F. and Forster, Provost, *Edmund Spenser: An Annotated Bibliography*, New Jersey and Sussex, 1975.

The brief following selection has been made in an attempt to combine accessible primary material with works of factual reference, and to suggest critical works, drawn largely from recent scholarship, that may themselves provide further general and particular guidelines. The Notes to the introduction contain further references; the most important editions of Spenser's work are listed in A Note on the Text, p. viii. A number of critical anthologies have been compiled dealing with varied aspects Spenser's work. Three of the most generally useful of these are:

Alpers, P.J. (ed.), *Edmund Spenser*, Penguin Critical Anthologies series, Harmondsworth, 1969.

Bayley, Peter (ed.), *Spenser: 'The Faerie Queene'*, Macmillan Casebook series, gen. ed. A.E. Dyson, London, 1977.

Kennedy, Judith M. and Reither, James A. (eds), *A Theatre for Spenserians*, Toronto, Buffalo and Manchester, 1973.

INTRODUCTION

(i) Spenser's life and times

Byrne, M. St Clare, *Elizabethan Life in Town and Country*, London, 1925, revised edn 1950.

Heale, Elizabeth, *'The Faerie Queene': A Reader's Guide*, Cambridge, 1987.

Morley, H. (ed.), *England Under Elizabeth and James the First*, Carisbrook Library, vol. 10, London, 1889. (Contains Edmund Spenser, *Veue of the Present State of Ireland*; Sir John Davies, *A Discovery of the true causes why Ireland was never entirely subdued*, 1612; F. Moryson, 'Description of Ireland', from his *Itinerary*, 1617.)

Neale, Sir John E., *Queen Elizabeth*, London, 1934.

—— *Elizabeth and her Parliaments*, 2 vols, London, 1969.

Quinn, David Beers, *The Elizabethans and the Irish*, New York, 1966.

Shires, Helena, *A Preface to Spenser*, London, 1978.

(ii) Language and style

Alpers, Paul J., *The Poetry of 'The Faerie Queene'*, Columbia and London, 1982.

Smith, Charles G., *Spenser's Proverb Lore*, Cambridge, Mass., 1970.

CRITICAL COMMENTARY

(i) Critical perspectives

Cummings, R.M. (ed.), *Spenser: The Critical Heritage*, Glasgow, 1971.

Frushell, Richard C. and Vandermith, Bernard J. (eds.), *Contemporary Thought on Edmund Spenser*, Illinois, 1975.

Hamilton, A.C. (ed.), *Essential Articles for the Study of Edmund Spenser*, Hamden, 1972.

Smith, Gregory (ed.), *Elizabethan Critical Essays*, 2 vols, Oxford, 1904. (Includes George Puttenham, *The Arte of English Poesie*, 1589; Sir Philip Sidney, *The Apologie for Poetrie* (1583), 1585; William Webbe, *A Discourse of English Poetrie*, 1586.)

Wurtsbaugh, Jewel, *Two Centuries of Spenserian Scholarship*, Baltimore, 1936.

(ii) History and religion

Harper, C.A., *Sources of the British Chronicle History in Spenser's 'Faerie Queene'*, New York, 1964.

Greenlaw, Edwin A., *Studies in Spenser's Historical Allegory*, London and Baltimore, 1932.

King, John N., *Tudor Royal Iconography: Literature and Art in an Age of Religious Crisis*, Princeton, NJ, 1989.

Pollard, Alfred W. (ed.), *Records of the English Bible: The documents relating to the translation and publication of the Bible in English, 1525-1611*, London, 1911.

(iii) Allegory and iconography

Freeman, Rosemary, *English Emblem books*, London, 1948.

—— *'The Faerie Queene: A Companion for Readers*, London, 1970.

Hieatt, Kent, *Short Time's Endless Monument: The Symbolism of Numbers in Edmund Spenser's 'Epithalamion'*, New York, 1960.

Lotspeich, Henry Gibbon, *Classical Mythology in the Poetry of Spenser*, Princeton, NJ, 1932.

Maccaffrey, Isabel G., *Spenser's Allegory: The Anatomy of Imagination*, Princeton, NJ, 1976.

Roche, Thomas P., Jr, *The Kindly Flame: A Study of the Third and Fourth Books of Spenser's 'Faerie Queene'*, Princeton, NJ, 1964.

Whitney, Geoffrey, *A Choice of Emblems* (1586), ed. J. Horden, Menston, 1969.

Williams, Kathleen, *Spenser's 'Faerie Queene': The World of Glass*, London, 1966.

Wind, Edgar, *Pagan Mysteries in the Renaissance*, London, 1958, revised edn 1968.

Yates, Dame Frances A., *Astraea and the Imperial Theme in the Sixteenth Century*, London and Boston, 1975.

(iv) Faerie land

Ariosto, Ludovico, *Orlando Furioso*, translated with an introduction by Barbara Reynolds, 2 vols, Harmondsworth, 1975, 1977.

Chaucer, Geoffrey, *Works*, ed. Larry D. Benson (The Riverside Chaucer), Oxford, 1988.

Malory, Sir Thomas, *Works* ed. E. Vinaver, revised edn Oxford, 1971. (This is now the standard edition of Malory's *Works*, based on the fifteenth-century manuscript discovered in the Fellows Library of Winchester College in 1934. Spenser would have known the text as edited and first printed by Caxton in 1485. Vinaver includes Caxton's Preface. A full discussion and comparison of the texts is given in the introduction to the second three-volume edition of the *Works*, Oxford, 1967.)

Rathborne, Isabel E., *The Meaning of Spenser's Fairy Land*, New York, 1937.

Tasso, Torquato, *'Geoffrey of Bolloigne': A Critical Edition of Edward Fairfax's Translation of Tasso's 'Gerusalemme Liberata', Together with Fairfax's Original Poems*, ed. K.M. Lea and T.M. Gang, Oxford, 1981.

Wells, Robert Headlam, *Spenser's 'Faerie Queene' and the Cult of Elizabeth*, London and New Jersey, 1983.